JOSEPHUS DANIELS IN MEXICO

Josephus Daniels signing agreements for settlement of American special claims in Mexico City on April 24, 1934, the first anniversary of his presentation of credentials as American ambassador to Mexico.

Josephus Daniels

IN MEXICO

E. DAVID CRONON

Madison, 1960

THE UNIVERSITY OF WISCONSIN PRESS

Published by
The University of Wisconsin Press
430 Sterling Court, Madison 6, Wisconsin

Printed in the United States of America by the
George Banta Company, Inc., Menasha, Wisconsin

LIBRARY OF CONGRESS CATALOG CARD NUMBER 60–5672

For my mother and father

PREFACE

In the spring of 1958 the Vice President of the United States visited Latin America on a much-heralded goodwill tour. Instead of cheers, he was greeted with jeers; worse yet, in several capitals he was stoned and spat upon and his very life endangered. What had happened, Americans asked themselves anxiously after the first surge of angry shock, to our once cordial relations with our southern neighbors? What about our vaunted Good Neighbor Policy? Was this its fruit? The answer seemed to suggest that the Good Neighbor Policy, like last Sunday's sermon, had fallen into a kind of half-forgotten limbo. Everyone approved of it, some even referred to it now and then, but as a nation we had not tried very hard to apply it in recent years. We had all been taking our Latin American neighbors pretty much for granted, living, as it were, on a stock of previously accumulated goodwill. The Nixon visit demonstrated that this stock was running low.

The story of the Good Neighbor Policy—of its evolution by the Roosevelt administration in the 1930's and its mellowing effect on our relations with Latin America—has not yet been adequately told. This book makes no pretense of telling the whole story. Rather, it concentrates on the one Latin American country—Mexico—with which the United States had the most trouble during the formative days of the Good Neighbor Policy. And the focus is on Josephus Daniels, the septuagenerian American Ambassador in Mexico City for nine troubled years between 1933 and 1941. Mexico, through its radical doctrines, strict anticlericalism, and, most of all, its defiant expropriation of American-owned oil and agricultural lands, gave the Good Neighbor Policy its severest trial in the 1930's. Yet throughout, Ambassador Daniels remained one of the most vigorous and outspoken champions of a true neighborly approach, frequently bypassing his less convinced superiors in the State Department to take his case directly to his good friend in the White House. The settlement reached with Mexico in late 1941, though there were a number of factors involved, was a fitting climax to Daniels' patient and persevering labors. In a real sense, too, it was the high-water mark of Good Neighbor diplomacy, contributing substantially to that stock of goodwill in Latin America which Vice President Nixon found so depleted a decade-and-a-half later.

Historians and political commentators have interpreted the Good Neighbor Policy in a variety of ways. To some, it has seemed at bottom simply a clever and sophisticated attempt to tighten up and extend United States dominance in the Western Hemisphere. Viewed in this rather cynical light, New Deal neighborliness was clearly expansionist; its means, the carrot rather than the stick. Others have been more inclined to accept the Good Neighbor Policy at face value, to see it as an idealistic yet realistic effort by a powerful nation to treat its weaker neighbors with understanding, tolerance, and restraint. If in the process the United States made friends and achieved a measure of political and commercial influence, these were merely the natural and well-deserved rewards of an essentially unselfish policy. In truth, the Good Neighbor Policy was a measure of both ideas. Never very precisely formulated or defined, over the years it was applied by the Roosevelt administration quite haphazardly, though with a good deal of pious drum-beating. There were those in the administration who construed neighborliness chiefly as a tool to promote American interests, just as there were those who stressed the idealistic impulse. At times even President Roosevelt himself seemed unclear as to which aim was primary. Neither in motivation nor in application, then, was the Good Neighbor Policy a simple, consistent doctrine. This book aims to show something of the complicated nature and problems of Good Neighbor diplomacy by examining the mission of one of its most dedicated adherents, Ambassador Josephus Daniels in Mexico.

Like every author I owe a heavy debt of appreciation to the many persons who have helped in various ways in the preparation of this book. The Henry L. Stimson Fund of Yale University generously financed a summer of research in Mexico in 1955 and later provided me with a year free from academic responsibilities while I was completing the manuscript. For this indispensable help and their other encouragement I can never adequately thank my two successive departmental chairmen at Yale, Harry R. Rudin and George W. Pierson. I wish to thank Mrs. William E. Borah for her permission to examine the Borah collection in the Library of Congress and William M. Geer for sharing with me pertinent items from his research in the O. Max Gardner Papers. Jonathan Daniels on a number of occasions kindly filled in some of the gaps in my knowledge of his father's career. Two of Ambassador Daniels' associates in the Mexico City Embassy, Robert Newbegin and R. Henry Norweb, graciously allowed me to interview them at length, and two other key Embassy staff members, Pierre de L. Boal and Stephen E. Aguirre, prepared long helpful memoranda in response to my queries. I received useful insights and information through interviews or correspondence with the following persons: Ramón Beteta, Francisco Castillo Nájera, Narciso Bassols, Emilio Portes Gil, Ezequiel Padilla, Salvador Duhart, Xavier Sorondo, José R. Colín, Frank P. Graham, Thomas H. Lockett, James A. Farley, and Harvey O'Connor. Robert C. Jones and Arturo Arnáiz y Freg helped particularly to make my stay in Mexico City pleasant and profitable. I would be remiss if I did not also mention a few of those who provided expert assistance during my labors in various libraries and manuscript collections: E. Taylor Parks of the State Department's Historical Division and

Mrs. Mary Ellen Milar of its Records Section, Herman Kahn and his efficient staff at the Franklin D. Roosevelt Library, Howard B. Gotlieb and Roy M. Mersky of the Yale Library, Margaret Hall of the Benjamin Franklin Library and Rafael Carrasco Puenta of the Hemeroteca Nacional in Mexico City, and Katharine Brand and many others at my favorite research center, the Division of Manuscripts of the Library of Congress.

Although I naturally take full responsibility for all errors of fact or interpretation, I have profited greatly from the constructive criticism of a number of uncomplaining friends and colleagues. I am especially indebted to Howard K. Beale of the University of Wisconsin, who originally suggested that I explore Daniels' career and then patiently read several early drafts of the manuscript with the same painstaking care and discrimination that is the hallmark of his own writing. My Yale colleague, Mario Rodríguez, cheerfully shared with me over several years his considerable knowledge of Latin American history; his careful reading of the manuscript not only caught a number of factual errors but also greatly improved its style and content. Other Yale colleagues, Howard R. Lamar, Sidney E. Ahlstrom, and William H. Goetzmann, also offered helpful suggestions after reading portions of the manuscript. Two student assistants at Yale, Richard P. Lewis and John J. Maresca, helped track down elusive items and generally checked the manuscript for accuracy.

Lastly, I must acknowledge the invaluable help of my wife, Jean Hotmar Cronon, who in addition to keeping the children out of my study at critical times also took over many of the thankless tasks of research, typing, filing, and proofreading. How scholars manage to get, let alone keep, their wives I shall never know.

E. D. C.

Lincoln, Nebraska
September 1, 1959

CONTENTS

LIST OF ILLUSTRATIONS

JOSEPHUS
DANIELS
IN MEXICO

Wonder whether the Mexicans remember that the man who ordered the United States navy to shoot the daylights out of Vera Cruz in 1913 [1914] was none other than Josephus Daniels.
—*Cleveland News*, March 23, 1933

Ambassador Daniels carries upon his shoulders the burden of the occupation of Veracruz. The memory of that iniquitous outrage against our sovereignty will cause the new representative to encounter a frigid atmosphere here.
—*Omega* (Mexico City), March 17, 1933

CHAPTER I

Shades of Veracruz

March 4, 1933, was a somber, oppressive day in Washington—skies leaden, weather chill and damp. Yet for many it was a day of buoyant hope and optimism. Across the tired land millions of frightened and discouraged Americans waited expectantly to learn what the new President, Franklin Delano Roosevelt, would offer the nation in its hour of grave economic crisis. Most of the President's brief inaugural address was a ringing promise of dynamic leadership in restoring the national economy. In fact, Roosevelt dismissed foreign affairs in one rather obscure sentence:

In the field of world policy I would dedicate this Nation to the policy of the good neighbor—the neighbor who resolutely respects himself and, because he does so, respects the rights of others—the neighbor who respects his obligations and respects the sanctity of his agreements in and with a world of neighbors.[1]

Thus was unveiled the Good Neighbor Policy, which was to become one of the truly significant achievements of the Roosevelt administration and a landmark in American foreign policy.

One of the many Democratic leaders who had high hopes for the new administration was Josephus Daniels, a prominent North

3

Carolina editor and the new President's former chief. As he listened to Roosevelt's solemn tones that cold March day, his eyes
damp with tears of pride, Daniels paid little attention to the
rather vague declaration on foreign policy. Like most of the great
crowd gathered before the east stairs of the Capitol, he was intent
on the chief executive's plans for handling the domestic economic
crisis. Brooding over the magnitude of the administration's domestic problems, Daniels gave scarcely a thought to the significance of the President's phrase, "I would dedicate this Nation to
the policy of the good neighbor." Nor did he guess that he himself would play an important role in making Roosevelt's pledge
a reality.

Josephus Daniels was no stranger to Washington, though he
had never run for elective office. Indeed, the seventy-year-old
North Carolinian was something of an elder statesman in the
Democratic party, having been active in national party affairs
since the 1890's. He had first gone to the capital in 1893 to serve
as chief clerk of the Interior Department under his friend Hoke
Smith of Georgia. The job was comparatively unimportant, but it
broadened the young editor's outlook and gave him a chance to
meet some of the men who counted in the Democratic party.
Daniels' first love was journalism, however, and he had stayed in
Washington only a year before returning to Raleigh to purchase
the moribund *News and Observer*. From the first, he and his
newspaper took an active part in North Carolina politics. Grad-
ually his rugged editorial independence gave the *News and Observer* its nickname "Old Reliable" and built for it a devoted following throughout the state. Editor Daniels was at the same time
a regular Democrat and an ever-vigilant democrat.

In 1912 Daniels had come out for Woodrow Wilson well before
the Baltimore convention and had labored hard to win the presidential nomination for the scholarly New Jersey governor. It was
doubtless this early support as well as Daniels' unstinting efforts
during the campaign that led Wilson to bring him into his cabinet
as Secretary of the Navy. For his chief assistant, Daniels chose a
young, comparatively unknown New Yorker named Franklin D.

Roosevelt. Like an earlier and equally impetuous Roosevelt in the same post, the high-spirited Franklin did not always agree with the ideas and policies of his superior. Often, in fact, he chafed with visible irritation and impatience at Secretary Daniels' unhurried deliberation on pressing matters, his much criticized efforts to reform and democratize the Navy, his refusal to be overawed by brass- and salt-encrusted admirals, and his ingrained landsman's distrust of the professional naval officers with whom the Assistant Secretary got on famously. "I am *running* the real work, although Josephus is here!" Roosevelt boasted unabashedly to his wife shortly after the outbreak of World War I in 1914. "He is bewildered by it all, very sweet but very sad!"[2]

Yet for all his disarmingly gentle manner, Daniels proved to be a shrewd judge of men and a capable administrator. Roosevelt soon found that while he hit it off much better with the admirals than did his landlubber chief, the tact and political experience of the Secretary were essential to guide Navy bills through a skeptical Congress. Indeed, it was under Daniels' wise tutelage that Roosevelt began to learn how to handle obstreperous congressmen, a faculty he was later to raise to the status of a fine art. Thus, in spite of an early youthful contempt for his superior, Roosevelt came in time to see that Daniels was efficient and effective in his own way, and the two men left the Navy Department with a real regard for one another. Their friendship, though for reasons of age and temperament perhaps never an intimate one, lasted throughout the rest of their lives. Roosevelt continued to refer affectionately to his "Chief" as in the old days, and Daniels on his part was one of the few to call Roosevelt "Franklin" with the latter's blessing.

A decade later when Roosevelt, now governor of New York, began his campaign for the presidency, Daniels gave warm encouragement. Fully a year before the nominating convention he conferred with Roosevelt about his candidacy and thereafter promoted it in the editorial columns of the *News and Observer*. When North Carolina Democrats met in June, 1932, to select their delegates to the Chicago convention, Daniels was instrumental in getting them to instruct the delegation for Roosevelt. "Perfectly delighted with good old North Carolina's action," the Governor wired that same afternoon; "my thanks with lots of love to you all."[3] At Chicago Daniels worked closely with Louis M. Howe and other Roosevelt field lieutenants, strongly opposing the fight waged by his own and other southern delegations in defense of the two-thirds rule governing nominations. This holdover from ante bellum days he considered both undemocratic and a definite handicap to Roosevelt's chances for nomination on an early ballot. Following Roosevelt's nomination, the Raleigh editor campaigned aggressively for his friend throughout the West and Middle West, afterward assuring him that the area could not "be taken away between now and election."[4] Roosevelt's sweeping victory on November 8 surprised even the congenitally optimistic Daniels, who would have been the last to claim any substantial credit for the triumph. But the President-elect was not unmindful of his old associate's efforts. "My dear Chief," Roosevelt wrote shortly after the election. "That title still stands! and I am still Franklin to you."[5]

On first-name terms with the new President, and considered by most North Carolinians as the state's most eminent and deserving Democrat, Daniels unquestionably hoped to receive a cabinet post in the new administration. He was suitably discreet about pressing his claim, but he clearly had his heart set on his old berth in the Navy Department. Roosevelt, however, had determined to be in effect his own Secretary of the Navy, and he knew better than to appoint someone as independent as his old boss. Unaware of this, Daniels sought and received the support of leading North Carolina Democrats. "If you have not written the President-elect, you could see him in New York if you deem it wise," he reminded retiring Governor O. Max Gardner, also a patronage hopeful.[6] Taking no chances, Daniels advised Roosevelt of the gist of Gardner's expected message: "that whatever position should come to North Carolina they desired you to give me first consideration." The value of such approval by local party leaders, he reminded Roosevelt, had been amply demonstrated during their joint administration of the Navy.[7]

Late in January, 1933, in a dispatch suppressed by his sensitive editor, the *News and Observer's* Washington correspondent reported "a very strong movement on foot to return Mr. Josephus Daniels to the Navy Department." "The Boss may not want this," he surmised correctly in a footnote, "but it is an accurate report."[8] Ironically, only a week later the United Press noted a rumor, this time dutifully published by Daniels, that Governor Gardner was being seriously considered for the same post.[9] Roosevelt declined to tip his hand on cabinet appointments, but toward the end of February James A. Farley, the Democratic National Chairman, announced that Daniels would soon be named to "an important post" in the incoming administration.[10]

Three days before the inauguration Daniels conferred with the President-elect in New York and learned what he had in mind for his old shipmate. The two men talked of the many problems that would confront the new administration, Roosevelt stressing particularly those of the hard-pressed transportation industries. He then asked Daniels to become head of the United States Shipping Board and to reorganize it into a general transportation agency concerned with railroads as well as maritime matters. This was a far cry from the coveted Navy Secretaryship, and Roosevelt tried to soften the blow somewhat by inviting the "Chief" to join him for the ride to Washington on the inaugural special. Concealing what must have been bitter disappointment, Daniels promised to study the situation before accepting or declining the post.[11]

It took him only two days to make up his mind. "I would be placed in an impossible position if I should become Shipping Board Chairman," he told Roosevelt on March 3. As a longstanding skeptic of independent agencies and an inveterate opponent of government subsidies to business, Daniels recommended instead that the Board be abolished and its functions transferred to the Department of Commerce.

I need not tell you what you know so well that my interest in the great

success of your administration is so deep and means that I would be
ready to aid in any way I can that may contribute to its being a blessing
to the republic. But the Shipping Board suggestion would not contribute
to that end and I could not undertake what I am sure could not work
well.[12]

A week of further study and reflection at Roosevelt's urging failed
to change his decision, though the interval produced a crop of
rumors, approving editorials, and even job applications. "You
have talked yourself out of a job," the President remarked when
Daniels returned with new ammunition to support his view that
the Shipping Board ought to be torpedoed. At the same time he
gave assurance that the "Chief" would not be allowed to remain
out of action for long.[13]

With the President apparently unwilling to offer him a cabinet
post, Daniels next showed interest in a diplomatic assignment. He
refused to comment on rumors that he was being considered for
an ambassadorship, however, and he politely declined to throw
his support behind movements on behalf of a couple of would-be
ambassadors to Mexico.[14] Truth was, Daniels himself had his eye
on that very post! From a friend in North Carolina came an
excited warning: "Some interests will move heaven and earth to
get you out of the U.S. *Don't let them do it.* Your paper would
also suffer if you should go outside the U.S."[15] But with the *News
and Observer's* revenue shrinking monthly under the impact of the
depression and with three capable sons eager to take over its
management, Daniels felt perfectly free to serve the new administration at home or abroad.

As with the Shipping Board, he lost little time in making up
his mind. "Daniels came to Mr. Roosevelt and to me and told us
what he wanted, the appointment to Mexico," Secretary of State
Cordell Hull recalled later, "and that settled it."[16] This was not
quite true, for the Raleigh editor was too experienced a politician
to embarrass the President, and perhaps himself, with such a
direct request. Instead he merely advised his friend Dan Roper,
the new Secretary of Commerce, that of the available diplomatic
missions he would prefer Mexico to any other country.[17] Daniels'

choice was somewhat awkward for President Roosevelt. Jim Farley recalls that Roosevelt had already promised the Mexican post to Ralph W. Morrison, a prominent San Antonio businessman and patronage protégé of Vice President Garner. According to Farley, both he and Garner were consequently "amazed" and "terribly disappointed" when the Daniels appointment was unexpectedly announced by the White House. Roosevelt told Farley he had completely forgotten about his promise to the Vice President, and he immediately issued orders to clear all future appointments with Farley. The President said that Secretary Roper had suggested the appointment, explaining that Daniels was disappointed over not being asked to head the Navy again.[18] Morrison's feelings were partly assuaged when Roosevelt named him to the American delegation attending the London Economic Conference.

Roosevelt may or may not have forgotten his previous commitment to Vice President Garner when he offered the Mexican mission to Daniels. If the oversight was really genuine, it is easily understood in view of the President's preoccupation with the banking crisis and other pressing matters. In fact, it would be surprising if he gave the appointment much thought. The "Chief" wanted to go to Mexico; he was capable and devoted; and Roosevelt would hate to hurt his feelings again by denying this comparatively modest wish. But whatever the motivation behind this rather haphazard selection, the long-run results for Mexican-American friendship were to prove surprisingly happy. Franklin D. Roosevelt chose more wisely than he knew when he named warm-hearted, unpretentious Josephus Daniels as his "Ambassador Extraordinary and Plenipotentiary to the United Mexican States."

Unlike many political ambassadors, Daniels was not a complete stranger to the history, problems, and aspirations of the land in which he had chosen to serve. True, his knowledge of Mexico was scarcely encyclopedic, and he knew not a word of Spanish. But ever since the troubled days of "watchful waiting" during the Wilson administration, he had followed Mexican af-

fairs with more than passing interest. His unhappy duty then as
Secretary of the Navy in ordering the Marines to occupy Veracruz in April, 1914, had not covered the United States with glory,
but it had served to bring the Mexican Revolution sharply to his
attention. He had supported the decision to take Veracruz out of
the belief that the reactionary regime of the usurping Victoriano
Huerta might be weakened and perhaps overthrown if it were
denied the munitions en route to Veracruz aboard the German
freighter "Ypiranga." Daniels had nevertheless questioned the
wisdom of Admiral Henry T. Mayo's ultimatum demanding that
the Huerta government salute the American flag, and he subsequently changed naval regulations so that navy commanders were
obliged to clear all such warlike acts through their civilian superiors and the president.[19]

There is no evidence in Daniels' correspondence at this time to
show that he, any more than President Wilson, had carefully
thought out the implications of an interventionist policy toward
Mexico. Nor is there reason to think that he ever questioned or
disapproved of Wilson's missionary diplomacy in Latin America,
though as Secretary of the Navy he naturally had more to do with
implementing than with making foreign policy. Both by conviction and temperament, however, Daniels was strongly opposed to
any action hinting of exploitation or old-fashioned imperialism.
As a vice president of the Anti-Imperialist League, he had long
been active in the fight to secure independence for the Philip-
pines, and he quietly used his cabinet influence toward that end.[20]
But he also shared Wilson's belief that the Mexican masses were
deserving of American sympathy and help in their struggle for
political and economic liberty. Thus he, like Wilson, considered
the hasty decision to occupy Veracruz a friendly move in the interest of the Mexican people, and was genuinely shocked at the
violence of the Mexican reaction. Daniels fully approved of many
of the goals of the Mexican revolutionary leaders, especially their
passionate interest in land reform. Carefully preserved in his
papers for this period is an eloquent if unlettered manifesto by
several leaders of the Yaqui Indians in northwestern Mexico de-

manding the return of their tribal lands, taken from them during the previous Díaz administration.[21]

On the other hand, throughout the revolutionary turbulence in Mexico, Secretary Daniels was generally unmoved by appeals from American business interests in Mexico that he send warships to protect their property. When, for example, a group of American refugees from Tampico called to protest a lack of naval protection, Daniels startled them with a stern lecture. "You men went to Mexico because you weren't satisfied with business conditions at home," he pointed out grimly. "You went there to get rich quick; and now you want the whole country to raise an army of 500,000 men and send it to Mexico at this country's expense to protect you, and you won't pay a cent to support it there."[22] Mexicans (and many Americans) might find it difficult to distinguish between gunboats sent to help elect good men and gunboats sent to protect foreign concessions, but Daniels and his chief were satisfied that their intervention was motivated by high moral purpose. And Daniels, for one, was determined to keep it always so. In 1918 he successfully opposed a move by Secretary of State Robert Lansing to send six thousand Marines to Galveston to be ready to protect the oil fields at Tampico. Advising President Wilson that conditions in the oil fields were quiet, he warned that any such intervention would be "an act of war against Mexico."[23] Eighteen months later, with Wilson ailing, Daniels again sought to restrain Lansing when he seemed about to provoke war with Mexico over the kidnapping of an American consul.[24]

Daniels' interest in Mexico had continued even after he returned to Raleigh and his editorial desk in 1921. Generally critical of all things Republican, the *News and Observer* found little it could commend in the G.O.P.'s Mexican policy. "This country has waited too long to recognize Mexico," Daniels complained editorially early in 1923. "Obregon is the best president Mexico has had .... But for oil Mexico would have been recognized long before this." When the Harding administration finally extended diplomatic recognition to the government of its southern neigh-

bor, the *News and Observer* suggested tartly that the action was
long overdue. "The strong republic to the North should stand
ready to extend a helping hand to the weaker republic to the
South which has come to its present standing through fiery trials,"
the paper declared. A good share of Mexico's difficulties Daniels
blamed on Washington's stubborn refusal to grant recognition to
the succession of revolutionary governments. "We waited for the
sign from concessionaires too long," he protested. A lifelong foe
of vested interests at home, Daniels was equally suspicious of
such interests abroad. He argued that the United States government should not support Americans who attempted to monopolize
the national resources of other countries, lest such action jeopardize larger interests. "In the long run," he warned, "resentment
for taking the resources results in loss of trade." Americans had
every right to invest in Latin America and elsewhere if they chose,
but they should do so with the understanding that their investments were subject to local laws. "The purchase of an oil well in
Mexico does not carry the right to a warship from Uncle Sam to
control the government of that country," he remarked drily in
1927. Characteristically, Daniels was suspicious when banker
Dwight W. Morrow was appointed U.S. Ambassador to Mexico
in 1927. But when the former J. P. Morgan partner died four years
later, the *News and Observer* joined wholeheartedly in the general editorial praise of his great work in bettering Mexican-
American relations.[25]

Daniels, then, would bring to his new post a basic sympathy
for Mexican social reform, plus a well-developed suspicion of
foreign concessionaires. This is not to suggest that he was hostile
to all foreign investment, for he was an ardent champion of an expanding American foreign trade. He merely believed that Americans who invested abroad ought to be satisfied with a reasonable
return and should not try to control local politics for personal
gain. His experience in the Wilson administration had convinced
him that not all American businessmen shared this noble sentiment. Unlike his immediate predecessors, Ambassadors Morrow
and J. Reuben Clark, Jr., Daniels had not spent long hours wres-

tling with the difficult problem of how to protect American economic and strategic interests in a land aflame with revolutionary
nationalism. So far as he had thought about the matter, Daniels
was convinced that American investors had nothing to fear if they
were reasonable and fair in their business dealings abroad. They
must, he thought, keep a sympathetic eye on local needs as well
as on their profit sheets. As for the American strategic interest in
maintaining control over the Mexican mining and oil industries,
Daniels believed that impoverished Mexico had a right to share
substantially in its rather limited national resources, and that if
this right were freely conceded the question of control would not
become an issue. In short, here was a devout Methodist who had
a deep and abiding faith in the efficacy of the Golden Rule.

Although publishing the *News and Observer* was normally a
fairly profitable enterprise, Daniels was not wealthy by the usual
standards governing diplomatic appointments. In fact, the business slump had so affected "Old Reliable's" advertising and cir-
culation revenues that he had recently been obliged to ask his
friend Bernard M. Baruch for a sizable loan.[26] He could not
afford a post that would require, as did many of the major embassies, any considerable personal expense. As soon as it was
rumored that he was interested in the Mexican assignment, Daniels received a warning from a well-posted friend in Congress that
the Mexico City embassy was "very costly to maintain."[27] To one
who sometimes wrote notes to his staff requesting them to watch
office expenditures for postage stamps and turn off unneeded
lights, this was doubtless alarming news. Daniels was consequently relieved to learn from Arthur Bliss Lane, the American
chargé d'affaires in Mexico, that with proper economy he might
be able to live within his $17,000 salary. Nevertheless, he pru-
dently advised Lane not to arrange "an expensive set-up for daily
living," so that the necessary formal entertaining might be done
"without too great a drain on the purse."[28]

Daniel's strict temperance views were to prove a big help in
keeping embassy expenses down, even if the two types of water
(plain and mineral) he served at formal dinners did little to keep

convivial spirits up. Retiring Ambassador J. Reuben Clark, Jr., was also a teetotaler, but the tradition was not so well established as to escape comment. "Look out, you Mexican drunkards," a North Carolina paper wisecracked just after Ambassador Daniels' appointment. "And if you don't know what that means, ask the United States Navy."[29] This last was a sly dig at Secretary Daniels' famous and controversial General Order 99 banning intoxicants from U. S. naval establishments. In Mexico City, where some of the late Ambassador Morrow's choice stock of spirits still reposed in the embassy's wine cellars, the news of Daniels' coming aroused both comment and hasty action. "I have a feeling that it might be just as well to have the wine taken out of the Embassy residence as soon as possible," Chargé d'Affaires Lane wrote Mrs. Morrow's secretary before Daniels' appointment had been announced publicly. "Some day, perhaps, you will realize the significance of this remark."[30] Even the Daniels family enjoyed the humor involved in sending a bone-dry ambassador to a land reportedly flowing with pulque and tequila. When Jonathan Daniels jokingly protested that the Mexicans would take one sniff of his mother's silver punch bowl, back away, and snort, "Humph, grape juice," Mrs. Daniels replied firmly, "Well, we won't serve liquor."[31] Fortunately, no diplomatic incidents were to arise on this score, and the Danielses even received occasional compliments for their virtually unique (in diplomatic circles) hangover-less hospitality.

After Daniels had told Dan Roper of his desire for the Mexico City post, events moved with unaccustomed swiftness, even in a capital used to the rapid turnover and sudden changes of a new administration. On the night of March 7, 1933, Secretary of State Cordell Hull telephoned Raleigh to ask Daniels if he would accept the Mexican appointment, a necessary formality in view of the indirect nature of his request. Daniels naturally accepted with suitable surprise and gratification, and Hull immediately cabled Chargé Lane in Mexico directing him to see if the appointment would be acceptable to the Mexican government. At noon on March 8 Mexico granted the *agrément* in a move of unusual haste which Lane called indicative of the government's desire "to show every consideration to President Roosevelt and to his administration." Lane quoted the Mexican foreign minister as saying that Mexico had agreed to the appointment "as soon as possible in order to demonstrate its desire to forget the Veracruz occupation which occurred while Mr. Daniels was Secretary of the Navy."[32]

Veracruz: 126 Mexicans killed, 195 wounded. Apparently both President Roosevelt and Daniels had overlooked the rather vital consideration that to Mexicans this diplomatic appointment would be an incredible insult. Mrs. Daniels had not forgotten Veracruz, however. "But you can't go to Mexico," she exclaimed when her husband told Secretary Hull he would accept the ambassadorship. Dining at the White House a few days later, she repeated to the President her amazement over the great irony of sending to Mexico a man whose name was so closely linked with the hated *yanqui* invasion of Mexican soil and sovereignty. Surprisingly, both men claimed then and later that they had completely forgotten about this aspect of the appointment. Roosevelt may perhaps be pardoned for overlooking so crucial a consideration, but it is hard to believe that Daniels, who had played such a prominent role in the Veracruz incident, could have failed to recall it now. To be sure, he had always regarded the Veracruz occupation as a well-intentioned move to aid the Mexican people in their struggle against an oppressive regime, but the gesture had not been so interpreted south of the Rio Grande. As recently as 1928 Mexico had refused to accept an American military attaché because he had served in the Veracruz occupation forces. And only a few months before Daniels' appointment the Mexican government had decorated the surviving defenders of Veracruz for their heroism in resisting Secretary Daniels' warships and Marines.[33]

President Roosevelt brushed aside any thought that Daniels might be unwelcome in Mexico, however, declaring that if the Mexicans would not do business with the "Chief" they could have no dealings with him.[34] The State Department, more sensitive to the delicacy of the situation, was nevertheless careful to thank Mexican President Abelardo L. Rodríguez for his desire "to forget the differences of the past between the two Governments." Lane was instructed to assure the Mexicans that Roosevelt had "complete confidence" in the new envoy, who was "an old and trusted friend," and that the selection of "so distinguished a national personage and close associate" indicated the President's deep interest in maintaining good relations with Mexico.[35] President Rodríguez was probably unconvinced, for he reportedly told an American businessman at this time that Mexico did not want to receive Ambassador Daniels but was forced to do so.[36]

The Daniels appointment was announced by the White House on March 13, and was quickly confirmed by the Senate without debate three days later. For the most part, the American press applauded this honor to one of its working members, though several of the conservative eastern dailies raised mild objections to Daniels' inexperience.[37] The Hartford *Courant* pointed to the Ambassador's "real friendliness and his sincere tolerance" and observed approvingly that he could not "be said in any way to represent the imperialistic finance that Mexico has most distrusted in the United States." Most commentators, indeed, recalled Daniels' well-known antipathy toward any sort of dollar diplomacy. "For the next four years at least," declared the *Winston-Salem Journal,* "big business will have to pull its own chestnuts out of the fire." Writing in the Baltimore *Evening Sun,* Gerald W. Johnson, a North Carolinian, also noted that unlike some of his predecessors Ambassador Daniels could not be accused of any partiality toward business. "The difficulty, indeed, will be to induce him to give big business interests a fair degree of consideration," Johnson suggested. "When oil, or ranching, or mining interests are under discussion, he will be liable to remember Buck Duke and see red." Nor should anyone be deceived by the Ambassador's deceptively mild exterior:

If any unscrupulous person develops the idea that because Daniels has the appearance of a simple countryman, therefore he is a Rube, that person will be destined to a rude and painful awakening. A man doesn't run a small-town newspaper and do battle constantly for a generation against the most powerful financial interests in his State if he is a simple, confiding child. Josephus Daniels has done business with some of the shrewdest crooks in America and come out unstung .... For being an Ambassador isn't going to change Josephus a whit; and any white-spatted young ornament of the diplomatic service who conceives the notion that he can handle and direct the old man is going to have a rough spin—oh, an exceedingly rough spin.[38]

Before departing for the Mexican capital, Daniels went to Washington for three weeks of intensive study about his new assignment. From retiring Ambassador Clark and from Herschel V. Johnson, a fellow North Carolinian in charge of the Mexican desk at the State Department, he learned much about the various problems and personalities with which he would soon be dealing. He also made plans for his trip to Mexico, requesting Johnson to book two steamship passages from New York to Mexico's chief Atlantic coast port, Veracruz. Johnson was horrified at the thought. One landing at Veracruz was enough for a lifetime, he protested. It would be tempting fate for the ex-Secretary of the Navy to make another, even on a mission of peace. Deferring to the infinite wisdom of the State Department, Daniels reluctantly consented to make the trip by rail. But even this mode of travel caused the Department some anxiety. Fearful of possible Mexican demonstrations against Ambassador and Mrs. Daniels while they were en route, both Johnson and Lane suggested diplomatically that it would be best "to make no stop" before reaching Mexico City.[39]

On March 30 Ambassador Daniels addressed the Pan American Society in New York, declaring that President Roosevelt's New Deal could well be applied to foreign policy with results that would benefit all of the Americas."Propinquity helps, but it must be propinquity of the heart as well as of the land or seas," he said. "Most misunderstandings, whether between individuals or nations, are based upon the premises of failure to know each other and to make adjustments which are dependent upon under-standing."[40] Beneath the commonplace generalities of this speech, one could detect a quiet but revolutionary determination to try to inject the Golden Rule into that most cynical of professions—diplomacy. Then, after a busy day that included farewell visits to Secretary Hull and to the North Carolina delegation on Capitol Hill, a review of the Army Day parade with President Roosevelt, followed by lunch at the White House, Daniels entrained for Raleigh on April 6 to complete his last-minute packing before departing for Mexico.[41]

Meanwhile, storm warnings were being raised south of the border. "Be prepared for a shock," was the terse comment of one American businessman in Mexico City as he spread the incredible news of Daniels' appointment.[42] Members of the large American colony in Mexico lost no time in voicing their surprise and dismay. "Why open old sore in Mexico's side by appointing Josephus Daniels ambassador to Mexico?" one American in Mexico City telegraphed the White House the day Daniels' name was sent to the Senate.[43] The president of the local American Chamber of Commerce wired Secretary Hull that the appointment was "being viewed with apprehension" in Mexico, and this statement was applauded by one of the less inhibited Mexico City newspapers as very much "in accordance with the truth."[44] Even when one of the leading Mexico City dailies, *El Universal*, published in its English-language section a letter from Newton D. Baker praising Ambassador Daniels as a "highminded, conscientious, patriotic, and hard working man," many American residents remained unconvinced.[45] Not only did the appointment seem an unbelievable affront to Mexican sensibilities; it also would bring to Mexico an ambassador well known for his suspicions of big business and corporate wealth. The American colony had little reason to cheer the arrival of Josephus Daniels.

But by far the loudest and angriest outcries came in a staccato Mexican accent, and the chorus was both impressive and alarming. Mexican President Rodríguez and Foreign Minister José M. Puig Casauranc had realized at once the political difficulties involved in the Daniels appointment. Whatever their personal feelings, they had concluded that Mexico dared not offend the new administration in Washington by refusing to receive President Roosevelt's close friend and associate. Foreign Minster Puig

Josephus Daniels and Mrs. Daniels (speaking to Arthur Bliss Lane) as they arrived in Mexico City on April 15, 1933. Below is the scene on the Avenida Juárez a few days later, April 24, as Ambassador Daniels and the embassy party proceeded to the National Palace to present his letter of credence.

Library of Congress photo

Sumner Welles and Daniels conferring about the Mexican oil expropriation in Washington on April 23, 1938. Below, Daniels at a Mexican party about 1940.

Library of Congress photo

urged, however, that the State Department announce the appointment as quickly as possible so that he could "give it to the press
with a helpful explanation."[46] Already several Mexican newspapers were noting rumors that Daniels was a leading candidate
for the ambassadorial post, and at least one had bluntly declared
that the news was causing a sensation in Mexico.[47] When the appointment was officially announced on March 13, Dr. Puig acted
swiftly to forestall any hostile criticism in the Mexican press, the
bulk of which was normally receptive to government suggestion.
"The Mexican Government is prepared to give Ambassador-desig-
nate Daniels a hospitable welcome," he told the nation. "I do not
know him personally but only through his articles and books. I
have two of his books. I should say that he was the inheritor of
Bryan—a defender of the masses against capitalism."[48]

This stress on Daniels' progressive views may have reassured
some Mexican liberals, like the deputy who was willing to concede in private that "what happened at Veracruz shortened the
Revolution three years and saved 100,000 lives."[49] A few thought-
ful Mexicans, including Foreign Minister Puig, even recognized
that the appointment had certain advantages, since Ambassador
Daniels might well feel obliged to go out of his way to prove himself a friend of Mexico.[50] But for many Mexican nationalists the
news of Daniels' coming was maddening proof of Washington's
arrogant unconcern for the dignity of its smaller neighbor. First
to take advantage of the chance to attack the United States and
embarrass the Rodríguez government was the small conservative
newspaper *La Palabra,* which in answer to Puig's statement retorted in banner headlines: "Daniels Is Not Acceptable to the
People." Also quick to join the attack was *Omega,* an unimportant
but vociferous right-wing, anti-government weekly. Charging
that the despoiler of Veracruz would no doubt "bring with him
secret demands," *Omega* warned grimly: "We should prepare
ourselves for anything." The three large Mexico City dailies, *Excélsior, El Universal,* and *El Nacional,* were either government-
owned or susceptible to government pressure, and were consequently less outspoken in their dissatisfaction. In fact, the govern-

ment requested the major newspapers not to comment at all on the appointment. When *Excélsior* did publish an editorial on the subject a week later, it was probably written in the Foreign Office. Reviewing the unhappy record of foreign intervention in Mexico, the editorial suggested delicately: "All this must be known to Ambassador Daniels, if he carefully studies the history of our country and, above all, if he observes the diplomacy of these late years between the United States and Mexico, which has been characterized by a decorous and beneficent cordiality."[51]

The Mexican Left also lost no time in getting into the act, with the small but active Mexican Communist Party stridently leading the assault. "Oust Daniels!" a party handbill urged on March 18:

Refuse the affront of Yankee imperialism. Mobilize the masses against Daniels! Organize meetings and demonstrations of protest!...The appointment of Daniels is a slap at the Mexican people and the spitting upon the memory of the dead who defended Veracruz.[52]

On March 24 demonstrators stoned the United States Embassy in Mexico City, breaking several windows.[53] A few days later posters appeared in the city denouncing Daniels and the United States:

The Yankee Government has named Daniels, who as United States Secretary of the Navy ordered the landing of foreign forces at Veracruz in 1914. His nomination can only be described as an insult to Mexico and to Mexico's remembrance of the death of her heroic defenders of the port of Veracruz .... Away with Daniels! Mobilize the masses against him![54]

Similar agitation developed in Monterrey, Mexico's third largest city, where three workers were arrested after a riotous street meeting to protest the Daniels appointment.[55]

The active opposition to Daniels was not confined to the Left, moreover. The right-wing clerical organ, *Omega*, continued to denounce not only Daniels, but also the Roosevelt and Rodríguez administrations for having appointed and accepted him.[56] The intensely nationalistic students of the National University in Mexico City required but little prodding from radical and other anti-government sources before they rioted against their government's acceptance of the former Secretary of the Navy. The situation was so serious, Lane told Daniels on March 28, that "the President has had to threaten them with force in order to compel them to cease their agitation against the Government."[57] There was more than a touch of irony in the fact that Foreign Minister Puig had to confer personally with student leaders before they would reluctantly agree to cease demonstrating against a man who was a devoted trustee of the University of North Carolina and a lifelong friend of students and education.[58]

On April 4 the Foreign Minister was obliged to appeal publicly in the name of President Rodríguez for Mexicans to ignore what he called the "absurd and even caluminous progaganda regarding the appointment of Mr. Daniels."[59] The pro-government dailies dutifully responded with editorials expressing confidence in the new Ambassador's good will, but *Omega* belligerently defended its right to criticize the architect of the outrage at Veracruz. Because of his guilt feelings over Veracruz, *Omega* suggested cannily, Daniels would "endeavor to make himself a creditor upon our sympathies." Therefore, instead of Mexicans carping at one another, "the Foreign Office and the press should endeavor to obtain from the present disagreeable circumstances whatever advantage may be possible."[60]

The Mexican attacks on Daniels did not go unnoticed in the United States, where the Ambassador's friends quickly rallied to his defense. The *New York Times* recognized that Mexican radicals were using the Daniels issue mainly to discredit the moderate Rodríguez administration. "Plainly this is a case of the Communists not loving the victims of Veracruz more," it pointed out, "but of loving the present Mexican Government less." The New York *Daily Mirror* was amused by the thought of this "kindly, genial and capable man" as a bloodthirsty imperialist. "Mr. Daniels is a Jeffersonian Democrat to the core and a vigorous champion of the Wilsonian doctrines of peace and good will." Noting the support given the anti-Daniels drive by American businessmen in Mexico, the *Mirror* observed sarcastically: "We could do with a little more courage and loyalty in the breasts of those who represent American business and financial interests in foreign countries." A Mexican resident of New York declared that the ruling Mexican Revolutionary Party and the great majority of the Mexican people understood and approved of Daniels' motives at Veracruz. "Ambassador Daniels will find an affectionate welcome from his fellow liberals in Mexico," he said.[61]

In North Carolina Daniels' friends and enemies alike were astonished at the violence of the Mexican reaction. The North Carolina General Assembly was so upset that it adopted a joint resolution expressing confidence in the Ambassador and commending him to the people of Mexico. "Out of this appointment," the lawmakers predicted, "will come a more sympathetic understanding between the republics of the western hemisphere."[62] The Durham *Sun* was amazed at the spectacle of a Red demonstration against Daniels. "Were the Communists of the land of Montezuma to pour over the list of eligibles to the Mexico City post, they probably could discover no more liberal prospect, no greater advocate of the cause of the masses," it asserted. "Mexico's liberals may well thank their stars they were lucky enough to draw the man they did."[63] With a trace of bitterness, the organ of the state's textile manufacturers, long unhappy over Daniels' pro-labor views, noted sardonically: "We are wondering who misinformed them, for certainly no good communist would wish to throw rocks at Mr. Daniels."[64] One editor suggested wryly that the Mexican critics "should at least have been considerate enough of Publisher-before-he-was-ambassador Daniels to use newspaper space instead of posters for their advertising."[65]

When Ambassador and Mrs. Daniels departed for Mexico on the night of April 11 nearly a thousand of their North Carolina friends were on hand to say goodbye. A drum and bugle corps and throngs of admirers crowded the station platform as the Danielses boarded their train. "Please note that four of these six bags are Mr. Daniels'," remarked Addie Daniels as the porter took their luggage onto the train. "I'm carrying only two."[66] If the affection demonstrated at their departure was any indication of their forthcoming reception in Mexico, Ambassador and Mrs. Daniels would have little to worry about.

Unfortunately, the welcome being prepared below the border was, like the climate, considerably warmer than the send-off in Raleigh. Apprehensive of trouble, the Mexican government took extraordinary care to prevent any untoward incidents from marring Ambassador Daniels' trip to Mexico City. War Minister Lázaro Cárdenas ordered local army commanders to exercise "special precautions" so that Daniels' train would enjoy "absolute security" once it entered Mexico. Foreign Minister Puig wired the Mexican consul at Laredo, Texas, to remain on the train until it left Nuevo Laredo, Mexico, meanwhile coöperating with Mexican civil and military authorities to insure the Danielses "perfect facilities and safety." President Rodríguez personally ordered a special detail of six army officers and a carful of soldiers to Nuevo Laredo to meet the ambassadorial train and accompany it to the capital. In addition, a heavy police guard was set up around the American Embassy in Mexico City.[67]

Ambassador and Mrs. Daniels were met at the border by the Embassy's second secretary, Stanley Hawks, who along with the Mexican security escort tried vainly to dissuade the Ambassador from leaving the train at various station stops. "I did not come to Mexico to be a prisoner," Daniels bluntly told them. Shrugging aside their protests, he left the train at Saltillo, Monterrey, San Luis Potosí, and other stations to accept the greetings of the waiting Mexican officials and American consuls. "I knew if I could not come into Mexico City in the regular way," he wrote his children back home, "I would be a prisoner in the Embassy after I got here." To President Roosevelt, himself a recent near-victim of an assassination attempt, Daniels explained: "You know, and I know, that there is no safety for any man in public life anywhere if there is in the hearts of men a desire to do him injury .... I think it is better to run some risk than to die of ... suffocation and fear."[68]

Just north of Monterrey a Mexican section hand discovered a broken rail barely a half hour before Daniels' train was to pass. The train was held up several hours while repairs were made, and thereafter it proceeded slowly while men ahead carefully scrutinized the roadbed. Officially, the accident was explained as warping caused by a sudden change in temperature. Any rise in tem-

perature had been more political than atmospheric, however, so
the incident probably represented a deliberate attempt to wreck
the ambassadorial train. Unperturbed, Daniels told a station audience at Monterrey: "Two neighboring countries have to be either
friends or enemies. Mexico and the United States, because of
their commercial, cultural and diplomatic relations, cannot be
enemies. I propose to work for the continuance of friendly relations."[69]

Heavily guarded, hours behind schedule, Daniels' train rum-
bled into Mexico City late Saturday morning, April 15. The Ambassador had paid no attention to the advice of a worried American resident of Mexico City that he quietly slip off the train at
an outlying station in order to frustrate any embarrassing demonstrations. The Mexican government was equally determined to
forestall any anti-Daniels agitation, however. Several hundred
police were on guard at Colonia Station, and secret service men
were conspicuous in the crowd of several hundred persons, Mexican and American, on hand to welcome the new United States
representative. Streets were blocked off, the dozen blocks between the station and the Embassy were lined with police, and a
motorcycle escort accompanied the Danielses to their new home,
itself surrounded by guards. The Embassy staff was nervous and
apprehensive over possible trouble. Clearly, the situation bore
little resemblance to the gay leave-taking celebration in Raleigh
four days before.[70] Yet perhaps the most serene and least troubled
souls in Mexico City that bright Saturday morning were Josephus
and Addie Daniels, the objects of all this extraordinary precaution. "My wife and I were both convinced there was going to be
no trouble," Daniels told President Roosevelt a few days later,
"and, conscious of our own feelings of friendliness, we expected
and received the same sort of courteous treatment as was in our
own hearts."[71]

Editor Daniels had scarcely arrived at the Embassy before he
called in his fellow journalists for an interview, thereby taking
a first and highly important step toward allaying Mexican distrust. Unlike many government officials, the Ambassador was wise

in the ways of the press, and felt completely at home with reporters. Accordingly, he discussed his hopes for the future with
the simple directness of one of his own editorials. The results
were impressive, as one of the correspondents present testified
privately to an American friend:

> Ambassador Daniels got off to an amazing start. He did it with one
> interview—newspaper interview. Disregarding the trivialities of the
> protocol, he discussed the bases for good relations, following closely
> in the footsteps of Morrow and Clark. He promptly subscribed to the
> principles of parity of sovereignties and mutual respect between the
> two governments in their dealings with each other. He elaborated a
> trifle by stating specifically that each country should respect the terri-
> torial rights of the other. He stressed common destinies. And he de-
> clared that neither country should prosper at the expense of the other.
> He thus got to the basis—to the fundamentals—of correct and friendly
> relations. This was no slobbery goodwill stuff. It was deep doctrine ....
> My observation is that Daniels within 36 hours after his arrival in Mexico
> City dissipated completely all the scattered dissatisfaction with his des-
> ignation ....
> Morrow laid down the basic principles for good relations between
> the United States and Mexico. He gained Mexican respect. But "pop-
> ularity" is too strong a word to use in Morrow's case. I think it quite
> possible that the simpático Daniels may actually gain popularity. He
> puts his personality over more definitely than Morrow did. He meets
> people with more ease. Here, his political experience and temperament
> stand him in fine stead. He revealed also in our half hour interview
> with him a depth of understanding that placed him high among states-
> men.[72]

The next day every newspaper in Mexico City gave front-page
coverage to Ambassador Daniels' remarks about the equality of
sovereignties, and nearly all applauded him editorially. Most of
the editorials followed the tone of the influential morning paper
Excélsior, which recalled the "certain amount of uneasiness in the
mind of the public to know the tendencies of the new Ambassador, especially since he was not unknown to us." "Fortunately, his
first words reveal the good will which animates him," the paper
declared, "and we can expect the relations between his country
and our own to continue respectful, cordial and beneficial." Even
the right wing *La Palabra*, which had begun the press campaign

against Daniels' appointment, admitted that he seemed to be "a
diplomat who does not seek to play politics or to defend the interests of special American groups." And the Mexican Confederation of Students, which had been involved in the earlier anti-
Daniels demonstrations, now did a sudden about-face, with one of
its leaders conceding that the Ambassador's press conference had
created "a magnificent impression" in student ranks.[73]

Daniels' initial coup might well have turned out differently.
Despite a number of Embassy warnings, the Navy Department in
Washington had perversely scheduled naval maneuvers off
Mexico's Pacific coast to coincide with the Ambassador's arrival
in the Mexican capital. The original plan had even called for a
contingent of naval officers in uniform to be on hand in Mexico
City to greet the former Secretary of the Navy! Fortunately, the
State Department managed to persuade the Navy to abandon its
plans to stop at strategic Magdalena Bay, on which Mexicans had
long suspected the United States of designs. And instead of de-
scending on politically conscious Mexico City, the fleet limited its
visit to the complacent resort city of Acapulco, where a large holiday crowd gave it a friendly welcome.[74]

Ambassador and Mrs. Daniels quickly demonstrated their conviction that they were among friends. After attending church the
day following their arrival, Daniels asked for an Embassy car to
take them around the city. Lane protested it would be wiser not
to leave the Embassy grounds until the agitation over the appointment had subsided, but the Ambassador firmly overruled him,
repeating his determination to lead a normal life. He also dismissed the police guard around the Embassy, lest their presence,
as he told Roosevelt, "indicate that we feared some of the im-
aginary things that had been published might take place."[75] This
cheerful unconcern, and its mellowing effect on Mexican suspicions, came as no surprise to the Danielses' friends back in the
United States. As their maid in Raleigh put it: "I knew if you
ever got there you would be alright. Your sweet and kind expressions would turn the hearts of your worst enemy."[76]

By no means were all Mexicans won over, however. The still

suspicious *Omega* warned of the probable hypocrisy of the Ambassador's gentle words of greeting, especially in view of the appearance of American warships at Acapulco at the time of his arrival.[77] And no doubt to emphasize its dignity and sovereign independence, the Mexican government kept Daniels waiting more than a week for the formal presentation ceremony that would officially inaugurate his ambassadorial duties. In the interval, by accident or design, President Rodríguez marked the anniversary of the Veracruz occupation by bestowing medals on some of the surviving defenders of the city.[78]

Late in the afternoon of April 24 the new United States Ambassador, somewhat uncomfortable in his unaccustomed striped trousers and cutaway, went to the National Palace to pay formal respects and present his credentials to President Rodríguez. At the outset Daniels shattered what he called "archaic" protocol by insisting over Lane's objections that Addie Daniels and the other Embassy wives attend the ceremony. Still taking no chances, the Mexican government provided an impressive escort of motorcycle police and a squadron of cavalry to accompany the Embassy party, and saw that plenty of plain-clothes detectives were among the sidewalk crowds. The Ambassador, who was understandably flattered by all this ceremony, discovered only later the real motive behind it. "In diplomacy, as in some other things," he observed with some amusement, "it is sometimes difficult to tell the difference between grandeur and a guard."[79]

After being presented to President Rodríguez, Daniels made the usual brief address expected of a new envoy, and here again he went beyond the customary polite but sterile generalities. Noting his determination to be "an Ambassador of Good Will," he declared that both Mexico and the United States had embarked upon programs of "new and well-considered" social reform:

Both are animated by faith that the social order now in the making in both countries will guarantee to all men equality, justice, liberty, and the full enjoyment of the fruits of their labor. Your nearest neighbors to the north have deep admiration for your marked advance in social reform, in public education, in agriculture, in transportation, in communications, and in all measures which promote the well-being of your nationals. The people and officials of my country feel that each Republic has much to learn from the other. It is in this spirit that I have come to Mexico.[80]

In reply President Rodríguez expressed his country's gratification that other nations were interested in Mexico's efforts at social betterment. His meaning, Daniels reported to Roosevelt, seemed virtually to be: "'We began this reform and we are glad Uncle Sam is following our lead.' Of course his language was much more tactful, but that was the tone of it."[81]

Ambassador Daniels' presentation speech won him more friends in Mexico. The Mexico City press generally hailed his remarks as denoting a new United States interest in Latin American social reform. Only the unreconstructed *Omega* intimated darkly that the speech might be interpreted in several ways, while a correspondent in the right-wing *La Palabra* declared that Daniels was a "humorist" to suggest that Mexicans might wish to imitate American gangsterism, divorce, and other vulgarities, or that the United States would care to copy Mexico's radical Constitution. *Excélsior*, on the other hand, called the speech "important," even "a eulogy (why not say it?) to the Mexican Revolution." The most independent of the major dailies, *El Universal*, noted that Daniels had again spoken simply and directly, avoiding the tendency of diplomats "to say as little as possible in the greatest number of amiable words."

What is chiefly to be gathered, in our opinion, from Mr. Daniels' speech, is that we have before us a man with a modern mind, capable of understanding the political and social innovations, and also anxious to contribute to them. A diplomat is ordinarily of a different calibre; under the outwardly mundane modernity he frequently hides the conservative. He seems convinced that his role is to make every effort to maintain unchanged the established order.

Ambassador Daniels, on the contrary, far from seeking to evade the reality of the profound social transformation which is going on on all sides, points out these changes, and rightly feels confident that the country which he represents and our own will maintain and strengthen their good relations .... We have left behind, we hope forever, that stagnant diplomacy which has done so much to obstruct the progress of our countries.[82]

The formal transformation from editor to ambassador was now complete. Over the next eight and one-half years Josephus Daniels would have ample chance to demonstrate his diplomatic capacities at what would turn out to be a most difficult post. Certainly his initial success in blunting Mexican suspicion and hostility augured well for the future. The anticipated riots and violence had not materialized to mar his entry upon his new duties. His calm assurance and evident good will had caused Mexicans to take a new mark of the man who had once ordered American Marines to invade their territory. Yet the situation, which might easily have had more tragic consequences, was not without a touch of wry humor, and back in Washington the Gridiron Club exploited it fully at its annual "roasting" banquet. In a skit that brought down the house, the club recalled for its guest of honor, President Roosevelt, a mythical conversation between Secretary of the Navy Daniels and his youthful assistant back in April, 1914:

DANIELS (*broad hat, string tie, etc.*): "I've ordered the fleet to take Vera Cruz!"

ROOSEVELT: "Mexico will love you for that."

DANIELS: "If necessary I'll march the Marines to the Halls of the Montezumas."

ROOSEVELT: "I can hear the Mexicans shouting: 'Viva Daniels!'"

DANIELS: "I'll drive Victoriano Huerta and the whole Mexican Government out of business."

ROOSEVELT: (*Laughs aloud.*)

DANIELS: "What are you laughing about?"

ROOSEVELT: "I was just thinking how funny it would be if I ever get to be President and send you as Ambassador to Mexico."

DANIELS: "I can't imagine anything as funny as that ever happening."[83]

CHAPTER II

Mexico for the Mexicans

Mexico in the 1930's was digesting a
revolution, one of the really significant and enduring social up-
heavals of the twentieth century. Like most Latin American
countries, Mexico has known many revolutions, some of the
ordinary palace-guard variety, some of greater consequence. But
to Mexicans there is only one Revolution, that which began in
1910 and ushered in more than a decade of turbulence, strife, and
radical social change. Always capitalized, it needs no other identi-
fication. Even today, a half-century later, such is the Revolution's
continuing force in Mexican life that no politician can hope to win
office without paying homage to its ideals. As Secretary of the
Navy between 1913 and 1921, Josephus Daniels was an interested
participant-observer of the Revolution's violent and prolonged
parturition. As U. S. Ambassador two decades later, he was to
find himself playing an even more important role in its stormy
adolescence.

To understand the Mexico of Daniels' ambassadorial years,
some background is necessary. The Mexican Revolution was as
much an outpouring of fervert nationalism as it was an irrepressible movement for economic and social reform. Through it,
Mexicans reasserted not only their sovereign independence—of

both foreign interests and the Church—but also their right to modify drastically the nation's lopsided property structure. Unlike most other revolutionary movements, the Mexican upheaval accomplished its major reforms in the decidedly unpromising period of post-revolutionary consolidation and reaction, in the face of strenuous opposition from native conservatives and foreign property holders, and over the anguished protests of international lawyers and foreign chancelleries. The Revolution had a decisive impact upon three major aspects of Mexican life: land tenure, exploitation of the country's rich subsoil resources, and relations between Church and State. Any move to change the status quo in these three areas affected substantial foreign interests and brought angry condemnation and more from those concerned. Since Americans were conspicuous among the foreign investors against whom the new revolutionary nationalism was directed, and since American Catholics reacted vigorously against the wave of revolutionary anticlericalism, the Revolution took on an anti-American character that was intensified by the bitter memory of past defeat and despoliation at the hands of the United States.

From 1910 down to World War II, therefore, Mexican-American relations ranged from uneasy suspicion to open hostility. Throughout this period mutual recrimination and distrust were the dominant notes in the foreign policies of the two countries. On more than one occasion war seemed possible, even imminent. Ironically, relations were most strained during the time Woodrow Wilson, an admitted friend of the Revolution, occupied the White House, and American military intervention in Mexico took place under the very men who professed a desire to help the Mexican people achieve at least some of their revolutionary goals. Despite this country's definitely hostile attitude towards Mexico at various times in the three decades after 1910, however, the United States never seriously threatened to overthrow the Revolution, though Republican and Democratic administrations alike strove to minimize its effects on American interests. Mexicans might well ponder this fact, for plainly Washington could at any time have crushed Mexico and protected Americans and their property by a variety of stern measures. Instead the Mexicans were permitted, grudgingly to be sure, to carry to new lengths the traditional nineteenth-century Latin American defense of economic national- ism and small-nation sovereignty. Mexico's stand, abetted by the United States' reluctance to intervene forcibly, prepared the way for the concepts of nonintervention and juridical equality made explicit at the Pan American Conferences at Montevideo in 1933 and Buenos Aires in 1936.

There were Americans, of course, who yearned for the "good old days" when annoying international problems could be "settled" by means of a gunboat or a detachment of Marines. Woodrow Wilson's New Freedom and Franklin D. Roosevelt's New Deal helped to reduce both the size and significance of this group, as acceptance of social and economic reforms at home made Ameri- cans increasingly aware of the importance of similar reforms in other lands. An American public grown suspicious of "malefactors of great wealth" and "economic royalists" could readily appre- ciate Mexican distrust of this same class, especially when the hostility was directed at some of the very individuals and corpora- tions that had incurred public disfavor in the United States. Washington did sometimes try to deal with revolutionary Mexico by means of bluster and threats. But in the long run American public opinion rejected both force and overt pressure as suitable tactics for the nation to use against its weak neighbor. Thus, in spite of the violence and property destruction of the Revolution, and the chain of expropriations and confiscations that followed in its wake, Americans generally came to believe that Mexico was striving for much the same political and economic democracy as that envisioned in the New Freedom and the New Deal.

With foreigners controlling nearly half of the national wealth in 1910, with most of rural Mexico carved up among a tiny number of great haciendas, it is not hard to understand why the revolutionary leaders were preoccupied with the problem of winning back their national patrimony. During the long dictator- ship of President Porfirio Díaz (1876–80, 1884–1911), Mexican resources were dispensed with a bountiful and profligate hand. In the process a small group of Mexican and foreign favorites was enormously enriched. Impressed by the rapid economic development taking place in Europe and the United States, Díaz alienated vast portions of Mexican agricultural and mineral lands in the hope of attracting foreign capital to build railroads and modernize Mexican agriculture and industry. Under this calculated benevolence foreign speculators and investors enjoyed a heyday in staking out claims, sometimes spurious, to rich Mexican resources.

By the time Díaz was overthrown, rural Mexico was in effect the private property of a small number of immensely rich and powerful *hacendados,* who between them owned most of the countryside. Less than 3 per cent of the Mexican people owned any land at all, and of this tiny minority 59 per cent held less than five hectares (1 hectare equals 2.47 acres), or an amount that in most of arid Mexico was insufficient for a bare living. The extent of some of the larger holdings, on the other hand, was enormous. For example, William Randolph Hearst, the wealthy American publisher, owned a million-acre ranch in Chihuahua, plus gold and silver mines and extensive tracts of oil and timber lands. Frank Tannenbaum has graphically described the great concentration of land ownership in Mexico at the close of the Díaz period:

Three haciendas occupied the 186 miles between Saltillo and Zacatecas. The properties of the Terrazas family in Chihuahua were comparable in extent to Costa Rica. In the state of Hidalgo the Central Railroad passed through the Escandón estates for a distance of about 90 miles. In Lower California foreign companies owned seventy-eight per cent of the land, an area greater than Ireland. The haciendas of La Honda and Santa Catalina in Zacatecas contained about 419,000 acres. The state of Morelos belonged to thirty-two families, and the census of 1910 recorded only 834 *hacendados* in all of Mexico.[2]

Under such conditions, it is not surprising that the Mexican peon eagerly rallied to the Revolution's battle cry: "Land and Liberty!"

Even more than with agricultural lands, ownership of Mexican mineral resources, especially oil, was concentrated in foreign hands. Mexico's rich petroleum deposits were known and used by the Aztec and Totonac Indian civilizations as well as by the early Spanish conquerors, though the Spaniards virtually ignored this source of wealth in their scramble for the more conventional precious minerals. Mexican oil did not become commercially important until the closing years of the nineteenth century, when British and American promoters began to explore Mexico as a likely source of the increasingly valuable black gold. The early efforts at commercial production, including one by the London Oil Trust with the ubiquitous Cecil Rhodes as a prominent stockholder, failed to discover oil in quantities sufficient to warrant commercial exploitation. As a result the fiction grew among Mexican and foreign geologists that the country was without any important petroleum resources.

Two men—an astute American oil promoter and a determined British public works concessionaire—nevertheless persevered in the search for Mexican oil. Around the turn of the century their respective gambles paid off handsomely. Edward L. Doheny, later to gain notoriety for some oily dealings in the United States, discovered the huge petroleum deposits in the Tampico area and secured drilling rights on more than 600,000 acres of oil land. Doheny's first commercially successful well was brought in at Ebano in 1901. At about the same time Weetman D. Pearson, later named Lord Cowdray by a grateful sovereign, began developing the oil wealth of the Tehuantepec fields. In 1910, Pearson's Compañía Mexicana de Petróleo "El Aguila" (Mexican Eagle Petroleum Company) brought in the largest producing well in the world, the fabulous "Potrero del Llano No. 4" in the Tuxpan region, which in 28 years produced 117,000,000 barrels of oil. In the next few years other amazingly productive wells were drilled, such as the "Casiano No. 7" (75,000,000 barrels in 9 years), the "Zurita No. 3" (21,000,000 barrels in 14 years), and the "Cerro Azul No. 4" (84,000,000 barrels in 21 years). Doheny's "Cerro Azul No. 1" is still going strong after more than 35 years and 88,000,000 barrels. Some of the oil strikes were so rich as to be uncontrollable. One gusher ran for six months before it was brought under control, overflowing makeshift reservoirs of more than 3,000,000-barrel capacity and following the Tuxpan River 34 miles to the sea, where it ruined fishing banks and oyster beds. Such finds quickly made Mexico one of the leading oil-producing nations.[3]

Under the hospitable Díaz regime, foreign oil companies received bountiful concessions and operated virtually free of any effective government control. The Díaz Mining Code of 1884, designed chiefly to promote coal mining to supply the country's burgeoning railway network, significantly promised that coal and petroleum deposits were to be considered "the exclusive property of the surface owner." This grant of private subsoil ownership marked a sharp break with Mexican juridical tradition. In colonial times the Spanish monarchy had carefully reserved to itself the ownership of minerals below the surface of the ground, demanding a share in the profits from their exploitation and retaining the right to revoke any concession if its owner did not fulfill certain royal requirements. After independence the various Mexican governments reiterated this claim that ownership of the subsoil was vested in the nation, the successor to the Spanish crown. But Díaz, interested in attracting foreign capital to industrialize Mexico, recognized that few foreign promoters were likely to invest in the country so long as there was any question of their right to exploit the mineral deposits they might discover. As the extent of the Mexican oil resources became apparent, the Díaz administration enacted a series of mining laws which not only affirmed exclusive ownership of subsoil mineral fuels by the surface owner but also provided liberal tax and tariff benefits to stimulate foreign investment.[4]

The immensely valuable concessions bestowed by Díaz on the oil promoters undoubtedly encouraged the rapid development of Mexico's petroleum industry in the early years of the twentieth century. At the same time, these benefactions did too little for the Mexican people and were productive of much future political trouble. Because most Mexicans did not at first believe that oil existed in commercial quantities in their country, and because the oil men were often dealing with ignorant Indian peasants who had slight comprehension of the potential value of their lands, the British and American oil companies were able to gain control of the fields for a small fraction of their real value. Where necessary, force and bribery were sometimes used to obtain "legal" leases and titles.

Roused by the nationalistic slogans of the Revolution, Mexicans of all classes began to question the wisdom of exporting a large share of their national wealth mainly for the benefit of a few foreign investors while the nation remained poor and backward. It did little good for the oil men to point out that the fields would not have been developed without foreign capital, that Mexico lacked both the financial resources and technical knowledge to operate the industry alone, or that the foreign companies had invested in Mexico only after the government had given certain explicit guarantees of their property rights. Mexicans could only see that their rich but exhaustible oil was rapidly draining out of the country. After 1910, therefore, successive revolutionary governments sought with increasing determination to recapture control of the nation's oil resources, which they claimed had been alienated illegally by the Díaz regime. The prize was worth fighting for, because by 1921 Mexican oil production had soared to an annual figure of more than 193,000,000 barrels, or better than a quarter of the world output.

The Mexican Constitution of 1917 was the major instrument by which the leaders of the Revolution had hoped to achieve and legitimatize their reform goals. Since very few basic reforms were accomplished during the Revolution's violent phase, the new Constitution mapped out a comprehensive program for the future, always stressing the primacy of the community over the individual. In this regard, Article 27 of the Constitution was perhaps the most important. Indeed, it represented a veritable revolution in the concept of private real property, a fact that the creditor nations of the world were quick to note and protest. Most of Mexico's difficulties with the United States during the next twenty-five years stemmed directly from Article 27 and its application to the property of American citizens.

Article 27 sought to make private property, especially land, subordinate to the public interest. The concept of private ownership was not obliterated, but it was now greatly restricted and circumscribed to accord with the broad and changing requirements of the public welfare. Under Article 27 an individual might still hold private property, but this right was conditional, not absolute as in Anglo-Saxon law. The Constitution set up various restrictions to govern the ownership and use of land; it claimed for the Mexican nation all rights to the subsoil wealth; and it carefully left the door open for further regulation by legislative action in the future. This new relationship between private property and the public interest was probably the most significant and far-reaching development of the Revolution.

"The ownership of lands and waters comprised within the limits of the national territory is vested originally in the Nation," declared Article 27. "The Nation shall have at all times the right to impose on private property such limitations as the public interest may demand, as well as the right to regulate the development of natural resources, which are susceptible to appropriation, in order to conserve them and equitably to distribute the public wealth." The Constitution specifically authorized measures "to divide large landed estates" and "to develop small agricultural properties." Villages that lacked land and water rights might secure them "from the adjoining properties." In a clause pregnant with meaning for foreign concessionaires, Article 27 further declared: "In the Nation is vested direct ownership of all minerals," including "petroleum and all hydrocarbons—solid, liquid or gaseous." This national ownership, the Constitution warned, "is inalienable and may not be lost by prescription." The federal government might grant concessions to develop mineral resources, but the legal capacity to acquire ownership of Mexican land was carefully hedged by some stiff constitutional requirements.

Only Mexican citizens or Mexican companies, for example, had the right to acquire agricultural lands or to obtain concessions to develop mineral lands. Foreigners might be granted such privileges only if they agreed to abide by the Calvo Clause,* that is, if they agreed "before the Ministry of Foreign Relations to be considered Mexicans in respect to such property, and accordingly not to invoke the protection of their Governments in respect to the same, under penalty, in case of breach, of forfeiture to the Nation of property so acquired." Recalling the gringo invasion of Texas and the subsequent defection of that territory, Article 27 shrewdly provided that no alien could acquire land within a hundred kilometers of the land frontiers or fifty kilometers of the seacoasts. Religious groups were forbidden to hold real property, and charitable organizations were adjured not to acquire more land than was absolutely indispensable for their intended purpose. The Constitution prohibited the holding of rural properties by commercial stock companies, and stipulated that companies exploiting mineral resources must acquire no more land than was actually needed for their operations.

Article 27 also declared illegal the previous alienation of village communal lands, or *ejidos,* which had been so characteristic of the Díaz period when the great haciendas increased their dominance over the Mexican countryside. At the same time it made provision for the restitution or dotation of agricultural lands to reestablish the old *ejido* system. Each village was guaranteed sufficient land to meet its collective needs. "All contracts and con-

---

* Carlos Calvo, an Argentine lawyer, in the 1870's sought to create a principle in international law that would protect weak states from stronger ones. Stressing the absolute sovereignty and equality of all states, Calvo declared that aliens were not entitled to different treatment than that accorded to a country's own nationals. Subsequently, many Latin American nations tried to implement the Calvo Doctrine by requiring aliens doing business in the country to promise not to call upon their home governments for protection in case of disputes with local authorities. Although widely accepted in Latin America, the Calvo Doctrine failed to receive general recognition as a principle of international law. The United States has consistently held, for example, that no American can sign away his claim to Washington's protection, and that regulatory measures may be applied impartially and still be arbitrary and confiscatory so far as American rights are concerned.

cessions made by former Governments from and after the year 1876," the Constitution warned, meaning specifically the Díaz administration, "which shall have resulted in the monopoly of lands, waters and natural resources of the Nation by a single individual or corporation, are declared subject to revision, and the Executive is authorized to declare null and void those which seriously prejudice the public interest."[5]

Mexicans claim with some justification that Article 27 was neither new nor revolutionary, that it was in fact derived from ancient and sound Spanish legal doctrine. They assert that the papal bull of 1493 vested control over Mexican territories in the persons of the Spanish kings, who thereafter never relinquished these vast personal properties. Each Spanish monarch made grants of his Mexican holdings to favored individuals, to be sure, but these grants were held only at the will of the crown and could in theory be revoked at any time at the royal pleasure. When Mexico achieved independence the royal prerogatives descended intact to the Mexican nation as the crown's successor, and these included the right of reversion over all private real property, as well as original title to the subsoil wealth. Any deviation from this legal concept during the nineteenth century, when Mexican governments made unconditional grants, was therefore illegal and void, because it was contrary to Mexican tradition and basic law. Nevertheless, although the Mexicans could muster sound legal, moral, and traditional arguments on behalf of the Constitution of 1917, Article 27 represented a revolution in property rights. Under it the state was given greatly increased powers to determine the kind, form, and amount of private ownership that might exist in Mexico. Unlike Anglo-Saxon law, the Mexican concept of property rights now became conditional and flexible, responsive to changing national moods and needs.[6]

Modern land reform in Mexico began with revolutionary President Venustiano Carranza's decree of January 6, 1915, ordering the restitution of communal lands to villages that had lost their holdings under the Díaz regime. Carranza also authorized the do-

tation or grant of public and private land to those villages lack-
ing legal evidence to prove the original village ownership. The
essence of this decree, as we have seen, was embodied in Article
27 of the Constitution of 1917, which called for a return to the
ejido system by asserting the basic right of villages to whatever
"waters, woods, and land" the members of the village in common
might need. Under Article 27 dotation of new land was recognized as equal in importance with restitution of previously held
land. Moreover, the Constitution specified that these new grants
could be taken from any public or privately owned lands in the
vicinity of the petitioning village instead of only from immediately adjoining lands as under the 1915 decree. This provision
greatly broadened the potential scope of the reform program and
vastly increased the amount of land available for distribution.
Any village could now petition the government for land on the
ground of collective need, and if a petition asking restitution of
previously held lands failed for lack of proof of village ownership, then the principle of dotation was to be automatically
invoked.

In spite of the brave words of the 1915 decree and Article 27,
however, the actual distribution of land proved to be a slow and
painful process. Carranza, who had been forced by the revolutionary ferment to pose as a champion of land reform, actually
had no real desire to implement the constitutional provisions to
which he had only reluctantly assented. Consequently, he distributed only about 180,000 hectares of land to 190 villages during the years 1915-20. His successor, President Alvaro Obregón,
moved with considerably greater vigor. The Obregón administration enacted important basic legislation that included in 1920 a
measure authorizing the issuance of federal agrarian bonds in
the amount of up to fifty million pesos as compensation for land
expropriated under the reform program. These agrarian bonds
were to run for twenty years at 5 per cent interest and were to
be acceptable as payment for land taxes. Obregón more than
tripled the number of villages receiving land during his four-year
term, distributing about 1,200,000 hectares. Under President

Plutarco Elías Calles (1924–28) the agrarian laws were broadened in 1927 to include grants to any *poblado* (populated place), rather than merely to those villages possessing political rights, a minority of rural communities. Calles also sought to round out the land-reform program with other related social and economic measures, such as the establishment of rural schools, rural colonization schemes, a national bank for agricultural credit, and local *ejido* agricultural banks. The Calles administration distributed more than 3,200,000 hectares of land, or approximately two and a half times as much as had been distributed by the preceding revolutionary governments.[7]

Since as late as 1923, thirteen years after the start of the Revolution, foreigners held more than one-fifth of the privately owned lands of the Republic, an area equivalent to all of New England, New York, and New Jersey combined, the Mexican land-reform program was bound to affect foreign interests. Of the total foreign holdings, Americans owned 16,558,000 hectares, or about 52 per cent. Spaniards held 6,233,000 hectares, or about 20 per cent, and the British owned 5,315,000 hectares, or 17 per cent. By the end of 1927, when the pace of land distribution slackened, nearly 700,000 hectares of foreign-owned estates had been expropriated for the agrarian program, of which more than half was taken from the Spanish holdings.[8] The heavy preponderance of Spanish expropriations, despite the fact that Americans owned much more land in Mexico, may have been due in part to the strong United States diplomatic objections of these years. A more likely explanation, however, is that most of the American properties were in arid and sparsely settled areas where the pressure for land was not so great as in the older, more humid, and more heavily populated parts of Mexico where the Spanish holdings were concentrated.

The revolutionary leaders also moved determinedly in asserting the nation's claim to ownership of the subsoil. The Constitution of 1917 stipulated that mineral concessions must actually be developed to remain in force; that is, the owner must demonstrate his intention to exploit his holding by some "positive act." Unworked claims would revert to the nation, which held original and inalienable title to the subsoil. Needless to say, any suggestion that they did not have clear title to the oil beneath their surface properties came as something of a shock to the foreign oil companies. The oil men received an even ruder jolt in 1925 when the Calles administration enacted a stringent new petroleum law that sought to give practical meaning to Article 27's nationalistic claims. Among other things, the law required the companies to apply for government confirmation of all concessions acquired before May 1, 1917, the date the new Constitution went into effect. In deciding whether to grant such confirmatory concessions, the government was to apply the positive acts test. Moreover—and this was the most drastic stipulation—the new confirmatory concessions were to run for only fifty years, not in perpetuity as before.

For a variety of reasons, not the least of which was the petroleum law of 1925 and all that it implied, Mexican oil production declined drastically in the 1920's. From the peak of 193,397,587 barrels in 1921, output dropped rapidly to a low of only 32,805,496 barrels in 1932.[9] One of the reasons for the decline was undoubtedly the exhaustion of the old fields and the fact that it was not until 1930 that any important new discoveries were made. In that year the British-owned El Aguila company (by now a subsidiary of Royal Dutch Shell) brought in the first well in the rich Poza Rica field, at that time the second largest oil pool in the world. Certainly of equal importance in the decline of Mexican oil production, however, was the companies' fear of the economic nationalism unleashed by the Revolution. Although exploratory drilling continued at a high rate during the twenties, the companies were reluctant to make any substantial new investments in a country where political developments were making them increasingly less secure. Instead they turned to the relatively safer fields of Venezuela and Colombia, where costs were lower and there was as yet no political agitation against foreign development of the oil industry. Except for El Aguila's efforts to develop the Poza Rica field after 1930, the companies concentrated on holding their Mexican concessions for a possible better day. Their policy was to realize as much as they could from their investments in Mexico, at the same time putting a minimum of new capital into the country. Such a course made good sense from the companies' standpoint, but it did little to endear them to Mexicans eager to speed their country's economic development.

The creditor nations, especially those with large investments in Mexico, naturally did not let Article 27 and its subsequent implementing legislation go unchallenged. If Mexico could successfully establish the legal principle that private real property was only a conditional grant, held at the pleasure of the state and easily revokable, then foreign ownership might be questioned in any debtor nation where caprice or malice dictated a drive against alien holdings. If permitted to stand, this principle would threaten foreign investment capital wherever an underdeveloped country might become infected with the virus of revolutionary nationalism. More was at stake than the holdings of foreigners in Mexico, substantial though they were. The threat was real, in a way perhaps as important as that posed by the contemporary Russian Revolution. Foreign investors and their governments reacted accordingly.

As is usually the case when the "haves" are threatened with an outbreak of discontent on the part of the "have nots," the creditor nations resorted to a combination of shocked appeals to law and morality, backed up by diplomatic and economic pressure, to protect their interests in Mexico. Washington, chiefly because of the size of American investments in Mexico and the peculiar responsibilities shouldered by the United States under the Monroe Doctrine, largely set the tone of the diplomacy of the creditor nations. Under Woodrow Wilson, Americans watchfully waited for the revolutionary dust to settle in Mexico, though Wilson sought to hasten the process by imprudent naval and military action. Even before the Constitution of 1917 was adopted, Wilson's Secretary of State, Robert Lansing, who did not share his chief's idealistic outlook, tried to get assurances that Article 27 would not be applied retroactively to American property. In

January, 1917, Lansing declared that the pending Constitution indicated "a proposed policy toward foreigners which is fraught with possible grave consequences," and he warned the Carranza government that the United States could not "acquiesce in any direct or indirect confiscation of foreign-owned properties in Mexico."[10] This was to be the key issue in Mexican-American relations for the next twenty-five years.

Whatever else his failings, President Carranza was not one to give ground in the face of outside pressure, especially from above the Rio Grande. Accordingly, he promulgated and began to enforce the new Constitution with scant regard for the anguished howls from foreign investors, notably the British and American oil companies, and their respective governments. In the United States the agitation by business and religious interests against the revolutionary Mexican Constitution provoked a Senate investigation of alleged outrages against American citizens in Mexico. The investigating subcommittee, headed by Senator Albert Fall, himself interested in Mexican oil, urged that the United States withhold diplomatic recognition from any Mexican government that failed to exempt Americans from certain provisions of Articles 3, 27, 33, and 130 of the new Constitution. In the event that Mexico failed to restore "order and peace" and extend "protection to our citizens," the Fall committee recommended, with more wrath than reason, that the United States "send a police force consisting of the naval and military forces of our Government into the Republic of Mexico."[11] Fortunately, the American public had had enough of naval landings and bandit chasing in Mexico, and the interventionists were never able to muster sufficient interest to carry out their plans to modify the new Constitution by force of arms.

If military intervention was ruled out, the United States could and did withhold diplomatic recognition to show its distaste for revolutionary Mexico. The Wilson administration granted *de facto* recognition during a brief honeymoon with the Carranza government in 1915, but Wilson, exasperated at Carranza's erratic behavior and studied insults, and concerned over some of the implications of the new Constitution, refused to extend complete *de jure* recognition until mid-1917. With the overthrow and murder of Carranza in May, 1920, tension between the two countries eased somewhat, and an accord seemed possible with the more conciliatory but equally nationalistic regime of General Alvaro Obregón.

It was largely the desire to appease foreign interests and pave the way for full diplomatic recognition, in fact, that led Obregón in 1920 to push through the law authorizing the issuance of fifty million pesos worth of agrarian bonds as compensation for expropriated agricultural lands. Mexican finances being in their usual chaotic state, however, only 170 persons with a total of 381 claims received relief under this law, and less than half of the total authorized amount of bonds was actually delivered to claimants in the eleven years the law was in operation. In 1931 the general world depression forced Mexico to stop issuing agrarian bonds and to suspend interest payments on those already outstanding. For a brief time thereafter the agrarian bonds were accepted at face value in payment of federal taxes or for purchases of public land, but when this provision was revoked, the bonds had little practical value.[12] The Obregón law of 1920 was thus merely a gesture—and an almost empty one at that—to try to convince the world of Mexico's long-run good intentions.

The Harding administration, brought to power on the promise of a return to normalcy, was unimpressed with Obregón's gesture, and was determined to set a stiff price for normal relations with its southern neighbor. Three months after taking office, Secretary of State Charles Evans Hughes submitted to the Mexican government a proposed treaty of "amity and commerce" which contained specific guarantees of American property rights in Mexico. Under the terms of the Hughes draft, in order to obtain American recognition Mexico would have to agree that neither the Constitution of 1917 nor any other Mexican law or decree had "any effect to cancel, destroy or impair any right, title or interest in any property, of whatever nature and wherever situated, which ... was owned in accordance with the laws of Mexico as then

existing or declared or interpreted." Moreover, Mexico was specifically required to concede American "ownership of all sub-
stances ... on or beneath the surface of lands in that country"
which were acquired "prior to May 1, 1917," the date the revolutionary Constitution went into effect. After reading Secretary
Hughes' proposed treaty, Obregón understandably decided he
could do without Washington's recognition, perferring to wait,
as his foreign minister observed candidly, "until the Government
of the United States becomes convinced of the reality of events."[13]

The apparent stability of the Obregón government, and the
patent failure of Washington's stern diplomacy, led Secretary
Hughes to agree to the Bucareli Conference in 1923, so named
because the sessions were held at No. 85 Bucareli Street in Mexico
City. Here representatives of both countries met and quietly explored their various differences. One immediate result of the
Bucareli Conference was the United States decision to grant full
diplomatic recognition to the Obregón regime. Another was the
signing of two claims conventions, one providing machinery to
adjust general claims by nationals of one country against the
other for the period 1868–1910, the other dealing with the special
claims arising from the revolutionary turbulence from 1910 to 1920.
Fully as important were the informal discussions of property
rights and international law carried on by the Bucareli conferees.
Although the two sides could not agree on all aspects of the
radical Article 27 of the Mexican Constitution, in the end the
American delegates accepted the Mexican doctrine of positive
acts—that is, the requirement of evidence of actual intent to
exploit a claim to the subsoil. On their part, the Mexicans reaffirmed a loose definition of the positive acts necessary to validate
a mineral concession, and agreed to issue agrarian bonds in payment for small agricultural properties expropriated in amounts of
up to 1,775 hectares (about 4,385 acres) and to pay cash for all
other land expropriations.[14]

Since the discussions of Article 27 were informal in character,
and since American diplomatic recognition preceded the signing
of the two claims conventions, the formal achievement of the

Conference, Mexico was later able to deny having made any binding promises in exchange for recognition. Subsequent Mexican administrations took the position that the discussions of Article 27 represented only informal exchanges of views, and that President Obregón's private assurances regarding the application of the Constitution were entirely personal in character, since no individual or government could so commit future administrations as to their interpretation of the nation's basic law.

The Bucareli Conference thus failed to settle definitely the vexing problems raised by Article 27. American oil companies in Mexico complied only unwillingly and haphazardly with the increasing number of regulatory measures, and they looked to Washington to protect their Mexican concessions, at that time among the most valuable in the world. The oil men objected particularly to the requirement of confirmatory concessions, which they believed would be used to deprive them of some of their rich but undeveloped holdings. They also complained that Mexican petroleum taxes were confiscatory (though other nations had higher tax schedules). In both requirements the companies professed to see the opening wedge of the nationalization threatened by Article 27. Unfortunately for good relations, when American diplomats intervened to protect the rights of the companies, they paid all too little attention to the questions of whether Mexican taxes were really confiscatory, whether the requirement of confirmatory concessions was actually unreasonable, and most important, whether there might be some justice in Mexico's demand to share more of the benefits of her most valuable but highly exhaustible natural resource.

The oil companies generally found sympathy and support in the Republican administrations of the twenties. In June, 1925, for example, Secretary of State Frank B. Kellogg issued a press statement sternly warning that the United States would continue to support the Mexican government only as long as it protected American lives and rights and complied with its international commitments. "The Government of Mexico is now on trial before the world," he declared. "We cannot countenance violation of her obligations and failure to protect American citizens."[15] Two days later Mexican President Calles angrily retorted that he would not permit any nation to determine Mexican domestic policy. Rejecting "any foreign interference contrary to the sovereignty of Mexico," Calles emphatically denied "that a Government of any nation may pretend to create a privileged situation for its nationals" abroad.[16]

Now began the interminable legal bickering that bulked so large in Mexican-American diplomacy down to World War II. The United States impatiently cited precedent after precedent from Anglo-Saxon and international law to demonstrate the sacred character of property rights. Mexico just as determinedly asserted that Spanish legal tradition, Mexican constitutional law, and the long-suppressed social and economic aspirations of the Mexican people all justified regulation of property ownership and readjustment of the nation's top-heavy property structure. Since neither side accepted the same premises nor defined its terms in the same way, the controversy often became a battle in confused semantics. The arguments at first were directed specifically at the regulatory agrarian and petroleum legislation passed by the Mexican Congress late in 1925, but the core of the dispute remained the revolutionary concept of flexible public control over private property rights by a nation too poor to pay adequate and immediate compensation for such holdings.[17]

U. S. Ambassador James R. Sheffield (1924–27), in private life a wealthy New York attorney, was unfortunately too friendly with old-regime Mexicans and with the American colony in Mexico City to have any real perception of the state of Mexican public opinion or the firm resolve of President Calles. Indeed, in private he described Calles as "a murderer, an assassin, a robber and a violator of his own pledged word."[18] Sheffield thus not only encouraged American oil and other interests in Mexico to stand firm against the regulatory legislation, but also advocated forceful measures to protect American rights against what he called Mexico's "violation of international law through confiscation."[19] "Calomel is more effective than pink lemonade when you have ills

to cure," he emphasized.[20] "There is a vast amount of policing to
be done in this world, and as the greatest and richest of the
nations, we will have to do our full share of it in the interests of
civilization and peaceful commerce."[21] Sheffield naturally had
little use for the Mexican Revolution, and he lamented its overthrow of the conservative President Díaz. "Of course, he had over-
ridden the Constitution, and was in truth a dictator with practically absolute power," he conceded. "But Mexico needed that
treatment. It was then and still is utterly unfit for self-govern-
ment."[22]

With these views, it is not surprising that Ambassador Sheffield
made few friends in Mexico, other than adherents of the old
regime. Nor was he notably successful in protecting American
interests, since his tough-talking approach belonged to a past
century. The American public refused to be stampeded by Secretary Kellogg's and Sheffield's warnings that the Calles regime constituted a dangerous Bolshevist threat to the Western Hemisphere.
Teapot Dome had made Americans suspicious of all oil men,
especially such Mexican concessionaires as Harry Sinclair and
E. L. Doheny. The oil companies threatened for a time to go on
drilling without the required confirmatory concessions, but they
cocked a wary eye on Washington to see how much backing they
would receive in their defiance of the Mexican petroleum law. It
was soon clear that the Coolidge administration had neither the
will nor the public support to intervene actively. In July, 1927,
Coolidge withdrew the unpopular Ambassador Sheffield and sent
Dwight W. Morrow to Mexico to try to do by peaceful persuasion
what years of bluster had failed to accomplish.

Ambassador Morrow (1927–30) did not resolve any of the basic
problems plaguing Mexican-American relations—probably no man
could have completely reconciled the conflicting points of view—
but he did manage to introduce a cooling breeze into the heavily
charged atmosphere of the diplomatic negotiations. Morrow's
eagerness to form personal friendships with influential Mexicans
like President Calles, his willingness to listen seriously to Mexican
arguments, and his genuine interest in Mexican problems and

aspirations soon convinced suspicious Mexicans that the American Embassy was neither the bastion of Standard Oil nor the center of counterrevolutionary intrigue. Consequently, Morrow was able to effect a compromise on agrarian and mineral legislation that would have been impossible under a champion of the old order like Ambassador Sheffield.

Under Morrow's prodding the State Department agreed to accept the Mexican definition of the positive acts necessary to validate old mineral claims. President Calles, in turn, induced the Mexican Supreme Court to declare the petroleum law of 1925 unconstitutional, reaffirming in the process the loose definition of positive acts enunciated in the Texas Oil case of 1921 and at the Bucareli Conference in 1923. The United States conceded that Mexico had a right to require confirmation of all concessions obtained before 1917, and Mexico promised to issue these confirmatory concessions in perpetuity. The informal Morrow-Calles agreement did not cover pre-1917 concessions of land upon which no positive acts had been performed to develop the property, the United States in effect refusing to back claims to these concessions. Nor did it settle definitely the question of subsoil ownership. This issue remained ominously in the background.[23]

Ambassador Morrow's personable diplomacy worked wonders in clearing up for a time some of the most difficult problems clouding relations between the two neighboring countries. Still, suspicious Mexican liberals soon noted that coincidentally with Morrow's arrival in Mexico the Revolution ground to a virtual halt. A month after the new Ambassador took over his post the Mexican Supreme Court knocked out most of the regulatory legislation affecting the nation's oil resources. Two months after the erstwhile J. P. Morgan partner reached Mexico the Mexican Congress authorized President Calles to modify the agrarian laws. And although Calles had previously distributed more land than any other Mexican president before him—land reform being one of the outstanding achievements of the Calles administration—not long after Morrow's arrival the so-called *Jefe Máximo* of the Revolution was calling for an end to further *ejido* grants. Morrow's shrewd, even brilliant, diplomacy won a temporary breathing spell for American interests in Mexico and earned for him the reputation of a sincere and devoted friend of Mexico. But at the same time Mexico's first significant reform movement more or less got lost in the shuffle. Eyler N. Simpson, a leading student of Mexican agrarian reform, has observed: "The Mexican who exclaimed 'God save us from the friendship of the United States' made a statement which the professional 'good-willers' may have some difficulty understanding, but it contains a deal of wisdom nonetheless."[24] The revolutionary impetus for reform would not begin to pick up speed again until 1935, when Lázaro Cárdenas ended the Calles domination of Mexican politics with a ringing call for a return to the sidetracked principles of the Revolution. Morrow's significant achievement was his very real contribution to Mexican-American friendship and understanding. At the same time he merely postponed a settlement of the basic problems that were to confront Josephus Daniels in the Mexico City Embassy.

In the field of world policy I would dedicate this
Nation to the policy of the good neighbor.
—Franklin D. Roosevelt[1]

We have had too much Dollar Diplomacy on this
hemisphere.
—Josephus Daniels[2]

CHAPTER III

A Neighbor Goes to Work

Ambassador and Mrs. Daniels lost no
time in making themselves at home in Mexico City. At first the
rarefied air of the Mexican capital caused them some discomfort,
but they soon got used to both the mile-high atmosphere and the
delightfully mild climate, which clothes the city in a floral
magnificence that warmed the heart of garden-loving Mrs.
Daniels. Before long they were boasting to friends sweltering in
Raleigh's summer heat that in Mexico City one slept under
blankets every night of the year. Climate-wise, had Daniels can-
vassed a whole library of Baedekers before choosing Mexico, he
could not have found a more pleasant post.

The Embassy, too, was all that even a seasoned diplomat could
desire. In fact, the Ambassador was so impressed with his new
home that in his first press conference he jokingly denied that its
luxurious appointments had been a factor in influencing him to
forsake journalism for diplomacy. The Daniels family home back
in North Carolina could hardly be called modest, but the large
Embassy residence, as Daniels described it to his sons, "seemed
a far cry from Raleigh." In addition to its drawing, reception, and
dining rooms—"all extremely large and well adapted to entertaining"—the residence contained two studies and five bedrooms and
baths, plus quarters for the servants and a large room and bath
on the roof "still called the Lindbergh room," after Ambassador

Morrow's famous son-in-law who had stayed there while courting
Anne Morrow. Opposite the residence, across a beautiful garden
that was the delight of Mrs. Daniels, was the Chancery, where
the day-to-day work of the Embassy was done. The lot on which
the Chancery stood had been given to the United States in 1923
by Mrs. Edward L. Doheny, whose husband had achieved both
fortune and fame (somewhat tarnished) in Mexican and American
oil operations. Good Democrat that he was, Daniels enjoyed the
Mexico City rumor that the Dohenys had given the Chancery lot
to the Harding administration in return for various favors rendered, including perhaps the Elk Hills naval oil reserve in California. The new tenant nevertheless recorded, doubtless with
some surprise, that there was "no smell of oil on the premises."[3]

Like most visitors since Cortés, the Danielses were immediately
enchanted by the rugged beauty, sharp contrasts, and changeless
customs of Old Mexico. Neither the Ambassador nor his wife
picked up more than a handful of Spanish words during the
decade they lived in Mexico, but they were soon using their
meager vocabulary with unabashed enthusiasm. Determined to
be *simpático*, Daniels had scarcely arrived before he got off a
letter to his friend, "Señor Don Franklin D. Roosevelt, Presidente
de los Estados Unidos de America," and he quickly got on first-
name terms with such national specialities as tortillas, frijoles, and
enchiladas. The Danielses even startled their gringo and Mexican friends by appearing on occasion in traditional Mexican cos-
tume—the Ambassador resplendent in dignified *charro* dress and
Mrs. Daniels somewhat less convincing as a stoutish *China Poblana*. More spry at three-score-and-ten than many a younger man,
the Ambassador also sometimes took his turn at the "Jarabe," a
famous old folk dance of the State of Jalisco. He drew the line at
bullfighting, however, and politely yet adamantly refused to attend such a spectacle during his entire stay in Mexico. In a land
where the *corrida* is a national pastime, such a course clearly demanded considerable diplomatic skill. No doubt there were Mexicans who were entertained and amused by the spectacle of an
elderly ambassador who was fearlessly "fluent" in his use of a few

words of their language and who sometimes went native in cos-
tume and dance, but Daniels' evident goodwill and geniality soon
made him many friends.[4]

Unquestionably, a knowledge of Spanish would have been a
great asset to Ambassador Daniels in his diplomatic work. That
he himself recognized this is apparent from his stipulation that
his counselor, or second-in-command in the Embassy, "should of
course speak Spanish fluently and should be heart and soul in
sympathy with the Good Neighbor Policy."[5] Still, it is surprising
how unanimous are members of Daniels' staff and Mexican officials in their agreement that his lack of Spanish was no real handicap. Both groups stress that it was far more important for him to
devote his attention to a sympathetic understanding of the Mexican people and their problems than merely to mastering their
language. Most of the Mexican leaders with whom Daniels had
contact spoke English, and where they did not, as in the case of
General Calles and President Cárdenas, the use of interpreters
proved to be no barrier to mutual regard and understanding. Indeed, one of the Mexican foreign ministers with whom the Ambassador dealt believes that his lack of Spanish was sometimes an
asset, since the frequent pauses for translation during a difficult
negotiation always gave Daniels plenty of time to weigh his words
before the next exchange.[6] Daniels recognized his linguistic limitations, however, and worked out a careful routine whereby every
morning his staff prepared a digest of the latest news and editorial
comment from a wide range of Mexican newspapers and periodicals. Apparently, few educated Mexicans expected a man of Daniels' age to learn a new language, though they would certainly
have been flattered had he made the effort.[7]

Daniels was past seventy when he went to Mexico and seventy-
nine when he retired because of his wife's ill-health, but he was
never handicapped by his age. As he had all his life, the Ambassador set a stiff schedule for himself and his associates. He was
fond of repeating the story of how the Embassy staff had at first
pictured him as a "tired old man" who would need lots of help
and supervision from the career men. His associates quickly
changed their minds, however, and after a particular full day one

of them sank wearily in a chair with the sarcastic comment: "Just had an easy day with the tired old man."[8] Daniels never thought of himself as old nor questioned his capacity for hard work. At seventy-four he thanked a Mexican admirer for sending him a carved walking stick, suggesting impishly, "Some thirty or forty years hence, when I begin to grow old, I shall find it a great comfort."[9] In 1939, when he was seventy-seven, Daniels asked President Roosevelt to appoint him Secretary of the Navy, and although Roosevelt apparently did not reply to this unusual request, it illustrates Daniels' conviction that his health "was never so good as now."[10] The great range of Ambassador Daniels' activities and interests during his stay in Mexico—troublesome as well as routine diplomacy, frequent speeches, travel throughout the country, close attention to political affairs back home, wide reading, extensive correspondence, preparation of book reviews and articles for his newspaper, plus work on five volumes of autobiography—testifies to an extraordinary zest for life and serves to dispel any notion that his age should have disqualified him for the Mexican post.

One of the first tasks Ambassador Daniels set for himself in Mexico was to win over the numerous critics of his appointment. Mention has already been made of the favorable reaction to his first press conference and his remarks when he presented his credentials. But Daniels was not content to charm with words alone. Following the practice begun by his predecessor, Ambassador Clark, he called on all the cabinet members, and then, going further, paid his respects to congressional leaders, the inspector general of police, and sundry other functionaries as well. "This made an excellent impression," reported one of the Embassy staff to Clark. "There has been a very favorable reaction here since it has been learned that he does not intend to land the Marines and capture the country. His charming personality and his considerate nature have had an excellent effect not only on the government officials but also on the others with whom he has come into contact."[11]

Ex-editor Daniels well knew the importance of a good press,

and after his official courtesy calls he made the rounds of Mexico City newspapers. He spent time chatting not only with the publishers and editorial staffs, but shrewdly went into the composing rooms and pressrooms and shook hands with the ordinary workers. *Excélsior* ran a picture of him tapping out a few words on a linotype machine to show that he still knew the trade. Daniels' easy-going informality made a big hit with the newsmen, who in any country are by profession allergic to stuffed shirts. One linotype operator commented afterward that here was "the first genuinely 'democratic' Ambassador" that the United States had sent to Mexico.[12] Even at the offices of *La Palabra*, the small rightwing paper that had led in protesting his appointment, Daniels managed to thaw the atmosphere a bit. "You won them over completely," he was told afterward by an enthusiastic Mexican priest, "and they are yours forever."[13] This was something of an overstatement, for *La Palabra* and its readers were by no means yet ready to forget Veracruz, but the paper did grudgingly begin to concede that Daniels was not the monster it had expected.[14]

Ambassador and Mrs. Daniels made one other visit not long after their arrival, one that touched Mexicans deeply. One afternoon they called upon Señora Sara P. de Madero, the widow of the martyred first president of the Revolution. To history-conscious Mexicans, this visit had, as one newspaper put it, "an exceptional and special significance." The last time Señora de Madero had seen a United States ambassador had been two decades earlier, when she had vainly begged Henry Lane Wilson to intercede with Huerta, after his counterrevolutionary coup, to spare her husband's life. To Daniels, the visit represented a chance to show his genuine admiration for Madero and his shame over Ambassador Wilson's ill-concealed hostility to the Mexican Revolution. Mexicans understood his gesture, and were impressed. "An Ambassador with deep understanding," commented *El Universal*. "And those who understand it must reciprocate the noble action with noble gratitude."[15]

Ambassador Daniels could be blunt as well as tactful, and he was rather less diplomatic in his first contacts with the American colony in Mexico, a group which, it will be recalled, had not been unanimously overjoyed at his appointment. He was well aware that some of the critics were disturbed less by his connection with the Veracruz occupation than by their belief that he was hostile to corporate wealth. At the traditional American colony banquet to welcome him to Mexico, therefore, the Ambassador decided to clear up any doubts as to his position. Knowing he was addressing an audience composed primarily of conservative Republicans, he proudly praised President Roosevelt's New Deal for letting "the country see that the physician lived in Washington and not in Wall Street." Worse yet from the standpoint of some of his listeners, he declared that Americans "ask nothing for themselves here except what their own nation guarantees to Mexicans residing in the United States." This sentence had more than ordinary meaning in a land where foreigners, notably Americans, owned about one-third of the national wealth, and overwhelmingly controlled such basic industries as oil, mining, and electric power. Accordingly, a number of Mexican City newspapers gave it headline attention, no doubt to the extreme discomfiture of Daniels' businessmen hosts.[16]

Several months later, in his Fourth of July address to the American colony, Daniels went even further. Departing from the customary banalities on patriotism and Old Glory, he called for a new Declaration of Independence, this time from "the yoke of Favoritism" and "the tyrannical rule of Privilege, strongly entrenched." He listed a number of self-evident truths applicable to modern times, among which was the stipulation that "the national resources of the country…are the property of all the people, not to be sequestered or transferred or monopolized for the enrichment of any group."[17] Daniels' speech presumably dealt with American conditions and problems, but both he and his listeners knew that it had wider application. "It is the first time that an Amabassador here has talked off the record," Daniels exulted to a friend afterward, "and has touched upon the inherent right of every nation to own its own natural resources and use them for the benefit of all the people and not for the enrichment of a few."[18] The Mexican press called the speech "sensational" and noted the consternation it caused in business circles. "Very good, Ambassador Daniels!" declared a Puebla newspaper.[19] From an upper-class Mexican woman in Monterrey came warm approval: "You must know that all Mexico is counting on every one of your words, even to the last of the common people, as everybody is expecting for a new era to dawn on our country .... You surely must be the instrument in God's hands for the fulfilment of His plans."[20] But in Salt Lake City, former Ambassador Clark's only comment was, "I wonder?"[21]

Despite sharp differences in political and economic views, Ambassador and Mrs. Daniels got along quite well socially with the American colony. They entertained frequently, and every Fourth of July the Embassy held open house for Americans in Mexico, complete with nonalcoholic punch, entertainment, and appropriate oratory by the Ambassador. In turn, the Danielses were always happy to grace a gathering of Americans, even one in which the New Deal was anathema. The Ambassador's private secretary recalls that American residents of Mexico City generally thought of Daniels in terms of amused affection, and at parties his prize would invariably be a bottle of Scotch or something of equal utility to a staunch prohibitionist.[22]

Nevertheless, Daniels' alleged radicalism probably kept him from attaining genuine popularity with a considerable element of the colony, and he heartily reciprocated the feeling of distrust. It galled him, for example, that the American Club in Mexico invariably went Republican by a wide margin in its straw votes before an American presidential election. When the club voted 111 to 37 in favor of Landon in 1936, Daniels told Cordell Hull he was not surprised, and offered a frank and revealing description of the American colony:

Most of them resent the Good Neighbor Policy. They wish Uncle Sam to hold a Big Stick over Pan America and protect them in their exploitation. The only use those who have gotten rich by obtaining concessions have for the department of diplomacy is to help them continue their big profits as they continue to pay wages that would mean starvation in our country. Three fourths of them rush to the Embassy when in trouble (some of their troubles they have brought upon themselves) and spend their time berating Roosevelt and all measures that look to social security. The American Club vote is typical of a belief in dollar diplomacy. It sometimes goes against the grain to be called upon to make representations for them as "American citizens" when I know they have no real American citizenship and feel no duty to the country they would like to see send soldiers here to protect their property or concessions some of them obtained under the rotten reign of Díaz.[23]

Before leaving Washington Ambassador Daniels had been carefully briefed on the political conditions he would find in Mexico. He had been advised not to be deceived by external similarities between the American and Mexican structures of government, for real political democracy was as yet largely unknown in Mexico. Mexican elections were frequently marred by violence and ballot fraud, and only the ruling party, which claimed all credit for the Mexican Revolution, had any chance of winning an election. Struggles for power thus nearly always took place within the existing governmental structure. One man above all others, Daniels was told repeatedly, he must cultivate if his mission were to be a success. This was former President Plutarco Elías Calles, nicknamed the *Jefe Máximo* (Supreme Chief) of the Revolution. General Calles currently held no public office, but he was universally recognized as Mexico's strong man. According to the State Department, Calles' word was "the last one on all important matters."[24]

General Calles, originally an impecunious schoolteacher from the state of Sonora in arid northwestern Mexico, had risen to power through the Mexican Revolution. As a lieutenant of General Alvaro Obregón, another native of Sonora, Calles helped to engineer his chief's election to the presidency in 1920, thereby paving the way for his own election four years later. Calles' presidential term began and ended with attempted revolts by dissident political and religious factions, and seemed on the verge of catastrophe during most of its fateful four years. Yet President Calles probably saved the Mexican social revolution by strengthening the labor movement, speeding land reform, and championing popular education. With significant help from Ambassador

Dwight Morrow, Calles also brought about a *rapprochement* between Mexico and the United States. And by declining to flout the constitutional ban against re-election, Calles took a significant step toward ending the *caudillo* tradition, thus strengthening political democracy in Mexico.

At the same time, General Calles remained very much in politics when his presidential term ended. He dictated the nominations of the dominant National Revolutionary Party and saw that his followers were rewarded with high positions in government. He personally selected the four presidents who succeeded to the office between 1928 and 1934. In 1932 he forced the resignation of President Pascual Ortiz Rubio in order to substitute a more loyal adherent, General Abelardo L. Rodríguez. Though in nominal retirement, the *Jefe Máximo* obviously enjoyed living up to his nickname. He still professed devotion to the principles of the Revolution, but he and most of the older revolutionaries who followed him had by this time lost the sense of urgency that had impelled their social reforms in the early days. Power and wealth had corrupted many of the leaders and tarnished the ideals of the National Revolutionary Party.

Ambassador Daniels' staff urged him to lose no time in getting on friendly terms with General Calles, emphasizing that Ambassadors Morrow and Clark had got nowhere until they had won Calles. This seemed especially important in view of newspaper reports that the General had pointedly left Mexico City before Daniels arrived to emphasize his displeasure with the appointment.[25] Only four days after presenting his credentials to President Rodríguez, therefore, Daniels sent off a friendly greeting to Calles at his Lower California estate. He was gratified to receive an immediate reply, in which the General promised, "It will be a real pleasure for me, on my return, to clasp your hand and to consider myself numbered among your friends."[26] A week later the Ambassador thoughtfully sent Calles a copy of a speech he had just made which contained a pertinent quotation from the General himself. This shrewd bit of homespun diplomacy had the desired effect, for the flattered Calles quickly responded that Daniels' remarks were "packed with truths."[27]

Late in July, after the Danielses were well established in the Embassy, General Calles returned to Mexico City, and in a homecoming address warmly praised the Roosevelt administration in the United States.[28] Two weeks later the General invited Ambassador Daniels for a conference at his villa in the nearby resort town of Cuernavaca. Closeted together for two hours on August 14, the smalltown editor and the schoolteacher general, so different in background yet each representing a similar tradition of agrarian radicalism, found themselves in close agreement in their basic social philosophies. Despite the language barrier that prevented any direct communication, Daniels came away greatly impressed with the Mexican strong man. "I have never come in contact with a Latin American," he immediately wrote Cordell Hull, "who seemed to have such a clear mind, so well informed, so frank, so courageous in expressing his views, and evidently so sincere in his readiness to take risks to bring about policies for the commonweal."[29] Quoting Calles as saying that a basic concern of government ought to be to see that every man received his fair proportion of the national wealth he helped to create, Daniels observed enthusiastically to his friend Claude Bowers: "Doesn't that sound like Jefferson and Wilson?"[30] The Ambassador apparently did not perceive (or perhaps did not care) that the words he found so stirring might have an ominous ring for some American investors in Mexico. It was enough that in General Calles he thought he recognized a congenial fellow-liberal with the same broad social ideals.

Ambassador Daniels got along well with President Rodríguez and other high Mexican leaders, but he continued in the belief, shared well-nigh universally by Mexicans and Americans alike, that General Calles was the real power behind the government. This attitude, at the same time realistic and a little naive, ultimately precipitated a near governmental crisis, though Daniels was only partly at fault. President Rodríguez, like most Mexican officials, was a Calles follower politically, but he nevertheless had strong convictions about the prerogatives of his office, and he was increasingly annoyed over what he fancied were slights to his presidential dignity. He could not, of course, risk an open break with the *Jefe Máximo*, for that would probably mean the same swift downfall that had been the fate of his predecessor, President Ortiz Rubio. So Rodríguez bided his time, waiting for a suitable but not too self-assertive chance to demonstrate that he, and not the powerful General Calles, was the actual head of Mexico.

The President's opportunity, and with it some rapid backstage maneuvering, came early in April, 1934, when he learned of a luncheon Calles was planning to hold at his Cuernavaca home in honor of Ambassador Daniels. The idea for this luncheon party had originated with Ralph W. Morrison, the Texas businessman who had been Vice President Garner's choice for the Mexican ambassadorship. Morrison's investments in Mexico had long ago brought him into contact with Calles and other prominent Mexicans, and he was eager to promote the budding friendship between Daniels and the General. His plan was simple and on the surface seemed productive of nothing but good will. He proposed that General Calles invite Daniels and a few other friends—other foreign diplomats and Mexican cabinet officials—to a luncheon just before Daniels' departure for the United States on his first leave of absence. As a highlight of the affair, the Ambassador would produce a letter of greeting to Calles from President Roosevelt, and the General in turn would entrust to Daniels' care a similar salute to the American President. Inasmuch as Daniels and Roosevelt were old friends, the Ambassador could no doubt secure the necessary letter outside the usual and probably more cautious channels of the State Department.

Morrison sold not only Daniels and Calles but also Roosevelt on the idea of the goodwill luncheon, and Foreign Minister Puig Casauranc, a strong *Callista*, undertook to handle the invitations and other arrangements. Apparently it never occurred to any of the participants that President Rodríguez might object to being left out of the party, particularly when it was being arranged by his own foreign minister. Certainly this thought never entered Daniels' head, for he assured Roosevelt that the luncheon-letter scheme "would bear good fruit."[31] He even drafted the proposed letter for Roosevelt's signature, which the latter accepted with one minor stylistic change. "Entirely satisfactory," Roosevelt cabled in reply. "Am mailing letter."[32]

The luncheon promoters did not reckon on the explosion from the National Palace when President Rodríguez learned of the plans, and especially of President Roosevelt's role in the affair. Highly indignant, Rodríguez bluntly informed Foreign Minister Puig that any message from another chief of state must come to the President of Mexico rather than to a private citizen, no matter how eminent. Under the circumstances, he delared, the luncheon must not take place.[33] On a scant two-days' notice, an exceedingly upset Dr. Puig notified Daniels and the other guests that the luncheon had been called off. It seemed that General Calles was "suffering from malaria, that his temperature was 104 and that his physicians had ordered him to the West Coast." All of the General's appointments had been canceled, and, regretfully, the luncheon was of course out of the question.[34] Ambassador Daniels, not yet aware of the real nature of Calles' "illness," immediately extended the General his sympathy and offered, "If you wish to send [President Roosevelt] any message through me I will be glad to take it to Washington."[35] But the luncheon itself, along with the speech the Ambassador had painstakingly prepared for the occasion, never came off. Later, after the whole story had been brought to light by President Rodríguez' biographer, Daniels termed the canceled luncheon a significant event in Mexican history. "I suspect it marked the beginning of true constitutional government," he noted, "without any 'Strong Man' standing in the scene behind the presidency."[36]

The luncheon incident, and a later erroneous and misinterpreted newspaper interview in which he purportedly praised General Calles as "the strong and vigorous man of Mexico,"[37] emphasized to Daniels the danger of appearing to be involved in Mexican politics. From this time on, though he followed Mexican political developments with lively interest, he was careful to avoid charges of Embassy partisanship. Yet, it was noteworthy that Daniels should need this lesson at all. He of all people, with his intimate knowledge of Wilson's frustrations in dealing with

Huerta and Carranza, ought to have remembered that Mexico hath no fury like a president scorned.

Aside from his understandable and commendable desire to make friends, one of Ambassador Daniels' chief concerns after he got to Mexico was to reorganize his staff. He was darkly certain that the Embassy suffered from years of Republican inefficiency, mismanagement, and worst of all, the callous practice of big-stick and dollar diplomacy. Some of his staff, he suspected, were hostile to the Roosevelt administration and contemptuous of its new Good Neighbor Policy. Daniels strongly believed that any man who could not give whole-hearted support to the new administration "ought to have the decency to resign and let those policies be carried out by someone who is in honest sympathy."[38] This problem of finding loyal subordinates, like himself devoted to the Good Neighbor Policy, remained a critical one for the Ambassador throughout his stay in Mexico. "I need not tell you that all of the career men are not in sympathy with that policy," he once reminded a high State Department official. "Some of them have been brought up in the old order of 'Speak softly and carry a big stick.' "[39]

At first, however, Daniels was mainly interested in rooting out waste and inefficiency, in line with the Roosevelt administration's proclaimed intention to prune the budget. He discovered in Mexico a bureaucratic jungle. Conflicting American agencies frequently duplicated each other's efforts, occasionally operated at cross purposes, and in some cases were virtually free of any supervision by the Ambassador, who was presumably the ranking American official in Mexico. Five separate offices reported to Washington on Mexican political and economic affairs: the Embassy itself, the consulate general, the various consuls, and the Embassy's military and commercial attachés. The American consuls stationed throughout the country, for example, reported either to the State Department or through the consulate general in Mexico City, which was not directly a part of the Embassy. Often their despatches contained information of value to the Ambassador, but he either got it secondhand or not at all. The commercial attaché, whose duties and prestige had flowered during the lush Hoover days in the Commerce Department, reported directly to the Secretary of Commerce. His accounts of economic conditions overlapped similar reports submitted to the State Department by the Embassy and the consulate general. Moreover, the commercial attaché maintained branch offices in several large Mexican cities—cities where an American consul was already reporting on commercial and other matters.[40]

As a beginning, Daniels sought, though without much success, to bring the commercial attaché under closer control of the Embassy. To this end he persuaded economy-minded Dan Roper, the Secretary of Commerce, to cut his staff in Mexico to what the Ambassador regarded as a more reasonable level.[41] Fortunately, Thomas H. Lockett, Daniels' commercial attaché, was able to forgive this sabotage. Lockett was the only Embassy staff member who served throughout the Daniels mission, no doubt partly because he and the Ambassador got along extremely well. Though he possessed some independence, Lockett consequently worked closely with the Embassy, often supplying Daniels with intelligence of real value. Thus the Ambassador managed to achieve a working, if not a formal, control over this important branch of his domain.

Daniels also tried, again unsuccessfully, to convince the State Department that all important reports should be channeled through the Embassy. This would make the Embassy, he told Secretary Hull, "the central agency for information and carrying out the policies of the Government."[42] Hull had more important matters on his mind, and Daniels never did get full jurisdiction over the consuls stationed in Mexico. Later, however, he instituted a series of annual consular conferences in Mexico City designed to brief the consuls on American policy and incidentally to enable the Embassy and the State Department to evaluate their work. Daniels made it a point at these conferences to preach the Good Neighbor Policy, and he and his superiors did not hesitate to weed out any man who seemed unable to comprehend the new era.[43]

Perhaps in part because he was an old Navy hand, Ambassador

Daniels was immediately suspicious of the work done by his military attaché, an army officer attached to the Embassy but responsible directly to the War Department. He was shocked to discover that the military attaché had a small expense allowance for intelligence work, and that he sometimes used these funds in a way that made the American government, as Daniels protested to Secretary Hull, "a party to bribery."[44] The War Department, moreover, had plans for expanding its staff in Mexico City, at the very time the Ambassador was doing his best to cut expenses and personnel in other agencies. Daniels therefore suggested to Secretary of War George H. Dern that he abandon the plan to send an assistant military attaché to Mexico, since such a move could hardly be justified "in an economical administration." Besides, the military attaché mainly collected information that the Embassy regularly furnished the State Department. "I cannot conceive," he told Dern, "why the data cannot be made available to all departments of the Government."[45] Privately, the Ambassador complained to Hull that much of the military attaché's work was "trenching upon the duties of the Embassy."[46]

Secretary Dern naturally did not take kindly to the thought that his representative's duties were unimportant, and his reply indicated that the good neighbor spirit had not yet percolated into the War Department. The military attaché, he explained, must continue to supply him with full reports on the political stability and war-making capacity of Mexico. Such information was needed especially "in the case of those countries with which we may become involved in war, or against which we may be compelled to take punitive measures."[47] This last phrase was too much for Daniels, who immediately remonstrated:

I tremble to think what would be the reaction in Mexico if the sentence quoted above were made public .... I am insisting to the State Department that placing Mexico in a status different from that of other nations should no longer continue. It is partly because we have pursued such a course in the past that Mexicans have felt that we were fruitful of words of fraternity but that often the acts were not in conformity with our professions.

Today we have no thought of "punitive measures." If your Military Attaché is making reports in contemplation of "punitive measures," is it not a wrong conception in these days of harmonious cooperation by the two neighbor republics?[48]

Dern's silence in the face of this pointed query suggested that the War Department was unconvinced. But the exchange also was proof that in Josephus Daniels the United States had a diplomat of a rather rare order, one who was idealistic, independent, and, when dealing with his superiors, unabashedly outspoken.

Ambassador Daniels again demonstrated these traits—idealism and forthright independence—in the fall of 1933, when Cuba was torn by violence and revolution and there were calls for American intervention to restore order. The United States possessed not only large economic interests but also special treaty rights in Cuba. Under the terms of the so-called Platt Amendment, which was imposed upon the island republic when it received its independence after the Spanish-American War, Cuba had consented that the United States might intervene both to preserve Cuban independence and to maintain orderly government. The political turmoil in Cuba, which eventually resulted in the overthrow of three successive governments, did not come under Daniels' direct purview, of course. He was soon drawn into the controversy, none the less, both because he had strong feelings about the proper American reponse to the Cuban revolt, and because the Mexican government took the lead in opposing any United States intervention, Platt Amendment or no.

The United States Ambassador in Cuba at this time was Sumner Welles, a professional diplomat of considerable skill and experience temporarily detached from his regular post as Assistant Secretary of State. Like Daniels, Welles had gone to Cuba professing his devotion to President Roosevelt's Good Neighbor Policy in foreign affairs. But the new Good Neighbor Policy was as yet unformulated and untried, scarcely more than a vague slogan taken from Roosevelt's inaugural address the previous March. The Cuban crisis provided its first real test and forced

Washington to spell out more precisely just what the new gospel of neighborliness meant. And in the process there developed a significant divergence between the views of Welles and Daniels, a difference that was to be of importance in later years when worsening relations with Mexico subjected the Good Neighbor Policy to its severest trial.

Ambassador Welles' initial approach to the troubled Cuban situation was to seek the voluntary retirement of the unpopular dictator, President Gerardo Machado, using a combination of soft persuasion and tough-minded firmness. As Machado proved unable to cope with the increasing unrest on the island, Welles raised the spectre of American military intervention under the Platt Amendment. He even asked Washington for authority to withdraw diplomatic recognition from the Machado regime if the President refused to step down, and when conditions grew worse recommended the dispatch of two American warships to Havana harbor.[49] Was this to be the practical meaning of the new Good Neighbor Policy—old fashioned restraint and benevolent supervision?

Across the Caribbean in nearby Mexico Ambassador Daniels fervently hoped not, for he now had second thoughts about even the well-intentioned and idealistically motivated intervention of the Wilson administration. His attitude had been spelled out in a recent letter of reminiscence to his one-time naval assistant, President Roosevelt:

You know that the things we were forced to do in Haiti was [*sic*] a bitter pill to me, for I have always hated any foreign policy that even hinted of imperialistic control .... I never did wholly approve of that Constitution of Haiti you had a hand in framing or the elections we held by which our hand-picked President of Haiti was put in office. I expect, in the light of experience, we both regret the necessity of denying even a semblance of "self-determination" in our control of Haiti, when we had to go in and end revolutions or see some European government do so. Your "Good Neighbor" policy will not, I hope, be subjected to any such emergency as we were up against ....[50]

On the very same day that Welles asked for warships, Daniels wrote Secretary Hull warning against the unfortunate effect on

Latin America if the United States intervened in Cuba. "Something ought to be done to get rid of Machado," he admitted. But Washington should not try to do the job alone. "Would it not be better," he argued, "for us to ask the cooperation of the ABC countries or a representative of Mexico and nearby Latin American countries, with a view to securing peace in Cuba than to act alone?"[51]

Ambassador Welles' prodding, powerfully reinforced by a crippling general strike and the defection of Cuban army units, finally convinced the reluctant President Machado of the wisdom of quitting both his office and his country. After a serious of anxious conferences between Welles and Cuban officials, it was decided that the new president should be Dr. Carlos Manuel de Céspedes, a former diplomat and cabinet member. For a time it seemed that the crisis was over. The day after President Céspedes took office two American destroyers arrived in Havana harbor, and their presence had a quieting effect. Within a week the situation seemed calm enough for Welles to recommend that he return to Washington soon. Now that Cuba was relatively quiet he was becoming somewhat embarrassed, he told the State Department, at "the measure of control over the Government" which the Embassy possessed.[52]

Despite Welles' optimism, Céspedes was too closely tied to the old order to inspire much popular enthusiasm. Strikes and scattered violence continued, and on the night of September 4 a group of army sergeants, led by Fulgencio Batista, deposed their officers, seized control of the army, and overthrew the three-week-old government. As the extent of the coup became apparent, Welles worriedly decided that destroyers were inadequate and he would need a cruiser or even a battleship. In a series of anxious telephone calls to the State Department he suggested that a small detachment of Marines be landed to protect the Embassy and the National Hotel in Havana, where he and other Americans were living. Welles was also in touch with leaders of the deposed Céspedes government, one of whom informed him of plans for a counterrevolution and intimated that its success would be mater-

ially advanced by the strategic landing of American troops. The
Ambassador immediately advised Washington that such support
would be "most decidedly...in the best interest of the United
States Government." He proposed a "strictly limited intervention"
to help restore the Céspedes regime, estimating that it would
"presumably entail the landing of a considerable force in Habana
and lesser forces in certain of the more important ports of the
Republic." No doubt there would be charges that the United
States supported Céspedes because he was friendly to American
interests, but Welles was convinced that the rest of Latin America
would accept the move as "well within the limits of the policy of
the 'good neighbor.' "[53]

Washington's response to this interventionist scheme was decidedly chill. Secretary Hull and President Roosevelt decided to
send several naval vessels to Cuba and authorized Welles to land
a Marine guard if he and his staff were in actual danger. But they
wanted no part in any counterrevolution. Hull cabled Welles to
maintain "strict neutrality," lest his actions have "disastrous effects" on current United States consultations with other Latin
American states over the crisis.[54] The Mexican government, which
might well be accused of a myopic Yankeephobia on the subject
of American gunboats and revolutions, had come out strongly
against any unilateral U. S. intervention in Cuba, and from Mexico City Ambassador Daniels repeatedly urged his superiors to
seek an inter-American solution rather than invoke the Platt
Amendment. "Wilson did this, you know, but belatedly," he reminded President Roosevelt. "To be effective, it should be done
promptly."[55] Roosevelt was enough impressed with Daniels' arguments to refer a similar letter to the State Department.[56] On
September 9 Secretary Hull telephoned Daniels to get more information on a Mexican effort to line up support from the ABC
powers of South America for a peaceful Cuban settlement. "They
are very tense down here," Daniels told him. "They feel that if
we intervene it will destroy the Montevideo Conference," the
Pan American meetings scheduled for the coming December.[57]
Daniels cautioned Hull against being stampeded by Welles's re-

ports of Communist control over the Cuban revolutionary movement. "If I were you I would accept with many grains of allowance the attempt to saddle on the comparatively few Communists
all that goes awry," he observed.

Army officers under a Machado are often the agents of repression and
have no heart-beat for the oppressed and distressed. May not the rich
and powerful in Cuba, and their allies in the United States, and imperialistic army officers, be behind the attempt to hide behind exaggerat-
ing the lawlessness of Communists? I do not know, but I submit the
question for your consideration.[58]

"Hungry mobs are dangerous and need to be suppressed—and
fed," he reminded the Secretary of State subsequently, "but swag-
gering militarists are more dangerous."[59]

Meanwhile, the Cuban revoluntionary junta had named as Provisional President Dr. Ramón Grau San Martín, a university professor whom Ambassador Welles described as "utterly impractical"
and an "extreme radical."[60] Welles therefore advised Washington
that "it would be highly prejudicial to our interests" to recognize
the new government.[61] In fact, after conferring with Cuban opposition leaders, he recommended that President Roosevelt issue
a public statement calling for the formation of a more representative (and conservative) government. Otherwise, he foresaw only
further revolutionary chaos, with consequent damage to American and foreign property, or the establishment of an even "more
radical" military dictatorship.[62] But despite two strong pleas,
Roosevelt and Hull declined to interfere.[63]

Ambassador Daniels heartily approved of Washington's hands-
off policy. "Your patience and wisdom are being justified in a
situation where it was easy to take a false step," he told President
Roosevelt. "I believe you will escape intervention and give Cuba
the opportunity to work out its own destiny."[64] To Cordell Hull
he repeated his concern, based on personal experience, lest the
United States be maneuvered into actions reminiscent of old-style
gunboat diplomacy.

During my years as Secretary of the Navy I was forced, as policeman,
to send ships and Marines into weak countries to carry out some State

Department policies with which I was not wholly in sympathy. I learned then that Mr. Lansing held to a policy that was semi-imperialistic and at one time would have welcomed war with Mexico. Wilson repudiated an act of Lansing's which might have led to hostilities between the two countries. It was humanity that sent our soldiers into Cuba, but the monopolization of Cuban resources and land by Americans since Cuba has been under our protection has not been wholly in keeping with the unselfish spirit of sacrifice displayed by the men who fought to free Cuba from Spain and selfish domination (both of us were ardently for Cuban liberty then). It was due to a like conception of high duty that sent us into Haiti, but we overstayed our time. Knowing my feeling about imperialism, Secretary Franklin Lane would mockingly refer to me at Cabinet meetings as "the King of Haiti." I know that we both wish to see our country wholly free from anything that savors of Dollar Diplomacy, and I am writing in jealous zeal that the New Deal in this part of the world will have no connection with former policies which have caused some of our actions to be viewed with suspicion south of the Rio Grande.[65]

Privately, Daniels thought the United States ought to recognize the new Cuban government, which he believed was leading a healthy social revolution, but he refrained from advice on this score. The State Department was impressed by Welles's reports of the instability and radicalism of the Grau San Martín regime, however, and Washington decided to withhold recognition and maintain its naval forces off Cuba.

The approach of the Seventh Pan American Congress, scheduled to take place in December at Montevideo, Uruguay, ultimately brought a reconsideration of American policy. The Cuban Provisional Government planned to send a delegation to Montevideo, and there were reports of heavy pressure in Latin America for a concerted move to recognize it before the Conference opened. Secretary Hull learned with "some anxiety," moreover, that the Mexican government planned at Montevideo to propose that the Monroe Doctrine be modified so as to prohibit not only European but also American intervention in the affairs of Pan American countries, a move that seemed clearly related to the Cuban crisis.[66] Daniels' second-in-command, Arthur Bliss Lane, reported after a visit to Washington that the State Department felt the Mexicans had "let us down badly." Some officials even believed that "unless Mexico plays ball with us it would be far better not to have a conference."[67]

Characteristically, Ambassador Daniels did not share such narrow pessimism. When Secretary Hull telephoned him about the Mexican proposal in mid-October, he argued boldly that the time had indeed come to convert the Monroe Doctrine into a general hemispheric policy. He urged that President Roosevelt renounce any unilateral United States action in Latin America. Such a step would not only "clear the atmosphere at Montevideo," he told Hull, but would be "another declaration that will be heard around the world, and which will cheer and hearten all who wish Pan American understanding and solidarity."[68] Hull was unimpressed by this suggestion, however, and he went to Montevideo devoutly hoping that the subject would not come up.[69]

Undiscouraged, Daniels made one further effort during the Conference to persuade the Secretary of State of the wisdom of modifying the traditional American view of the Monroe Doctrine. To dispel any Latin American notion that the United States merely reserved for itself what it forbade Europe, Daniels recommended that Hull announce a kind of Good Neighbor corollary to the Doctrine: "This country will never on its own motion send troops into any country in this hemisphere and if cases arise where it is needful that neighbor countries assist in the preservation of orderly government in any Pan American country, the United States will confer with other nations and cooperate with them for preservation of peace and order."[70] Hull was evidently unwilling to go this far, but he did cast an affirmative U. S. vote, subject to a future definition of terms, for the list of Rights and Duties of States drawn up by the Conference. The most significant of these Rights and Duties, adopted in a session the Secretary of State described as "more or less wild and unreasonable," was embodied in Article 8: "No state has the right to intervene in the internal or external affairs of another."[71] This was not so explicit a pledge as Daniels had proposed, but it was far more than Secretary Hull had contemplated before the Conference opened.

Several considerations lay behind Hull's historic step at Mon-

tevideo. For one thing, he had been amazed and upset by the
angry denunciation of past United States intervention in the
speeches of various Latin American delegates during the debate
over Article 8.[72] Perhaps more important, Hull's assent to Article
8 reflected President Roosevelt's own keen desire to put his administration's relations with Latin America on a genuine good-
neighbor basis. While his Secretary of State was en route to Montevideo, Roosevelt had quietly intervened in the stalemated Cuban situation. After a conference with the by now controversial
Ambassador Welles at Warm Springs, Georgia, the President announced that Welles would shortly return to his Washington post
and that his successor would be career diplomat Jefferson Caffery.
As soon as Cuba had a stable provisional government enjoying
broad popular support, Roosevelt declared, the United States
hoped to negotiate mutually beneficial commercial and economic
agreements. But of greatest interest was the President's promise
to discuss "a modification of the permanent treaty between the
United States and Cuba."[73] This could only mean that he contemplated relinquishing some of the American rights under the Platt
Amendment. "I cannot but feel," Undersecretary of State William
Phillips cabled the absent Hull, "that the President would now
like to find some excuse to alter his policy if a way can be found
to do so without prejudice to his former position."[74] Thus when
the Latin American delegates at Montevideo bitterly attacked
past United States meddling, Secretary Hull was able to cite Roosevelt's recent offer to reconsider the Platt Amendment as proof
of the sincerity of Washington's new good-neighbor spirit.[75]

Only a few days after the Montevideo Conference had formulated the nonintervention rule, President Roosevelt reaffirmed in
categorical terms his administration's compliance with the ban.
Addressing the Woodrow Wilson Foundation, he conceded that
Latin Americans were suspicious of United States motives and
intentions, and in the past sometimes justifiably so. To clear up
any doubts, he declared that "the definite policy of the United
States from now on is one opposed to armed intervention." The
maintenance of law and order was a domestic concern, Roosevelt

observed. "It is only if and when the failure of orderly processes affects the other Nations of the continent that it becomes their concern; and the point to stress is that in such an event it becomes the joint concern of a whole continent in which we are all neighbors."[76]

To a delighted Ambassador Daniels in Mexico City, the President's explicit renunciation of the role of policeman in Latin America signified that the Good Neighbor Policy would indeed be far more than a slogan. "The Monroe Doctrine, the Wilson Mobile utterance and your declaration," he immediately telegraphed Roosevelt, "constitute the trinity embodying a noble American policy on this continent which confers glory upon our country."[77] Diplomats and reporters in Washington speculated that Daniels himself had inspired Roosevelt's dramatic pledge.[78] Actually, there is no conclusive evidence linking Daniels with the President's address to the Wilson Foundation, and very likely neither he nor Secretary Hull knew of it in advance. The State Department took no part in preparing the original draft of the speech, and saw a copy only after Roosevelt had worked it over carefully. Twice Daniels had proposed precisely such a presidential declaration to Hull, but there is no reason to believe that the Secretary of State passed the idea along to the White House. Certainly Daniels' frequent letters to Roosevelt during the Cuban crisis left no doubt of his conviction that the time had come to abandon unilateral intervention in Latin America for more neighborly joint action. But just what role, if any, he had in shaping the President's views is unclear.

With Washington's nonrecognition policy unchanged, by January, 1934, President Grau's support in Cuba began to weaken, and he finally resigned to make way for a more conservative government headed by Colonel Carlos Mendieta. In less than a week Secretary Hull extended "formal and cordial recognition," and the long crisis seemed over.[79] But in Mexico City Ambassador Daniels was not so sure, and he questioned whether the United States had behaved like a proper good neighbor in Cuba. "I do not think that Cuba is going to become quiet or stable until they have a President of their own choosing," he told Cordell Hull in the summer of 1934.[80] All too frequently since the Spanish-American War, he asserted, U. S. representatives in Cuba had been more concerned with protecting private American investments than in helping the Cubans achieve genuine independence:

I could wish we had as Ambassador in Cuba a man of a new type. Welles and Caffery are of the old school of diplomats, who never saw anything wrong in the sort of diplomacy which cost us the confidence of the people of Pan America in the past years. What we need in all Pan American Embassies and Legations are men of our type, who will change the whole atmosphere and have welcome in their hearts for a New Deal in those countries such as we wish for our own.[81]

On another occasion during his first year in Mexico, Ambassador Daniels' strong views as to the good neighbor responsibilities of the United States came into conflict with the more narrow approach of his State Department superiors. This was in connection with his negotiation of a claims settlement, a major achievement in improving Mexican-American relations. The State Department had warned Daniels before he went to Mexico that his first big task would be to dispose of the mountain of claims being pressed by nationals of both countries. Some of these claims dated back to 1868, the date of the last claims settlement, and had been neglected so long that the original nineteenth-century claimants had long since gone elsewhere for their reward. In the sixty-five-year interval, claims against both governments had been steadily accumulating, weighted in favor of the United States due to property depredations of the revolutionary years and the subsequent land reform programs. In fact, the claims by Americans against Mexico amounted to a half billion dollars, while Mexican claims against the United States totaled nearly half as much.

These totals were not to be taken seriously, however. Some of the claims, like the one by the American inventor who demanded $42,000,000 from Mexico for antipicated profits on a patent, or that of a group of Mexicans who claimed ownership of a sizable chunk of Los Angeles, Daniels soon decided were absurd or grossly exaggerated. When he discussed the matter with Senator

Key Pittman, chairman of the Senate Foreign Relations Committee, Pittman recalled that one American claimant "had filed papers for $300,000 and would be glad to get $30,000." Daniels asked if the man would not accept $3,000 cash, and Pittman laughed and said he thought he would.[82]

Everyone agreed that this obstacle to close relations between the two countries ought to be removed, but the question was how this could be done with justice to both the American claimants and the impoverished Mexican government. The Bucareli Conference of 1923, it will be recalled, had established two claims commissions of mixed membership, one to process and value general claims, and the other to handle the special claims arising out of the turbulent revolutionary period from 1910 to 1920. Yet down to 1932 the two commissions, operating at a cost of more than two-and-a-half million dollars to the United States, had made little progress toward a final settlement, and American claimants and the State Department alike despaired of obtaining satisfaction under the ponderous commission system.[83] Daniels' predecessor, Ambassador Clark, had therefore begun informal conversations looking toward an *en bloc* or lump sum settlement, similar to those negotiated by various European governments equally dissatisfied with the slow-moving claims commission method. These lump sum agreements had scaled down claims originally totaling 382 million pesos to about 10 million pesos. The percentage of return varied with the country, from a high of 7.92 per cent for Belgium to a low of 2.46 per cent for Spain, but the average return for the six nations involved was 2.65 per cent.[84]

Both Daniels and the State Department agreed that he should try to get a lump sum settlement of the troublesome claims issue. "At the present rate of progress," the Ambassador told President Roosevelt shortly after he got to Mexico, "your son Franklin's grandchildren would be gray headed before all these claims could be heard and determined."[85] But, like most of his predecessors, Daniels quickly found that the Mexicans were, understandably, hard to pin down to specifics. Early in the negotiations, he advised the State Department that Puig had promised some "concrete

proposals to be delivered three or four days after May 1st."[86]
Nevertheless, it was October before Puig got around to presenting
his first serious offer, and by the end of the year, when Daniels
summed up progress to date in a letter to a former Embassy staff
member, he concluded pessimistically, "But you know better
than I do the Mañana troubles."[87]

From the first, Ambassador Daniels showed himself more disposed than the State Department to take Mexican poverty into
account in reaching a claims settlement. When the Foreign Office
finally proposed a lump sum settlement of $13,500,000 for the spe-
cial claims dating from the revolutionary period 1910–1920, to
be paid over thirty years at no interest, Daniels urged his superiors to give the offer serious consideration. This sum would
amount to a recovery of 2.65 per cent for memorialized claims
(those that had been formally accepted by the claims commission)
and 1.25 per cent for unmemorialized claims. The former figure
was based on the average recovery by six European nations for
similar claims, the latter on the average recovery by the United
States in its claims conventions with Mexico in 1839 and 1868.
"I feel it my duty," Daniels told Secretary Hull, "to say that...
our Government should be ready to go more than half way."[88]
But the State Department hesitated, not convinced that this was
the best Mexico could do, and Daniels felt obliged to point out
once more that in as much as six other countries had accepted an
average recovery of 2.65 per cent the United States could not "with
good grace and with sound argument press for a larger amount."
He disapproved, moreover, of the Department's reasoning that
since Mexico could not afford to pay substantial amounts on both
general and special claims, it would be better to hold off settlement of the former until some future time. "My own opinion is
that the wisest course is to do everything reasonably possible to
reach an en bloc settlement on all claims and not take two bites at
this cherry," he advised. "Some day there must be recognition of
the true situation and a willingness to meet the Mexicans more
than half way on these claims controversies."[89]

After more than a month of indecision, the State Department

rejected the Mexican offer on special claims, at the same time instructing Daniels to negotiate a protocol that would have the effect of postponing a settlement of the general claims for several years.[90] The Ambassador undertook to carry out orders, but he continued to argue that it would be wiser to settle both sets of claims in order to be rid of the disagreeable issue. And he advocated a kind of diplomatic Golden Rule. "I have tried to go beneath pleadings and agreements, forced or voluntary," he reminded the Department, "and ask what we would expect Mexico to demand of our country if conditions were reversed."[91] Privately, he told Cordell Hull that were it not for the 1923 Bucareli claims convention, in which the Mexicans had admitted liability for the property damage of the Revolution in return for United States recognition, he "would not feel that Mexico should be held responsible for what occurred when there was no responsible government in operation."[92]

In February, 1934, Foreign Minister Puig Casauranc came up with a new proposal. Among other things, he offered to pay off the special claims over a fifteen-year instead of a thirty-year period. Daniels urged acceptance. "In a day when no European government is paying back what it borrowed from our government, and all creditors, individual and public, are either granting moratoriums or making generous adjustments," he advised Hull, "I feel that we should meet this country more than half way."[93] In Washington, Herschel V. Johnson, head of the Mexican desk at the State Department, concurred: "I am heartily and without reservation in agreement with you that we ought to accept. I promise you that I will do what I can to this end. It seems to me it is futile to attempt to carry on these negotiations any longer."[94] But discussions dragged while lawyers in both capitals haggled over details, those in the State Department insisting that Mexico should be charged interest as an incentive to regular payments.

Final agreement seemed in sight when suddenly State Department claims experts raised new objections. They had discovered that the proposed special claims convention, although ostensibly based on the average Mexican settlement with European coun-

tries, did not take into account certain American claims that for
one reason or another had been excluded before the totals were
calculated. This meant that the Europeans had been paid for some
claims similar to ones for which the United States would not. The
difference was only about 0.5 per cent in Mexico's favor, but since
the American claims totaled about $300,000,000, it would mean a
difference of perhaps $1,500,000 less in the final award. The Mex-
icans denied that this was unfair discrimination, pointing out that
the American and European settlements could not really be compared. The Europeans, except for Belgium, had agreed to accept
payment in Mexican pesos without interest, while the United
States demanded payment in dollars with interest.[95] Hull cabled
Daniels to remind Foreign Minister Puig of the need for "concessions on both sides," since no time remained "for protracted
discussion of minor technicalities."[96]

But in a tense two-hour session at the Foreign Office, Daniels
found Dr. Puig adamant. The Foreign Minister declared he
would rather let the whole negotiations lapse than compromise
further.[97] In a private letter to Cordell Hull the same day Daniels
expressed his deep concern lest the fruits of an entire year's work
be lost:

I was greatly disappointed ... that the Department did not see its way
clear to following the last recommendation which I wired the Department. Negotiations have been going on a whole year and I thought, and
still think, we had obtained the best possible adjustment of a very difficult situation .... I must say to you, my dear friend as well as superior
officer, that I have felt that in some details insistence by the Department
upon the strictly technical approach has been made paramount to the
larger questions of policy which would affirmatively have shown that
we are actually and practically practicing the generous good neighbor
policy. There are other long standing difficult problems between the
two countries which must be taken up....By insisting upon our own
point of view in debt collections for individuals (some of them questionable) I have feared that we might render it more difficult to reach
agreements upon larger questions.[98]

After discussing the matter with Daniels by telephone, the
State Department finally capitulated, though in authorizing the

Ambassador to sign the agreements Undersecretary William Phillips reminded him unhappily that the approval was "given with reluctance."[99] This was not the feeling of the staff at the Embassy in Mexico City. "All of us here regret that the Department's authorization was given with reluctance," wrote Daniels' claims adviser to a Department lawyer. "Being on the ground and in personal touch with the different officials of the Foreign Office, we were in a better position to know the situation and estimate the outcome .... Moreover, we are convinced that any further discussion would not have secured any more concessions, and would have had a bad effect on other prospective negotiations."[100]

On April 24, 1934, exactly a year from the day he had presented his credentials to President Rodríguez, a jubilant Ambassador Daniels joined Foreign Minister Puig in signing the convention on special claims and the protocol covering the future disposition of general claims.[101] "Today witnessed the consummation of the hope cherished upon my appointment," Daniels noted happily in his diary. Now he could feel that in his first year he had "done something of value."[102] The two agreements were quickly ratified, Daniels himself being on hand in Washington to help convince a few skeptical senators that the settlement was as much as the United States could expect from poverty-stricken Mexico. And early in the new year the Ambassador received Mexico's first half-million dollar check as part payment for the damage to American property during the Revolution.[103] There was no telling what troubles lay ahead, but one thing was certain: the Good Neighbor Policy had been put to work, and Josephus Daniels had shown himself to be perhaps its most dedicated and persistent advocate.

CHAPTER IV

A Nearly Fatal Speech

The Roman Catholic Church has been a powerful force in Mexico since the days of Hernán Cortés and the conquest. Much of recent Mexican history, in fact, is incomprehensible without an understanding of both the historic influence of the Church and the rising determination of Mexican secular leaders to wrest from it some of its great power. Owner of half the land in Mexico and holder of mortgages on much of the remaining property, in firm control of education, exempted from civil justice, the Church in the colonial period was a formidable force. After Mexico achieved its independence in 1822 anticlericalism tended to become a staple element of Mexican politics, and throughout the nineteenth century a series of governments, most notably that of President Benito Juárez in the 1850's, sought with varying success to whittle down the special privileges and political and material power of the clergy.

But the most serious challenge to the Church came with the outbreak of the Mexican Revolution in 1910. The revolutionary leaders were passionately determined to set drastic limits to the clergy's influence over the life of the nation. The new Mexican Constitution adopted in 1917 frankly aimed to drive the Church

82

out of politics and to restrict it to narrowly defined religious functions. Among other restraints, it authorized the state legislatures
to limit the number and activities of priests in each locality, and
declared that primary education should henceforth be secular in
character and under strict government control.

Leaders of the Church could hardly be expected to let the new
Constitution go unchallenged, and their opposition to its religious
and educational provisions was made plain from the first. But
here the Church found itself aligned with the large landowners
and foreign interests that also were threatened by the Revolution,
and many Mexicans judged it accordingly. Had the Church
leaders, without siding with the other enemies of revolutionary
Mexico, limited their protest to a convincing defense of religious
freedom, had they come out strongly for the social reforms of
the Revolution, and had American Catholics not lent color to the
charge that the Church was seeking foreign intervention to destroy the Revolution, subsequent Mexican history would undoubtedly have been different. As it was, the men who came to power
through the Revolution and who governed Mexico in the 1920's
and 1930's remained convinced that the Church was irreconcilably
opposed to the new Mexico.

In 1926, during the administration of President Calles, the sim-
mering conflict between Church and State erupted into open revolt—the so-called Cristero Rebellion. For the next three years
there was sporadic fighting between government and clerical
forces. Although militarily the advantage lay with the government, the Church was not without important support. Ever since
the beginning of the Revolution Catholics in the United States
had watched the developments in Mexico with mounting concern.
Indeed, Catholic resentment of President Wilson's Mexican policies was a factor of some importance in the American national
elections in 1916, and throughout the twenties American Catholics had continued to keep an anxious eye on Mexico. The Cristero
Rebellion, with its bloody excesses on both sides, enflamed Catholic opinion in the United States and led to American efforts to
end the religious controversy. In April, 1928, Rev. John J. Burke.

a prominent American priest noted for his liberal social views, conferred secretly with President Calles at Veracruz in an attempt to mediate the dispute. The following year an uneasy peace was arranged with the quiet support of American Catholic leaders and U. S. Ambassador Dwight Morrow.

The Church was still very much on the defensive, however, and to the faithful intolerably so. A number of Mexican states, exercising their powers under the Constitution, passed laws severely limiting the number of priests and making it almost impossible for them to function. In Veracruz, to use one of the more extreme examples, only one priest was permitted for every 100,000 of population, while in Tabasco, one of the most anticlerical states, all clergymen were required to be married. The effect of this anticlerical legislation was to close churches in many parts of Mexico and to curtail drastically the number of priests operating legally.

Of equal import to the hierarchy, which had to think in terms of centuries, was the government's determination to secularize education, traditionally the domain of the Church. Before the Revolution popular education had been sadly neglected in Mexico, and the comparatively few schools had catered mainly to the small upper classes of the cities. In 1910 only 2.9 million out of a population of 15.1 million could read or write, and there were parts of Mexico where even Spanish was unknown. The leaders of the Revolution were determined to change this. In the Constitution of 1917 they were explicit as to the kind of training they wanted for the children of the new Mexico. Reserving for the State exclusive control over education, they forbade any religious teaching in the schools and declared that instruction must be rational and socialistic in content. Thereafter, a succession of Mexican governments waged war against the nation's shockingly high rate of illiteracy, greatly expanding the public school system, and in the process implementing many of the constitutional restrictions on the activities of religious schools.[1]

In 1933, when Ambassador Daniels arrived in Mexico, the struggle between Church and State was still bitter and intense, notwithstanding a deceptive surface calm. Daniels had been carefully briefed on the touchy religious situation before he left the United States. Herschel Johnson, who had served with Ambassador Morrow and was now head of the Mexican desk in the State Department, told him frankly: "The whole history of the Roman Catholic Church in Mexico demonstrates the determination of its hierarchy to participate in, and if possible, control the political trend of the country .... It has always supported the reactionary forces and aligned itself with the property interests." Johnson also expressed enthusiasm for the progress being made by the Mexican government in extending primary education to the Indian masses. "Despite all the grossness and selfishness of the leaders of the revolution," he observed, "there is a germ of sincerity that you trace all through the movement, even with the worst of the leaders. They desire to uplift the illiterate Indian peasant."[2]

From American Catholic leaders Daniels received a rather different assessment. Only two months before his appointment the Catholic bishops of the United States had publicly protested against "the sustained persecution of the Church in Mexico."[3] And shortly before he left for Mexico City the editor of the Jesuit weekly *America* published a long open letter urging the new Ambassador to intervene actively in the Mexican religious controversy. "In any case the precedent exists," Daniels was reminded, "and if you go about it the right way, in the name of common humanity, you can confer a service on mankind."[4] From his friend Father Burke, the head of the National Catholic Welfare Conference and the American intermediary in the 1928–29 religious negotiations in Mexico, Daniels got a grim warning that the situation there was becoming critical. Burke assured him that the Vatican frowned not only on armed rebellion but also on Church interference in politics. He emphasized, however, that Mexican Catholics were permitted to have the services of only a "ridiculously small number of priests." "The situation with regard to religious liberty in Mexico," he declared, "continues, as you must see, to be deplorable."[5]

A prominent Methodist layman, Ambassador Daniels had a deep personal concern for religion. Despite the demands of a busy

schedule, for over a quarter of a century he had found time every
Sunday to give Bible lessons to successive classes of young people
at his Raleigh church. But unlike some southern Protestants, he
was in no sense anti-Catholic. As Secretary of the Navy in 1915
he had appointed a Catholic to be Chief of Naval Operations and
had increased the proportion of Catholic chaplains in the Navy.
During the twenties, he had fought the Ku Klux Klan in North
Carolina, and at the Democratic national convention in 1924 he
was one of the tiny handful of southerners who had supported a
resolution condemning the Klan. He had campaigned loyally for
Al Smith in 1928 even though he deplored Smith's views on pro-
hibition. American Catholics, therefore, had good reason to suppose that Ambassador Daniels would strongly disapprove any
religious persecution he might find at his new post. One priest
assured Daniels that his "breadth of Christian charity" was
"enough for me to understand your feeling in regard to things un-
Christian in Mexico."[6]

Still, Daniels' past record was to provide him with no immunity
from criticism by anxious American Catholics once he got to
Mexico. Catholic editors in the United States watched the Ambassador closely from the moment he crossed the Rio Grande,
and, in fact, his first official words brought a pained and angry
outcry. In presenting his credentials, Daniels politely remarked to
President Rodríguez that Americans had "deep admiration for
your marked advance in social reform, in public education, ... and
in all measures which promote the well-being of your nationals."[7]
For this rather perfunctory praise he was roundly rebuked by the
Catholic press back home. One of the strongest critics, the influential *Baltimore Catholic Review,* bluntly asserted that Daniels
"does not know what he is talking about," and declared that his
ill-considered words merited "the condemnation of everyone who
is familiar with conditions in our neighboring republic."[8] Several
of the Ambassador's Catholic friends arranged to kill a hostile
dispatch about the incident sent out by the news service of the
National Catholic Welfare Conference, and saw to it that his remarks on freedom of religion a few months later were well publi-

cized. But one of them, Colonel Patrick H. Callahan of Louisville, nevertheless advised Daniels to "go rather slowly for, to be frank, it is my thought no matter what you say you are going to be criticized by some of these editors."[9]

Although the brief flurry over his praise of Mexican social reform demonstrated the concern of American Catholics over the religious situation, neither Ambassador Daniels nor his superiors wanted to involve the United States in the Church-State struggle in Mexico. Indeed, with the lesson of Veracruz behind him, Daniels had good reason to reflect on the frustrations involved in trying to help the Mexicans settle their domestic disputes. "The Republic of Mexico belongs to the people of Mexico," he reminded a North Carolina Catholic shortly after his arrival in Mexico City. "We cannot enforce our views upon them and of course we would not permit them to enforce their views upon us."[10]

By word and deed, however, Daniels tactfully tried to show his interest in religion. From their first Sunday in Mexico he and Mrs. Daniels set an example by regularly attending the Union Evangelical Church in Mexico City, and in his first Fourth of July address to the American colony the Ambassador pointedly observed that freedom of religion was one of the very cornerstones of American liberty. Daniels did not hesitate to confer with Archbishop Pascual Díaz, the Primate of Mexico, and other Mexican Catholic leaders, and at Archbishop Díaz' request he intervened with American consular authorities to permit Mexican Catholic girls to enter the United States to study nursing in American hospitals.[11] Nevertheless, he tried to stay clear of the touchy Mexican religious controversy. "At this time there is nothing an official could do," he replied to an officer of the National Catholic Welfare Conference in the United States who urged that he mediate the dispute.[12] The Ambassador's determination to offend no one led one Mexican priest to declare with respect: "You are an old fox, you know the game; you tell your jokes and say nothing."[13]

As a trustee of the University of North Carolina and a longstanding champion of popular education in his home state, Ambassador Daniels was much less circumspect in commenting on Mexican educational matters. This was not surprising, since he and most Americans accepted without question the professed goal of Mexican government leaders: universal education through secular public schools. During his first year in Mexico Daniels visited a number of schools of various types and levels. He talked at length with teachers and school administrators and throughout evinced a keen insight into Mexican educational problems. As might be expected of a man who within the last year had led a drive for a longer school term in North Carolina, the Ambassador quickly showed an interest in governmental efforts to increase the number of Mexican schools. "There is a strong feeling here in and out of the Government," he told an interested Catholic friend back home, "that no effort should be spared to have schools that will give the rural children an opportunity of education and thus reduce and finally end the illiteracy which is so great in Mexico as to make difficult such participation in government matters as is necessary in a free republic."[14]

Like most Americans, the Ambassador considered it axiomatic that education was an obligation of the State, though this did not preclude, of course, suitably regulated private schools. Daniels believed that free government was impossible without an educated citizenry, and only the State had the resources to assure a decent education for all children. "Every child born into this world has the inalienable right of an opportunity to go to a school, supported by public taxation, so that he may burgeon out all that is in him," he told an audience at one of the Mexican schools he visited. "Experience has taught that the only guarantee of education of all the people is the operation of public schools as the essential factor of democratic government."[15]

Daniels consequently approved of the educational goals announced in the Six Year Plan drawn up by the ruling National Revolutionary Party late in 1933. Intended as a manifesto for the coming Mexican presidential election, the Six Year Plan promised among other things a federal program to build six thousand new schools by 1940.[16] This worthy undertaking, Daniels predicted to reporters, would "lead to an educated and trained population" which would "bring about the best development of the country."[17]

But many Catholics in Mexico and the United States did not share the Ambassador's enthusiasm, for the Six Year Plan also reiterated the constitutional doctrine that education must be under government direction and must be nonreligious and socialistic in character. Nor were Catholics reassured, moreover, by some of the inflammatory speeches made by leading Mexican politicians during the election campaign in the summer of 1934. Speaking at Durango late in June, General Lázaro Cárdenas, the presidential candidate of the National Revolutionary Party, vowed: "I shall not permit the clergy to intervene in any manner in the education of the people."[18] A few weeks later at Guadalajara General Calles, the *Jefe Máximo* himself, demanded that the government eradicate the hostile influence of the clergy and other conservative groups in Mexican schools. "We must now enter into and take possession of the minds of the children, the minds of the young," Calles warned, "because they do belong and should belong to the Revolution."[19] Late in July, after General Cárdenas' expected sweeping victory at the polls, a government commission presented a report calling for the amendment of the Constitution to purify Mexican education by prohibiting church schools and the teaching of religious dogmas.[20] Catholics above and below the Rio Grande expressed fear that a new anticlerical campaign was under way in Mexico.

Somewhere Ambassador Daniels came across a translation of the catchy sentence from General Calles' Guadalajara speech quoted above without seeing the rest of the General's strong attack on the Church. He was impressed by what he considered its earnest plea for universal education. It would, he decided, fit admirably into an address on education that he had been asked to give before the members of Professor Hubert Herring's annual American Seminar for the study of inter-American problems. The scholars and educators attending the Seminar would surely appreciate the important role played by public schools in a democracy and would understand the significance of the educational progress made by Mexico since the Revolution.

Daniels' speech to the Seminar on July 26, 1934, was merely a brief statement of his educational philosophy—exactly the sort of address he had made over the years in every corner of North Carolina without arousing so much as a ripple of protest. Rereading his words today, one wonders how they could have caused such a storm of controversy in the United States, where most Americans shared his devotion to the principle of universal public education. In the course of his remarks, Daniels quoted Jefferson on the correlation between freedom and education, and then noted recent Mexican educational advances. Private and religious organizations had done good work in educating some of the Mexican people and in promoting a love of learning, he observed, but "experience through many centuries has taught mankind that no other agency than Government has brought the advantages of education to all the children of any country." This was a lesson of history that the Mexican leaders of today recognized:

General Calles sees, as Jefferson saw, that no people can be both free and ignorant. Therefore, he and President Rodríguez, President-elect Cárdenas and all forward-looking leaders are placing public education as the paramount duty of the country. They all recognize that General Calles issued a challenge that goes to the very root of the settlement of all problems of tomorrow when he said: "We must enter and take possession of the mind of childhood, the mind of youth." That fortress taken, the next generation will see a Mexico that fulfills the dreams of Hidalgo, Juárez, Madero and other patriots who loved their country.[21]

Although his remarks were delivered at the Embassy to a group of visiting Americans—none of whom found them exceptional or offensive—Daniels soon discovered that in Mexico his speech was both unwise and indiscreet. Mexican Catholics, some of whom read a published English version of the address the next day, were quick to resent the Ambassador's apparent interference in the current struggle between Church and State. Catholics were incensed at his favorable reference to Benito Juárez, one of the leading nineteenth-century anticlericals, and at his quotation from General Calles, the prime mover behind the current assault on the Church. The small but vociferous Catholic newspaper *El Hombre Libre* of Mexico City at once indignantly protested Daniels' apparent support of a government campaign "to uproot from the mind of childhood, from the mind of youth, a belief in God and to convert our children into atheists and materialists even against the wishes and protests of parents."[22] The surprised Ambassador hastened to point out that he was praising only universal education, not any particular kind of instruction, and that he had not previously seen all of General Calles' remarks. "I did not even remotely touch upon the character of the instruction imparted, or that should be imparted, in the schools of this Republic," Daniels declared. "That is a matter for Mexicans alone to determine. I was simply declaring my faith in universal education and holding with Jefferson that 'if a nation expects to be ignorant and free, in a state of civilization, it expects what never was and never will be.' "[23] But the angry editor of *El Hombre Libre* kept the issue alive for nearly a month before grudgingly accepting the explanation.[24]

The interval was long enough to insure that the Ambassador's blunder would not be overlooked by Catholics in the United States. Daniels' well-meant but imprudent Seminar address now became a convenient way by which American Catholics could enter the Mexican religious controversy with some hope of rousing non-Catholic opinion and perhaps forcing action by the American government to persuade Mexico to stop harassing the Church. The Jesuit weekly *America* led the way late in August by denouncing as "shameful" Ambassador Daniels' endorsement of "the tyrannous designs of Calles upon the children of the nation," and vowing: "If this was actually Mr. Daniels' intention—and it will be verified—then the very least our own Government can do is to recall him; and this Review, at least, will not rest until he is recalled."[25] By the next issue the editor of *America* had made up his mind, though without consulting Daniels in the meantime as to his actual intent. "Daniels Should Resign!" proclaimed *America* in a leading editorial on September 1. "Ambassador Daniels did say the words attributed to him, and they show that he is no longer capable of representing the American people in Mexico."[26]

Most other Catholic papers showed more Christian restraint in not at first demanding the Ambassador's head. After contacting Daniels the news service of the National Catholic Welfare Conference sent out a story on the incident that included a fair statement of his intended meaning, though the effect of this was partially offset by the stress put on *America's* demand that he resign.[27] The *Baltimore Catholic Review*, diocesan organ of Mexico-conscious Archbishop Michael J. Curley, contented itself with a wry expression of sympathy for President Roosevelt because he did not have "an Ambassador in Mexico who 'knows what it is all about.' " At the same time its editor thoughtfully sent a copy to the White House to make sure the President was aware of this ominous solicitude.[28]

But as the debate in the Mexican Congress throughout September and October of 1934 showed that government leaders were determined to push through a constitutional amendment abolishing religious education, Catholics in the United States anxiously began to demand action to aid their coreligionists below the border. Largely as a result of the political developments in Mexico, American Catholics stepped up their attacks both on Ambassador Daniels and on official Washington's hands-off attitude. "What detestable cowardice on the part of the official representative of the mighty nation to the North," fumed one indignant priest, "to jump with both feet upon the weak children of a nation that is being harassed to death in its religious belief and practice by a persecutor that compares favorably with a Nero and a Stalin."[29] Late in September the Holy Name Union of Richmond voted unanimously to censure Daniels and to send copies of the rebuke to President Roosevelt and Secretary of State Cordell Hull. A few days later the National Council of Catholic Women sent to the White House a similar resolution deploring Daniels' approval of Mexico's godless school system.[30] Even in the Ambassador's home town, where his true feelings concerning religious freedom were well known, his indiscretion came in for sharp criticism. In his

Sunday sermon on October 6, Bishop William J. Hafey said he hoped Daniels had quoted General Calles only "thoughtlessly and unintentionally," but he nevertheless termed the action a "serious error" which warranted Catholic appeals to President Roosevelt "to deny this interpreted endorsement of Communistic Atheism in Mexico."[31]

Not all Americans were so quick to condemn the Ambassador, especially those who knew him best. Colonel Patrick H. Callahan, Daniels' stout defender against Catholic attacks during his first few months in Mexico, again jumped into the fray, suggesting that the present issue was being raised largely to provide political capital for the enemies of the Roosevelt administration.[32] "Could you not send me a copy of the address itself," he begged Daniels, "so I can see whether it is 'a mountain' or 'a mole hill'?"[33] After reading the much maligned speech, Callahan, who had been decorated by the Pope for his work in Catholic lay organizations, admitted to a friend: "There is nothing in this address but what I would have said myself under the same circumstances."[34] William F. Montavon, the legal adviser of the National Catholic Welfare Conference, also requested a copy of the speech, as well as Daniels' letter to the editor of *El Hombre Libre*. After reading both, he agreed that Daniels' remarks had been "misunderstood by some Catholic commentators."[35] North Carolinians professed themselves amazed that anyone could consider Josephus Daniels intolerant or anti-Catholic. The *Greensboro Daily News* recalled that in the past he had "offended many a Prostestant by his undisguised liberality toward a religion against which he could have made considerable capital in this severely Prostestant Eastern North Carolina .... Raleigh people would be astounded if President Roosevelt did anything to Mr. Daniels."[36]

But by mid-October the angry tone and growing volume of protests against Ambassador Daniels' alleged support of Mexican religious persecution had reached such proportions that the administration in Washington could no longer ignore the situation. At his press conference on October 17, President Roosevelt was asked whether he intended to recall Daniels as a result of the

furor, but he merely referred reporters to the State Department
and dismissed the question with an airy wave of his hand, saying
that the complaints sounded "fishy" to him.[37] The State Department could not get off the hook so easily. That same day Undersecretary of State William Phillips telephoned Daniels in Mexico
City, explaining that there had been "a little flurry in the press the
last day or two," and "in view of the political strength" involved,
he believed the Department should attempt to clarify the Ambassador's position.[38] Shortly after receiving Daniels' permission,
Phillips called a press conference and read to reporters the Ambassador's statement emphasizing his devotion to "the principles
of our country with reference to public schools, the freedom of
religion and the freedom of the press." Phillips indicated that the
State Department planned no further action in the matter, and
in an off-the-record comment reiterated the administration's fer-
vent desire to keep clear of entanglement in foreign church problems.[39] His remarks and the Daniels statement were given wide
press coverage in the United States and Mexico, and a number of
secular newspapers expressed the hope that the misunderstanding
could now be forgotten, because, as the *Dallas News* explained,
"Ambassador Daniels has so kindly a heart that he would be the
last man to arouse intentionally religious animosity."[40]

If the administration hoped this move would calm the mounting tide of Catholic indignation, it soon lost its illusions. Far from
forgetting Daniels' blunder, many American Caholics continued
to misinterpret and magnify it out of all proportion. *Commonweal's* rather uncharacteristic reaction to the Phillips press conference, for example, was to charge that Ambassador Daniels had
addressed "the Seminario, the official directors of Calles' educational storm troops," and to suggest that his remarks, if not officially repudiated, foreboded similar antireligious treatment in the
United States under the New Deal.[41] The journal *Ave Maria* was
darkly certain that if the Mexican persecution had involved Protestants Daniels would not "be so carefree in his approval of Calles
and his henchmen...or if he were, he would be recalled."[42] Even
the American hierarchy, at its annual meeting in mid-November,

issued a thinly veiled reprimand plainly intended for Ambassador Daniels. "We cannot but deplore," declared the bishops, "the expressions, unwittingly offered at times, of sympathy with and support of governments and policies which are absolutely at variance with our own American principles. They give color to the boast of the supporters of tyrannical policies that the influence of our American Government is favorable to such policies."[43]

Daniels' mail now grew heavy with rebukes and personal abuse, and the White House and State Department were flooded with petitions and protests. "If you have one bit of decency in you or the least hope of Eteranal Salvation," one bold anonymous writer stormed, "you will resign your post immeadiately, and opalogize for the wrong you have done."[44] From a North Carolina priest came the angry query: "How can you expect to save your soul, Mr. Daniels, when you aid and abet the godless gangsters of Mexico?"[45] Normally, the Ambassador did not answer the more extreme attacks, but he was obviously hurt by the frequent accusations that he was intolerant. "If you and your friends had heard my address," he replied soberly to one critic, "you would not have written me the letter you did. I have always stood for religious liberty and have said nothing in this country contrary to my life conviction."[46] By December the volume of mail to the State Department had become so heavy, and seemed so largely the result of organized propaganda efforts, that Secretary Hull told his staff not to bother acknowledging most of it. Over the next six months the Department received more than ten thousand communications dealing with the Mexican religious controversy, many of which were petitions bearing a number of signatures. One mammoth petition, in fact, was signed by twenty thousand persons. Two-thirds of the correspondents demanded the removal of Ambassador Daniels (only twenty-seven defended him), while most of the rest favored some other form of American protest against Mexican persecution.[47]

Daniels and his hapless superiors were also roundly condemned at a series of Catholic protest rallies. Monsignor Hugh L. Lamb, chancellor of the archdiocese of Philadelphia, denounced Daniels as a "consummate jackass" for approving of Mexico's "socialistic and communistic educational program." "If the embargo on arms were lifted, and rifles put in the hands of the majority," he declared ominously, "Calles and his band of minions would be blown to smithereens."[48] Other Catholic zealots, including at least two bishops, were similarly critical of the administration's alleged arms embargo, which one Knights of Columbus officer charged was actually "a form of intervention" favoring the godless Mexican government.[49] Relying more on emotion than reason, the famed radio priest Rev. Charles E. Coughlin managed to link Daniels, Woodrow Wilson, President Roosevelt, American oil concessionaires, and Moscow in what he termed "the rape of Mexico." Father Coughlin indignantly reminded his large radio audience that in 1914 Wilson and Daniels had run "the guns in for the mobsters and...won the dirtiest revolution this world has ever known." Small wonder that Daniels was now "practically" telling the Mexicans that "Americans are Communists and haters of Christ."[50] From New York to Spokane, Catholic groups organized a generally fruitless boycott of Mexican goods, and in Manhattan Catholic students picketed the Mexican Consulate.[51]

Not all of Daniels' mail was hostile, however, and from friends and strangers alike he received expressions of confidence. Several members of the now famous Seminar voiced astonishment that he should be attacked for statements they had found thoroughly American and completely inoffensive. The group's leader, Professor Hubert Herring, told Daniels: "I have been applauding you from the sidelines for your handling of that ticklish church situation. Now that the lunatics are breaking loose in Washington it is good to know that you are on the job in Mexico. I hope you won't let the firebrands get us into trouble."[52] Daniels' Catholic friends were no less concerned about Mexican religious persecution than his critics, but they deeply resented the slurs on his integrity and Christian devotion. "I want to say that I have been literally 'burned up' at the ravings of some of our Catholic editors," protested one. "Ambassador Daniels...is one of the finest, most sincere and greatest Americans we have today in America."[53]

A North Carolina Catholic professed utmost confidence in Daniels' "fairness and broadmindedness," explaining: "I wanted you to know how the Catholics of North Carolina feel about this matter. We love, honor, and respect you."[54]

The indefatigable Colonel Callahan was worth a small army in combatting the anti-Daniels propaganda, carrying on an extensive correspondence with some 1,500 Catholic editors, members of the hierarchy, and important laymen. Callahan pulled no punches in expressing his disgust over the ugly misrepresentations of his friend's conduct in Mexico. "If he were the direct representative of the Holy Father and on the payroll of the Vatican he could hardly do all the things that some of the Catholics in this country want him to do in Mexico," he expostulated on one occasion.[55] To a critical Catholic editor he admonished: "I see no reason why Calles should not be complimented for any good he might have done if we are to have any regard for free speech. I myself think he did fine in having two and in some places three children going to schools where only one went before."[56] Callahan delighted in offering hundred-dollar bonuses or items of clothing to errant Catholic editors if they could back up their wild charges. He promised one particularly flagrant offender an overcoat "if you will show me where Ambassador Daniels 'Blames the Church' for the conditions in Mexico," and raged: "As a builder of prejudices against Catholics I think you are entitled to a Pulitzer Prize for this year."[57] To Daniels himself Callahan declared wryly: "It is my thought that we will succeed in making a martyr out of you, in which event you will be known in history as 'St. Josephus.' "[58]

The drive to aid Mexican Catholics also quickly assumed a political character. The Mexican issue had not played a significant part in the 1934 American elections, but Catholic congressmen soon joined in the general denunciation of Mexican religious policies. In mid-December Representative John P. Higgins, a newly elected Democrat from Massachusetts, asked the President to intervene on behalf of the Church in Mexico. One of Higgins' first acts after the new Congress convened was to introduce a resolution demanding the recall of Ambassador Daniels and the with-

drawal of diplomatic recognition of Mexico. "Ambassador Daniels'
actions, during recent months," the irate Catholic congressman
told Roosevelt, "is an indictment of every principle of honor and
decency that America has stood for during the past one hundred
and fifty years and warrants his immediate removal."[59] Catholic
papers generally applauded the Higgins move, though one editor
warned that it might result in a Pyrrhic victory:

If a certain element of Catholics in America persist in their endeavor,
Mr. Daniels may really lose his position. At best, this would be a dubious redress even for an aggravated wrong. Those who know Mr.
Daniels best are agreed that he is in no sense anti-Catholic. However,
it is not inconceivable that he might be made into one .... Nor must it
be overlooked for Mr. Daniels that he was fearless in declaring the right
of conscience, the necessity of religion, and the belief in God. The over-
enthusiastic amongst us might readily be tricked into an action that
subsequent developments might bring sincere chagrin and sorrow.[60]

The secular press was also decidedly unenthusiastic, the Louisville *Courier-Journal* asserting that "few things could be more
injurious to Catholicism in America than the prosecution of such
charges."[61] The administration made plain, however, that it contemplated no change in either its Mexican envoy or its Mexican
policy. Secretary of State Hull cautioned Higgins that his proposal would almost certainly provoke such Mexican resentment as
to defeat his purpose, and President Roosevelt told him that his
interpretation of Ambassador Daniels' conduct was "as unjust
as it is unwarranted by the facts."[62]

"You must not worry if you hear that some member of Congress
proposes some drastic action with reference to our relations with
the Mexican Government," Assistant Secretary of State Walton
Moore advised Daniels early in January. "All sorts of remarkable
proposals are, of course, going to be made and with no result
beyond some little ineffective discussion."[63] Moore proved to be
right on both counts. Throughout January the political pressure
increased. New York's influential Democratic (and Catholic) Senator Robert F. Wagner put on record a series of resolutions framed
by Knights of Columbus groups demanding that the United States

sever trade and tourist relations with Mexico. Catholic organizations in Massachusetts petitioned Congress for action, and the New York State Senate sent a resolution to Washington urging that the United States condemn Mexican religious policies. On January 21 a delegation of the national leaders of the Knights of Columbus, headed by Supreme Knight Martin H. Carmody, conferred in Washington with Secretary Hull, demanding a blunt warning to Mexico that diplomatic relations would be broken unless "persecution and murder" of Catholics ceased.[64]

Ten days later Idaho's unpredictable Senator William E. Borah startled his colleagues and the nation by introducing a resolution calling for a full-dress Senate investigation of religious conditions in Mexico to determine whether the rights of American citizens were being violated.[65] The political importance of this move was underscored by the fact that Borah was a Protestant, the ranking Republican member of the Senate Foreign Relations Committee, and a statesman of national prominence. Catholics were, of course, jubilant that a non-Catholic of Borah's stature had enlisted on the side of the Church in Mexico. But some observers were struck by certain aspects of Borah's sudden interest in Mexico. For one thing, the Idaho Senator did not have many Catholic constituents, nor had he previously paid much attention to the Mexican religious controversy. He was, moreover, one of the country's leading isolationists, and for years had battled to keep the United States out of foreign disputes. In fact, only two days before he introduced his Mexican resolution Borah had led a successful fight to block Senate approval of American participation in the World Court. It seemed a little odd, therefore, that he should now become, as the *New York Times* put it acidly, "a screaming eagle of intervention in the domestic affairs of another nation."[66] Capitol Hill buzzed with rumors that the Borah resolution was a political pay-off for powerful Catholic support in defeating the World Court proposal.[67]

Whatever the motivation, Borah's move soon drew heavy fire. The *Milwaukee Journal* spoke for a number of secular newspapers when it asked pointedly: "What manner of Americanism is it that preaches 'isolation' when the other nations concerned are something like our size, but is ready for any degree of meddling with a smaller neighbor?"[68] A number of Protestant groups went on record against the Borah resolution, including the Federal Council of Churches of Christ in America, the National Council of the Protestant Episcopal Church, and the board of foreign missions of the Methodist Episcopal Church.[69] At Senator Borah's office the volume of protest mail rivaled his heavy Catholic support, and some of the opposition came from old and respected friends. Professor Edwin M. Borchard of the Yale Law School, for example, the Senator's longstanding adviser on international law and a recent visitor to Mexico, warned of the dangerous implications of the proposed investigation. "The appeal to 'human rights' in Mexico," he declared, "should be taken with a grain of salt, for so far as I was able to discover, the persecution consisted not in denying persons the right even to attend Church if they wished, but the disability of Church dignitaries to undermine the state by their hold upon ignorant Indians and others."[70]

In Mexico the opposition to Borah's proposal was virtually unanimous. *El Hombre Libre,* the Catholic paper that had helped set off the furor by publicizing Ambassador Daniels' Seminar address, indignantly rejected any American interference. "We earnestly beg our sympathizer," it implored Borah, "to leave us alone in our task of remedying the evils which assail us."[71] As a clincher, the Primate of Mexico, Archbishop Díaz, asserted privately that any American intervention like that proposed by Borah "would be very injurious to the interests of the Church in Mexico," and he expressed the hope that the State Department "would not allow such measures to be carried out."[72]

Actually, Borah's demand for a Senate investigation of Mexico never resulted in more than what Assistant Secretary of State Moore had predicted would be "some little ineffective discussion." In firm control of a Democratic Congress that was, after all, more interested in domestic economic problems, the Roosevelt administration kept the resolution effectively bottled up in committee.

"I have from the outset been giving every attention to the defeat of the Borah resolution," Secretary Hull assured Daniels in mid-February.[73] Hull virtually disposed of the matter when, with President Roosevelt's approval, he advised the friendly chairman of the Senate Foreign Relations Committee that there was no substance to Borah's charges and that his proposal was "unwise from every point of view."[74] And although throughout the following year Catholic groups made repeated attempts to secure action on the resolution, Senator Borah himself seemed to lose interest and never tried to force a vote on his measure.

The Borah resolution was only one of a number of congressional efforts to intervene in the Mexican religious dispute. As Catholic pressures mounted, other congressmen sought to aid Mexican Catholics (and please local constituents) by calling loudly and often belligerently for action by the United States. Representative John J. Boylan of New York told the House on February 5, for example, that five thousand residents of Mexico City had recently been kidnapped or murdered because of their opposition to the government, an assertion that seemed unsubstantiated outside the American Catholic press. "That country is today unsafe for American visitors," Boylan declared.[75] Three days later a debate on the general subject of Mexico degenerated into a noisy free-for-all, with Representative William P. Connery of Massachusetts shouting over heated objections from southern Democrats that Ambassador Daniels favored communism and was "cooperating with the tyrants of Mexico to enslave the Mexican people."[76] Daniels' friends promptly rejected such charges. The *New York Times*, in an editorial entitled "Maligning a Good Man," asked indignantly: "What can have happened to turn a kindly and benevolent man, as we all knew Josephus Daniels to be, into an enemy of democracy and humanity?"[77] Over the next several months Catholic congressmen repeated their intemperate charges against Daniels and the administration, with a few going so far as to attack the President himself. In a widely circulated speech entitled "Red Mexico," Representative Clare G. Fenerty of Penn-

sylvania asserted that Roosevelt "knows Americans have been
murdered in Mexico, but smiles and plays Pollyanna while men
and women die and little children suffer in body and soul."[78]

Throughout the first six months of 1935 no less than fourteen
resolutions were introduced in the House of Representatives demanding some kind of action with respect to Mexico. Like the
Borah resolution in the Senate, most of them called for an investigation of religious conditions, but two explicitly asked the recall
of Ambassador Daniels and one directed the Secretary of State
to demand freedom of religion in Mexico.[79] At the same time,
Catholic lobbyists were successful in getting the state legislatures
of New York, Illinois, Massachusetts, and Arizona to petition
Washington for action.[80] The high point of organized political
action came in July, when a delegation of congressmen visited the
White House and presented President Roosevelt with a petition
signed by 250 members of the House of Representatives requesting an official investigation of the religious rights and facilities
available to American citizens in Mexico. With unconscious irony,
the two Catholic leaders of the delegation declared in an explanatory memorandum that "the committee is unalterably opposed to
any semblance of interference or intervention in Mexico."[81]

As with the Borah resolution in the Senate, the Roosevelt administration set itself firmly against the similar agitation in the
House of Representatives. The harassed chairman of the House
Foreign Affairs Committee, Representative Sam D. McReynolds,
assured Daniels privately that despite heavy Catholic pressure,
he planned no action on the various resolutions before his committee.[82] Nor was the President particularly responsive to Catholic appeals. When he met with the sponsors of the congressional
petition for an investigation of Mexican religious conditions, he
declined to do more than issue a mild reaffirmation of the American belief in religious freedom. It was evident that Roosevelt preferred to take a calculated political risk at home in order to avoid
any suspicion in Latin America that the United States was scut-
tling the Good Neighbor Policy. The President was convinced,
moreover, that there were more effective methods of persuasion

than congressional investigation and name-calling. "I have had a talk with the Knights of Columbus people and a number of others who wish to 'resolve', start conferences, etc., etc.," he wrote Daniels at the height of the uproar. "I think they see the danger to Catholics and to future relations if we Yankees start telling the Mexicans what to do."[83]

The President's admonition notwithstanding, throughout the noisy agitation in the United States Ambassador Daniels had been working quietly but effectively behind the scenes in Mexico to secure greater religious freedom. Maligned and misunderstood at home, Daniels deserved considerable credit for the eventual lessening of religious tension in Mexico. Other factors, to be sure, were also important in bringing about a relaxation of governmental restrictions on the right to worship. Notable among these was the determination of the new Mexican President, Lázaro Cárdenas, to concentrate on a positive program of land reform and labor advancement rather than the negative anticlericalism of his predecessors, an attitude that soon led to his open break with General Calles. But the persistence of Ambassador Daniels in arguing for religious freedom must not be overlooked, nor its effect on Mexican leaders underestimated.

Even before President Cárdenas took office in December, 1934, Daniels had sought to convince government leaders that many of the restrictions on the Church were both unwise and unnecessary. He warned Foreign Minister Puig Casauranc that the pending constitutional amendment strengthening the ban on religious education, as well as the actions of certain states in expelling priests and closing churches, hurt Mexico's reputation throughout the world. Daniels even tried to convert the stubbornly anticlerical General Calles, though his staff warned him that Calles had told Ambassadors Morrow and Clark to stay out of Mexican religious matters. At the risk of offending the man he believed to be the real power in Mexico, the Ambassador paid a special visit to the General's Cuernavaca villa to suggest to him "that anything that savored of denying the right to worship was a backward step

fraught with loss of prestige." He found Calles so "very definite
and inflexible," however, that he gave up trying to make progress
in that quarter.[84] By this time Daniels was used to unjust criticism, but it still must have rankled when news of his quiet visit
to General Calles leaked out and American Catholics flayed him
for having "clasped cordial hands with the bitterest persecutors
of the Church."[85]

Ambassador Daniels' official courtesy calls upon cabinet members of the new Cárdenas administration, actually routine social
obligations, were also badly misunderstood in the United States.
His visit to Tomás Garrido Canábal, the new Minister of Agriculture, for example, was condemned by one Catholic paper as "this
hobnobbing, palsy-walsy spirit of our Ambassador with Mexico's
greatest atheist."[86] Yet after this customary call Daniels had noted
in his diary: "It is a pity a man of his force is so unwise as to
close churches and try to outlaw religion."[87]

In his talks with the new Foreign Minister, Emilio Portes Gil,
the Ambassador repeatedly urged that the government open more
churches, sometimes arguing on broad moral grounds, other times
stressing Mexico's world prestige, occasionally referring to the
political pressures against the Roosevelt administration in the
United States. After one such interview, the pleased head of the
Mexican desk at the State Department called Secretary Hull's
attention to the fact "that Mr. Daniels has again taken up the
cudgels for religious freedom in Mexico and this time obtained
a confidential intimation from the Foreign Minister that his Government is considering measures to ameliorate the situation in
States where freedom of worship is denied."[88] Nor did Daniels
hesitate to carry his arguments to the doors of the National Palace, pressing upon President Cárdenas himself the view that
Mexico would gain world stature by removing the state restrictions on the right to worship. The Ambassador took advantage of
the Calles-Cárdenas break in June, 1935, to remind Cárdenas
that now was a good time to modify the government's religious
policy.[89] "There is no hope of changing the educational policy,"
he reported to Roosevelt. "My thought has been to quietly con-

vince the authorities that the first thing to do is to permit churches to be opened and priests to officiate in those states where churches are now closed. That is the most important step."[90]

Nowhere was Daniels' sincere interest in religious liberty better demonstrated than on the occasion of the death of Archbishop Pascual Díaz in May, 1936. Mexican law prohibited religious processions in the streets, and Church leaders lamented that this would prevent their holding a proper funeral procession so that services for the dead Primate could be held in the Cathedral. Daniels had known and liked Archbishop Díaz, and he believed that this was one time when the law might be stretched. When he learned of the impasse, he went at once to the home of the Foreign Minister, who was entertaining guests at dinner, and quietly declared his intention to carry the matter directly to President Cárdenas if necessary. Within hours the government had granted the necessary permission.[91] "Mexicans do not have a government which listens to them," declared the Catholic paper *El Hombre Libre* afterward. "The Government listens more to Mr. Daniels, and the Mexicans, as a result, are protected by Mr. Daniels."[92] Unfortunately, the Ambassador's successful intercession in this matter did not receive anything like the publicity given some of his other acts. Few American Catholics ever learned of his action, though when one priest did, nearly a year later, he wrote humbly to apologize for ever having doubted Daniels' Christian spirit.[93]

Although Ambassador Daniels' efforts to settle the religious controversy were little known or appreciated in the United States, those who were familiar with his role gave him credit for much of the spirit of moderation shown by the Cárdenas administration. Indeed, one member of the diplomatic corps told Daniels that the improved situation could largely be ascribed to his influence.[94] This was a conclusion shared by a three-man inter-faith delegation sent from the United States in the summer of 1935 to investigate Mexican religious conditions. The group's report was highly critical of Mexican policy (Daniels considered some of its sweeping conclusions unjustified) but the three representatives were unanimous in praising the Ambassador.[95] The Catholic member of the group, William Franklin Sands, himself a former American diplomat, was particularly outspoken in his defense of Daniels, reporting to the White House on his return:

From Mexican Government officials, in the Foreign Office and elsewhere, we had repeated statements that the Ambassador has never ceased consistently and persistently, to try and bring about a better condition and an ultimate solution of the religious problem. He is well liked by Mexicans and trusted—even by the opponents of the present government. If I may say so, after serving three administrations in those countries, the President could not have a better man in Mexico at this moment. There is not the slightest justification for the attacks on him in the United States, and as the Catholic member of our delegation I would have been glad to say so publicly—if Mr. Daniels had not preferred to let it die.[96]

Despite noticeable improvement in the Mexican religious situation throughout 1935 and 1936, Democratic Party leaders in the United States remained apprehensive lest the Mexican issue prove damaging in the 1936 national elections. To be sure, the Catholic vote in key eastern states was traditionally Democratic, but no one could be certain that it might not be lost as a result of dissatisfaction with the Roosevelt administration's handling of the Mexican problem. Some Catholics were openly threatening political reprisals if Washington did not act to clean up Mexico. "If you don't do something," one of them warned Ambassador Daniels, "you will find out in the next election what will happen."[97] Archbishop Michael J. Curley charged at a rally in Washington that President Roosevelt was personally responsible for blocking an investigation of the Mexican situation. "Twenty million American Catholics are getting pretty tired of the indifference shown by the Administration," he declared ominously.[98] In Congress Representative Fenerty demanded to know how long the President expected Catholic patience to last: "If, as a statesman, he will not think of human rights, let him, as a politician, think of the next election."[99] Supreme Knight Martin Carmody of the Knights of Columbus made a series of slashing attacks on both President Roosevelt and Ambassador Daniels for their failure to do something about "bleeding and oppressed Mexico."[100]

The continuing Catholic criticism of the Roosevelt administration worried most Democratic leaders, but it disturbed no one more than Josephus Daniels, a loyal party man from the day he cast his first vote for Grover Cleveland in 1884. Daniels knew that he was the victim of misunderstanding and perhaps calculated misinterpretation, but he also realized that he was clearly a political liability to the President. Convinced, however, that he did not deserve the violent abuse of his detractors, he was reluctant to resign under fire, at least without presenting some plausible excuse. While home on leave in the summer of 1935, at the height of the attacks upon his work in Mexico, the Ambassador seems to have discussed with President Roosevelt the possibility of quitting his post. Over the next few months he considered the matter further, eventually concluding that he could leave Mexico without too much loss of face if he resigned to run for the Senate from North Carolina. This possibility was especially appealing, because if he won he would replace Senator Josiah W. Bailey, a conservative Democrat with a long record of opposition to important New Deal measures. He might thus be of service to the administration on two fronts: by removing himself as an irritant in the Mexican issue, and by waging a vigorous campaign on behalf of the New Deal's social reforms.[101]

But when Daniels broached the idea to some of his close friends when he returned home for the Christmas holidays in 1935, he received mixed advice. Some of them reacted enthusiastically, while others warned frankly that Senator Bailey had too strong a political machine for anyone to beat. As when he had contemplated running for governor in 1932, Daniels' family was strongly against his entering this race. The Ambassador remained genuinely concerned, none the less, that his continued presence in Mexico City might be, as he put it candidly, "a weakness to the party in the election."[102] Throughout February and March of 1936, therefore, as the deadline for filing in the senatorial primary approached, he pressed President Roosevelt and his friend Secretary of Commerce Dan Roper for an inkling of what the administration would like him to do. Wary of mixing in a primary fight, especially where the outcome was reportedly in doubt, Roper intimated that the White House could offer no more than restrained moral support, though he assured Daniels he could count on another ambassadorship should he lose the race.[103] The President was no more helpful. He admitted that he would like to see the "Chief" in the Senate, where his militant liberalism could aid the New Deal, but declared he would hate to see Daniels make the race and be defeated.[104]

With party leaders evidently doubtful of his chances against Senator Bailey, the Ambassador had another idea. Secretary of the Navy Claude Swanson was dangerously ill, and newspaper accounts indicated that he might not recover. "It occurred to me that I might fit in by being recalled to the Naval portfolio," Daniels hinted broadly to Roper. "It might soften the K[nights] of C[olumbus] criticism if I were changed from Mexico to Washington."[105] To Roosevelt himself, Daniels declared: "As I have twice told you, I am ready to resign at any time rather than permit my presence here to be a weakness to our ticket in November .... Under no circumstances would I be willing to remain in a position that would endanger success in November, even though I am conscious that I have done nothing—quite the contrary—to justify the criticism by Mr. Carmody and others." Referring to press speculation that he was scheduled to take over Swanson's post when the ailing Navy Secretary resigned, Daniels allowed that the change would be agreeable. "In the event of Swanson's resignation and you should wish me to resume the old position and it would be politically wise," he promised, "I would, of course, say 'Aye, aye, Sir.'"[106]

But the President paid no more heed to this suggestion now than he did three years later when Swanson died and the navy secretaryship was clearly vacant.[107] Late in February he casually reported to Daniels that although Secretary Swanson was very weak he nevertheless had "all the old light of battle in his eyes," and would, Roosevelt thought, "get well by sheer will power."[108] Rebuffed in both of his proposals, in the end Ambassador Daniels decided to ride out the storm in Mexico, which both he and ad-

ministration leaders in Washington hoped might now be sub-
siding.

Daniels continued to express concern about the political effects
of the attacks against him, bombarding Roosevelt and other administration leaders with suggestions as to patronage and other
means of counteracting the Catholic opposition, and warning
especially against any intemperate replies to the critics.[109] There
were more important issues in the campaign, but the Ambassador
might be pardoned for being rather sensitive to this one. Having
been active in every national election since 1896, Daniels was
delighted when Jim Farley, the Democratic National Chairman,
wrote him in July that "it would be a good idea for you to come
home in September or October after the campaign gets under
way, as you can render splendid service in many sections of the
country."[110] He immediately accepted an invitation to address the
September convention of the American Legion, and told Sam
Rayburn, the chairman of the Democratic speakers bureau, that
he "could speak right on then every day until the election."[111]

After further reflection, however, apprehensive party leaders
decided to keep their controversial Mexican envoy safely out of
the country and the campaign. Dan Roper probably spoke for
the White House when he suggested early in September that
Daniels could be "rendering continuously very valuable services"
by staying in Mexico City and campaigning by mail. [112] It was left
to Secretary of State Hull to make the point more explicitly.
"Have conferred with White House and Jim Farley and conclusion is reached that possibility of matters arising which would
call for urgent attention by you," he told the Ambassador abruptly
in a code telegram. "Suggest that for the present it would be best
for you to remain there."[113] Since there was nothing urgent on
tap in Mexico, this cryptic message required further elaboration,
which Hull supplied somewhat apologetically a few days later.
"The extreme partisan republicans, especially in the K. of C.," he
explained, "are watching every pretext to foment the religious
situation."[114]

As it turned out, the Democratic victory in 1936 assumed such

landslide proportions that it seems inconceivable that Daniels'
presence in the United States could have affected it much one
way or another. Administration leaders simply overestimated the
disposition of American Catholics to vote as Catholics in this
election, though their concern is understandable in view of the
violent outbursts throughout 1934 and 1935. President Roosevelt
himself was surprised and no little awed at the massive nature
of his vote of confidence. "I am beginning to come up for air after
the baptism by total submersion," he wrote Daniels after the
election—then scrawled as an afterthought, "The other fellow was
the one who nearly drowned." Perhaps a little guiltily he added:
"My greatest regret of the whole campaign was that you could
not have been in the thick of the fray yourself, and I missed you
much."[115]

Although the Catholic agitation over Mexico did not affect the
1936 American elections, nor force the resignation of Ambassador
Daniels or some other action by the United States in the religious
dispute, the effort can hardly be called a failure. Catholic pressure
made American officials—in Mexico City and Washington alike—
acutely conscious of the religious situation in Mexico. Undoubtedly it led Daniels and his superiors to take a more active role
in quietly persuading the Mexican authorities to call off the campaign against the Church. American Catholics thus deserve some
credit, however one views their tactics, for the improved religious
conditions in Mexico after 1935.

The episode is also of interest because it involved the first
sustained attack on President Roosevelt's Good Neighbor Policy.
For the first time, large numbers of Americans openly criticized
the hands-off precept of the Roosevelt administration. By portraying the Mexican government as atheistic, communistic, and a
dangerous threat to American values, the Catholic criticism of
these years helped to create an unfavorable public opinion in the
United States that was a barrier to good relations not only with
Mexico but with other Latin American countries. The Mexican
stereotype publicized by American Catholics during these years

was to be of great comfort to American oil companies after the expropriation crisis in 1938. Yet though the fabric of the Good Neighbor Policy was severely strained by the bitter Catholic attacks of 1934–36, the Roosevelt administration nevertheless demonstrated a firm resolve to stay well within neighborly limits in handling the crisis. In spite of powerful opposition, the Good Neighbor Policy, along with its badly bruised yet unembittered apostle in Mexico, continued on active duty.

Mexico 7 April 16 1938

THE FOREIGN SERVICE
OF THE
UNITED STATES OF AMERICA

AMERICAN EMBASSY

Dear Franklin :—

It may be that the action of the Chamber of Deputies yesterday may not have been reported to you. Therefore I have caused to be translated and am enclosing an extract from today El Universal. It must warm your heart to know in what esteem you are held by the American people. They have the sincerest admiration for you as a man and as the apostle of the Good Neighbor policy.

Faithfully —

Josephus Daniels

I think of you often these days, particularly as I have a goodly portion of what little I have left, after thirty years of being my own executor, in some Mexican Railroad Mining stocks. I confess my personal sympathies have always been with Mexico as regards exploitation of land by aliens so that although I may be made very uncomfortable by the outcome, I shall recognize the difficulties faced by the officials.

—George Foster Peabody to Josephus Daniels[1]

I wish all Americans had the same attitude toward Mexico that you have, but it is too much to expect, and when they have invested money here and are not protected most of them have no willingness to compromise any more than extreme socialists here are willing to meet the foreign investors half way.

—Daniels to Peabody[2]

CHAPTER V

Dollars and Diplomacy

Between 1934 and 1940, under the restless, driving leadership of President Lázaro Cárdenas, Mexico moved perceptibly to the left. This was a time of general social ferment, when much of the world was more or less painfully substituting new institutions for old. Mexico was thus very much in the current of the times. But Lázaro Cárdenas knew little of the world outside Mexico; he was an unlettered soldier, a man of impatient action rather than a brooding intellectual. His uncomplicated ideas derived more from the Mexican Revolution than from contemporary experiments in Washington or Moscow or Berlin. Cárdenas was young—only thirty-nine when he took office —but already this strangely gentle revolutionary knew his country and his people as have few Mexican presidents. It was not for this, however, that the dominant Calles group had picked him for the presidency. Rather it was because the Calles clique, grown wealthy and complacent in power, needed a man of Cárdenas'

112

known honesty as a candidate, and believed he would be as easy
to control as his predecessors. Calles, who had made and broken
presidents at will for a decade, little suspected that this quiet,
unimaginative former subordinate and comrade-in-arms would
within six months of his inauguration repudiate both the system
and the machine, and send the *Jefe Máximo* himself into exile.

Unlike so many veterans of the Revolution, Cárdenas was not
corrupted by the power and preferment of high office. Nor did
he ever forget the revolutionary commitments to the people.
What distinguished Lázaro Cárdenas was his abiding faith in the
principles of the Revolution, his unshaken determination to accomplish that which other Mexican politicians only promised. As
President, he drove himself and his aides mercilessly, regularly
putting in eighteen-hour days. By plane, train, automobile, and
even horseback, he toured every corner of the Republic, personally
estimating needs, drafting plans, and supervising the progress of
reform. During his administration he was away from the capital
on such inspection trips fully a third of the time. Always he was
available to those, no matter how poor or insignificant, who required help; he decreed that between the hours of twelve and
one each day any person in Mexico might use the national
telegraph free of charge in order to notify the President of a need
or grievance. What is more, he was responsive to such communications. Of course, Cárdenas could not attend to everything himself, and in his inexperience and zeal he sometimes made mistakes.
Moreover, his administration, like most before it, was weakened
by corruption, incompetence, and indifference in the Mexican
bureaucracy. Yet one is inclined to agree with the judgment of
Ambassador Daniels, when he told President Roosevelt at the
end of Cárdenas' term: "He is the best President Mexico has had
since Juárez."[3]

So far as possible during his six-year term, President Cárdenas
was determined to build a modern democratic Mexico that ful-
filled the promises of the Revolution to the workers and peasantry.
This required money: increased expenditures for schools to end
the nation's shameful illiteracy, investment in dams to provide

electricity for industrialization and water for parched farm lands, funds for the construction of roads, bridges, and other badly needed public works. It also demanded a drastic speed-up in land reform, which had lagged since Calles lost interest in the late twenties, and official backing for a revival of militant trade unionism. These goals naturally threatened powerful vested interests in Mexico—native and foreign—and aroused bitter hostility on the part of those adversely affected. Cárdenas, the critics charged, was a dangerous communist, or at best the naive tool of communists. Ambassador Daniels discounted such talk. "Of course you hear that Cárdenas and Mexico have gone communistic," he told George Creel in 1936,

but you and I have lived long enough to know that you have to define communism before you can call a man a communist. There are undoubtedly communists in this country—more in proportion than in the United States—but Cárdenas and his administration deny that they have any sympathy with communism. He said to me one day: "This country and this government are not communistic and have no sympathy with communism. How can a country be communistic when the chief desire of the campesino is to get a piece of land for himself and his family."[4]

Whatever one's view of the controversial Mexican President, there is no question that the effect of some of his programs was to damage or even destroy American and other foreign economic interests in Mexico. This was particularly true of the land reform program, which Cárdenas considered the most important project of his administration. Foreign businessmen and industrialists complained, moreover, that the President's support of radical labor demands was equally destructive of legitimate property rights. Americans who suffered property losses in the name of reform, or who merely feared an uncertain future, naturally turned to Washington and to the U. S. Embassy in Mexico City for help. Their appeals raised a number of difficult questions concerning the Roosevelt administration's Good Neighbor Policy, questions that were increasingly to occupy the attention of Ambassador Daniels and his superiors. How far should a good neighbor go, for example, in protecting the rights of its nationals? To what extent should these private rights be balanced with a proper neighborly concern for Mexico's own problems and aspirations? Should a government dedicated to a New Deal at home object when a poverty-stricken nation like Mexico demonstrates a similar desire to reform its institutions?

Josephus Daniels had some definite and resolutely held ideas about the proper duties of an American diplomat abroad. Such duties did not normally include collecting debts due private interests, nor seeking special protection for risk capital that had been invested in the expectation of earning larger profits than were available at home. Daniels was no narrow nationalist, and he was eager for broader commercial ties between the United States and Mexico. But he construed his office as something more than a mere appendage of American firms doing business in Mexico. From the first, he politely rebuffed suggestions from American bankers and businessmen as to how the Embassy might best represent them in Mexico. For too long, he was convinced, the United States had followed the seductive logic of Dollar Diplomacy in supporting questionable practices and "rights" of American citizens and corporations in Latin America.

The Ambassador was perfectly willing to intervene on behalf of Americans who had what he considered legitimate grievances against Mexican authorities, but he rejected the notion that the Embassy should automatically assume the validity of all American complaints. Nor did he think the Mexicans should be portrayed as all black or all white, though he was personally inclined to sympathize with Mexican nationalist and reform aspirations. Many Americans, he once lamented, returned from a hasty visit to Mexico convinced "there is nothing here but cactus and bandits and dire poverty." These critics consequently found nothing to disturb their conviction that the Mexican government was atheistic or communistic or just plain incompetent. "Others come down thinking that Mexico has found a perfect solution of economic problems and is a sort of Utopia. Of course we know that this conception is not true. The truth is, Mexico is a country of contrasts; many delightful and many otherwise."[5]

Daniels believed that the State Department, as the agent of

all the American people, ought to move very cautiously in seeking to promote private economic interests abroad. What might be of benefit to a small group of American investors might not be in the interest of the United States as a whole, nor, for that matter, of debtor countries like Mexico. In particular, he was highly critical of past encouragement by Washington of the sale of Latin American and other government bonds to American investors. During the twenties American banking houses had promoted the lucrative sale of foreign bonds in the United States. With more or less open support from the State Department, the bankers had marketed several billion dollars worth of such securities. The worldwide economic collapse after 1929 found many of the bond-issuing governments, especially in Latin America, unable to pay even the interest charges on their swollen foreign debt, with consequent loss to investors. During the campaign of 1932 Roosevelt had attacked the preceding Republican administrations for their encouragement of these improvident loans, and the Democratic platform had declared: "We condemn the usurpation of power by the State Department in assuming to pass upon foreign securities offered by international bankers as a result of which billions of dollars in questionable bonds have been sold to the public upon the implied approval of the Federal Government."[6]

Ambassador Daniels was consequently shocked when he learned from a newly assigned staff member that the State Department was tabulating the amounts due American bankers and other holders of foreign government bonds, evidently with the thought of seeking payment. With characteristic bluntness, he immediately remonstrated to Cordell Hull:

Why should our Government undertake this work and press collections due to those who pressed loans upon South American governments and got big rake-offs? We have not taken the laboring oar to save other creditors. Why jeopardize larger trade in these countries by helping to collect money due private parties?

Recalling the Democratic campaign charges in 1932, Daniels suggested that Hull instead launch a thorough investigation to determine "what 'good offices' and other help was given by diplomats accredited to those countries to American bankers when they negotiated...the reprehensible loans which ought never to have been made, and which imposed heavy burdens on the borrower and resulted in heavy losses to the purchasers of the bonds." Such a probe, he suspected, would turn up "near corruption" on the part of some former American officials.[7] But Secretary Hull, as was often the case with Daniels' off-the-cuff suggestions, showed no interest in reviving old campaign charges which might have the effect of disrupting or discrediting his department.

In the fall of 1933 the State Department sponsored the formation of an unofficial Foreign Bondholders Protective Council, composed of noted citizens like Newton D. Baker, Frank O. Lowden, and Philip F. La Follette, to try to work out a general settlement of Latin American indebtedness to private creditors in the United States. The move was partly to head off a campaign by the Mexican government to line up support at the forthcoming Montevideo Conference for a drastic reduction and moratorium on foreign debts. When Hull discussed the plan with him by telephone, Ambassador Daniels' first reaction was favorable, since the proposed council would be a private agency operating with only nominal State Department support. But he soon began to question whether the scheme would not, as he pointed out to Hull, "dig up more snakes than it will kill." His chief objection was that the Department's plan set up a wholly American body "to deal with a matter in which both the debtor and creditor are vitally concerned and whose mutual cooperation is essential to any measure of success." Latin Americans would probably object if they were not represented on the council. "I may be all wrong about it," Daniels declared, "but it looks to me that there will be some resentment at what will be called Uncle Sam's initiating another form of the much hated Dollar Diplomacy which has cost us lack of confidence in Latin American countries." He thought it would be wise in any event not to announce the creation of the bondholders' council until after the Montevideo Conference, and he urged Hull to discuss the matter first with repre-

sentatives of the countries concerned, in order to assure them that
the United States wished to be fair to creditors and debtors alike.
In the past, Latin Americans had rightly objected because "we *tell*
them instead of *consult* with them. There is a world of difference,
particularly to sensitive nations or individuals."[8]

There already was in existence such a bondholders' protective
group concerned with Mexico's external debt. In 1919, with the
State Department's blessing, the major holders of Mexican bonds
had formed the International Committee of Bankers on Mexico,
headed by Thomas W. Lamont of J. P. Morgan and Company, to
look after the bondholders' interests. Ostensibly a private group
representing European and American investors, the bankers'
committee did not hesitate to work through official channels
whenever possible. It made periodic efforts to persuade the Mexican government to resume payment on the quarter of a billion
dollars of old defaulted bonds, but with little success. Not even
the moral support of former Morgan partner Dwight Morrow
during his tenure at the American Embassy was of much help.
Indeed, Mexico stopped making payments on its external debt in
1927, the year Morrow arrived.

It was perhaps significant that before Ambassador Daniels left
for Mexico in April, 1933, Lamont offered to call and brief him
on Mexican matters, an opportunity of which Daniels did not
avail himself.[9] Congenitally suspicious of bankers, throughout his
stay in Mexico Daniels declined to support the claims of the
Lamont committee. He took the position that investors who
bought dubious foreign bonds ought not to expect their government to underwrite the obvious risks involved. The threadbare
Mexican treasury clearly could not satisfy all claimants, and
Daniels believed that Americans who had suffered losses of real
property—through revolutionary violence or government expropriation—should have priority over the bondholders. He suspected,
too, that the bankers had already been well paid for handling the
initial sale of the bonds, and that any settlement now would
mainly benefit speculators and not the original bondholders. Be-

sides, this was like any bad debt, a matter to be worked out between the borrower and his creditors.

Regardless of priorities, however, Daniels hoped that necessary social reform in Mexico would not be frustrated by the nation's crushing burden of debt. "This country is a laboratory for trying out new, and what we would call radical, policies," he noted in 1934, shortly before Lázaro Cárdenas' inauguration. "If Mexico can have quiet and progressive policies in the interests of Mexicans and not of foreigners, it may solve some problems here which may benefit other nations less able to try experiments."[10]

During 1935 and 1936 the International Bankers Committee on Mexico made a determined effort to arrange a debt settlement with the Mexican authorities. After several months of fruitless private talks, the bankers appealed to Ambassador Daniels for support. He refused to intervene without specific instructions from Washington, and he suggested to the State Department that such intervention would be inadvisable. Daniels pointed out that it had required a year of concentrated negotiation to persuade the Mexican government to begin payments to Americans who had suffered losses during the revolutionary period between 1910 and 1920. Furthermore, the United States was currently pressing for a settlement of general claims dating from 1868, and was also trying to get the Mexicans to recognize their obligations to Americans whose lands had been expropriated under the land reform program. "These three claims, in my judgment," he told the Department frankly, "should be given priority by our Government over the claims of foreign bondholders, pressed by private interests, and for the payment of which our Government has assumed no responsibility."[11]

In reply, Assistant Secretary of State Sumner Welles agreed that "we are not, in any sense of the word, a collection agency." He reminded Daniels, however, that the Mexican government would find it difficult to borrow foreign capital for new construction projects until it had resumed payment on the old bonded debt. And he suggested that it might be well to let the Mexicans know quietly and unofficially that American financing of Mexico's share of the second section of the Pan American Highway was "dependent upon the satisfactory conclusion of Mexico's negotiations with the Bondholder's Committee." Daniels evidently disapproved of such tactics on behalf of the bankers, for he refrained from carrying this veiled hint to the Foreign Office.[12] Reminding Welles that the Lamont committee represented substantial European as well as American interests, he declared: "Not long ago the French Minister said to me: 'We knew we could not collect them and were glad to let the Americans have them.' "[13] The bankers committee carried on spasmodic negotiations with the Mexican government during the rest of Ambassador Daniels' stay in Mexico, but it got little encouragement from the Embassy.*

Daniels firmly believed that businessmen operating abroad had no right to expect their government to secure for them special advantages or protection. Of course, Washington might properly object if American interests were discriminated against, but as a general rule it should not seek to exempt its nationals from laws applying impartially to local businessmen. The Ambassador was delighted when he thought he discerned support for this view within the State Department. He carefully saved a foreign policy address by Sumner Welles in January, 1935, in which the Assistant Secretary of State declared that "American capital invested abroad should, in fact as well as in theory, be subordinate to the authority of the people of the country where it is located."[14] If

---

* Daniels may even have sabotaged the bondholders' efforts to get a settlement in 1936. The Mexican Ambassador in Washington, Dr. Francisco Castillo Nájera, told Welles three years later that President Cárdenas had actually been ready to sign an agreement resuming debt payments when Daniels let it be known that the United States was not backing the bankers' claims because a large percentage of the bonds involved were held by Europeans. This was certainly Daniels' view, and he may well have stated it to Mexican officials. It is unlikely, however, that he went out of his way to block the agreement, as Castillo Nájera, implied. The latter occasionally sought to ingratiate himself with State Department officials at Daniels' expense.—Welles, memorandum of conversation, November 24, 1939, in Department of State, *Foreign Relations of the United States, 1939* (Washington: Government Printing Office, 1957), V, 711–12.

this was Washington's real policy, there was no conflict between it and its strong-minded representative in Mexico City.

Daniels probably thought he was on safe ground, therefore, when he suggested the following year that Americans doing business in Mexico ought to live up to their pledges under Mexico's Calvo Clause. Article 27 of Mexico's Constitution, it will be recalled, specifically required foreign businessmen to promise not to call upon their home governments for help in disputes with local authorities. The State Department had never accepted the validity of a Calvo pledge, and accordingly in February of 1936 it expressed concern over a bitter and protracted strike by the workers of the American-owned Guanajuato Reduction and Mines Company. At the Department's request, Daniels conferred with officials of the company, afterward promising Washington that the Embassy would "lend its good offices in some proper way...when and if it becomes necessary." He left little doubt, however, that he did not think much of an American who violated "his signed pledge not to call upon the Embassy but to submit to the ruling of the Mexican authorities."[15] The possible implications of this off-hand observation were not lost on the property-conscious State Department. Speaking for Secretary Hull, Sumner Welles immediately responded:

I remind the Embassy that this Government has uniformly held that an American citizen cannot, by entering into an agreement of this sort, divest his Government of its right to extend to him its protection abroad. While maintaining this position the United States could not consistently decline in a proper case to exercise the right in question. It should perhaps be borne in mind in this relation that an agreement of the nature mentioned is presumably in effect extorted from interested American citizens, at least in many cases, the alternative confronting them being the threatened expropriation of property rights theretofore obtained in accordance with the laws of Mexico.[16]

Unquestionably, there was both logic and experience to support the State Department's position, but Daniels continued to believe that there was also some justice in the Calvo Doctrine.

Similarly, the Ambassador was something less than enthusiastic when Welles requested him to arrange an interview between

President Cárdenas and Curtis E. Calder, head of the American
and Foreign Power Company, a subsidiary of the giant Electric
Bond and Share Company, which operated extensive electric
utility properties in Mexico and ten other Latin American countries. Calder was very much concerned over a bill to regulate
electric utilities which the Mexican Congress had under consider-
tion. Daniels secured the desired conference, but he refrained
from pressing the company's suit himself, except to point out to the
Foreign Office several features of the bill that he considered unjust. Instead, he told Welles:

I have examined the measure, and while I would not say so to any
Mexican or utility officials, it seems to me in the main to be a wise
method of regulating public service corporations. If attention is called
to the provisions that are unwise, by utility officials, they might secure
their deletion from the measure before passage .... If the United States
had enacted somewhat the same legislation (omitting some features)
when light and power companies were in their infancy, we would have
escaped the Insull scandals and Roosevelt would not have been compelled to wage a hard fight to secure legislation which, in a sense, could
do no more than lock the stable after the horse was gone .... Mr. Calder
is in effect asking our Government to step in and tell the Mexican Government what sort of utility laws it should put upon its statute books.
That is going far beyond any request that has heretofore been made by
American investors in this country.[17]

The Ambassador had done battle with power interests in North
Carolina for too many years not to sympathize with Mexican
feelings.

In the fall of 1936 the Cárdenas administration submitted for
almost certain congressional approval the draft of a new law to
govern the expropriation of private property. Government leaders
asserted that it was necessary to revise the existing expropriation
law, passed under the Díaz regime in 1905, in order to bring it
into conformity with Article 27 of the Constitution. Foreign investors and businessmen were not persuaded of any such need,
however, and they noted with alarm rumors that the measure
would grant the government considerably broader powers than

the old law. Even before the exact terms of the bill were known, Daniels discussed the matter informally with President Cárdenas, whom he regarded as fair but singleminded in his determination to carry out the mandate of the Revolution. Daniels pointed out that "unless the measure was drawn with great clearness and gave assurance that private property would be protected,...there would be such fear as would decrease investments and manufacturing plants and purchase of property here." Cárdenas, normally quiet and aloof, was emphatic in declaring that his country needed and wanted American capital, and that "in every case of *bona fide* investment in Mexico, complete protection would be afforded the investors."[18]

As soon as he could, the Ambassador secured a copy of the proposed law and sent it to the State Department, which promptly drew up a long list of objections. Acting Secretary of State Walton Moore, in charge while Secretary Hull was out of the country attending the Buenos Aires Conference, complained that the bill frankly admitted that one of its purposes was to redistribute the country's wealth. Nor was its scope limited to agrarian matters; it granted sweeping authority to expropriate all classes of property. Moreover, it fixed, as the basis of compensation for property taken, the value declared by the owner for tax purposes, which might be well below the market value. And although it promised compensation within ten years after expropriation, the bill was vague as to the manner and terms under which such compensation would be made. Moore declared that it was "indeed unfortunate" that Mexico should propose "this almost unlimited extension of the right of expropriation," and he instructed Daniels to take up the matter again confidentially with President Cárdenas as soon as possible.[19] In a private letter to Daniels the same day, Moore declared that the new law "might very properly be called a confiscation law," and he urged the Ambassador to "do everything that may be possible in the direction of enabling the Mexican authorities to see what a troublesome situation is being created."[20]

Ambassador Daniels was well aware that the expropriation law did not contain any explicit guarantees of the sort mentioned by

President Cárdenas in their earlier conversation. The difference between protection and confiscation would largely depend, he admitted, "upon the action of the President."[21] But he thought it too late for further remonstrances. The new law had gone into effect several days before the Embassy received Moore's instructions, and all of the arguments made by the Department had previously been presented by the bill's opponents while it was being considered in Congress. In the circumstances, he doubted that he could get anything "more reassuring" than the informal promises already given by the Mexican President. He pointed out, too, that "the Mexican Constitution of 1917 carries the identical provision against which the Department has instructed me to make representations."[22] President Cárdenas was currently out of the city, but Daniels promised to see him when he returned, though he expressed doubt "that anybody can have any influence now, since the act has passed both houses of Congress and been approved by the President."[23]

Acting Secretary Moore was not interested in explanations; he wanted action. To the absent Secretary Hull at Buenos Aires he repeated his apprehensions over the new Mexican law. Moore put little stock in President Cárdenas' verbal assurances to Daniels that American investors would be treated fairly. As he saw it, the United States had two courses of action open. It could either follow Daniels' advice and let the matter rest until the intent and application of the law were more clearly apparent, or it could make strong representations now in the hope that the Mexican government would think twice before taking American property under the act. There was no doubt that Moore favored the latter course.[24]

So did Cordell Hull, whose view of the sanctity of a vested right was as stern and flinty as the hills of his native east Tennessee. "Please inform Ambassador Daniels," he promptly cabled, "that I entirely agree with you as to desirability of his seeing President Cárdenas and putting matter up to him as strongly as possible. I think Daniels might at the same time discuss recent agrarian expropriations."[25] Daniels had already declared his intention to see Cárdenas upon his return to the capital, but he warned again that there was "no reasonable hope for a change in the law officially enacted in accordance with Mexican procedure." Stung, no doubt, by the inference that the Embassy was not doing its job, the Ambassador reminded both Hull and Moore that he had been the only member of the diplomatic corps to raise objections to the expropriation law before its passage.[26]

Before returning to the United States for the Christmas holidays, Daniels had a long talk with President Cárdenas about Mexico's expropriation policy. The conversation was relaxed and friendly, over tea and cookies at the President's suburban home, Los Pinos. Among other things, Daniels asked Cárdenas frankly how he intended to apply the new expropriation law. The President replied emphatically that he "would not engage in any suicidal policy." Recalling his earlier assurances, Cárdenas repeated his conviction that Mexico needed to encourage American investment. "The Government would not be so childish or short-sighted as to engage in any policy which would prevent this," he declared. "It would not, for instance, endeavor to take over the oil fields or the mines, since that would be impractical and would place the Government in the situation with regard to foreign investment which it intended to avoid." The main reason for the passage of the expropriation law, he explained, was that the government "wished to be equipped legally so it could, if necessary, take over an industry or factory which had shut down, thus paralyzing a business or enterprise necessary for the public welfare."[27] From unofficial but usually reliable sources the Embassy learned that another purpose of the new law was to enable the government to move against certain members of the old Calles clique who had acquired great wealth under suspicious circumstances while in power.[28]

These assurances clearly did not constitute the ironclad promise the State Department would have liked. Nevertheless, President Cárdenas had given about as strong a guarantee as could be expected of any Mexican chief executive, especially one as conscious as Lázaro Cárdenas of the national dignity. The proof of

Mexico's attitude toward foreign investment would lie in future developments.

Already, however, there were indications that Ambassador Daniels and his State Department superiors looked at the problem in quite different ways. Daniels was inclined to take a long-run view. Mexico, he believed, badly needed the reforms Cárdenas and other revolutionary leaders were instituting: more rural schools, higher wages for the industrial workers, and land tenure for the peasantry. "With this trinity of opportunity open to the Indians, Mexico faces a new day," he told a friend in 1940. "If this trinity can be advanced, the United States in another generation or two will be proud to have Mexico as its nearest neighbor."[29] In other words, what was called for during this trying period of Mexican reform and readjustment was neighborly patience and understanding and even concrete help. Such a policy would in the long run pay off in both stronger ties and increased trade between the United States and a stable, prosperous Mexico. Daniels accepted at face value President Cárdenas' assurances that Mexico needed foreign capital for its economic development, and consequently had no intention of harming legitimate foreign investments. He and Cárdenas were probably not far apart in their ideas as to what constituted a legitimate investment, one designed to contribute to the Mexican economy for a fair and reasonable return, as opposed to one that was primarily exploitative.

The State Department found it hard to make such fine distinctions. Secretary Hull usually took a practical, short-run view of the problem, operating on the premise that all American interests, of whatever character and wherever located, were entitled to diplomatic protection. Hull believed that Washington could not adopt a makeshift policy of protesting here and acquiescing there; nor could it look upon Mexico as a special, isolated case, for what happened there might have a definite bearing on the treatment of American investments in other countries. Certainly Mexico had problems, and an administration seeking to accomplish a New Deal at home had to admit that a measure of reform was probably a good thing elsewhere. But the State Department's first concern must be for the rights of Americans under its protection. It must insist, for example, that any expropriation of American-owned property, no matter how worthy or necessary the motives behind it, must be accompanied by fair, effective, and immediate compensation.

The Mexican expropriation law of November, 1936, was twice used by the Cárdenas administration to take over foreign-owned properties involving substantial American investments. On June 23, 1937, Mexico expropriated the Mexican National Railways, a partly foreign-owned company operating about 55 per cent of the railroad trackage of the country. Nine months later, on March 18, 1938, President Cárdenas nationalized the almost wholly foreign-owned oil industry. In both cases the amount of foreign capital affected was approximately the same, with American investors accounting for about half of the total. Yet the expropriation of the National Railways brought only the merest flutter of concern in the United States compared with the violent storm raised by the oil seizure the following year.

The reasons for the strikingly different reactions are not hard to find. For one thing, the expropriation of the National Railways applied only to that railroad system and not to other more profitable foreign-owned roads. The American investors affected by the move had long thought of their holdings as of dubious value, in view of the chronic state of near bankruptcy enjoyed by the National Railways. Since the days of Díaz, moreover, the Mexican government had owned a controlling interest in the road. Hence the position of the minority stockholders and bondholders could hardly be worsened by the government's assuming full ownership of an enterprise that had long since ceased to attract risk capital. There was, in fact, some reason to accept the government's explanation that the move was necessary to stave off the road's impending bankruptcy. The outlook for the foreign investor was admittedly bleak, but he was about as likely to get his money back under government as under private management.

The expropriation of the oil industry, on the other hand, involved the taking of valuable revenue-producing properties. Unlike the railroad bondholders, who were widely scattered and poorly organized, the foreign oil companies affected by the seizure included such corporate giants as Royal Dutch Shell and Standard Oil of New Jersey, whose total assets far exceeded the puny resources of the Mexican government. This not only made the oil companies formidable antagonists, but assured them of more than ordinary support from interested foreign chancelleries. Furthermore, the oil seizure, if successfully carried through, threatened American and British control over important oil supplies not merely in Mexico but elsewhere in Latin America and the world. For these reasons, the oil expropriation brought a major crisis in good neighbor diplomacy that will be treated in detail later in this study.

Ambassador Daniels was not in Mexico when President Cárdenas surprised both his cabinet and the nation with his decree expropriating the National Railways.[30] Instead he was touring Europe as a member of the American Battle Monuments Commission to dedicate cemeteries and war memorials honoring the American dead of World War I. In his absence the Embassy was headed by career diplomat Pierre de L. Boal, Daniels' able counselor and second-in-command. Boal reacted to the sudden expropriation of the railroad exactly as his chief would have had he been in Mexico City. He immediately advised Washington of the situation, noting that the Mexican action seemed based on a desire to forestall the complete bankruptcy of the road. He pointed out, too, that the expropriation law had been applied on the basis outlined in the Cárdenas-Daniels talks of the previous December. He reported that Mexican officials had given assurances that the claims of foreign investors would not be jeopardized by the action, and would, in fact, probably be improved through more efficient government management, a view also advanced by the Mexican ambassador in Washington in a conversation with Sumner Welles.[31] Privately, however, Boal warned that the expropriation of the railroad might be taken as a significant harbinger "of a further movement towards socialization, at least of all public service corporations, and a warning to private industries that their profits will be watched and controlled by the Government."[32]

Harbinger or not, Ambassador Daniels was too busy laying wreaths and making speeches in Europe to pay much attention to Mexico's nationalization of the National Railways. Like Boal, he did not consider the move a violation of President Cárdenas' promise to protect legitimate American interests. And by the time Daniels returned to Mexico City in September, 1937, the brief flurry of excitement over the expropriation of the railroad had subsided. Secretary of State Hull did not even mention the incident in a long letter briefing Daniels on current Mexican problems.[33] The Ambassador on his return found the Embassy staff and State Department officials much more interested in two other matters: the increasing number of agrarian expropriations arising from the Cárdenas government's ambitious land reform program, and a bitter labor dispute involving the American and British oil companies. These two issues—land and oil—would occupy most of Daniels' attention for the next four years. Alone and in combination, they would strain Mexican-American relations to the point of very nearly wrecking the Good Neighbor Policy.

My residence in Mexico has made me more interested than ever in problems of putting the tenants on the land and giving them a stake in old mother earth. ... We must find a way, in fairness to the land-owner who himself is often impoverished by owning too much land, as an essential foundation of our future democracy to help the man who tills the soil to own the soil.

—Josephus Daniels[1]

In the event you are convinced that division of American owned lands is imminent you are directed to insist vigorously that contemplated expropriation proceedings be deferred until satisfactory arrange-ments have been made for prompt payment of ade-quate and effective compensation to American owners.

—Secretary Hull to Ambassador Daniels[2]

CHAPTER VI

Yanquis in the Yaqui Valley

From the very start of his mission Ambassador Daniels recognized that his most difficult problems would probably arise from the Mexican agrarian program. "You may not have observed that in my address on presentation to President Rodríguez I mentioned all reforms except land," he commented to President Roosevelt shortly after assuming his ambassadorial duties in 1933. "It is the acute question here under the surface. Mexico can never really prosper until there is a larger opportunity for the average man to own land."[3] Land re-form was indeed the acute question throughout most of Josephus Daniels' stay in Mexico. For during the 1930's the Mexican govern-ment made its most determined effort to fulfill the promise of the Revolution to the peasantry: "The land belongs to those who work it."

To the casual observer, Mexico might appear to be land rich. Much of the country is virtually unoccupied; 70 per cent of the population, in fact, is concentrated on only 7 per cent of the land.

But this 7 per cent represents Mexico's cropland. And by any standard, most of it is poor—infertile, hilly, arid. Two-thirds of Mexico's land surface is mountainous, and nearly all of the rest is hilly and rolling. Of the comparatively small amount of arable land, most lies in regions of scarce rainfall, where crops are dependent upon the brief and agriculturally inefficient rainy season. Only about 13 per cent of the country has enough rain through the year, and these parts are tropical and poorly inhabited, where the rainfall is itself a curse.

At the outbreak of the Revolution in 1910, land ownership in Mexico was unbelievably concentrated, perhaps to a degree unequaled elsewhere in modern times. Only 3 per cent of the Mexican people owned land at all—this in a country where nearly three-fourths of the population was directly engaged in some form of agriculture. The remaining 97 per cent was landless and mostly destitute, able to count on possessing a bit of ground only at death.

Beginning with Venustiano Carranza in 1915, the revolutionary governments moved with ever increasing vigor and determination to break the dominance of the great haciendas over the Mexican countryside. Once the process had begun, it became difficult if not impossible for any government to resist the peasants' demands for land. But it was Lázaro Cárdenas who between 1934 and 1940 shifted the land reform program into high gear. Cárdenas not only stepped up the pace of land distribution, but also greatly expanded the number of those eligible under the program. An indication of Cárdenas' zeal is shown by the unprecedented amount of land distributed during his administration. Previous Mexican presidents from Carranza through Rodríguez had granted a little over eight million hectares (about twenty million acres) of land over a twenty-year period. Cárdenas distributed nearly two-and-a-half times this much in his six years in office. By the end of Cárdenas' term, the beneficiaries of the land reform program numbered 51 per cent of the total agricultural population and held 47 per cent of the cropland in Mexico. In a few brief years Cárdenas had drastically altered the structure of land ownership in Mexico, and had pushed land reform to the point where it would be extremely difficult for any future government to undo his work.[4]

The very magnitude of the land reform program meant that it could be carried out only at the expense of the previous land-owning class. By 1940, with the program still under way, the revolutionary governments had distributed land amounting to 15 per cent of Mexico's total area, much of it the best cropland. Presumably, few if any nations have ever been rich enough to purchase, at market rates, that large a portion of their national territory. Yet Mexico was desperately poor. The country had suffered more than a decade of revolutionary strife; the great mass of the people had an appallingly low standard of living; and the government lacked money or credit and possessed only modest revenues. In 1937, for example, a year of record government expenditures in Mexico, the city of New York spent more on its police, fire, and sanitation departments, and nearly twice as much on its school system, as did the Mexican government in *all* its activities on behalf of a population two-and-a-half times as large. Clearly the Mexican government was in no position to buy all the land it felt obliged—for moral, social, and above all political reasons—to distribute.

But since Mexico very early had acknowledged an obligation to pay compensation for lands taken under the program, the big question was how. Initially, the revolutionary leaders thought that the villages should pay for whatever land they received. This idea was soon dropped as impractical, and in 1920 the Obregón administration recognized the central government's responsibility for the agrarian debt and authorized the issuance of long-term, interest-bearing federal agrarian bonds as compensation for lands taken. In practice, however, this was of little benefit to the affected landowners. Between 1920 and 1933 bonds issued totaled less than 25 million pesos, indemnifying 170 persons whose claims covered only 223,000 hectares of land. Yet by 1933 the government had distributed approximately six million hectares of land, which meant that by this time Mexico had a potential agrarian debt of anywhere from a half billion to a billion pesos. Even before the advent of Lázaro Cárdenas, when the pace of land distribution quickened, it was abundantly clear that Mexico would never acknowledge the full debt, nor pay more than a fraction of the real value of whatever part of the debt it chose to recognize. By the time Ambassador Daniels arrived in Mexico, the government had ceased to issue further agrarian bonds, and had suspended interest payments on the outstanding bonds.[5]

From the start of the Mexican land reform program, the United States consistently held that while Mexico had the right to expropriate private property, no American-owned lands should be taken unless prompt, adequate, and effective compensation was made. Both the Embassy in Mexico City and the State Department in Washington kept a sharp watch over the progress of the agrarian program and were quick to intervene on behalf of American landowners who were threatened with the loss of part of their lands. The extremely vague character of the Mexican agrarian laws, however, and the fact that after 1932 Mexican courts ruled that the agrarian program was not subject to judicial review, made it difficult for the United States to do more than issue ineffectual protests against the injustices and illegalities of the program. What American and other landowners in Mexico were up against may be seen in Articles 177 and 178 of the Agrarian Code of March 22, 1934:

> The proprietors affected by resolutions granting or restoring lands or waters handed down in favor of communities or which may be handed down in the future shall have no ordinary right or legal recourse, nor may they apply for an *amparo* [court injunction].
>
> Parties affected by dotations shall only have the right to petition the Federal Government to pay them the respective indemnity ....
>
> Any cases of doubt arising from the application of this Code shall be solved by the Federal Executive.[6]

Without going beyond the bounds of polite, or even fairly intemperate diplomacy, Washington could only demand that Mexico pay immediate and effective compensation to American citizens affected by the program. And as the land reform became broader in scope, such payment was obviously beyond the nation's ability to provide.

Strenuous (but largely unheeded) demands for compensation did little or nothing to save American lands from expropriation, since under the agrarian laws the question of compensation did not arise until after the transfer of ownership had actually taken place. The aggrieved landholder then had a year in which to file his claim with the government. From his staff Ambassador Daniels learned that the Embassy in the past had limited its efforts to seeing that Americans received the full protection of existing Mexican laws. "There is never a question of asking the Mexican Government to violate their own laws," the Embassy's expert on agrarian matters informed him. "The position of the Embassy has been and is that an American landowner in Mexico is bound by the laws of Mexico and that the only thing that he can demand and the only way in which the Embassy or an American Consul in Mexico may aid him is to see that he receives justice under the existing laws."[7]

Such intervention had not been notably successful in protecting American interests. An Embassy staff memorandum reported gloomily in 1936 that in no case had United States representations ever saved the property of an American citizen from expropriation, nor had demands for compensation been effective. "It seems useless, certainly at this time," the report concluded pessimistically, "to hope that the Mexican Government will pay for lands already expropriated because the total agrarian debt is now beyond its capacity to pay and the Mexican Government is averse to paying foreigners without paying its own citizens. It is likewise ineffective to intervene in expropriation proceedings where slight irregularities are alleged because the law is so elastic as to permit these to be legalized when the case is reviewed by the Agrarian Department."[8]

From his boyhood days in rural eastern North Carolina, Josephus Daniels had interested himself in agricultural problems. As

a newspaper editor he had vigorously championed the disadvan-
taged classes in southern agriculture: the apathetic sharecropper,
the struggling tenant, and the poor but fiercely independent yeo-
man farmer. His Jeffersonian view of the importance of the small
landholder in a democratic society naturally led Daniels to sympathize with the aims of the Mexican agrarian program. Land reform, he was convinced, was "the basis of a future stable and
prosperous Mexico."[9] Indeed, he believed it was the great en-
grossment of land under the old hacienda system that was "the
real reason for the poverty of the people and the backwardness
of the country."[10] The breaking up of the big estates promised not
only new economic opportunities for the Mexican masses, but the
hope of political stability and responsible democratic government
for the Mexican nation as well. "In some things, as for example,
giving land to men who work the haciendas," Daniels observed
candidly to President Roosevelt in 1934, "Mexico is looking to do
more for the forgotten man than you have been able to do."[11]
When a rash American consul at Monterrey casually reported that
farmers in his district seemed content to work on a sharecrop or
wage basis, the Ambassador replied bluntly: "You may be right
about this but I have never seen a man who lived next to the soil
who did not wish to own and control the land he tilled. Business
men who live in the cities may think otherwise, but they have
not looked beneath the surface."[12]

Regardless of his private view that Mexico desperately needed
some program of land reform, Ambassador Daniels dutifully followed State Department instructions to press for a halt in the
taking of American-owned lands unless adequate compensation
was paid at the time of expropriation. "In cases where the land
belonged to Americans," he informed Roosevelt in 1936, "I have
insisted that none should be taken until [the Mexican] Congress
made provision for additional bonds." In the same breath he
warned, however, that no government in Mexico "could long
endure if it did not give the lands to the people who have long
tilled them."[13] The problem was of a sort to tax a Solomon. Popular pressure for land in Mexico was enormous, perhaps irresis-

tible. It could be ignored only at the risk of renewed disorder and violence. But it was equally clear, as Daniels remarked to a friend, that President Cárdenas had "not yet found the key to carry out his agrarian policy without being unjust to owners who purchased land in good faith."[14]

During Ambassador Daniels' first year in Mexico, he had repeatedly urged a settlement of all outstanding claims between the two countries. His State Department superiors, with an eye on Mexico's precarious financial situation, had instead concentrated on securing a convention disposing of the special claims for damages suffered by Americans during the revolutionary years, 1910–20. For the time being, the Department had decided to defer a settlement of the general claims covering the period 1868–1927, believing that Mexico could not afford to pay adequate compensation on both sets of claims. Accordingly, in a protocol Daniels had signed along with the special claims convention, the two governments had agreed to extend the life of the general claims commission to continue adjudicating these claims. This was admittedly a stopgap measure, for the claims commission had made little progress toward a final settlement in a decade of expensive deliberation.

The general claims protocol of 1934 specified that the two governments might try to settle agrarian claims outside of the claims commission. Exercising this option, in April, 1935, the State Department sent two claims experts to Mexico to try to reach a separate agrarian settlement.[15] Since most of the claims involved dated before the period of extensive land reform in Mexico, the negotiations aimed merely at winding up an old problem. State Department officials may have felt, however, that some judicious diplomatic pressure on behalf of the older agrarian claims might cause the Mexicans to think twice before taking any additional American properties.

Ambassador Daniels and the Embassy staff were not at first directly involved in these negotiations, other than to introduce the two State Department negotiators, Joseph R. Baker and Peter H. A. Flood, to the appropriate Mexican officials. Daniels neverthe-

less tried without success to win a commitment from the Mexican
Foreign Office that no further American-owned lands would be
expropriated while the conversations were in progress.[16] Unfortunately for the negotiations, Baker and Flood proved not to be
the most tactful of diplomats in the face of dilatory and evasive
Mexican tactics. In July, after three months of exasperatingly
fruitless discussions, the two State Department emissaries sent
the Foreign Office a strongly worded note threatening to break
off the conversations. Charging that the discussions had in effect
already "terminated fruitlessly," they declared that Mexico was
thus "obligated to proceed with the arbitration of these claims."[17]
Daniels and old hands at the Embassy could have given some
good advice on the "mañana" difficulties inherent in any claims
negotiations with the Mexicans, but Baker and Flood did not
consult them before taking this extreme step.

The Mexican Foreign Office had only a few days earlier informed Daniels that it was about to submit a settlement offer. It
consequently declined to accept the Baker-Flood memorandum
unless its offensive language was toned down. Ambassador Daniels did what he could to soothe ruffled Mexican sensibilities, but,
as he reported to Secretary Hull, "The whole matter is difficult
enough; condemning the attitude of the Mexican officials only
jeopardizes a satisfactory solution."[18] Whether he knew it or not,
Daniels' complaint was actually a rebuke to the State Department
itself, for the sentences in question had been written in Washington. Secretary Hull could only explain somewhat lamely that "it
was not intended that the paragraph should be included in a
communication to Mexican officials."[19]

Baker and Flood were recalled to Washington in August without having accomplished anything worthy of note other than the
preparation of a number of memoranda stating the well-known
American position on expropriations. After their departure, Daniels and the Embassy staff carried on the stalled negotiations, with
more patience but no better success. Daniels also continued to
remind the Mexican authorities of their obligation to compensate
Americans whose lands were currently being taken. When the

Mexican Congress convened in September, 1935, the Ambassador used the occasion to suggest to the Foreign Office that no more American lands be taken until Congress had authorized compensation.[20] For this he was commended by Secretary Hull, who told him that "the Department depends upon you to keep the matter actively before the Mexican Government until a satisfactory outcome has been assured."[21]

At one point in the discussions, Ambassador Daniels managed to elicit a tentative pledge by the acting Foreign Minister, José Angel Ceniceros, that the government might be willing to halt further seizures of American-owned land without prompt compensation. Ceniceros admitted that President Cárdenas was "very much concerned" over Daniels' protests. The Ambassador urged his superiors to accept even a temporary expedient to protect Americans from further expropriations in the hope that Mexico might ultimately be persuaded to adopt "a more rational land policy in which public lands and those already taken may be fully utilized before more private property is taken."[22] Secretary Hull quickly agreed that Daniels should try to get a commitment exempting American lands from expropriation, but he warned that it must not be conditioned on any acquiescence in Mexico's failure to pay for American properties already taken.[23] The Foreign Office did not repeat the Ceniceros offer, however, and it seemed evident that he had been speaking without authority.

Daniels had even less success in the negotiations for a settlement of the old agrarian claims dating from the period prior to 1927. His task was not made easier by the State Department's rigid, uncompromising attitude toward various Mexican proposals for an agreement.[24] Always impatient with legal wrangling that obscured what he thought were the larger issues, Daniels took a dim view of the Department's insistence upon the right to question the legality of Mexican agrarian expropriations under international law. "It is doubtful whether it is good policy," he pointed out, "to embark upon a legal discussion with the Mexican Government as to its rights to enforce its Constitution and laws upon foreigners within its borders." On this point the position of both governments was well known.[25] If Washington really wanted to secure some relief for American claimants, Daniels believed, it should seriously explore the Mexican offers for a lump sum settlement, which would at least provide partial compensation for Americans who had been waiting years, and in some cases decades, for payments. But the State Department declined to abandon the position that Americans must receive fair and full compensation for their lost properties. Assistant Secretary of State Walton Moore declared: "I do not think anything should be said or done that will imply in any way our abandonment of the principle of international law that entitles Americans whose lands are taken to be fully compensated, precisely as compensation in this country is made to owners whose lands are taken for public purposes."[26]

Despite his private misgivings, Daniels carried out the Department's policy. Late in November, 1935, he warned the Foreign Office that unless it showed a greater willingness to meet the United States' objections, "there would appear to be no alternative but to consider the negotiations at an end and to proceed with the filing of the memorials of the agrarian claims with the General Claims Commission."[27] Over the next two months the Mexicans made several vague offers of a lump sum settlement of the agrarian claims, while Daniels and the State Department vainly tried to pin them down to satisfactory terms. In January, after returning from a conference with officials in Washington, Daniels informed the Foreign Office that unless the two governments reached an agreement by February 1 the United States intended to turn the problem over to the General Claims Commission.[28] If the State Department intended this as a threat, it had little effect. Mexico merely expressed polite regret that no agreement had been reached, and agreed that the United States had every right to file its claims before the commission.[29] Negotiations for a separate agrarian settlement thus came to an end on February 1, 1936, though Secretary Hull hopefully held the door open for "any further proposals."[30]

Perhaps Hull and Moore and other State Department officials

were right. Perhaps their insistence upon the full legal rights of American claimants served to protect foreign-owned property not only in Mexico but elsewhere throughout the world, though this is hard to demonstrate so far as Mexico is concerned. Certainly the State Department's position had the merit of logic and simplicity, requiring little or no understanding of the political forces at work in post-revolutionary Mexico. But in light of the comprehensive claims settlement agreed to by the United States in 1941 —to be considered later in this study—one is inclined to wonder whether the American claimants really benefited by the delay resulting from Washington's failure to take advantage of every chance for a lump sum agreement at this time. It is also worth asking whether the State Department's simple black-and-white view of the problem was entirely appropriate for a government dedicated to good-neighbor principles in its foreign relations. Both the claimants and Mexican-American rapport might have been the richer as a result of more imaginative (and at the same time more realistic) diplomacy in 1936.

Indeed, Washington officials probably played right into Mexico's hands when they reluctantly decided to refer the American agrarian claims to the General Claims Commission. It is quite unlikely that the Cárdenas government, its budget already strained to capacity, wanted any immediate settlement of the old agrarian debt, though it might well have agreed to moderate lump sum payments in order to be rid of a troublesome issue. From the Mexican standpoint, the delays involved in processing claims through an international tribunal were infinitely preferable to the disquieting prospect of substantial new charges against a chronically threadbare treasury. If the history of previous claims commissions was any guide, moreover, Mexico had every reason to expect that the agrarian claims would eventually be scaled down to a figure far below what the United States was demanding. President Cárdenas was determined that land distribution should go forward regardless of protests from *hacendados* of whatever nationality. As Ambassador Daniels so frequently pointed out, any policy that did not take this fact into account was unlikely to get very far.

With the General Claims Commission responsible for the pre-1927 American agrarian claims, Ambassador Daniels next concentrated on securing a pledge from the Mexican authorities not to take further American-owned lands until they had first paid for the properties already expropriated. He had little success. Foreign Minister Eduardo Hay intimated that his department lacked the power to act independently in agrarian matters, and declared, "I will make you no promises I can't fulfil."[31] Daniels had already concluded that he was largely shadowboxing in his weekly conversations with the Foreign Office, which plainly had little influence over agrarian policy. President Cárdenas evidently felt that its chief mission was to pacify and sidetrack foreign protests against the Mexican reform programs. In recognition of this situation, the Embassy frequently bypassed the Foreign Office to deal directly with the autonomous Agrarian Department, or even on occasion with the President himself.

Although American protests, whether by Ambassador Daniels or the State Department, were generally ineffective in blocking scheduled expropriations, not all American-owned properties were under immediate threat from the land reform program. Some of them were located in the sparsely settled parts of Mexico where the pressure for land was not great. An Embassy dispatch to the Department noted in mid-1935, for example, that if anything, Americans seemed to be receiving favored treatment over Mexican and other foreign landowners, considering that the million-acre Hearst ranch in Chihuahua and certain other large estates had not yet been divided.[32] The Embassy and the State Department recognized, moreover, that not all the American agrarian claims were above suspicion. Sumner Welles frankly conceded to Mexican officials that some Americans "had acquired land for practically nothing and…were claiming fantastic sums for compensation."[33]

If the titles to some of the large American holdings were sometimes embarrassingly cloudy, both Daniels and the State Department showed greater enthusiasm for protesting the seizure of moderate-sized properties, especially those where the American owner was living in Mexico as an active farmer or rancher. This greater concern for the rights of the small resident landowner was amply demonstrated when the Cárdenas administration instituted expropriation proceedings against a number of American-owned farms in the Yaqui Valley of arid northwestern Mexico. During the last years of the Díaz regime a group of about fifty American citizens had been granted sizable tracts of unimproved land along the Yaqui River under a hospitable colonization law. By means of extensive irrigation improvements over the years, the Americans had developed prosperous winter wheat and rice farms. Their holdings were large by ordinary American standards; they could be considered small only when compared with the old-fashioned Mexican hacienda.

During 1936 the peasants who lived in the Yaqui Valley began petitioning the government for grants of the irrigated American lands, spurning the unimproved land which the worried American farmers were willing to help clear for them elsewhere. In September, 1936, the U. S. Consul at Guaymas reported that the American farmers in the valley hesitated to plant their winter wheat crop lest they subsequently lose both the crop and their lands. "The agrarian situation in the Yaqui Valley," he warned the State Department, "is said to be coming to a head right now."[34] Secretary Hull immediately cabled Ambassador Daniels to look into the matter, and to insist that the Mexicans not proceed with the Yaqui Valley expropriations unless they agreed to make "prompt payment of adequate and effective compensation."[35]

Daniels discussed the agrarian problem with President Cárdenas early in October, repeating once again the by now standard objections to the seizure of American-owned property without adequate compensation. Cárdenas replied that Mexico intended to pay for lands taken under the land reform program, and said that he was planning to provide for some compensation in the

1937 budget. "With due regard to our educational and economic needs," he promised, "we will pay as much on the agrarian claims as we possibly can, and when payments are begun, they will be kept up."[36] Daniels did not get into specifics over the Yaqui Valley situation at this meeting, using the occasion rather to urge a further moderation of the religious laws and to express concern over the expropriation bill pending in the Mexican Congress.[37] He informed the State Department, however, that other Mexican officials were "seemingly agreeable" to an adjustment of the Yaqui Valley problem to allay the American fears.[38] Continued Embassy warnings that seizure of the Yaqui Valley properties "would cause a terrific stir at home," produced a Mexican report that President Cárdenas was "deeply concerned" to avoid any crisis with the United States in the matter.[39] Foreign Office spokesmen repeated Cárdenas' pledge to budget as much as possible for agrarian compensation in 1937, and informed Daniels that the President intended to make a personal visit to the Yaqui Valley in order to try to work out a settlement that would be fair to both the landowners and the petitioning peasants. Daniels told the State Department he was convinced that the Mexicans were making a sincere effort "to solve a very delicate situation in a way that would satisfy our Government."[40] His superiors were more skeptical. Acting upon anxious dispatches from its consul at Guaymas, the Department directed Daniels to keep a close watch over the situation, and if necessary to "make vigorous representations with a view to preventing expropriation unless adequate compensation is to be paid promptly."[41]

In December Ambassador Daniels saw President Cárdenas again, and had a long discussion of Mexico's expropriation policies. This time he paid special attention to the Yaqui Valley. Cárdenas advanced the view that the American farmers in the valley had now made a profit on their holdings and thus had "reimbursed themselves for the benefit they brought to the country in instituting this irrigation system and developing the Valley as a cultivable area." He reminded Daniels that the Agrarian Code exempted from expropriation a certain portion of an owner's land,

the so-called *pequeña propriedad* or "small property."* The President suggested that the American landowners should divide up
their holdings among their families in order to preserve legal title
to as large a proportion of their properties as possible. The remaining lands might then be divided among the several thousand
Mexicans who were petitioning for farms in the valley.

Daniels was accompanied at this meeting by his counselor,
Pierre de L. Boal, who wrote out a report of the conversation for
the State Department afterward. Boal's account, written in the
calm impersonal style of the career diplomat, nevertheless cap-
tured some of the Mexican President's compelling force and dedi-
cation:

President Cárdenas then said he wished to ask a personal favor of the
Ambassador. He said that his people had existed for many years in a
state of appalling misery and poverty. It had been the ambition of the
great mass of the poor agrarian workers to own the land on which they
worked, and he and his government had sought faithfully to carry out
this purpose. Would it not be possible for the Ambassador to enlist the
assistance of President Roosevelt and of the American Government to
get the American landowners in Mexico to cooperate with the Mexican
Government so that this end might be achieved?[42]

It seemed quite clear, Boal commented to Daniels afterward, that
President Cárdenas' primary interest was "in improving the condition and the opportunities of the poverty-stricken Indian population of his country."[43]

Daniels could make no commitments as to Washington's policy,

---

* Ordinarily, the owner facing expropriation proceedings had a right to
select 150 hectares (about 370 acres) of irrigated land or 300 hectares (about
740 acres) of nonirrigated, seasonal land as his small property, which was
exempt from further seizure. The law provided, however, that should there
not be sufficient land available in the area to satisfy the needs of the agrarian
petitioners, the size of the small properties left to the original owners might
be reduced to 100 and 200 hectares, depending on whether or not the land
was irrigated. The amount of land left to the owner may be contrasted with
that granted to a Mexican petitioner. Each agrarian petitioner was legally
entitled to a maximum of 4 hectares of irrigated land or 8 hectares of seasonal land.—"Agrarian Code," Articles 47 and 51, quoted in Eyler N. Simpson, *The Ejido: Mexico's Way Out* (Chapel Hill: University of North Carolina Press, 1937), pp. 770–71.

though he assured Cárdenas that "President Roosevelt had an interest in the forgotten man and would give sympathetic consideration to this request." He pointed out, however, that Roosevelt had to consider American public opinion, which was strongly opposed to the seizure of property without compensation. To this, Cárdenas responded that he and his associates were deeply appreciative of Roosevelt's and Daniels' sympathetic understanding of Mexican problems, and considered themselves under heavy obligation to the Roosevelt administration. Then he made a surprising offer. He promised that "even though it should involve a discrimination in favor of American citizens which would be very embarrassing to the Mexican Government," Mexico would make whatever settlement in the Yaqui Valley that Roosevelt desired, "in order to save him from embarrassment and difficulty in the United States." In any event, he said, the government would take no further action in the matter until Daniels returned from consultations in Washington.[44]

During his stay in the United States over the Christmas holidays in 1936, Ambassador Daniels carefully went over the recent developments in Mexico with his superiors in the State Department. Some officials thought that Washington should take advantage of the Cárdenas offer to abide by President Roosevelt's wishes in settling the Yaqui Valley controversy. Acting Secretary Walton Moore even asked Daniels to urge Roosevelt to tell Cárdenas that he was deeply concerned over "the continuance of a policy in Mexico which amounts virtually to confiscation of American-owned lands." In this proposed statement, as drafted by a State Department bureau chief, Roosevelt would also declare that he hoped "not as a favor but as a matter of right [that] from now on there may be a cessation of expropriations of American-owned lands in Mexico unless prompt and effective compensation based upon the actual loss to the owners of such lands is to be paid."[45]

Daniels conferred three times with President Roosevelt before returning to Mexico in mid-January, 1937. There is no record of what he told his one-time assistant, but it is quite unlikely that he gave much support to the State Department's attempt to turn

President Cárdenas' Yaqui Valley offer into a general guarantee of American property, regardless of the effect on Mexico's land reform program. In fact, immediately after Daniels left for his post Roosevelt sent a sharply worded memorandum to Moore emphatically rejecting the Department's draft statement. This he had "read with some surprise," the President said, because it did "not represent the policy of the Government." According to Ambassador Daniels, the proposed statement also misrepresented Cárdenas' recent offer, Roosevelt declared:

Secondly, the statement at the bottom of page 1 and at the top of page 2 that the United States cannot acquiesce in the expropriation of lands of Americans unless compensation based on the actual loss to the owner is paid, represents perhaps a policy of many years ago but certainly not the policy of today.

Finally, the suggested instructions to the Ambassador at the foot of the page are also wholly out of line with present policy.

I think our policy can best be stated as follows:

"In the matter of expropriation of American owned property of any kind in any foreign country the United States expects prompt and effective compensation to be paid to the owners on not less than the same basis that payments are made to the nationals of the country making the expropriation."

Please inform the Division of Mexican Affairs and all other Divisions of the State Department of this policy.[46]

Shocked State Department officials did not let the new Roosevelt doctrine go unchallenged. Secretary Hull sent the President a long memorandum warning of "extremely dangerous" consequences should the United States take the view that Americans were under no circumstances "entitled to better treatment in foreign countries than the nationals of those countries." In many parts of the world national law was below the standard of international law, he pointed out. The United States had therefore always held that if the payment offered was *manifestly and substantially less than reasonable, fair or just compensation, or if nothing at all is offered,* this Government cannot leave its nationals to the mercy of debtor countries contrary to reason, the holdings of all international agencies and tribunals and the principles of long-established international law." An announcement of Roosevelt's policy, Hull declared, "would certainly amount to an incentive to foreign governments now encroaching upon the rights of aliens to go much further than they have otherwise gone in the direction of confiscation. It can hardly be doubted that it would produce world wide repercussion."[47]

President Roosevelt apparently did not pursue the matter further, and official United States policy concerning expropriations remained unchanged. The incident is of interest chiefly as an illustration of Daniels' influence with the President and of his independence of the State Department. It also pointed up the division of opinion within the administration on how to deal with Mexico. Both Daniels and Roosevelt were inclined to sympathize with President Cárdenas' efforts to carry out a Mexican New Deal for his countrymen. They tended to take a long-run view of the problem, hoping that the Mexican reforms would result in political stability and a higher standard of living which would benefit not only the Mexican people but the United States as well. For Daniels especially, the question was not simply one of compensation versus confiscation, of law versus larceny; it was necessary to balance the rights of the great mass of the Mexican people against the vested rights of the small minority that had come into possession of most of Mexico's resources. The State Department was generally not troubled by such considerations, believing that its first obligation was to protect the interests of Americans who had invested their money abroad.

While he was in Washington, Daniels learned from his staff that President Cárdenas had kept his promise to resume payments on the agrarian debt. Pierre Boal reported that the new federal budget provided for the issuance of two million pesos' worth of new agrarian bonds, which would be granted in order of priority to those landowners whose claims had been approved. Holders of the now practically worthless old agrarian bonds, moreover, could exchange them at par for regular government bonds, which, although they paid no interest, at least had a current market value. The sum involved was small, but Boal believed the action indicated "a sincere desire to arrive at an adjustment of the question of agrarian compensation within Mexico's present capacity of payment."[48]

President Cárdenas also kept his word not to move hastily in the Yaqui Valley dispute. Indeed, the controversy dragged on for nearly another year before Mexico took final action. In the interval, the American farmers in the valley, supported by the Embassy and the State Department, proposed a number of compromises designed to preserve the bulk of their lands. But the two sides were unable to agree, and in the fall of 1937 the negotiations reached crisis stage. On October 22 President Cárdenas informed Daniels that the government was making final arrangements for the distribution of the Yaqui Valley lands. He promised that each American owner would be allowed to retain with guaranteed water rights a tract of 100 hectares (about 250 acres) as his *pequeña propriedad* (small property) exempted from expropriation by the Agrarian Code. In view of the great backlog of older agrarian claims, Cárdenas said the government could not offer compensation in either cash or bonds, but he proposed that the landowners accept payment in the form of nonirrigated land near the unfinished Angostura Dam. When completed in 1939 the dam would provide an ample water supply to irrigate the new lands. He recommended that when the dam was finished the owners sell the new lands in small parcels so as to avoid future expropriations.[49] A few days later the President outlined this settlement to the affected American landholders, Cárdenas indicating that "discussion of any other proposals would be useless."[50]

Daniels immediately delivered a long formal protest to the Foreign Office, pointing out that the government had classified the American lands "in two different ways in the same decision, to the disadvantage of the American landowners and without following the Agrarian Code." Each agrarian petitioner was being given a tract of eight hectares, as though the land was not irrigated. The owners, however, were being permitted to retain only 100 hectares, the smallest amount permitted by law, on the

ground that their lands were irrigated. Daniels also objected that
the expropriation decree said nothing about compensating the
owners for their irrigation canals and other improvements, nor
did it take into account their losses unless they were permitted
to continue preparations for planting and harvesting the 1938
crop. "In most cases," he declared, "practically all of the financial
resources of the American farmers in the Yaqui Valley are tied
up in their lands, their equipment, and the preparations already
made for sowing wheat."[51] Daniels advised the State Department
that Cárdenas was unlikely to agree to a delay until after the
1938 harvest, since his expropriation decree had already been
published in the press. But he thought the United States might
yet obtain some helpful concessions for the owners if it pressed
"for other points connected with the transfer of non-irrigated
lands."[52]

The Foreign Office's reply to Daniels' protest was for the most
part a model of specious logic, but it contained one possibly important new guarantee. In lamely attempting to justify the government's dual standard in classifying the Yaqui Valley lands,
Undersecretary Ramón Beteta pointed out that the Americans
were being given perpetual grants of free water "both for the
small properties left to them and for the new lands which are
given to them for colonization purposes."[53] At the moment this
was small comfort to the American owners. But after Mexican
officials had had time to consider the full implications of this
grant of free water rights, they concluded the government had
probably made a bad bargain. Beteta admitted rather unhappily
to the Embassy that "free water to the landholders would result,
in a few years, in their having in fact acquired much more value
than that of their properties."[54]

While continuing to try to get additional concessions for the
Yaqui Valley owners, Ambassador Daniels also tried not to lose
sight of larger issues. He reminded Undersecretary of State Sumner Welles of the deep-seated Mexican determination to carry
through the land reform program, regardless of foreign objections.

"When we ask the Government not to dotate land owned by Americans," he commented, "we ask the President to violate his own pre-election and after-election pledges and the promises of the Revolutionary Party." The Yaqui Valley grants had originally been made by the Díaz regime, and Americans should remember that Mexicans were united in their bitterness toward the Díaz gifts of Mexican resources to foreigners. And even though the Embassy had failed to prevent the Yaqui Valley expropriations, it had managed to get the government to defer them for nearly a year, and then to grant the owners some unusual concessions. Daniels pointed to the seventeen treaties and conventions Mexico had negotiated with the United States since his arrival in 1933. These should not be overlooked, he told Welles, as evidence of the Mexican government's desire "to cooperate upon the large mutually beneficial measures."[55]

Welles evidently did not fully share this view, because several weeks later he made a speech in the United States which was widely interpreted as a public rebuke and warning to Mexico. The Undersecretary of State conceded that Latin American nations had a legal right to expropriate foreign-owned property, but he warned that any American citizen who suffered such a loss was entitled to fair compensation. "In that contention he will be supported by this Government," he promised firmly.[56] The always sensitive Mexican press quickly concluded that Welles was referring to Mexico, and there was much speculation below the Rio Grande that the United States might be contemplating a get-tough policy.[57]

Alarmed, Daniels wrote at once to remind Welles again that the Cárdenas administration was bound "by the most solemn pledges" to proceed with land reform. "No Government could endure here which failed to do this," he declared. Mexicans believed that a hundred hectares of land was enough for any owner so long as a large part of the population was landless. The government also recognized the nation's obligation to pay some compensation for lands taken, but this was not a simple matter. "The lion in the path is that if the Government issues bonds to pay the United

States, it will have to issue bonds to pay Mexicans, Spaniards, and others in the sum, perhaps, of a billion dollars," Daniels noted. Government officials were willing to concede in private that American landowners generally had more right to compensation than Mexican and Spanish *hacendados,* many of whom had received their lands for nothing, but "they do not see how they can discriminate against their countrymen."[58] In any event, Daniels told Welles in a subsequent letter, it was wishful thinking to hope for adequate compensation for American landowners, since "the Mexican Government could not by any device known to governments raise so much money."[59]

A few weeks later Daniels summed up his views in a private letter to Laurence Duggan, the chief of the State Department's Division of American Republics. Duggan had recently visited the Embassy in connection with a consular conference, and the Ambassador had rightly sized him up as more understanding of Mexican problems than either Cordell Hull or Sumner Welles. Land reform was the key to understanding modern Mexico, Daniels declared:

You learned when you were here, and the whole history of Mexico since the Revolution shows that Mexicans are determined to subdivide the great estates, as Mr. Hull is determined to have better trade relations. Zapata is rapidly becoming the patron saint of fourteen million Indians, mestizos and other people of small means in Mexico. A statue of him has been erected in Cuautla and another one is being erected in Veracruz, and it will not be long before there is one of him in Mexico City. His cry of "Land and Liberty" makes him a popular hero. As you know, he broke from Madero when Madero surrounded himself with large land owners who were not ready to give the Indians the land which he had promised them. Carranza failed largely because he was of the old land owner class and whatever he did toward breaking up the old estates was forced upon him. Obregón and Calles came into power promising this. Calles got rich and repudiated it. Rodríguez did something, but only under pressure. Cárdenas was elected on the platform supporting it and took the platform seriously. For us at this stage of the game to try to get Mexico to back stream on the plan of giving land to the people would be to go up against a stone wall. Any public man who would advocate the repudiation of the agrarian policy would be doomed to defeat. Strong as he is, Cárdenas would soon fall into the same place that Calles is in if he were to fail to carry out the agrarian policy. It is more firmly entrenched in Mexico than the Monroe Doctrine is in our country. We should not make that the chief issue in our discussions with Mexico, but seek to ameliorate it and obtain such compensation as we can, as we are doing in the Yaqui Valley.[60]

In his handling of problems arising from the Mexican agrarian program, Ambassador Daniels showed a consistent point of view that was more in keeping with the spirit of the New Deal's Farm Security Administration than that of the State Department. He frankly considered it unreasonable for the United States to expect that American landowners in Mexico could be spared from division of their lands, nor was it realistic to assume that impoverished Mexico could compensate them fairly, at least in the immediate future. The wisest course was to try to get special concessions, as in the Yaqui Valley, for those Americans who had especially good claims against Mexico. A reading of Daniels' private correspondence gives one the strong impression that he agreed with the Mexican authorities that in a healthy agricultural society there is no place for million-acre haciendas. Undoubtedly he sometimes found it difficult to muster personal conviction when called upon officially to defend the property rights of certain large American landowners, when all the while he believed with Zapata and Cárdenas that the land should belong to those who work it.

The taking of some American-owned lands in the remote Yaqui Valley was not the only, nor even the most extensive, agrarian expropriation with which Daniels had to contend during his unusually eventful stay in Mexico. The Yaqui Valley dispute has been described at length chiefly because it illustrates the difficult and complex nature of the problems created by the Mexican land reform. It also highlights the divergent attitudes within the Roosevelt administration on how to deal with the radical Cárdenas regime in Mexico. Moreover, the Yaqui Valley expropriations later figured prominently when the State Department applied strong diplomatic pressure after Mexico took over the foreign-owned petroleum industry in March, 1938. Viewed in the light of oil stakes reportedly worth several hundred million dollars, the few thousand hectares of Yaqui Valley wheat lands take on a vastly increased significance that will be treated in a subsequent chapter. The stage was now partly set for a serious crisis in Mexican-American relations, a crisis that would turn out to be the major test of the Good Neighbor Policy.

Personal,   Mexico, D.F. April 8. 1938.

Dear Franklin :-

In these hectic days I have been digging into claims filed by Mexico against the United States and claims filed by American citizens against Mexico. I ran across two which will interest you :

1. An American citizen files a claim for forty odd million dollars which he says he would have cleared on a patent but for the revolution in Mexico —

2. Mexico files a claim for over $400000 for the damage the American fleet did to the property and person of Mexican civilians when Fletcher landed. They may make this bill personal and expect me to pay it. If so, I serve notice that I will draw on you for half the amount for we were partners then.

Faithfully

Josephus Daniels

CHAPTER VII

Too Little, Too Late

No event during Ambassador Daniels'
stay in Mexico caused more of a stir than the expropriation of the
foreign-owned oil industry in March, 1938. This abrupt and
largely unexpected action by the Cárdenas government not only
endangered Mexican-American friendship; it threatened for a
time to destroy the Good Neighbor Policy. Daniels' role throughout the long, angry dispute was sometimes central, more often
peripheral, but always conciliatory. His insistence that the United
States try to understand the Mexican side of the complicated oil
question, his determination not to allow the needs of the oil companies to dictate American policy, and his rejection of any form
of coercion unquestionably helped to set the tone of American
diplomacy. His presence in Mexico City was one of the reasons
why the oil controversy did not bring about an open break between the United States and Mexico, and, in the long run,
strengthened rather than weakened the Good Neighbor Policy.

There were few problems concerning oil during Daniels' first
year in Mexico. The breather secured by his famous predecessor,
Dwight W. Morrow, was still in effect, and the Rodríguez administration showed no apparent disposition to press Mexico's
claim to the subsoil. In a few important cases, such as the Cerro
Azul field of Standard Oil of New Jersey, and Royal Dutch Shell's
rich Poza Rica holdings, the government had not yet issued the
confirmatory concessions promised, at least implicitly, in the informal Morrow-Calles agreement of 1928. Technically, Mexico
still owned the subsoil, but aside from uncertainty, the companies

154

faced no real obstacle to the effective exploitation of their hold-ings. Approximately two-thirds of the foreign-held oil properties had been confirmed, and the companies continued to operate the rest pending confirmation.

In the spring of 1934, however, the situation began to change. Daniels had a series of visits from company representatives, who expressed alarm over the government's failure to continue issuing confirmatory concessions under the Morrow-Calles agreement, and its increasingly strict scrutiny of oil titles. They were also concerned over the establishment of a government corporation, Petróleos de México, S.A., to exploit the government's oil reserves. This government-sponsored rival, they believed, would not only cut into their markets in Mexico; it might also, by training Mexi-can technicians, prove to be the means of easing the foreign com-panies out of the country entirely. Daniels declined to intervene in what he considered essentially a domestic matter, advising the oil men that they must first take their case to the Mexican courts if they believed they were being treated unjustly.[2]

In Washington, too, the companies were active. A Jersey Stand-ard official told the State Department in September, 1934, that the situation in Mexico was rapidly deteriorating. "More and more pressure is being brought to bear upon American and other for-eign companies," he declared, and "the Mexican Government is making every effort which ingenuity can devise to circumvent the spirit and intent of the so-called 'Morrow Agreement of 1928.' "[3]

Anxious to head off any threat to the status quo, the companies decided to take their case directly to General Calles, the recog-nized strong man of Mexican politics. In November, 1934, Allen (Jack) Armstrong, the general secretary of the Association of Producers of Petroleum in Mexico, the trade association of the foreign oil companies, approached Daniels with an interesting plan. He suggested that Daniels invite his predecessor, J. Reuben Clark, Jr., to come to Mexico to try to iron out the current diffi-culties. Clark had worked with Ambassador Morrow on the oil agreement of 1928, and following Morrow's retirement had suc-ceeded him as Ambassador. He thus had first-hand knowledge of the informal Morrow-Calles discussion of oil matters. Armstrong said that the companies would pay all of Clark's expenses and fees, but he proposed that Ambassador Daniels formally invite him to Mexico so that his mission would have semiofficial status. Armstrong left a memorandum with Daniels outlining the scheme:

We are advised that Mr. Clark is unwilling to capitalize his knowledge or influence as former Ambassador to Mexico, but we believe, if asked by you to do so, he will seek an interview with General Calles and will endeavor to secure confirmation of the verbal agreement expressed above. To do this successfully, it is respectfully suggested that you might invite him to Mexico to discuss the antecedents of this matter; for him to take this opportunity to present his respects to General Calles and to use that opportunity to tell General Calles of the doubts and fears that exist and to ask him frankly what he may tell you as regards the understanding referred to.[4]

Regardless of any other merits of this plan, it showed remarkably little understanding of the current occupant of the Embassy. Josephus Daniels had long had strong feelings about the propriety of retired government officials making use of their special knowledge or former status for private purposes. His expressed disbelief that ex-Ambassador Clark could be "seduced," and left no doubt that he considered such a possibility "scandalous" and "reprehensible." "In fact, unless directed otherwise by the Department," he commented grimly, "I would feel like advising him to go home and not stand on the order of his going." Moreover, Daniels did not put much stock in the informal Morrow-Calles understanding. "There is no record here of any agreement," he noted. "If one was reached it was not of record and its terms are not on file …. In the absence of written agreements, the oil companies should carry their contentions to the courts or other officials without involving our Government."[5] Daniels warned Cordell Hull to beware of the companies' plan:

I do not agree with the public man who said "all oil stinks," but we have seen so many evil practices growing out of the greed for its possession and the power it gives (as, for example, the Doheny-Fall scandal) that we are warned to be cautious when we are asked to further the desires of the oil interests ….

Recently the Mexican courts have held that owners must show a legal chain of titles and the Huasteca [Standard Oil Company (New Jersey)], Aguila [Royal Dutch Shell] and other companies are affected. It is because of this decision that application is now made to the Embassy to come to the assistance of the oil companies. My feeling is that the request should not be granted, and that the oil companies should engage their own lawyers and abide by the decision of the Mexican courts ....

It would seem that the highest ethics would cause attorneys to refuse to appear in any case when their public service gave them knowledge which they could not otherwise have obtained.[6]

The Ambassador's counselor, career diplomat R. Henry Norweb, was also dubious about the propriety of the suggested Clark mission. "Personally I feel the plan will not get to first base," he advised Daniels from the United States, "but if it should I think we can put the runner out at second with a fast double play."[7] After conferring with State Department officials in Washington, Norweb reported: "I can assure you that the Department sees eye to eye with us as regards the Clark suggestion. Also I learned that Armstrong's idea in approaching the Embassy was not well received by the American interests. Possibly Armstrong has been hooked by the British group."[8]

Norweb was mistaken in thinking that the parent American oil companies frowned on the move to secure the good offices of ex-Ambassador Clark. Indeed, it seems quite unlikely that the Mexico City managers would have approached the Embassy without first getting the approval of their superiors. Far from disapproving, the major American company, Standard Oil of New Jersey, tried to get State Department backing for the Clark mission. Harold Walker, a vice president of the Huasteca Company, Jersey Standard's chief Mexican subsidiary, assured a Department official that Clark would have no difficulty in convincing General Calles that his agreement with Morrow was being disregarded. "A word from General Calles in the proper quarter would immediately straighten matters out," he declared confidently. Walker was equally certain that Ambassador Daniels could be won over, since he was "not a man to let personal pride stand in the way of the removal of an international sore spot."[9] The State Department declined to sponsor or endorse the companies' plan, however, agreeing with Daniels that if Clark decided to see Calles it should be as a private attorney, with no suggestion of official backing.[10]

The coolness of the State Department and Ambassador Daniels evidently gave the companies pause for a time. Harry Norweb reported from New York that Clark was opposed to the idea, and that even Walker was now inclined to be skeptical.[11] But in the end the companies decided to go ahead with the scheme. Ex-Ambassador Clark duly arrived in Mexico City and conferred with ex-President Calles (soon to be an ex-iron man after his break with President Cárdenas the following June). Clark was entertained privately by the Danielses at the Embassy and more elaborately by the American colony. He did not, however, achieve anything like the results hoped for by his clients. The Clark mission might have succeeded earlier, but it was unfortunately based on a now outdated view of Mexican politics. It overlooked the fact that Mexico had just inaugurated a new president, a man who was in nobody's pocket. The days were gone when the *Jefe Máximo* could, even if he wished, settle a disputed oil title.

Notwithstanding its decision to stay clear of ex-Ambassador Clark's negotiations, the State Department was definitely on the alert for any Mexican attempt to change the status quo in the oil industry. In March, 1935, at the behest of Standard Oil of New Jersey, Secretary Hull informed Ambassador Daniels that the Department was rather concerned over recent Mexican tax increases and the government's failure to grant confirmatory concessions to the oil companies. He suggested:

Pertinent inquiries and allusions made casually by you and the senior members of your staff in personal conversations with Mexican officials might be helpful as indicating the extent of our interest in the matter.

It is also considered desirable that the Embassy maintain close contact with the responsible representatives of the American companies whose interests have been or may be adversely affected. They should be assured of the Embassy's willingness to cooperate with them and they should be rendered such informal assistance as may be possible and proper in the circumstances.[12]

Daniels considered this instruction quite improper. He believed Mexico's tax policy was "purely a domestic question" to which the United States had no more right to object than Mexico would have with respect to American taxes. "As a matter of fact," he remarked, "the Mexicans feel that former administrations sold the patrimony of their people to foreigners and that the only way Mexicans can obtain any benefit from their rich oil supplies is by resort to taxation." Nor did the United States have any right "to demand any specific decree by the courts" regarding confirmatory oil concessions.[13] Dutifully but unenthusiastically, the Ambassador undertook to carry out Hull's instructions, and a Standard Oil official soon expressed his company's gratitude to the State Department.[14] Daniels' representations had little effect, however. The new Cárdenas administration, dedicated to fulfilling the promises of the Revolution, was no more willing than its predecessors to relinquish Mexico's claim to a substantial share in the nation's subsoil wealth.

From 1935 on, the oil controversy entered a new phase, as the companies became embroiled in a bitter labor dispute. This clash between the companies and their workers, represented by a newly militant petroleum workers' union, ultimately led the companies to defy a ruling of the Mexican Supreme Court, and brought President Cárdenas' decision to nationalize the oil industry. Thus after all the years of argument over ownership of the subsoil, Mexico in the end took over the oil fields not under the famous and feared Article 27 of its Constitution, but instead under Article 123, dealing with labor rights. This was grim irony, indeed.

To understand the labor dispute in the oil industry, some background is necessary. Under the prerevolutionary Díaz regime, Mexican workers had been discouraged from joining trade unions, but with the advent of the Revolution, organized labor naturally sought to expand its power and influence. In 1918 a group of labor leaders organized the Confederación Regional Obrera Mexicana, better known as C.R.O.M. In the twenties this organization

enjoyed the official blessing of the Obregón and Calles administrations, and grew to occupy a position in Mexico something like
that of the American Federation of Labor in the United States.
The leaders of C.R.O.M., headed by Luis N. Morones, stressed a
program of practical trade unionism combined with evolutionary
socialism, but after the confederation rose to be the dominant
voice of Mexican labor, its leadership became increasingly content, conservative, and corrupt.

In 1932 a young former teacher and Marxist intellectual, Vin-
cente Lombardo Toledano, withdrew from C.R.O.M. and organized the more militant General Confederation of Workers and
Peasants (Confederación General de Obreros y Campesinos). At
first skeptical of President Cárdenas because he was the hand-
picked candidate of the Calles oligarchy, the Lombardo Toledano
group and other radical trade unions rallied quickly to Cárdenas'
support when he broke with Calles in the summer of 1935. Out of
the temporary unity achieved during this political crisis emerged
a new labor organization, the Confederation of Mexican Workers
(Confederación de Trabajadores Mexicanos, or C.T.M.), under
the leadership of Lombardo Toledano. The new confederation,
based on aggressive industrial unionism like its counterpart in
the United States, the Congress of Industrial Organizations,
quickly became the dominant force in the Mexican labor movement. The C.T.M. furnished a good share of President Cárdenas'
effective political support; the Cárdenas administration, in turn,
willingly provided a favorable climate for trade union growth.

The foreign-owned oil industry was among the first to experience the new militancy of Mexican labor. Jersey Standard's chief
Mexican subsidiary, the Huasteca Petroleum Company, complained to the Embassy in May, 1935, for example, that the demands of striking workers at its Tampico refinery were so excessive that the company might ultimately be forced to suspend operations. If the Mexican government did not adopt a more friendly
and understanding attitude, a Huasteca official warned, the Standard Oil interests might withdraw entirely from the country.[15] This
threat to pull out of Mexico, made by the oil men many times over

the course of the next several years, must be regarded as at least partly bluff. Judging by the vigor with which the companies fought to retain their properties after expropriation, it seems inconceivable that they ever seriously considered leaving Mexico voluntarily.

The Tampico refinery strike was only a harbinger of worse trouble for the companies. Early in 1936 the twenty-one independent oil workers unions merged their organizations into a single industrial union called the Syndicate of Petroleum Workers of the Mexican Republic (Sindicato de Trabajadores Petroleros de la República Mexicana). This merger had the support of the Cárdenas administration, and the new organization quickly affiliated itself with Lombardo Toledano's aggressive Confederation of Mexican Workers. In July the new petroleum workers' union called a special convention to map a drive for an industry-wide labor contract, which, when drafted, called for substantial wage increases and fringe benefits. Among other demands, it specified union jurisdiction over all but a small number of technical and managerial employees, union control over hiring and firing, a forty-hour week, improved health services, a pension plan, better housing in the oil fields, eighteen compulsory days of rest per year, vacations of twenty-five to sixty days annually depending on the employee's length of service, free first-class transportation anywhere during vacations, and larger opportunities for Mexicans in technical and managerial posts. The wage increases asked by the union amounted to about 28,000,000 pesos annually; with fringe benefits included, the union demands were estimated to raise labor costs by more than 65,000,000 pesos.[16] Though by Mexican standards the oil workers were already reasonably well paid, some of the syndicate's demands seemed justified. Others were clearly excessive and unreasonable, and were doubtless advanced as bargaining points. It was evident that the oil companies were in for some rough collective bargaining.

The oil workers' syndicate presented its contract to the fifteen major oil companies (including the government corporation, Petróleos de México) on November 3, 1936, threatening an industry-wide strike unless the companies promptly agreed to negotiate a collective contract along the lines of the union proposals. The companies, which had meanwhile established a common strategy, rejected the union's contract as wholly unacceptable. Fearful of the economic consequences of a petroleum strike, President Cárdenas on November 27 persuaded both sides to agree to a cooling-off period of 120 working days, during which contract negotiations could be carried on. The companies accepted the principle of an industry-wide contract, and the syndicate in turn promised not to strike during the talks.

So far apart were the two sides, however, that they were unable to reach any agreement by the time the negotiation period expired. A few days later, on May 28, 1937, the oil workers went out on strike, shutting down the industry. Ambassador Daniels was home on leave when the strike began, and he did not return to Mexico until September, following his tour of Europe as a member of the American Battle Monuments Commission. During his absence the Embassy staff, under Chargé d'Affaires Pierre Boal, kept both Daniels and the State Department informed of developments in Mexico, especially with reference to the oil controversy.

The effects of the oil stoppage were quickly noticed in other sectors of the Mexican economy, and the government was soon under heavy pressure to get the men back to work. Ten days after the walkout began, therefore, the union instituted "economic conflict" proceedings before the federal Board of Conciliation and Arbitration.* Under Mexico's labor law, this procedure automati-

---

* Under Article 123 of the Mexican Constitution and subsequent legislation, labor was guaranteed many rights for which workers in more highly industrialized countries were still struggling vainly. This seeming paradox was more apparent than real, however. Mexico was a predominantly agricultural nation whose nascent industry was largely foreign-owned. Any economic gains by Mexican workers would thus be borne mainly by foreign capitalists. In other words, a liberal labor code was another way by which Mexico could be returned to the Mexicans under the mandate of the Revolution. The law established certain basic minimum standards in industrial employment and fully guaranteed labor's right to organize, bargain collectively, and strike. It also created Boards of Conciliation and Arbitration, composed of representatives of labor, the employers, and the government, to handle difficult

cally required the appointment of a committee of experts to audit the companies' books and determine their financial capacity to meet the union's demands. This was a distinctly unpalatable prospect for the companies, needless to say, and Boal reported them "very determined in their decision to resist any forced investigation." He predicted a period of "lengthy and extensive litigation and some claim on the part of the companies that they have been denied justice."[17] The board quickly accepted the union's petition and the strike ended. To conduct the inquiry into the financial condition of the oil companies, the board appointed a commission of three experts, composed of two high government officials and a university professor, who were given thirty days in which to carry out an investigation. "It seems pretty certain that the Board will at least give the workers the amount of increase offered by the companies," Boal advised Daniels, "and possibly something more if they can find justification for it in their economic investigation."[18]

In the meantime, more trouble loomed for the beleaguered oil companies. On June 16 Boal reported that the government was considering an important change in its petroleum policy. It planned to resume the liberal issuance of drilling permits, but intended to exact a royalty of from 10 to 15 per cent of the production of the new wells. After further investigation Boal learned that the new policy, embodied in a decree awaiting President Cárdenas' signature, would apply to new wells on all concessions, including those already confirmed by the government.[19]

Secretary Hull quickly instructed Boal to let the Mexicans know

---

labor disputes. Since the government's vote was decisive on these boards, it in effect became the arbiter between capital and labor. The boards had broad powers and quasi-judicial status. In disputes where the power of one of the contending parties was clearly superior to that of its antagonist, the weaker party (in practice almost invariably labor) might appeal to the board to protect its rights. Or in an "economic conflict" where the employer claimed financial inability to meet the demands of the workers, the board was empowered to investigate the employer's actual financial condition and determine the proper settlement. Its findings as to the facts were binding, and its decisions virtually unappealable in the regular Mexican courts.

"of our deep interest in the proposed decree." If the rumors were true, Mexico was undertaking a drastic revision of the informal Morrow-Calles agreement of 1928, which neither the companies nor the State Department wanted to see overturned. Such a unilateral step, Hull declared, "would probably lead to a revival of the petroleum controversy, which this Government is most anxious to avoid."[20] The oil men emphatically agreed. Representatives of the five largest American companies operating in Mexico told the State Department that payment of oil royalties to the government would "not only deprive them of their property rights but would impose upon them heavy financial losses and irreparable injury." It would, in fact, "make the continuance of operations extremely problematical."[21]

The Mexican move appeared to have at least two motives behind it. "There seems to be no doubt that the Mexican Treasury is in dire need of funds to meet the expenditures incidental upon the Government's program of public works, agrarian reform, etc.," Boal informed the Department. "This primary need of the Treasury is probably the driving force behind the Government's determination to obtain a greater part of the profits from oil and to make sure that these profits will be substantial."[22] The Cárdenas administration also seemed anxious to stimulate new production and to arrest the evident decline of Mexican oil fields to the status of standby reserves. Ramón Beteta, the Mexican Undersecretary for Foreign Affairs, told the Embassy that the new decree would contain penalties designed to force the companies to exploit their concessions fully or risk losing them.[23] But Boal reported that General Francisco J. Múgica, a cabinet member and confidant of President Cárdenas, had privately declared that the government had no intention of nationalizing the petroleum industry.[24] The government seemed more interested in a larger share of the oil profits than in assuming the burdens of management.

Washington officials were well aware of Mexico's great financial problems, but they also were reluctant to see the Morrow-Calles agreement upset. Secretary Hull informed Boal that any Mexican move to force the companies to exploit their concessions fully "would unquestionably result in the reopening of the Morrow arrangement." He suggested that Mexico merely ask the companies to increase production, and promised that the State Department would urge them "to adopt a cooperative attitude." Hull declared, moreover, that he would consider the imposition of an oil royalty a violation of company rights, but he observed that the United States might not object to "a reasonable tax on the production of oil."[25] A simple petroleum tax would have less dangerous implications than an oil royalty, which was predicated on Mexican ownership of the subsoil.

Perhaps because of the strong American objections, President Cárdenas decided not to issue the proposed oil decree until after a settlement of the industry's labor troubles.[26] The companies had little chance to catch their breath, however. On the night of August 3, the Board of Conciliation and Arbitration's commission of experts submitted its report. It was a massive document of more than a million words, containing a wealth of historical background and statistical data, and reportedly was largely the work of Professor Jesús Silva Herzog, an economist with Marxist leanings. The staggering length and impressive detail of the report suggested that much of it had been in preparation long before the beginning of the thirty-day period allotted for the investigation, a point the oil companies were quick to note.

The experts had not granted all the petroleum workers' demands, but their findings reflected a marked anticompany bias, nevertheless. The report recommended the creation of a mixed petroleum commission, composed of representatives of the companies, workers, and the government, to settle future labor disputes and to draft certain parts of the labor contract for the industry. The experts also called for a number of specific benefits: the establishment of an eight-hour day and forty-hour week; annual vacations of twenty-one to thirty days, depending on length of service; increased death and pension benefits; improved hospital and medical facilities in the oil fields; and the deduction of 10 per cent of the workers' wages for a savings fund with a matching contribution by the companies. The report stipulated

that the companies must pay all wages due during the period of
the strike, and set the minimum daily wage at 5.40 pesos (approximately $1.50) as compared with the 2-peso minimum (about $.56)
offered by the companies. The union was also given a large degree of control over changes in personnel, and what amounted to
a union shop. Only a limited number of so-called "confidential"
positions could be filled by nonunion men.* The experts asserted
that the oil companies were "perfectly able" to pay their workers
an increase "up to an amount of approximately 26,000,000 pesos
a year."[27]

To justify this award, the experts charged that the companies
had made "enormous profits" in the past, and that their current
earnings were substantially higher than in the American oil industry. The report put the companies' average annual surplus
reserves at 79,000,000 pesos. "The majority of the companies re-
covered their invested capital more than a decade ago," it declared. The experts conceded that the companies were paying

* In view of later company charges that this provision would make effective management impossible by permitting labor to take over vital managerial
functions, it is pertinent to note that certain categories of workers were exempted by the experts from union control. These included: members of
boards of directors; general, divisional, and local managers; sales managers
and assistant sales managers; comptrollers and assistant comptrollers; general
or divisional accountants and assistant accountants; auditors; treasurers; general cashiers and general paymasters; representatives; general and divisional
chief engineers, chemists, and heads of medical services; chief drillers; attorneys; physicians; geologists and geophysicists; licensed chemists; draftsmen,
timekeepers, and watchmen; general, divisional, and local superintendents,
field bosses; sales agents and subagents in charge of branch agencies; labor
agents and subagents; heads and assistant heads of departments; technical and
general inspectors; land agents. In addition, two out of every three drillers and
engineers could be nonunion employees, and up to 50 per cent of the personnel of the labor and legal departments. Each of these "confidental" employees
might have one or two secretaries or assistants, depending on the position,
who also did not belong to the union.—*Mexico's Oil* (Mexico City: Government of Mexico, 1940), pp. 593–94.
The parent Board of Conciliation and Arbitration subsequently modified
these recommendations to the extent of requiring the companies to replace
their foreign technicians with Mexican employees within three years, but the
companies had the right to select the Mexicans to be trained for these positions and they did not have to be members of the union.—*Ibid.*, p. 771.

relatively high monetary wages to their workers, but asserted that in real terms the oil wages were less than in the mining and transportation industries and had declined by as much as one-fifth since 1934. The interests of the oil companies, the report charged, "have always been alien, and at times even opposed, to the national interests." As an example, it cited the companies' pricing policies. Mexican oil invariably was sold abroad at prices below the world level; yet the companies marketed their refined petroleum products inside Mexico at prices well above the prevailing world price. The Royal Dutch Shell subsidiary, El Aguila, was especially criticized for such behavior, the experts claiming that it sold its oil in Mexico at prices ranging from 134 to 350 per cent higher than it sold the same products abroad. Professor Silva Herzog, the chief author of the report, subsequently charged that El Aguila, which produced over half the oil extracted in Mexico, in 1936 had sold all its oil abroad to a Canadian subsidiary at a price averaging about 40 per cent less than the market price at Tampico. This, he said, was plainly a device to transfer profits so as to evade Mexican taxation.[28]

As might be expected, the local oil men promptly took sharp exception to many of the experts' findings and recommendations. Nevertheless, it was significant that Boal reported to the State Department: "Companies feel that report is severe enough but not as unsatisfactory as had been anticipated."[29] Both the companies and the oil workers' union were unhappy with certain features of the award, Boal noted. The union thought the wage increase was too low, and resented the number of employees exempted from union membership. The companies objected particularly to the experts' estimate of their profits, which they claimed were closer to 18,000,000 pesos a year than 77,000,000 pesos.* Company offi-

---

* Boal, Mexico City, to Secretary of State, August 6, 1937, in Department of State, *Foreign Relations of the United States, 1937* (Washington: Government Printing Office, 1954), pp. 661–62. The question of computing profits is, of course, enormously complicated. It is beyond the scope of this study to do more than suggest the obvious—that the true figure doubtless lies somewhere between the figures supplied by the two sides. The Mexicans estimated company profits at three to four times what the oil men admitted.

cials in the United States also protested that the award was absurd. A high official of Jersey Standard flatly told the State Department that if put into effect it would put the companies out
of business. "The findings and recommendations are of such an
arbitrary and impossible nature as that the oil companies operating in Mexico will be forced to cease operations if the Board
makes a favorable award based on the Commission's recommendations," he declared.[30] In the middle of August the local managers
of the oil companies were hastily summoned to New York to help
draw up a policy statement, in order, an Embassy official predicted, "to prepare a case before the Department of State in an-
ticipation of a denial of justice."[31]

On August 18 an impressive delegation of oil men, representing
Standard Oil of New Jersey, Standard Oil of California, and the
Consolidated Oil Company (Sinclair), conferred at the State Department with Undersecretary Sumner Welles and other officials.
Speaking for the group, Thomas R. Armstrong of Jersey Standard
urged that the State Department intervene on behalf of the companies. The oil men warned that Mexico's real object was to take
over the oil industry; its policy was "obviously one of confiscation
by strangulation." They declared that the imposition of the wage
award "would place the companies in the position of being absolutely unable to continue to operate." This would be most unfortunate from the standpoint of American national interest, they
noted. It might, indeed, set a precedent that could "ultimately deprive the United States of petroleum reserves controlled by

---

They explained the difference as due to such improper practices as sales to
affiliates at below market prices, the charging of expenses to wrong years in
order to decrease profits for the years in question, high depreciation costs,
and high buying costs from affiliates. The companies denied these charges,
claiming that it was unfair to base the wage award on the three-year period
1934–36 when earnings were higher than usual. The two sides were equally
far apart in their estimates of what the award would cost. The experts
thought it would amount to about 26,000,000 pesos annually; the companies
estimated it at about 42,000,000 pesos.—See Wendell C. Gordon, *The Expropriation of Foreign-Owned Property in Mexico* (Washington: American
Council on Public Affairs, 1941), pp. 111–12; *Mexico: Labor Controversy,
1936–1938* (New York: Huasteca Petroleum Company, 1938), pp. 73–85.

American nationals in South America and other parts of the world, in the face of limited proved domestic reserves." Despite this gloomy estimate, Welles was noncommittal as to the amount of support the companies could expect. He rejected Armstrong's suggestion that the State Department use its influence to delay the final decision of the Mexican Board of Conciliation and Arbitration. The only ground for action by the Department, he pointed out, "would be a denial of justice."[32]

The oil men continued to stress that what was good for Standard Oil was also good for the United States. Walter C. Teagle, chairman of Jersey Standard's board of directors, reminded Secretary Hull that Mexico's policy was threatening United States oil supplies throughout Latin America:

We are hopeful that representations may be made which will lessen this possibility, realizing that it will be most difficult to secure relief once definite action is taken .... The present difficulties faced by the oil companies in Mexico have a significance to our country much broader than is implied in the local issue. Both existing oil fields and the country yet to be explored in the Gulf-Caribbean region are of vital importance to the United States and if Mexico nationalizes the oil industry, such action may set a precedent for similar steps by other nations in Latin America. In that case, the United States would be deprived of its only readily available foreign source of supply.[33]

The companies were obviously basing their strategy on the assumption that the labor demands were only a cover-up for the real Mexican aim—nationalization of the oil industry.

At this juncture Ambassador Daniels returned to his post, arriving back in Mexico the first week in September, 1937. He had been thoroughly briefed in advance by the State Department on the developments in Mexico during his three months' absence. Secretary Hull had stressed the Department's concern over the petroleum controversy. "It would be extremely unfortunate," he declared, "if any action should be taken precipitately by the Mexican authorities which would jeopardize the industry in any manner."[34] Oil circles made much of Daniels' press conference remark, which they noted came after he had seen President Roosevelt at Hyde Park, that the United States hoped Mexico would not upset the Morrow-Calles agreement of 1928. The reporters all but ignored his other comments, to the effect that the United States continued to believe in the Good Neighbor Policy and would enter the oil controversy only if there were a denial of justice for the American companies.[35]

At Secretary Hull's request, Daniels lost no time in discussing the petroleum situation with Mexican officials. Within hours after his return, he arranged a luncheon with Dr. Castillo Nájera, the Mexican Ambassador to the United States, who was home for consultations with President Cárdenas. "I impressed upon him," Daniels reported to Hull afterward, "the importance of reaching an agreement for the good of all parties, and stressed my strong feeling and the attitude of my Government that the arrangement made in the so-called Morrow-Calles agreement, upheld in five decisions of the Mexican Supreme Court, should not be disturbed, and that the status quo there entered upon should continue."[36] Daniels repeated this view several days later in a talk with Foreign Minister Eduardo Hay. He emphasized that the United States "wished only that its nationals should be treated with justice and no more exacted of them than was exacted of Mexicans in like situations."[37]

Over the next two months the oil dispute simmered while the Board of Conciliation and Arbitration reviewed the report of its commission of experts and considered the objections filed by the companies. Ambassador Daniels reported that the local managers were opposed to a Washington suggestion that the companies send a negotiator to Mexico to try to work out a settlement. Daniels, however, thought a single negotiator might win an acceptable agreement if empowered to make greater wage concessions than the local managers had thus far been willing to grant. "The oil men should divest themselves of the maze of holding companies and like devices," he told Hull, "and be satisfied with fair returns on their actual investment. Heretofore, they have cried that every demand for better wages would work confiscation, and have not been able to establish that assertion." In any case, Daniels thought that a company negotiator should not "have the imprimatur or backing of our Government."[38] To his one-time assistant, President Roosevelt, Daniels was even more critical of the companies' hold-the-line policy:

Having made big money on absurdly low wages from the time the oil gushers made Doheny and Pearson rich, all oil producers oppose any change in taxes and wages, and resent it if their Governments do not take their point of view. Mexico can never prosper on low wages and we must be in sympathy with every just demand .... I need not tell you that as a rule the oil men will be satisfied with nothing less than that the United States Government attempt to direct the Mexican policy for their financial benefit. They are as much against fair wages here as economic royalists at home are against progressive legislation. They would like to have an Ambassador who would be a messenger boy for their companies, and a Government at Washington whose policy is guided by Dollar Diplomacy. No matter what their attitude is, our course is to seek in all proper ways to aid American investors in securing just treatment, and protest if there is a denial of justice.[39]

To Daniels, what was good for Standard Oil must also be good for Mexico, if the oil men and the United States were to benefit over the long run.

The Ambassador's outspoken views made few converts at the State Department, where as a rule the figures and facts supplied by the oil companies were accepted more or less uncritically. This was particularly true of the Department's legal section, whose opinions carried considerable weight with Secretary Hull, the one-time Tennessee circuit judge. One notable exception, however, was Laurence Duggan, the head of the Division of American Republics. Duggan characteristically tried to keep an open mind with respect to the oil dispute. He turned down, for example, a suggestion by the Department's legal adviser that Ambassador Daniels be instructed to support the companies' objections to the labor award. "I still wonder," he remarked pointedly, "whether the Department has sufficient data to have enabled it to give consideration to all sides of this complicated controversy."[40]

By the end of October it was apparent that the oil dispute was completely deadlocked. In a meeting with President Cárdenas company representatives repeated their threat to cease operations if the experts' recommendations were put into effect.[41] The local manager of Jersey Standard's Huasteca Petroleum Company informed Daniels that his company was prepared to shut down before it would pay the wage increase proposed by the experts. When Daniels pointed out that this would give the Mexicans the legal right to take over the Huasteca properties, the oil official indicated his contempt for the technical capacity of the government. Mexico had no tankers or tank cars, he noted, and could neither operate the oil fields nor find a market for any oil it might produce. "I hope the matter will be adjusted without having that impasse," the Ambassador wrote in his diary, "but you can never tell."[42] In their public statements the oil men were equally firm. They informed reporters that the companies had "definitely decided not to pay a cent more" than their recent 13,500,000-peso offer to the union.[43]

Thoroughly alarmed over the ominous drift of events, Daniels wrote Hull at great length on October 29. The situation was now complicated, he said, by the fact that in recent months the companies had removed nearly all of their surplus funds from Mexico. This had stimulated a general flight of capital from the country that had greatly weakened the peso. Mexicans believed this accounted for the companies' intransigence, since the oil men apparently thought that by weakening Mexico's credit they could force the government to back down. But regardless of the maneuvering by each side, Daniels pointed out, the dispute was still essentially a domestic labor question "where it is inadmissible for us to take any part." The United States should intervene only if impartial experts could show that the wage increase would be a denial of justice to the companies. "I do not see how, except for seeking cooperation and fair concessions," he declared, "we could go further and abide by our declarations at the Montevideo and Buenos Aires Conferences and our Good Neighbor policy." Daniels rejected the companies' argument that the labor dispute was only a trumped-up excuse to let Mexico seize the oil fields. "I do not think the President wishes to take over the oil business," he advised, "and I think that the oil operators are mistaking an insistence upon better wages with a desire to nationalize the oil industry."[44]

Hull and Welles decided this letter required more than a perfunctory acknowledgment, since Daniels evidently had a notion that the State Department was not sufficiently neutral. Hull's reply was carefully drafted by Welles and the Department's legal staff, and was thus an important policy statement. It professed complete impartiality in the oil dispute, but revealed at the same time that the companies had managed to get some of their arguments accepted by the State Department. Hull carefully distinguished between an ordinary labor dispute and the present conflict in Mexico, where a government agency was apparently taking sides in favor of the workers. In such a case the United States had a right to ascertain whether its nationals were being treated fairly, and to make appropriate remonstrances. "It is not always easy," he conceded, "to draw a sharp line between matters purely of an internal and domestic character and those of an international character." (One wonders how Hull would have reacted, for example, to a British protest against an "unfair" decision by the National Labor Relations Board in the United States.) The Secretary of State repeated company assertions that the oil industry's scale of wages was "greater by far than that paid by any other industry in Mexico." He suggested, as had the oil men, that the question was thus not how much the companies could afford to pay, but "whether as a matter of justice the demands of the workers are reasonable or unreasonable."

We, of course, are not in sympathy in the slightest degree with any effort or supposed effort by the companies to take advantage of the Mexican Government's financial situation by threatening to close their plants, nor can we close our eyes to any unreasonable position of the Mexican Government designed, as the companies have alleged, to force them to abandon to that Government their investments in Mexico.

In the circumstances, however, Hull agreed that for the time being Daniels should do no more than to advise both sides to cooperate in reaching a fair settlement. Stronger American action would "depend entirely upon whether there is a showing of unfair treatment."[45]

Meanwhile, the united front of the British and American oil interests threatened to collapse. In mid-November, 1937, word leaked out that the Mexican government had concluded a major oil agreement with British interests. El Aguila, the Mexican subsidiary of Royal Dutch Shell, announced a pooling arrangement allowing the government a share of oil production in return for confirmatory concessions in its rich Poza Rica fields. A group of British and American independents at the same time declared their readiness to invest new capital in Mexico for exploratory drilling and the construction of pipe lines, refineries, and tankers.[46] The American oil men did not conceal their bitterness over this coup by their erstwhile allies. El Aguila, they feared, would now be much more inclined to settle with the oil workers union. Daniels, always something of an Anglophobe when American interests were at stake, reported his suspicion "that the British Legation was cognizant of the negotiations both of the Aguila and of the independent oil group."[47] He informed Hull, however, that the Mexican Finance Minister had promised to show no partiality and was hopeful that the American companies would agree to the same terms as the British. The reason for the unexpected oil agreements, Daniels thought, was Mexico's desperate need for new revenue.[48]

Mexican finances were indeed in bad shape by the end of 1937. First the depression, then the heavy demands of the Cárdenas reform programs, and finally the recent flight of capital from the country had put mounting strains on the never robust Mexican treasury. Government officials were especially indignant over the oil companies' role in the financial crisis. President Cárdenas told an American friend he was thoroughly disgusted by the companies' withdrawal of their cash reserves, as well as their refusal in recent months to sell oil in the domestic market on credit, as had previously been customary.[49] The companies no doubt considered their strategy both clever and prudent, but it was hardly calculated to win friends in Mexico.

Ambassador Daniels, along with Mexican officials, recognized that quick action was necessary to bolster the sagging Mexican peso. In mid-November he privately urged Secretary Hull to take up the matter with Secretary of the Treasury Henry Morgenthau, Jr., noting that there was a precedent for American financial aid.[50] Two years earlier Morgenthau had come to Mexico's support in a similar financial crisis by agreeing to purchase five million ounces of Mexican silver each month, and to accept on deposit a large amount of silver against which Mexico could draw dollar exchange.[51] The atmosphere was considerably different now, however. American oil men and their sympathizers believed that the United States ought to use its economic power to force a favorable decision in the petroleum dispute.[52] Daniels thoroughly disagreed with this logic, and told Sumner Welles that the United States ought to expand its trade with Mexico, with American financial aid if necessary, lest the Mexicans be driven to barter deals with the totalitarian nations of Germany and Japan.[53]

In the middle of December a Mexican delegation, headed by Finance Minister Eduardo Suárez, went to Washington to ask for a direct loan and a commitment to purchase a large quantity of Mexican silver. The State Department suspected the Mexicans had been encouraged by Ambassador Daniels. Herbert Feis, the Department's economic advisor, noted drily that Daniels had "a benevolent outlook on his wards down there so anything they do he perchance has a tendency to approve."[54] The prevailing view in the Department was that the Mexican financial crisis offered the United States an excellent opportunity to get a settlement of the agrarian and oil controversies on favorable terms. Early in the Suárez discussions, therefore, Department officials brought up the oil dispute and bluntly asked what Mexico's intentions were "with regard to the exploitation of the petroleum resources of Mexico by foreign companies." Feis informed Suárez that while the companies might be willing to grant Mexico a larger share of oil profits, they "would want to be assured in advance that their labor costs were not going to be continually increased."[55] The implication was clear that a satisfactory oil settlement would not hurt Mexico's chances for economic aid.

Secretary Morgenthau had ideas of his own about Mexico and about the Treasury's silver-purchase program, however, and he also had a low opinion of the State Department's willingness to take advantage of a neighbor's financial weakness. Like Daniels, Morgenthau concluded that the democratic Cárdenas government ought to be supported in this emergency lest it go elsewhere for help. "We're just going to wake up and find inside of a year that Italy, Germany, and Japan have taken over Mexico," he complained in his diary on December 16.[56] Twice Morgenthau reported his fears to President Roosevelt, urging quick action to forestall Mexico's turning to the fascist nations.[57] Another likely factor in the Treasury Secretary's thinking was the knowledge that American interests controlled more than 70 per cent of Mexican silver production. If the Treasury were to bail out the oil companies by ceasing its purchases of Mexican silver, the silver interests, well represented in the powerful silver lobby in Congress, would surely be unhappy.

The financial negotiations in Washington were interrupted on December 18 by news from Mexico that the Board of Conciliation and Arbitration had handed down its award in the oil dispute, largely following the recommendations of its commission of experts.[58] The oil companies immediately announced plans to appeal to the Mexican Supreme Court, claiming that they would "be forced into bankruptcy" if the award were put into effect.[59] One of the local managers again told Ambassador Daniels emphatically that the companies would not pay the increased labor costs.[60] On December 29 the Standard Oil Company of New Jersey issued a press statement bluntly rejecting the labor board's decision. "It will show the Mexican Government and the people that we mean what we say," a company official told the State Department. "They don't appear to believe it."[61]

Meanwhile, against State Department objections, Secretary Morgenthau had won President Roosevelt's approval for his program of financial assistance to Mexico. There would be time enough to discuss other problems after the Mexicans were helped over this emergency, he believed. On December 29 Morgenthau agreed to purchase 35,000,000 ounces of Mexican silver on deposit in the United States and to continue the regular monthly purchases for the time being.[62] The oil companies, and their sympathizers in the State Department, had lost a trump card. The intense gratitude of the Mexican delegation, however, convinced the Treasury Secretary that his decision was wise. "I think with any kind of sympathetic treatment, intelligent treatment, we may be able to help them pull through and have a friendly neighbor to the south of us," he wrote in his diary. "And I think it's terribly important to keep the continents of North and South America from going Fascist."[63]

Officially, both the State Department and the Treasury Department denied that they were concerned with Mexico's internal affairs, though both, of course, had approached the Suárez negotiations with political considerations very much in mind. On the very day that Morgenthau decided to go ahead with the Mexican silver purchases, Sumner Welles blandly informed the British Ambassador that the United States had "adopted no attitude" in the oil dispute, and would intervene only if, "after the Mexican Supreme Court had passed upon the question, there should exist a denial of justice." He consequently declined a suggestion that Ambassador Daniels work with the British Minister in Mexico City in support of the oil companies, declaring that the matter seemed "entirely within the jurisdiction of the Mexican Government."[64] This did not prevent Welles the next day from following up a Standard Oil request for the State Department's help in obtaining a suspension of the labor award until the Mexican Supreme Court could rule on the companies' *amparo* (injunction) plea.[65] The Department also endeavored to arrange a satisfactory bond to be furnished by the companies pending the court ruling. Upon urging by Finance Minister Suárez and Ambassador Castillo Nájera, both very amenable to United States desires as a result of the recent silver agreement, the Mexican government agreed to postpone the operation of the wage award until after the Supreme Court had passed on the companies' *amparo* petition, provided the companies paid their workers 1,300,000 pesos

in back wages. Feis privately advised a Jersey Standard official
that the Mexican offer was "probably the limit of their willingness to make concessions."[66]

Ambassador Daniels reported from Mexico City, however, that
the Mexicans had agreed to postpone the labor award only reluctantly and under what they considered to be "pressure applied
by our Government."[67] Both Undersecretary Welles and Secretary
Hull quickly tried to set Daniels straight. "There has been no attempt directly or indirectly on the part of this Government to
bring any pressure to bear on the Government of Mexico," Welles
cabled indignantly. The State Department had, it was true, discussed a number of pending problems with the Suárez mission in
the hope "that the way could be cleared towards reaching in the
year to come a satisfactory and friendly understanding." But
it had not gone further than to express the hope that the oil dispute could be settled in a way fair to both sides.[68] Secretary Hull
complained to Suárez and Castillo Nájera of the Mexico City
report, and informed Daniels that they had advised President
Cárdenas and the Foreign Office "that far from there being any
pressure applied by the Government of the United States, the
position assumed by this Government was entirely friendly and
very understanding."[69]

"All the right is not on either side," declared an unhappy Ambassador Daniels of the deadlocked petroleum dispute early in
January, 1938.[70] With leaders of the petroleum workers union
loudly demanding that the government enforce the labor board's
decision, Daniels thought the companies should "soften their
position and be willing to make some concessions."[71] Daniels'
hopes rose when Thomas R. Armstrong of Jersey Standard, representing the major foreign companies in the oil controversy, arrived in Mexico City on January 14 for a final effort at a negotiated settlement. "I have had a hunch all the time that there
would be some adjustment or compromise," the Ambassador told
his commercial attaché, "and the fact that the President has
agreed to see Mr. Armstrong, who has full powers to act, would

indicate that this hunch will be borne out—but you can never tell."[72]

The qualification was wise, for Armstrong proved to be a rather inept choice to conduct the companies' last-ditch negotiations. Either he did not have complete freedom to act or he lacked the imagination and broad outlook needed at this stage of the dispute. He relied heavily on advice from local company officials, although they had already demonstrated their inability to reach a settlement. Armstrong told the Embassy he believed the local oil men had acted wisely—"but of that I am not so certain," commented Ambassador Daniels to the State Department. Like the local managers, Armstrong was convinced the Mexicans were really out to nationalize the oil industry. "I do not think such is the purpose of the Cárdenas Government, certainly at this time," Daniels declared. "The present controversy is primarily a wage dispute."[73] Armstrong's fears were doubtless reinforced by a conversation with Antonio Villalobos, the Mexican Minister of Labor, who advised him that although President Cárdenas sincerely desired an adjustment with the companies, he could not be pushed too far. If Cárdenas felt he had to defend the national honor by taking over the oil industry, Villalobos warned, he was "a man of great personal and moral courage and in such a case he would undoubtedly take such a step."[74] Characteristically, Daniels was much more optimistic over the success of the negotiations than was Armstrong. Cavalierly mixing his metaphors, the Ambassador wrote an absent staff member: "You know these things go very slowly here and when you think everything is going to the bow-wows, somehow a parachute comes down and prevents destruction on the rocks."[75]

The Armstrong discussions ultimately broke down over the question of the 26,300,000-peso wage increase ordered by the labor board. Armstrong and the local managers continued to insist that it would break the companies to pay the full amount; and though in one session Finance Minster Suárez offered to prove to them from tax records that they could well afford this amount, the oil men did not avail themselves of this opportunity.[76] After Arm-

strong had left Mexico City empty-handed, Daniels learned from
the Foreign Office that Ambassador Castillo Nájera was still conferring with him in Washington. Castillo Nájera was convinced,
Daniels reported, that Armstrong had not realized "how far the
Government would be willing to go to meet the petroleum companies on other points if they would agree to pay 26,000,000 pesos
annually specified in the award."[77] After all the publicity in Mexico
on the wage award, the government evidently felt it could not
compromise on that issue, but it seemed prepared to adjust other
matters affecting managerial rights in favor of the companies.

The local managers were definitely opposed to the thought of
further concessions or negotiations. They informed Daniels on
February 24 that Armstrong "had no intention of coming to
Mexico City." Afterward Daniels cabled the State Department:

I suggested that they should make every possible concession to avoid
an impasse. After this they discussed the general situation with me
making it clear that they had no intention of acceding to the 26 million
figure, first, because they thought they could not do so, second, because
they feel it would simply be used as leverage to try to obtain further
concessions and would not lead to an adjustment of the other questions.[78]

L. L. Anderson, the manager of Jersey Standard's Huasteca Petroleum Company, told Pierre Boal, Daniels' second-in-command,
that the companies "would never be able to get on with the present Government here." He was equally confident that Mexico
could not operate its oil industry without the foreign oil men.
Anderson predicted that the Cárdenas regime would very soon be
overthrown, to be succeeded by a more conservative government
with which the companies could do business.[79] Boal saw little
likelihood of a successful revolution in Mexico, and he doubted
that President Cárdenas had "any desire to have the operation of
the companies on his hands in addition to his other troubles." He
recommended that the companies pay the wage increase, "in
which event the Government might come around on other things
to try to ease up the situation for them .... It is absurd that the
question of 3½ million pesos a year should mean the life or death
of the oil companies in Mexico."[80]

Obsessed with the idea that Mexico's real aim was to national-ize the oil fields, during February Anderson came up with a scheme that seemed to bear out Boal's belief that he had been "worn a bit ragged by the situation here."[81] He suggested to a representative of the American Smelting and Refining Company, the largest mining interest in Mexico, that it force a dispute with its workers and bring about a labor crisis in the mining industry. The government would then be confronted with trouble in two of the country's major industries, both largely foreign-owned. If, as expected, the Supreme Court ruled against the oil companies, President Cárdenas would probably hesitate to expropriate the petroleum industry, since he would face the prospect of taking over the mining interests as well. But American Smelting was en-joying the current silver prosperity and declined to jeopardize its position in Mexico to suit the convenience of the oil men.[82]

On February 25 Daniels reported that President Cárdenas had decided to take no further responsibility for an oil settlement but to leave the matter up to the Supreme Court.[83] Four days later the high court handed down its long-awaited decision, unani-mously upholding the ruling of the labor board and denying the companies' plea for an injunction against the award.[84] The oil companies immediately issued a defiant statement:

The companies have made it abundantly clear during the past months to their employes and to the general public that the conditions recom-mended by the commission of experts that served as the basis of the Labor Board decision are of such a nature that it would be impossible to comply with them. Their inability to comply remains unaltered by today's verdict ... which cannot but have serious consequences for the companies, for their employes and for those dependent on the indus-try.[85]

Ambassador Daniels tried to impress upon the Foreign Office that the companies were adamant in their refusal to pay the re-quired wage increase, which they feared would run far higher than the 26,300,000 pesos stipulated by the labor board. But both Foreign Minister Hay and Undersecretary Beteta argued that the companies could well afford the higher labor costs, pro-vided they did not conceal their profits through improper book-keeping practices. Daniels warned that Mexico would have trouble selling its oil if it tried to operate the industry alone, but he had no answer when Hay asked what the United States would do if a Mexican company were "ordered by your Supreme Court to obey the laws of your country and refused to do so."[86] Later the Foreign Minister reminded Daniels that President Cárdenas had personally guaranteed the oil men that the wage increase "would under no circumstances exceed the 26,300,000 pesos and that a Mixed Commission would decide upon the administrative points to which the operators objected."[87]

"This has been a very strenuous week," Ambassador Daniels wrote dejectedly in his diary on March 5. "It looks like a complete impasse .... When people are so wide apart in their beliefs of each other and distrust each other it is very difficult to find a common ground. I hope for the best but it doesn't look very bright now."[88] Daniels put his hopes on the British interests, which produced about two-thirds of the Mexican oil output. Officials of El Aguila, the Royal Dutch Shell subsidiary, were reported nervous over the possibility of losing their concessions in the Poza Rica field, Mexico's richest oil pool. These had been confirmed by the Cárdenas government only four months earlier, after a wait of more than seven years. "If they have to get out it would involve a heavy loss," Daniels noted, "and I have felt all along that they would find a way or make one."[89] Most of the American companies were under less compulsion, since their Mexican properties were older and some were nearing the point of exhaustion. The Jersey Standard men in particular continued to argue against any compromise. On March 15, more than a week after the deadline set by the labor board for compliance with its ruling, the oil men announced: "The companies are unable to put the award into effect. It would ruin their business."[90]

The following day Mexican newspapers headlined a ruling by the head of the Board of Conciliation and Arbitration holding the companies guilty of *rebeldía* (defiance). Mexican law provided in such cases that the recalcitrant employer's property might be turned over to his workers. With most to lose, the

British oil men showed corresponding concern. The British Minister immediately arranged an appointment with President Cárdenas, who suggested that it would be wise for the companies to withdraw their refusal of the previous day and offer to pay the 26,300,000-peso wage increase, provided that other administrative features of the award could be adjusted satisfactorily. The Aguila men promptly bestirred themselves in an effort to persuade the American companies to agree to a renewal of negotiations on this basis. They evidently had some success, for Ambassador Daniels reported that the companies had decided to present another statement:

With reference to the "escrito" [brief] presented to the Labor Board on the 15th instant the undersigned companies desire to make clear the fact that they are prepared to agree to increase their total labor costs up to the sum of 26,300,000 pesos .... The companies are unable to accept the administrative and other clauses laid down in the *laudo* [award] but are prepared to sign a contract as per copy enclosed in which the aforementioned increase is embodied.

The American oil men told Daniels the companies had secretly made a similar offer to the union on March 11, but that it had been rejected.[91]

Whether this offer to pay the full 26,300,000-peso increase represented a bona fide effort at compromise is hard to say. It seems to have been a case of too little, too late. Some months later Finance Minister Suárez told the Embassy privately that the companies' various proposals, including this final offer, always had important strings attached. The oil men claimed that their revised wage schedule would equal the required increase, while union leaders estimated that it would fall short by about 2,000,000 pesos. To break this deadlock, Suárez said he had proposed that the companies pay according to their schedule and put the 2,000,000-peso difference in escrow, to be returned to the oil interests if the wage increase equalled 26,300,000. If not, the money would be given to the workers. Both sides could thus be assured that the increase would reach, but not exceed, the figure set by the labor board. The fact that the companies rejected this proposal, Suárez declared, was "the best proof" that they had never agreed to the full wage award.[92] Suárez was hardly a disinterested source, but several years later an American oil man, one of the leaders of the old Petroleum Producers Association in Mexico, admitted in private that the British interests had been prepared to accept the Mexican government's terms. They were persuaded not to give in, he said, by the American companies, which in a showdown were counting on strong backing from Washington. Pierre Boal, Daniels' counselor, recalls that when President Cárdenas offered to give the companies certain assurances for the future if they would meet the wage award, one company representative asked how Cárdenas proposed to guarantee that his promises would be carried out. Cárdenas reportedly replied: "You have my word." The oil man considered this a moment and then said: "That is hardly sufficient."[93]

To the last, the American companies, even more than the British, seemed convinced that the Mexicans were bluffing. On March 16, the same day President Cárdenas made his compromise proposal to the British Minister, a Jersey Standard representative remarked to Laurence Duggan at the State Department that the continued hesitation of the Mexicans demonstrated "that the government lacked nerve to enforce the decision of its own Supreme Court."[94]

An interesting but dangerous theory. For whatever Lázaro Cárdenas lacked, he had plenty of nerve.

The oil and other big interests here have no sympathy with the Good Neighbor policy .... They go to bed every night wishing that Díaz were back in power and we carried the Big Stick and had Marines ready to land at their beck and call. The Mexican Government is so super-nationalist that it has regarded the Good Neighbor policy as a one-way road without feeling that its lasting success is conditioned upon reciprocity. Between these two points of view, our situation as a great and friendly nation is extremely difficult.

—Josephus Daniels to Cordell Hull[1]

The Mexican Government has driven us to the very edge of the precipice, so that in the interest of international law and order, and as one of its constant upholders, this Government finds itself obliged to speak or act.

—Hull to Mexican Ambassador Castillo Nájera[2]

CHAPTER VIII

A Bolt from the Blue

At 8:20 o'clock on the evening of March 18, 1938, radio stations throughout Mexico canceled their scheduled programs to broadcast an extraordinary message by President Cárdenas. The government had decided, Cárdenas announced in solemn tones, to end the eighteen-month-old oil controversy by expropriating the property of the companies:

This is a clear and evident case obliging the Government to apply the existing Expropriation Act, not merely for the purpose of bringing the oil companies to obedience and submission, but because, in view of the rupture of the contracts between the companies and their workers pursuant to a decision of the labor authorities, an immediate paralysis of the oil industry is imminent, implying incalculable damage to all other industry and to the general economy of the country.

Only by this drastic step could the nation assert its sovereign right to compel respect for its courts, the President declared.

But the road ahead would not be easy, for Mexico was incurring a heavy indebtedness:

Nevertheless, we shall, if necessary, sacrifice all the constructive projects on which the Nation has embarked during the term of this Administration in order to cope with the financial obligations imposed upon us by the application of the Expropriation Act to such vast interests .... I ask the entire Nation to furnish the necessary moral and material support to face the consequences of a decision which we, of our own free will, would neither have sought nor desired.[3]

Aroused at the Embassy by excited reporters after the presidential broadcast, Ambassador Daniels admitted unhappily that he had received no advance warning of the move. The seizure had come as "a bolt from the blue." At the very worst, the Embassy and the State Department had thought the President might put the industry under the temporary operation of a government receiver. Daniels called the expropriation "very regrettable" and declared that the two sides "should have gotten together after the companies agreed to pay the full amount the Supreme Court ordered." He refused to speculate on the effect of Mexico's action on the Good Neighbor Policy, but he was plainly troubled on this score.[4] "This has been a most hectic week in Mexico," he wrote sadly in his diary. "A step so far-reaching and the expropriation of property which the companies hold is worth 400 million dollars, has created a very serious situation here."[5]

Above the Rio Grande there was likewise stunned dismay over the boldness of the Mexican coup. In New York William S. Farish, president of the Standard Oil Company of New Jersey, grimly promised that the companies would not stand idly by while Mexico confiscated their properties, which he valued at $450,000,000. Farish expressed hope that President Cárdenas would reconsider and let the companies resume activities on the terms they had offered earlier, which, he said, "were fair to all interests concerned." If not, he predicted that Mexico could not operate the industry successfully alone. Harry F. Sinclair, considered a spokesman for the smaller operators in Mexico, declared that the companies could neither pay wages amounting to twice the industry's profits nor surrender management prerogatives to the oil workers' union. He bitterly accused the Mexican government of championing extreme labor demands, which he said arose "not so much out of a desire to improve the condition of the workers as to take over the properties."[6]

At the State Department the surface reaction was somewhat more restrained. A spokesman told reporters that the Department contemplated no official action until the companies had exhausted all appeals to Mexican courts and had made a formal request for diplomatic support.[7] Behind the scenes, however, there was considerably more activity. Within a few hours after the announcement of the expropriation, Secretary Hull directed Ambassador Daniels to cable his reports rather than entrust them to the slower diplomatic courier. "Is there any possibility of a settlement being arrived at in the near future," Hull asked. "In following developments please consider the possibility of German, Italian, or Japanese activities, such as negotiations for the purchase of oil."[8] Daniels' reply was not reassuring. "In my opinion," he cabled on March 20, "the extent to which the President and the Government have committed themselves in making this expropriation practically eliminates the probability of a settlement in the near future."[9]

The State Department had no intention of waiting for a decision on the expropriation's legality from the hardly impartial Mexican Supreme Court. Sumner Welles summoned Mexican Ambassador Castillo Nájera to the Department on March 21 and lectured him at length on the "absolutely suicidal" policy of his government. Pointing out that the United States only a few weeks earlier had helped Mexico through a serious financial crisis by purchasing a large quantity of silver, Welles noted drily that this neighborly act was now repaid by the seizure of American properties "amounting to many hundreds of millions of dollars in value." He declared it "a notorious fact" that Mexico could not operate the oil industry at a profit, warning that the oil companies controlled most of the world's oil tanker fleet and would boycott Mexican oil in the world market. Mexico would be able to sell its oil only at ruinous prices; it might, in fact, have to dump its oil in Japan, Germany, and Italy, the very totalitarian nations President Cárdenas professed to abhor. On further reflection, Welles suggested, Cárdenas might conclude that it would be in Mexico's best interest "to rescind the decree of expropriation and to permit the companies to continue operating." Dr. Castillo Nájera made no effort to defend his government's action, which he plainly felt had been ill-advised. He expressed doubt, however, that President Cárdenas could be persuaded to back down.*

Through Ambassador Daniels the State Department also sought to express its grave displeasure at the Mexican move. Secretary Hull telephoned Daniels on the morning of March 21, instructing him to see President Cárdenas at once and protest the expropriation in the strongest terms. Daniels immediately got in touch

---

* Sumner Welles, memorandum of conversation, March 21, 1938, in Department of State, *Foreign Relations of the United States, 1938* (Washington: Government Printing Office, 1956), V, 729–33.

In this interview with Welles, Ambassador Castillo Nájera resorted to a rather discreditable tactic he was to use again in the future: trying to raise his stock at the State Department at the expense of Ambassador Daniels. He told Welles that his own opposition to the oil expropriation was being undercut by Daniels' statements in Mexico City, which his superiors interpreted as meaning that the United States would not object to the seizure. "What can I do under these conditions?" he asked plaintively. "If I should say any more without communicating an official message from this Government I would merely lay myself open to the charge that I was favoring American interests whereas the American Ambassador in Mexico was making it clear that the American Government was not concerned."—*Ibid.*, p. 731.

Actually, Daniels had made it plain that the United States was very much concerned, though he had reminded reporters of Washington's public commitments not to intervene in the domestic affairs of another nation. In fact, his press interviews had followed rather closely the statements issued in Washington.—*New York Times*, March 19, 20, and 21, 1938; Daniels, Mexico City, to Secretary of State, March 19, 1938, 3 P.M., DS, 812.6363/3093. Moreover, he had already advised the Department of a Mexico City report that Castillo Nájera had told Cárdenas prior to the expropriation that the United States would follow a hands-off policy.—Daniels, Mexico City, to Secretary of State, March 19, 1938, 4 P.M., in *Foreign Relations, 1938*, V, 725–27.

with Ramón Beteta, the ranking official at the Foreign Office, and arranged an interview with the President. He told Beteta that Hull was "surprised and shocked" at Mexico's action, and believed that President Cárdenas had embarked on a course that "would prove disastrous to Mexico and extremely embarrassing to the United States."[10] Daniels repeated these objections to the President the next day, again stressing United States concern and embarrassment. Cárdenas said that he, too, was worried about the effect of the controversy on Mexico's friendly relations with democratic nations, but he blamed the "rebellious attitude of the companies" for the impasse. He proposed that Mexico begin immediate compensation payments to the companies by allotting them a share of the government-produced oil, to be credited against a final settlement based on a joint government-company valuation of the properties. As he had in his expropriation message, Cárdenas emphasized that Mexico wanted to reserve its oil for the democratic nations, and he offered to make a long-term agreement with the United States for whatever part of Mexican oil production Washington might want. He apologized for any embarrassment his action might have caused the United States, but asserted flatly that "no road was now open but to make compensation."[11]

In long private letters on March 22 Daniels urged Secretary Hull and President Roosevelt to move cautiously in the crisis. "I see no course open but to seek to aid the companies in securing compensation," he advised Hull.

The controversy began as a labor dispute not unlike those we have in our own country. It eventuated in excessive demands on the one hand and unwillingness on the other hand to obey the decree of the Supreme Court, and caused many Mexicans to believe the issue affected national sovereignty .... Between you and me—I wonder at the ineptness of the representatives of the oil companies who are their spokesmen here. Some of them are so dumb that if they had to start a business of their own it would be foredoomed to failure. Initiative and tact are not in their vocabulary—or if so, they conceal it.[12]

He reminded Roosevelt of the long history of wrangling over the ownership of Mexico's subsoil wealth, and the deep-seated

Mexican belief that the foreign oil companies had no interest in the country's welfare:

The feeling here harks back to the days when Doheny and Pearson obtained oil leases for a song from the corrupt Díaz government and when the oil companies backed Huerta and the United States later refused to recognize Mexico unless it upheld the subsoil ownership of oil and silver by Americans. These things have rankled .... If we must have troubles with Mexico about anything, it would be most unfortunate for it to come over oil.

President Cárdenas had made a serious mistake in expropriating the oil properties, Daniels declared, but for the moment he had the solid support of his countrymen. "This Mexican situation will test our Good Neighbor policy," the Ambassador warned. "The upholding of that policy, however, is of the highest consideration in a mad world where Pan American solidarity may save democracy. Oil ought not to smear it."[13]

Daniels' arguments carried little weight at the State Department, where sentiment strongly favored some kind of crackdown on Mexico to emphasize United States displeasure. The *New York Times* reported on March 23 that the Department was in touch with the Treasury on the subject of halting American purchases of Mexican silver. The report may have been slightly premature, but the next day Herbert Feis, the State Department's economic adviser, tried to persuade Secretary Morgenthau to end the Treasury's silver purchase agreement with Mexico. Feis admitted that the effect of this move would be largely psychological—"as indicating the American attitude towards the Mexican expropriations." He also recognized that a silver boycott would have little economic effect so long as the Treasury supported the world price at its present high level, since Mexican silver could still be disposed of abroad. For real pressure on Mexico, Feis urged Morgenthau to combine a boycott of Mexican silver with a progressive lowering of the world price. He listed the "various consequences of importance to Mexico" that this policy might be expected to produce:

(a) Discouragement of silver mining and less employment in silver markets.

(b) Decline in the direct revenue obtained by the Government through the purchase and sale of silver.

(c) Probably some decline of activity in the silver smelting industry with consequent indirect results on Government revenue.

(d) Lowering in the purchasing power of the silver making up part of the reserve of the Mexican Central Bank.

(e) For all the preceding reasons, probable further weakening of the peso.

Inasmuch as a number of friendly silver-producing nations would be hurt by a lowering of the world price, Feis suggested that the Treasury might wish to "make certain purchase arrangements before permitting the rate to decline."[14] Morgenthau was asked to look at the matter from the standpoint of the wrong being done by Mexico to American interests, and to read the State Department's reports on the subject if he had any doubts.[15]

The Treasury Secretary, as we have already seen, had his own views on foreign policy, and he declined to be enlightened by the State Department's data. Morgenthau felt strongly that the Treasury's silver program ought not to be used as a weapon against Mexico. Reluctantly, he agreed to follow the State Department's wishes, but he demanded a formal request to that effect. In his diary Morgenthau noted that Secretary Hull seemed to be motivated by fear for the safety of American oil holdings in Colombia and Venezuela if Mexico were permitted to carry through the expropriation.[16] On March 25 the State Department sent Morgenthau a suggested announcement of the proposed new silver policy: "In view of the decision of the Government of the United States to re-examine certain of its financial and commercial relationships with Mexico, the Treasury will defer continuation of the monthly silver purchase arrangements with Mexico until further notice." Morgenthau immediately conferred with Sumner Welles and Senator Key Pittman, the chairman of the Senate Foreign Relations Committee. He was surprised to find that Pittman, who was also the leader of the powerful silver bloc in Congress, supported the State Department. Outnumbered and outgunned, the unhappy Treasury Secretary took the precaution of sending a telegram to the vacationing

President Roosevelt at Warm Springs, announcing that he intended to comply with the State Department request "unless you advise us to the contrary."[17]

The President made no move, however, and on March 27 Morgenthau issued the terse announcement that the Treasury was halting its purchases of Mexican silver.[18] The next day he lowered the Treasury's price for foreign silver from forty-five to forty-four cents an ounce, and the following day dropped the price another penny, moves that helped to accelerate the downward plunge of the Mexican peso.[19] Morgenthau had understood that responsibility for the new policy would be shared jointly by the State and Treasury departments. He was thus terribly upset when he learned that Cordell Hull had blandly declared at a press conference that silver purchases were primarily a Treasury matter, but that in this case the Treasury had obligingly informed the State Department of its decision before notifying the Mexicans of the action![20]

The silver boycott was only one phase of the State Department's offensive against the errant Cárdenas regime. On Saturday, March 26, the day before the Treasury was scheduled to announce the new silver policy, Hull cabled Daniels the text of a long protest note, instructing him to deliver it "not later than Monday noon." Behind a façade of diplomatic courtesy, the language of the State Department note was stern:

The position which my Government has so frequently presented to the Mexican Government regarding the payment of just compensation for land taken pursuant to the agrarian policy applies with equal force with respect to the oil properties that have just been expropriated. This does not mean that the Government may later pay as and when it may suit its convenience. Having in mind the treatment that has been accorded the American owners of land, my Government must of necessity view with concern and apprehension the most recent act of the Mexican Government.

The note described past expropriations under the agrarian program as "confiscation," and declared that the time had come for a settlement of those claims, too. "In the event that the Mexican

Government persists in this expropriation," the note said pointedly, the United States wished to be informed as to "what specific action with respect to payment for the properties in question is contemplated by the Mexican Government, what assurances will be given that payment will be made, and when such payment may be expected." The State Department warned that it expected "a very prompt reply to this inquiry."[21]

An hour after dispatching this telegram, Hull cabled Daniels to return to Washington for consultation immediately after presenting the American protest. He also instructed Daniels to let the Department know as soon as he had delivered the note so that its text could be released to the press. Hull revealed that the publication of the American note would be timed to coincide with the Treasury's announcement of the suspension of Mexican silver purchases. "Please telegraph me likewise the date on which I may expect to see you at the Department," Hull requested.[22] The outlines of State Department strategy were clear: a stiff diplomatic protest, followed by a silver boycott and the withdrawal of the American Ambassador. If these moves did not produce the desired results in Mexico, they would at least be a timely warning to other Latin American governments with covetous thoughts or sticky fingers.

Ambassador Daniels received these various instructions with heartsick misgivings. He was not surprised at the position taken in the State Department's note, but he deplored its sharp language, which he took as evidence that Cordell Hull's Tennessee temper had gotten the better of his reasoned judgment. Three days earlier Daniels had watched while more than two-hundred-thousand cheering Mexicans paraded past President Cárdenas in the Zócolo, the great public square before the National Palace. Throughout the country more than a million Mexicans had demonstrated in support of the government that day, eloquent proof of the great popularity of Cárdenas' move. Even the Catholic clergy, long at odds with the revolutionary governments, joined in the appeals for national unity to defend Mexican sovereignty. The oil expropriation had brought a powerful resurgence of Mexican na-

tionalism. Except for some border towns, however, this sentiment was not yet anti-American, but Daniels recognized that the
great resentment against the oil companies could easily be transferred to the United States, should Washington take a strongly
partisan stand in their behalf.[23]

Desperately, Daniels stalled for time, hoping to convince Hull
of the dangers of a get-tough policy. In a rapid succession of
telegrams, he requested further instructions, though nothing could
be plainer than the orders he had just received. At 1 A.M. on
March 27 he asked:

Before publication of your note and announcement about silver purchase
with all its implications do you wish me, in view of the very serious
reactions, to point out to the Minister, when I deliver your note, the importance of Mexico's giving the prompt assurances you demand? If so
how far should I go in indicating the steps the Department will take in
the absence of assurances? Or would it not be wise for me to acquaint
Hay with your firm position and seek assurances and then let me fly to
Washington for consultation before anything in the nature of an ultimatum is delivered? I ask these questions because I believe every possible step should be taken to prevent the threatened break in relations
between the two countries. Nobody can foresee what will occur upon
the publication of the position of our Government outlined in your note
accompanied by the statement by the Secretary of the Treasury.[24]

Several hours later he cabled a stronger appeal, marked "Rush,
for the Secretary":

If there are conditions which justify Morgenthau [to] take measures
[to] cease buying silver he could take that course any time without a
public statement concurrent with your note. It would be regarded by
Mexico and all the world in the nature of a reprisal. Knowing the disposition of Mexicans I fear it may produce an impasse and prevent
possible future negotiations for payment.

Do you not feel that I am entitled to fly to Washington for personal
consultation before a final decision is reached and made public in a
situation fraught with unpredictable consequences? I do not like the
idea of delivering the note and leaving here immediately. It would be
construed that I am not willing to face any condition that may arise.[25]

Considering Daniel's prominence in the Democratic Party and
his long friendship with President Roosevelt, he could hardly

be ordered about like an ordinary foreign service officer. Yet Hull refused to retreat much in the face of the frantic appeals from Mexico City. He insisted that the strong American note must be presented on schedule, though he agreed that the word "very" might be dropped from the request for a "very prompt reply." He also authorized Daniels to say that the note would be withheld from publication "for the time being, and definitely if a satisfactory solution is found." For reassurance, he declared confidentially that the Department saw no reason to anticipate a break in friendly relations if Mexico adopted a conciliatory attitude toward the requests in the American note.[26] Hull pointed out that Ambassador Castillo Nájera had already been advised of the Treasury action, and declared that the proposed procedure was "more conciliatory in nature than cessation of silver purchases without any explanatory statement."[27]

In an extraordinary call at the Foreign Office on Sunday afternoon, March 27, Ambassador Daniels presented the American protest note to Foreign Minister Hay, who promised to give it to President Cárdenas at once. Hay reiterated the government's resolve to compensate the oil companies, but said it would be impossible to make the payments in cash. He emphasized that Mexicans were "ready to make any sacrifice to meet their obligations." Daniels told him that in view of the promise of an early reply the United States would for the time being keep the note secret, and Hay gratefully promised to do likewise.[28]

Two days later, however, Hay informed Daniels that President Cárdenas had requested that the American note be "withdrawn and altered," because it ignored his compensation offer to Daniels on March 22. Cárdenas believed the note should recognize that he had promptly given assurances of compensation, both privately to Daniels and in three public statements since the expropriation. "I recommend last page of note be altered in conformity with request," Daniels cabled Hull. "Please take no action on this until I have telephoned you."[29] After a telephone conference on the afternoon of March 29, Secretary Hull finally agreed with the Ambassador's argument that "it is results we desire." Daniels thereupon decided with Foreign Minister Hay that the American note should be regarded as not formally presented, merely an unofficial expression of American views.

This was quite a departure from the original State Department strategy, and there is good reason to believe that Daniels had no authority to water down the Department's protest to this extent. Several months later President Cárdenas off-handedly told reporters that the United States had not presented any formal notes or demands, only informal questions, concerning the oil expropriation.[30] When Hull learned of this, he was furious, and indignantly informed Daniels that he had "never remotely contemplated" the withdrawal or suspension of the note, and that if Cárdenas persisted in denying its existence, the State Department would reconsider its promise not to publish the protest. The State Department even drew up a press release summarizing the note.[31] Daniels admitted that he might have misinterpreted Hull's telephone remarks, but he pleaded with him not to initiate a controversy that would serve no useful purpose now and might only delay an agreement on compensation:

In assenting to General Hay's statement that "We will then consider the note as not having been delivered" I felt justified, after our telephone conversation, in consenting to such action as the best course to reach a settlement. I thought and I still think I was acting in harmony with the objective of the Department in accepting the assurances that payment would be made—that is, a satisfactory settlement .... never did I suppose my action was not in accordance with the spirit of the policy of the Department.[32]

Daniels' show of innocence was not very convincing, but Hull nevertheless decided to keep the note secret, provided the Mexicans clearly understood that the State Department regarded it as "regularly delivered and valid in every respect."[33] To this day the State Department has kept its promise not to publish the text of the March 27 note, though during the long controversy over the oil expropriation a number of American journalists and oil men claimed to be familiar with its contents.

With the American protest filed away, on March 30 Foreign

Minister Hay gave Daniels a memorandum outlining President
Cárdenas' verbal promise to compensate the oil companies for
the "irrevocable expropriation" of their properties. Hay proposed
that the companies meet with the Minister of Finance to discuss
the matter, and promised that Mexico would not wait for a final
appraisal before beginning payment.[34] The next day President
Cárdenas called Daniels to the National Palace and formally
expressed his government's appreciation of the understanding
attitude adopted by the United States in the crisis:

By this attitude, Mr. Ambassador, your President and your people have
won the esteem of the people of Mexico. The Mexican nation has lived
in these past few days through moments of trial in which it did not
know whether it would have to give rein to its patriotic feelings or to
applaud an act of justice of the neighboring country represented by
Your Excellency .... You may be sure, Mr. Ambassador, that Mexico
will know how to honor its obligations of today and its obligations of
yesterday.[35]

In forwarding this statement to Secretary Hull, Daniels declared:
"I fully believe the President and his advisers, after sweating
blood for a week and reading and rereading your note of March
27th which you authorized to be held in suspense at the Foreign
Office for a time, seriously intend to seek means to meet agrarian
as well as other obligations. I purpose to press the matter."[36] In
the circumstances, he decided to ignore Hull's instruction to return to Washington, convinced he could accomplish more at
his post, and a few days later received belated authorization to
remain in Mexico City.

Daniels' objections, delay, and generally independent course
had effectively sabotaged the State Department's plan for a
stern public rebuke of Mexico. His actions were clearly insub-
ordinate. Yet in Daniels' defense, it should be noted that he was
convinced the Department was not sufficiently aware that its
course would very likely lead to an open break between Mexico
and the United States, a break that might destroy the fruits of
five years of good-neighbor diplomacy. No one can be certain, of
course, what might have been the result if Daniels had not

blunted the force of the State Department's protest. A leading Mexico City newspaper, apparently speaking with inside knowledge, later described the note as "so strong that, if it had been accepted, it would have ruptured relations with the United States."[37] This impression is confirmed by Ramón Beteta, Undersecretary for Foreign Affairs in the Cárdenas government, who has advised the author that Mexico would have broken diplomatic relations if Ambassador Daniels had presented the note officially. Ever sensitive to reflections on their national honor, the Mexicans took just that step a few weeks later in retaliation for a similar strong British protest. Beteta believes that Daniels almost single-handedly prevented a break between the United States and Mexico at this time, and he suggests that both countries owe a heavy debt to the Ambassador's willingness to endanger his career in the furtherance of the Good Neighbor Policy.[38]

Although Ambassador Daniels was able to soften the official United States reaction to the seizure of the oil properties, he had less success in forestalling the move to suspend the Treasury's purchases of Mexican silver. This step he regarded as ill-advised economic coercion, which would accomplish nothing for those Americans with valid claims and would only embitter United States relations with Mexico. "I cannot convey to you the feeling here," he wrote Roosevelt after a sleepless night, "that a friend has struck a blow more devastating than he can conceive. It hurts economically and reduces ability to give employment and meet obligations, but it hurts worse in a conviction that it is the end of the Good Neighbor policy and its replacement by the old policy of the Big Stick and the patronizing Big Brother policies, for which you substituted one of neighborliness." Daniels urged that the Treasury reconsider the boycott, and announce the resumption of Mexican silver purchases. He even drafted a proposed statement for Secretary Morgenthau to issue, if Roosevelt approved. He reminded the President:

We are strong. Mexico is weak. It is always noble in the strong to be generous and generous and generous. The weak are afraid of demonstrating their weakness if they openly practice that virtue. Your Good Neighbor policy, the noblest conception of preserving unity in the Western Hemisphere in a mad world, is in danger. I know it is your heart's desire to preserve it and undergird it, and I pray you may be given wisdom and divine direction.[39]

Daniels' fears aside, the Treasury boycott against Mexican silver was never very effective. From the first, Secretary Morgenthau resented the State Department's manipulation of silver policy, and he disagreed sharply with its premise. Consequently he gave only grudging coöperation. A Treasury study prepared in late March concluded that Mexico, if helped over a long financial crisis, would be able to make full compensation to the oil companies, but that pressure tactics would "result only in driving Mexico to seek assistance elsewhere and/or into political and economic chaos."[40] The new silver policy had been in effect less than a week when a State Department official remarked privately that the Treasury was not firmly committed to the ban and that its future course was uncertain.[41]

In the middle of April Morgenthau admitted at a press conference that the Treasury was still buying any Mexican silver offered on the open market, despite the cancellation of the special purchase arrangement with the Mexican government. "We have continued to buy all spot silver offered to us at the Treasury price," he said, "and so far as I know we will continue to buy all spot silver that is offered. We don't know where it comes from, and we don't care. It's an open market, and a free market, and we buy all that is offered." Under questioning, he conceded that Mexican silver might even be sent directly to the United States for Treasury purchase without first being sold abroad.[42] If this was a boycott, its effect, as Herbert Feis had suggested, was largely psychological! A few days later when the Treasury indicated its intention of buying more than 200,000 ounces of Mexican silver—the first large lot since the announcement of the suspension—Feis and the State Department raised no objection.[43] Either the Department had begun to have second thoughts about the effectiveness of the silver manipulations, or it may have been influenced by the fact that the silver in question came from the mines of the American Smelting and Refining Company, the largest American mining interest in Mexico. Treasury purchases of Mexican silver did decline significantly after the oil expropriation (from 88 million ounces in 1937, for example, to 44 million ounces in 1938, to only 500,000 ounces in 1941), but the suspension was by no means a crippling blow to the Mexican economy. It not only failed to intimidate the Mexicans; it infuriated the owners of Mexican silver mines, mostly Americans, who felt they were being made to suffer for the deeds of the oil men.[44]

Over the next few weeks Morgenthau continued to argue against a punitive policy. The Treasury even drew up a proposal for a large low-interest loan to Mexico, in return for a satisfactory settlement of all outstanding Mexican-American disputes. Morgenthau interested President Roosevelt in the idea, but he met with strong State Department opposition. Feis, the Department's economic adviser, warned that the Mexican government was irresponsible and could not be trusted to carry out such an agreement. Besides, no oil settlement ought to leave control of the industry in the hands of the technically backward Mexicans. Feis also thought a loan to Mexico would be difficult to justify to public opinion at home, and expressed fear of the effects of such a precedent on other Latin American governments.[45] The State Department's arguments were persuasive, and they prevailed for the time being.

President Roosevelt, vacationing at Warm Springs, Georgia, during the hectic days immediately following Mexico's seizure of the oil properties, was content to remain aloof from the policy arguments going on in Washington. He kept abreast of the situation, however, and in a press conference on April 1 revealed that he did not wholly subscribe to the State Department's all-out support of the oil companies. Seated comfortably behind the wheel of his new car, which he had driven onto the east portico of the main building of the National Infantile Paralysis Foundation in order to escape a drenching rain, the President yielded to a reporter's plea for one of his famous background briefings, this time on American policy toward Mexico. Speaking off-the-record, Roosevelt observed that some Americans who had suffered property losses under the Mexican agrarian program had claimed damages far in excess of the capital they had actually invested. "We have not got much sympathy with trying to collect that excessive sum," he declared. Nor should the oil men expect compensation for prospective profits:

Oil companies have gone down there and they have invested money. Now, the Mexican Government would expropriate their property; they are condemning it. We feel that these oil companies should get payment from the Mexican Government for the actual sum invested in the oil lands and in the drilling operations and the pumping and the refining, and so forth and so on, less depreciation, so that they would come out with a whole skin.

President Cárdenas' pledge to compensate the oil companies seemed to be, Roosevelt said, "a very satisfactory thing."[46]

This optimism was hardly shared by the State Department. Only the day before, Sumner Welles had informed Ambassador Castillo Nájera that the Mexican offer was "not responsive to the specific requests and inquiries...we had very plainly asked."[47] Moreover, although Roosevelt assumed that an oil settlement ought to be based on actual invested capital, less depreciation, Welles had already told Dr. Castillo Nájera that the oil properties were worth "many hundreds of millions of dollars," an estimate obviously based on prospective profits on oil in the ground.[48] The very day the President's press conference remarks—attributed to a high administration official—hit the newsstands, Secretary Hull summoned Ambassador Castillo Nájera to the State Department in order to stress "the impossible position in which these proposed or threatened steps by the Mexican Government are placing this Government and this country."[49] Hull and Welles were willing to concede Mexico's abstract right to expropriate private property, but they plainly thought President Cárdenas had no business taking over the petroleum industry. If the stubborn Mexican chief executive could not be induced to back down, the State Department was evidently prepared to support the oil companies' claim for multimillion dollar compensation based on the subsoil wealth of their seized properties.

Here, then, were the makings of a long and acrimonious Mexican-American dispute, as well as a spirited policy debate within the Roosevelt administration. A get-tough policy must in the last resort be based on some form of sanctions. If the State Department view prevailed, the United States must be prepared to apply some unneighborly pressure against Mexico. Yet already it was abundantly clear that such a course would be strenuously opposed by Ambassador Daniels in Mexico City, and by Treasury Secretary Morgenthau, among others, in Washington. President Roosevelt himself appeared to be unwilling to sacrifice the Good Neighbor Policy in an attempt to win back the oil properties. Hull and Welles seemed to be overlooking a cardinal rule of diplomacy. As Ambassador Daniels wisely reminded his friend in the White House at this time: "Never draw unless you mean to shoot."[50]

The taking of property without compensation is not
expropriation. It is confiscation. It is no less confiscation because there may be an expressed intent to
pay at some time in the future.
—Cordell Hull[1]

Our State Department is vigorously demanding payment by this poor country and saying nothing to
Britain and France. I cannot understand such diplomacy. It is not even tenth cousin to Wilson's "self-
determination," the Buenos Aires declaration against
intervention "direct or indirect," and the spirit
of the Good Neighbor.
—Josephus Daniels[2]

CHAPTER IX

"Before Final Action"

The State Department's reaction to
Mexico's defiant expropriation of the oil industry—a strong diplomatic protest backed by economic pressure—brought no immediate results. President Cárdenas clearly had no intention of
backing down in the face of rebukes from Washington. But if
Cárdenas could not be persuaded to hand back the oil properties,
the next logical step was to make sure he paid for them. Here
the United States position was unequivocal. Washington recognized Mexico's sovereign right to expropriate the property of
American citizens, provided she paid prompt, adequate, and effective compensation. This was a goal more easily stated than
secured, for the Mexican government was richer by far in debts
than it was in cash.

While Secretary Hull and his aides in Washington pondered
this dilemma, Ambassador Daniels in Mexico City continued to
advocate a policy of caution. In a long private letter to Hull on
April 2 he warned against letting the oil companies set the tone
of American policy:

Every proper influence should be brought to bear upon the American oil interests to sit down with Mexican authorities and try to reach an equitable and just arrangement by which Mexico can pay for the oil properties in the only coin they have—oil .... I find some of the less responsible men in the oil companies, British and American, instead of trying to have them meet and reach an agreement by which they may take the oil, are disposed to wage a bitter fight, and some of the Mexican people believe they are trying to foment trouble in the hope that it may drive Cárdenas out of office .... It is inconceivable, though it is not impossible, judging by Mexico's past, that we might have another Spain here. It is certain that Cárdenas could not be ousted from office unless the opposition were supplied with arms by powerful interests, and that if that happened it would be the worst crime that has occurred in the Western Hemisphere since the days of Huerta.

Daniels believed the oil expropriation was a great mistake, but thought it must be considered as accomplished and irrevocable. "I do not believe there is any power under the sun that could make Cárdenas recede from his decree," he declared.[3]

The oil companies were not interested in any settlement that left control of the industry in the hands of the Mexican government. On the contrary, they grimly prepared to fight the expropriation with every weapon available. On April 4 they started *amparo* proceedings in Mexico City for a court injunction against the seizure of their properties. Finance Minister Suárez told Daniels the oil men had made it plain they would not discuss compensation until after the outcome of their legal suit.[4] Sources close to the companies reported they were in no mood to compromise. George Rihl, a Pan American Airways executive, advised the Embassy early in April that the question of money was unimportant; the companies were "chiefly concerned with the precedent, because it would affect their properties in other countries."[5] Rihl suggested another reason for the companies' strategy of delay. He told Daniels confidentially that he had been assured by a Jersey Standard vice president in New York that "there was certain to be a revolution or uprising against Cárdenas in Mexico within thirty days." After a quick survey, Rihl decided this prediction was based largely on wishful thinking, a conclusion the Ambassador fully shared.[6]

The companies' unwillingness to discuss a settlement rather complicated the State Department's position in the dispute. The United States, having recognized Mexico's right to expropriate, could legitimately take issue only with the amount and method of compensation Mexico might offer. If the companies refused even to discuss this question with the Mexicans, the State Department's talk of confiscation lost some of its force. The companies were undoubtedly correct in asserting that Mexico could never scrape together a half billion dollars in cash, which was the optimistic price tag the oil men had put on the properties. On the other hand, the Mexicans could point to their repeated invitations to the companies to discuss a settlement, as well as to President Cárdenas' promise not to take advantage of his right under Mexican law to defer compensation for ten years. With this in mind, Sumner Welles warned the oil men early in April not to adopt "an attitude of intransigence."[7]

The British government was much less reticent about demanding a return of the seized oil properties. London was well aware that British interests had suffered the greatest loss in Mexico. It was painfully aware, too, that with Hitler menacing the peace in Europe, El Aguila's rich Poza Rica fields might some day be of vital importance to the Royal Navy. Unlike the United States, therefore, the British did not concede Mexico's right to take over the oil industry. On April 8 the British minister in Mexico formally demanded the return of El Aguila's holdings, charging that the expropriation was an illegal political move to seize control of the oil fields.[8] Over the next month the two governments argued the matter with mounting tempers. Finally, on May 11, the British presented an icy request for payment of a comparatively small sum overdue on a claims agreement since the previous January, noting sarcastically that if Mexico could not meet her existing debts, she obviously could not pay for the oil properties.[9] Foreign Minister Hay quickly submitted Mexico's check for the required sum and announced that Mexico was breaking its diplomatic ties with Great Britain. As a parting shot he reminded the discomfited British minister that "even powerful States and those who have ample resources cannot pride themselves on the punctual payment of all of their pecuniary obligations."[10] In Washington President Roosevelt chuckled over this thinly veiled reference to the failure of the British to honor their large American war debt, calling the Mexican reply a "peach."[11] Daniels termed it a "palpable hit."[12]

With the British outmaneuvered and relegated to a sidelines position, the State Department was left with major responsibility for a settlement of the oil controversy. Realists in the Department were reported to be thinking in terms of a settlement that would recognize Mexico's ownership of the oil fields, yet permit the companies to control marketing and perhaps production, while receiving compensation from oil sales.[13] On May 9 Sumner Welles told Ambassador Castillo Nájera that the Department would be glad to transmit any Mexican offer to the companies. Welles emphasized that he was not speaking for the companies, but he outlined several possible solutions to the dispute, one of which involved Mexico's leasing the oil fields to the companies for an extended period.[14] Perhaps in response to this continued prodding from Washington, a few days later, in a rare press interview, President Cárdenas offered to negotiate a long-term agreement allowing the companies to export 60 per cent of Mexico's oil output. From this they might take whatever was necessary over the next ten years to recover the value of their expropriated properties. Cárdenas insisted firmly, however, that he would never permit the companies to regain control over production, and with it the opportunity to meddle in Mexican domestic affairs.[15]

Ambassador Castillo Nájera explained the Mexican offer in an hour-long conference with Welles on May 26. He proposed the immediate valuation of the companies' properties by a commission of three experts: one to be named by the Mexican government, one by the companies, and the other by mutual agreement. The value of the properties would be fixed in U. S. dollars. Meanwhile, a government-controlled trust would operate the industry, selling oil at a discount to the companies for export abroad. Through this discount, the amount of which was unspecified, the companies would ultimately receive whatever settlement was determined by the experts.[16] Ambassador Daniels, who had recently returned to the United States for those belated consultations, thought the offer ought to be explored, and he urged Secretary Hull to win the coöperation of the American oil interests.[17]

This proved to be no simple matter. On May 31 Hull and other high Department officials conferred with officers of Standard Oil of New Jersey, the largest of the American firms affected by the Mexican seizure. Jersey Standard's plain-spoken president, William S. Farish, wasted little time in declaring the Mexican offer unacceptable. The Mexican situation must be considered, he said, in the light of his company's large holdings elsewhere in the world. Farish and his associates were convinced the company would be "lost," if it accepted a settlement that compromised its right under international law to immediate compensation. Other countries would quickly follow Mexico's example. When Hull asked what would be their reaction to a "more reasonable" plan, such as an international trusteeship, the oil men reiterated that their major concern in any settlement would be its effect on their other foreign holdings. Hull thereupon suggested that there were two alternatives open to the companies. They could either negotiate some agreement now with the Cárdenas government, or let matters drift in the hope that it might be possible to win a more favorable settlement in the future. Farish declared he would "prefer to let things go than to accept a proposal which compromised the doctrine of compensation."[18]

With minor variations, watchful waiting was to be the companies' strategy for the next three-and-a-half years. The companies were convinced they could accept nothing less than immediate compensation for their properties, including subsoil rights, without jeopardizing their position in other countries. They were certain, too, that the Mexicans could not successfully operate the oil industry alone. In any event, Mexico must be dealt with firmly so that no other country would be tempted to follow her lead. "If Mexico can get away with its present arbitrary act there is no safety for American property anywhere in Latin America or elsewhere," warned Thomas R. Armstrong, a Jersey Stand-

ard vice president early in July, "and, sooner or later in some part
of the world, drastic action will be called for."[19] Laurence Duggan
believed the oil men were anticipating the early collapse of the
Cárdenas regime, but Daniels, who passed this report on to
President Roosevelt, declared, "To me this looks like a vain
hope."[20]

Vain or not, the oil companies were doing everything possible
to make President Cárdenas' position untenable. Immediately
after the expropriation they launched a boycott of Mexican oil
based upon their control of most of the world's tanker fleet and
their obvious capacity to retaliate against independent tanker operators. By legal action they sought to tie up Mexican oil shipments abroad. They also persuaded a number of American manufacturers to refuse Mexico's prepaid cash orders for equipment
needed to operate the oil industry.[21] By 1940 this boycott was
even being applied to American export firms suspected of supplying Mexico. When Westinghouse closed down its Mexican branch
in 1939, Daniels reported that the local company representative
believed the move was the result of pressure by Rockefeller and
power interests.[22]

The companies' boycott of Mexican oil was helped by quiet
support from the State Department. In 1939, for example, Secretary Hull blocked the purchase of Mexican fuel oil by American
ships on a naval cruise, explaining in a policy directive: "This
Department as a policy matter of considerable importance would
not consider it desirable for any branch of the United States Government to purchase Mexican petroleum products at the present
time."[23] The State Department continued this ban on government
purchases of Mexican oil until early 1942, some months after the
general diplomatic settlement with Mexico. Moreover, it encouraged Latin American governments to take a similar stand
against Mexican oil.[24] Even when they were low bidders, American suppliers who offered Mexican oil were unable to get U. S.
government contracts. When one such firm protested, it was told
by the State Department's legal adviser that Mexico must not
thus "reap the fruits of this wrongful act."[25] The Sinclair interests

discovered to their surprise and great unhappiness that acceptance of a settlement with Mexico in 1940 did not necessarily re-
move the taint from their oil. Jersey Standard quickly objected
when Sinclair underbid it on a large Navy contract in the fall of
1940, and received State Department help in getting the Sinclair
bid rejected.[26] The Department also frowned on private operations in Mexican oil. An official advised the T. A. D. Jones Company of New Haven, when it sought approval of a profitable import deal, that it was "fishing in troubled waters."[27] It seemed
hardly a coincidence, too, that the representative year used by the
Department to set import quotas for foreign oil was 1939, when
because of the boycott Mexican imports were at a minimum.[28]

The oil interests also went to considerable pains to mobilize
American public opinion. Jersey Standard's company magazine,
The Lamp, began portraying Mexico as a strife-torn land of revolutionaries and brigands. Through their service stations, the
companies warned American tourists against undertaking a trip
into Mexico. Motorists were advised that there was danger of an
uprising, their personal property might be in jeopardy, travel by
car was unpleasant and hazardous, and even the Mexican railroads were unsafe.[29] Wide publicity was given to the claim that
Mexican gasoline was dangerously inferior. Its octane rating was
alleged to be only 48, barely adequate to operate an automobile
engine at minimum power.*

---

* Jim Marshall, "Mexico Cuts Off Her Nose," *Collier's,* CIV (November
25, 1939), 16. The Mexicans claimed, on the other hand, that the oil companies had always exported all of the higher octane gasoline produced in
Mexico, leaving only an inferior grade for the domestic market. Consequently, motorists could now obtain gasoline with an octane rating of 58-63,
"the best gasoline the public of Mexico has ever enjoyed."—I. M. Quintana,
"Mexican Oil—a Statement of Facts," *Facts on Mexican Oil* (January, 1940),
p. 10.
An independent Fort Worth laboratory, conducting a test for the Ameri-
can Automobile Association, reported late in 1939 that a sample of Mexican
gasoline had an octane rating of 57.—Romeyn Wormuth, Nuevo Laredo, to
Secretary of State, January 31, 1940, DS, 812.6363/6480. See also Ruth
Sheldon, "Mexico Faced Many Problems in Operating Refineries," *Oil and
Gas Journal,* XXXVIII (May 18, 1939), 40.
By today's standards an octane rating of 57 is low, but it should be noted

Standard Oil of New Jersey made a special effort to publicize
the companies' side of the dispute, sending a public relations expert to make the rounds of leading newspapers and magazines. At
least one reporter, Seward R. Sheldon of the *Cleveland Press,*
was offered an all-expense trip to Mexico if he would write a
series of articles to "put the people right."[30] Sheldon declined the
invitation, but others went to Mexico to write highly partisan reports. For example, newspaper publisher Henry J. Allen, a former
Republican governor of Kansas, toured Mexico briefly in the summer of 1938, and returned with a series of articles charging that
Cárdenas was a dedicated Communist who was determined to
establish a Soviet Mexico. One news service refused to handle
the Allen articles as too obviously propaganda, but they were ultimately syndicated by the New York *Herald Tribune,* excerpted
in the *Reader's Digest,* and sent out in pamphlet form by the
Committee on Mexican Relations, an obscure group financed by
Jersey Standard.[31] After having thus qualified as an expert on
Mexican affairs, Allen traveled about the United States demanding that the administration abandon the Good Neighbor Policy
and force Mexico to return the oil properties.[32]

Perhaps the most ambitious attempt to promote the cause of the
oil interests came in July, 1938, when the *Atlantic Monthly* published a special issue entitled "Trouble below the Border." Like
the Allen articles, this was a thoroughly pro-company analysis of
the controversy, designed to persuade its readers that Mexico was
sliding into dangerous chaos as a result of radical leadership.
Daniels called it "rotten oil propaganda," a view that was reinforced after he learned from Duggan that the issue had been paid
for by the companies.[33] When the *Nation* exposed the source of
the oil used to lubricate the *Atlantic*'s presses for this particular

that at this time the major oil companies in the United States had only recently raised the octane rating of their lowest priced gasoline to 67. In January, 1938, a University of Minnesota researcher had found that the octane
ratings of this grade of gasoline sold by four companies in the Twin Cities
ranged from 51 to 55.—Burton J. Robertson, "An Investigation of Motor
Gasolines," University of Minnesota Engineering Experiment Station, *Bulletin,* No. 13, XLII (May 3, 1939), 31.

United Press International photo

Mexican President Lázaro Cárdenas on March 23, 1938, reviewing a massive six-hour parade of workers celebrating the expropriation of oil properties. Below, a year later a similar crowd gathered again at the National Palace to celebrate the first anniversary of the oil expropriation as a symbol of national economic independence.

United Press International photo

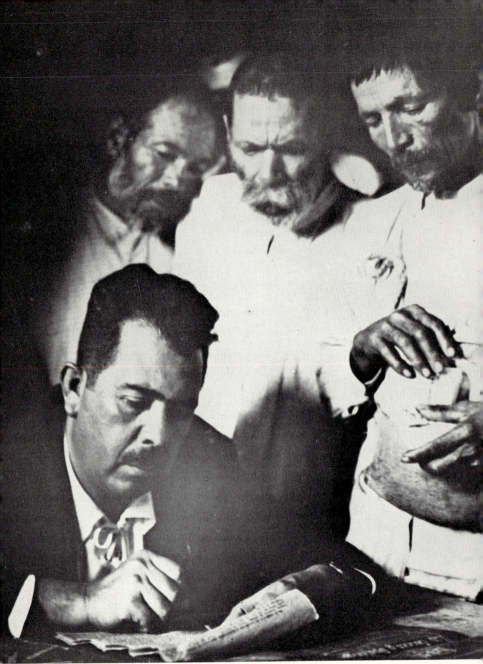

President Cárdenas signing over land to a group of
Mexican peasants.

run, the magazine's embarrassed publisher could only retort lamely, "Well, we have our racket and you have yours."[34] *Collier's* published a highly partisan article repeating company claims that Mexico's oil industry was rapidly breaking down under incompetent government direction, and charging that to Mexicans the term expropriate was "a polite, international word for 'steal.'" But when Mexico submitted an article in reply, *Collier's* refused to print it.[35]

Writers who tried to be more objective in their reporting sometimes found it difficult to get their material into print, at least without significant editing. Anita Brenner, well qualified by years of residence in Mexico, did a blanced and informative article for *Fortune,* but after Daniels compared her original draft with the published version he predicted, "she will not recognize her own baby." Himself a journalist for more than half a century, Daniels winced at such threats to the integrity of his profession. "I do not know why Munchausen is given access to newspaper columns, unless the oil barons have called him back to life," he complained to Duggan. "I can make no official comments on such articles unless the Department furnishes a large supply of asbestos!"[36] In view of the companies' careful efforts to mold public opinion, it was hardly surprising that a detailed survey of American publications in 1939—paid for by Standard Oil of New Jersey— showed that the press was overwhelmingly on the side of the oil interests in their dispute with Mexico.[37]

Just how far the companies were prepared to go in trying to bring about the collapse of the Cárdenas government is not clear. The local company representatives were confident that the Cárdenas regime would soon be overthrown. One official went so far as to tell a visiting American that his firm was "prepared to place on the barrel head a million dollars or more" to achieve this result.[38] It is evident, however, that the top management of the companies was much more cautious. If, indeed, company executives ever considered the possibility of underwriting a revolution in Mexico, their thinking was doubtless tempered by uncertainty over the reaction of the Roosevelt administration, as well as by knowledge of President Cárdenas' popularity with the great mass of Mexicans. When General Saturnino Cedillo, the strong man of San Luis Potosí, launched a right-wing uprising in May, 1938, the army remained loyal and Cárdenas had little difficulty in putting Cedillo's forces to flight. The government claimed to have proof that Cedillo had sought aid from the oil interests, promising to return their properties, but the present writer has found no evidence that they gave him more than moral support. Company aid seems to have been limited to radio broadcasts and advertisements in the Mexico City newspapers during the revolt emphasizing the determination of the oil men to defend their rights.[39] President Farish of Jersey Standard assured Secretary Hull at this time that his company had turned a deaf ear to all proposals to support a revolution in Mexico.[40]

The attitude of President Roosevelt was probably decisive in forestalling any significant attempt to overthrow the Cárdenas regime. During the Cedillo uprising the President warned that American pilots faced the loss of their licenses if they enlisted in a revolt against an established foreign government. The Justice Department later secured an indictment against Cedillo and his top aides, including two American pilots, for conspiring to violate the 1937 American Neutrality Act.[41] Roosevelt made the point even plainer, when, in the company of Ambassador Daniels, he informed Donald R. Richberg, a Standard Oil attorney, that there would be no revolution in Mexico.[42] The President apparently wanted no Western Hemisphere re-enactment of the tragedy in Spain.

With the oil men determined to sit tight for the time being, the State Department decided to press for a settlement of other claims against Mexico. The oil problem might settle itself if, as expected, the Mexicans ran into trouble in operating the industry. If Mexico could be induced to pay off American agrarian claimants, moreover, she would find it difficult to refuse a similar settlement on oil. And once committed to a schedule of regular payments on the agrarian debt, the Mexicans might discover that they could not also shoulder an expensive oil settlement. They might then be more willing to consider returning the oil properties to the foreign companies. In effect, State Department strategy called for soft-pedaling the oil issue while stressing the urgency of an agreement on agrarian claims.

Ambassador Daniels recognized that he was in for another period of protracted haggling over claims. Jokingly, he reminded President Roosevelt that the Mexicans had on file a demand for over $400,000 damages done when the American Navy occupied Veracruz in 1914. "They may make this bill personal and expect me to pay it," he told his one-time assistant. "If so, I serve notice that I will draw on you for half the amount, for we were partners then."[43] The remark was half jest, but it suggested that its author intended to take a long-run view of the current claims negotiations, with an eye on the past as well as the future.

The close tie between agrarian and oil claims was apparent to the Mexicans, too. President Cárdenas and his advisers recognized that the oil expropriation made it necessary to pay more attention to United States requests for an agrarian settlement, if Mexico's offers to compensate the oil companies were to carry conviction. With this, as well as Washington's recent stern remonstrances, in mind, a few weeks after the oil expropriation Cárdenas offered to begin making monthly payments on the agrarian debt, giving special priority to Americans with hardship claims. He promised that the nation would pay "to the limit of its possibilities, in order that there may not be among the people of the United States a person who feels that he has received unjust or arbitrary treatment from Mexico."[44] In Washington Ambassador Castillo Nájera elaborated on the offer. Cárdenas was particularly anxious to take care of the small claimants, the Ambassador told Welles. As a beginning, Mexico intended to set aside 120,000 pesos a month to pay for the lands recently taken from the American farmers in the Yaqui Valley, in whose plight the State Department had shown great interest. Other small landowners would likewise be compensated in cash before the end of the current presidential term in 1940. Large landowners, who generally could afford to wait, would have to be content with agrarian bonds. Welles thought the offer only partly encouraging. The United States could not agree, he declared emphatically, "to the drawing of any distinction between one group of Americans whose properties had been expropriated in Mexico and another group solely because one group happened to own larger tracts than the other."[45]

The State Department, it seemed, had a rather different view of a proper agrarian settlement. On June 29 Welles proposed to Dr. Castillo Nájera that Mexico place in escrow the sum of $337,000 a month for the next two-and-a-half years, so that all American agrarian claims, which Welles totaled at more than $10,000,000, could be settled before the end of President Cárdenas' term. He reiterated the State Department's objection to any discrimination among American claimants, such as that contemplated in the Mexican offer to compensate the Yaqui Valley landowners separately. "Compensation on a basis of fair equality is required for all expropriated American property," Welles noted. "The right to take is thus dependent upon the willingness and the ability at that time to pay the appropriate compensation." This principle, he pointed out, applied equally to the recently seized oil properties.[46]

Ambassador Daniels, who had returned to his post only the day before, was as surprised as the Mexicans when he learned of Welles' proposal. He quickly reminded Welles that for the past two years the Embassy and the State Department had insisted that the Yaqui Valley landowners merited special treatment, both because their properties were comparatively small and because they had originally been granted under a colonization contract. Now the Department seemed to be saying that it would not accept compensation for the Yaqui Valley claimants unless the money was part of a general agrarian settlement. This to Daniels was completely unrealistic; worse, it meant sacrificing the prospects of an especially deserving group of claimants. "It is as impossible for the Mexican Government in so short a time to pay this ten million dollars," he remonstrated, "as it would be for Great Britain and France and other countries to pay the United States the full amount, in the same period, of the debts incurred by them in the World War." Washington ought not to throw away this chance to help the Yaqui Valley landholders. Instead, it should use this settlement as "an argument for the payment of other claims," as and when Mexico's financial condition improved.[47]

Daniels' view was shared by Frank Tannenbaum, a Columbia University Latin American expert and close friend of President Cárdenas. Tannenbaum, who was currently visiting Mexico, reported that Cárdenas was deeply disappointed over the negative reception of his offer to pay for the Yaqui Valley and other small American properties. "It was a kind of spontaneous, friendly gesture of good will on his part, to meet what he thought would be the interest of President Roosevelt in the little man," he told Daniels. "To have this act on his part become the basis for raising a series of issues which the Mexican Government feels it is not prepared to face, has led to a kind of psychological slump." The demand for agrarian reform in Mexico was irrepressible, Tannenbaum warned. Even if the United States were to take the ultimate step, and send troops into Mexico, it would soon discover that the country could not be administered without continuing to give the people the land they craved.

Unless we are prepared as a Government to go to extremes, I feel fairly confident that both sides will merely indulge in a series of embittering gestures that will end, as all such gestures have ended in Mexico in the last twenty-five years, by leaving the problem about where it was when the exercise began. As I have said before, even intervention could end only in our doing what the present Government is doing and paying for it .... Recognizing as I do the very difficult position in which the State Department finds itself, and the obvious justice of the demands of Americans for compensation, I have nothing but sympathy for the difficulties of the Department—but in the long run we may get some compensation by following a policy of understanding Mexico's difficulties and helping her solve them rather than by assuming a quite opposite attitude.[48]

Daniels forwarded Tannenbaum's letter to the State Department, where it was read by Hull and Welles and other top officials. Secretary Hull, for one, was unimpressed. Ambassador Castillo Nájera had already rejected the Welles proposal, declaring that Mexico could not possibly pay off all agrarian claims within the short space of thirty months. Exasperated, Hull asked Treasury Secretary Morgenthau to lower the world price of silver another penny, explaining: "Well, we are having lots of trouble in Mexico and you know the President and Daniels have given the Mexicans the impression that they can go right ahead and flaunt everything in our face. Daniels is down there taking sides with the Mexican Government and I have to deal with these Communists down there and have to carry out international law." Morgenthau was not persuaded; this time he refused to interfere.[49]

Hull was quite right in thinking that Ambassador Daniels thoroughly disapproved of the State Department's stern approach. Daniels did not believe the Mexican Revolution, and its aftermath of social reform, could be dismissed as a tortillas-and-frijoles brand of communism which needed to be contained or stamped out. Besides, such a course would imperil the Good Neighbor Policy and embitter United States relations with the rest of Latin America. He saw, moreover, that the demand for a full agrarian settlement dovetailed neatly with the oil companies' campaign of economic pressure against Mexico. Daniels suspected that some Washington officials shared the belief of the oil men that a strong line would force Mexico to hand back the properties. No Mexican government would agree to this, he reiterated to both Hull and Roosevelt. "Patience is the virtue essential in a Good Neighbor policy," he reminded the President. "The delicate situation here is putting that doctrine to a severe test. It is more important that it be maintained than that any particular debt collection be pressed."[50]

Well aware that his advice carried little weight with Hull, on July 14 Daniels offered to fly to meet Roosevelt at Panama, where the latter was headed on a fishing cruise, to discuss the developing crisis *"before final action by the State Department."*[51] He was quite sure the President understood better than Hull the complexities of the Mexican agrarian situation. Daniels had, in fact, carefully saved the published accounts of Roosevelt's press conference at Warm Springs right after the oil expropriation. At that time, speaking off-the-record, the chief executive had gone out of his way to distinguish between certain kinds of American land-owners in Mexico:

The first is the small fellow, the small American, who has gone down there to ranch and farm, etc., and has put everything he has had into his ranch or farm. Under the Mexican policy of distribution of land ownership, quite a number of those poor Americans have been stripped, and their property has been taken, and so far, they have not been able to realize on a settlement. Those people, the Mexican Government assures us, are going to be taken care of. They are the real hardship cases.

Then you come to another type of American investment, the Americans who went to Mexico, like William Randolph Hearst, and bought a state legislature, bribed officials and acquired title—this is all background—acquired title to hundreds of thousands of acres of land for practically nothing except the cost of the bribe, or they paid three cents on the acre for it, things like that, and then claimed all kinds of damages in a sum far in excess of the amount of money that he had actually put in. We have not got much sympathy with trying to collect that excessive sum for him.[52]

Roosevelt had repeated these views to the Mexican Ambassador a few days later, chuckling over the fact that the press, while playing up the rest of the interview, had carefully ignored his reference to Hearst.

Roosevelt had either changed his mind by July or, more likely, had no desire to let a minor foreign policy row interfere with his vacation. In any case, he brushed aside Daniels' plea for a conference. A week later, on July 21, Secretary Hull summoned Ambassador Castillo Nájera to the State Department and handed him a note strongly protesting Mexico's long record of seizing American-owned lands "without making prompt payment of just compensation." Hull conceded that Mexico had recently offered to settle a small number of American claims, but he indicated that the United States would be satisfied with nothing less than an over-all agrarian settlement:

We cannot question the right of a foreign government to treat its own nationals in this fashion if it so desires. This is a matter of domestic concern. But we cannot admit that a foreign government may take the property of American nationals in disregard of the rule of compensation under international law.

Hull challenged Mexico to agree to arbitrate the question of whether she had complied with international law in compensating American landowners, and if not, to let the arbitral commission set the amount and terms under which such compensation should now be made.[53] The State Department took the unusual step of releasing the text of the note even before it was transmitted to Mexico City. Hull was taking no chances that Mexico would regard *this* note as suspended, withdrawn, or not received!

In the United States the demand for arbitration was seen as evidence of a virtual breakdown in diplomatic negotiations. Reporters forecast a similar exacting stand in the oil dispute, noting that Hull had conferred with Jersey Standard's Thomas R. Armstrong shortly after handing the American note to Dr. Castillo Nájera.[54] Armstrong, for one, was so pleased with the Department's firm stand on agrarian claims that he instructed Standard Oil representatives in the major Latin American capitals to cable summaries of the local press reaction to the note, which he then passed along to Hull—a precaution, perhaps, against inadequate or tardy reporting by the Department's own personnel.[55] Senator Key Pittman, the influential chairman of the Senate Foreign Relations Committee, told newsmen that the United States stand was "final and positive." Pittman denied, however, that Washington had any thought of resorting to armed force, noting suggestively: "Our Government is sufficiently powerful financially and in resources to enforce fair treatment by any government without calling on military resources."[56] Most American business spokesmen heartily approved of the tougher State Department line, though a few, like the New York *Journal of Commerce,* questioned the wisdom of stressing an agrarian settlement instead of concentrating on the immediate return of the oil properties.[57]

The reaction in Mexico, on the other hand, was one of shock, concern, and defiance. As always, the Mexican press bristled angrily at the suggestion of arbitration, recalling sarcastically that the United States still had not complied with the 1911 Chamizal ruling, which awarded Mexico part of El Paso.[58] Even before the government had drafted its reply, President Cárdenas declared at a press conference that Mexico was prepared to pay its debts, within the time limits permitted by its laws. Although immediate compensation for all claimants was impossible, he said, the government was determined to pay its creditors within a reasonable time—"ten years or perhaps less, maybe even five years"—provided Mexican exports were not boycotted, in which case payment would be uncertain. Asked about the oil controversy, Cárdenas declared emphatically, "Mexico will not return the properties under any conditions."[59]

Ambassador Daniels was deeply concerned lest the State Department's new firm policy degenerate into empty namecalling, with no more result than the futile break in diplomatic relations achieved by the British in May. While awaiting the Mexican reply (meanwhile urging the Foreign Office to accept arbitration), Daniels sought to convince his superiors that they were demanding the impossible. The Mexicans were afraid to arbitrate the agrarian dispute, he told Hull, because they were sure it would be followed "by insistence upon prompt payment of the General Claims and—what is for Cárdenas the hardest nut to crack—a demand for arbitration of the oil expropriation."[60] Nor could the government conceivably pay off the entire agrarian debt within the period specified by the State Department. "In Mexico's financial condition it is utterly impossible for it to make such payments," he reminded Welles.[61] The present State Department course, he warned President Roosevelt, threatened the Good Neighbor Policy—"the only hope of permanent friendly relations, increase of commerce, and the sound basis of amity and peace." For in the final analysis, if the United States undertook the unpopular job of collecting private debts, "it must be ready to use the Big Stick or advertise its impotency."[62]

Mexico's reply, handed to Daniels by Foreign Minister Hay on August 3, was unexpectedly blunt. So firm was its tone, indeed, that the State Department decided not to release a translation of its contents until after a thorough study of the Spanish text. Re-

porters had to be content with a translation furnished by the less
reticent Mexicans.[63] The note conceded that Mexico was obligated by its own laws to pay compensation for expropriated
property. It denied, however, that there was any universally accepted rule of international law requiring immediate payment.
If, as Hull had pointed out, the United States had followed such
a rule in its own program of social reform, this merely was proof
of its more favorable economic condition. "Certainly it could not
have postponed or abandoned those reforms, even in case such
conditions had not been favorable," Hay declared. Mexico's land
reform program had been applied without discrimination to Mexicans and foreigners alike, the note pointed out. While Mexico
could not admit that Americans had a right to favored treatment,
it was nevertheless prepared to compensate certain small claimants immediately. To evaluate the other American claims, Hay
proposed that the two countries appoint a mixed claims commission.[64]

With characteristic optimism, Ambassador Daniels thought he
saw in the Mexican offer the basis of a neighborly settlement.
The United States could accept compensation for small landholders, he suggested to Hull, without conceding discrimination
as a principle. It could, moreover, condition its acceptance of a
mixed claims commission on the appointment of an impartial
arbitrator to settle any differences between the two sides. Welles
had proposed such a course to Ambassador Castillo Nájera on
June 29. True, there was danger of procrastination and delay.
"Even so, in what better position would we be to reject the proposal to begin *at once?*" Daniels asked. "We may refuse this offer,
but what then? An impasse will follow with strained relations
that will imperil Good Neighborliness. Or we may accept it and
follow up with insistence upon prompt compliance and promise
of payment."[65] Knowing that his advice was not overly welcome
at the State Department, Daniels sent copies of his several letters
to Hull to the White House. He reminded Roosevelt of his own
Warm Springs press conference remark that the United States
was mainly interested in protecting the rights of small landowners

in Mexico. "The majority of the claims," Daniels emphasized, "are not for small properties but for large properties, one exceeding $900,000."*

But the President had other matters on his mind: his intended purge of conservative Democrats in the fall congressional elections, for example, to say nothing of Hitler's menacing gestures towards Czechoslovakia. And within the State Department only a handful of officials, led by Laurence Duggan, shared Daniels' conciliatory point of view. Pierre Boal, Daniels' counselor, reported after a visit to Washington that most of the Department from Secretary Hull down were convinced that the Mexicans had no serious intention of reaching a settlement. "There seems to be a strong desire to write a reply 'for the record,' " Boal said, "to show all of L[atin] A[merica] and our people on what principles we stand."[66] Some officials, indeed, were openly critical of Daniels. *Newsweek* published a story, obviously based on inside information, that the Department was furious over the "shoddy and inaccurate" translation supplied by Daniels of the recent Mexican note. News commenator Upton Close, just back from a trip to Mexico, immediately protested to Hull:

Ridiculous to imply that an Ambassador is responsible for a job of translation! ... I believe common every-day run of Americans can be thankful to God that so human and wise an old chap as Josephus Daniels is in the Mexico City Embassy. He's as bright as a new dollar and about

---

* Daniels, Mexico City, to Roosevelt, August 8 and 12, 1938, Daniels Papers. Daniels subsequently pointed out to the State Department that of the 265 American claims on the list given Castillo Nájera by Welles, only about 24 could be considered small properties. He also warned that some of the claims would have to be eliminated completely. Among these was the largest, that of the Agricola Industrial, Colon, Limitado del Tlahualilo, S.A., for $999,000. This company was largely British-owned and entirely British-controlled, with only minority American stock ownership. As a matter of fact, this claim, constituting nearly a tenth of the total claimed by Welles at the outset of the notewriting, was quickly dropped by the United States after the two countries reached an agreement in November.—Daniels, Mexico City, to the Secretary of State, August 30, 1938, dispatch no. 7281, cited in Daniels to Hull, September 22, 1938, Daniels Papers [possibly not sent]; *New York Times*, November 24, 1938.

ten times as alive as his critics. I heard him give the best, absolutely neutral, most complete summary of a certain complex situation that I was able to get anywhere.— From the standpoint of a correspondent who has worked all over the world.

If anything, Daniels ought to be given more adequate help, Close suggested, "instead of watched for bum translations by certain boys in the State, War and Navy Building whose sympathies in certain present issues are far from [above] suspicion."[67]

Secretary Hull, as Boal had suggested, was determined to put the United States' principles deeply into the record. On August 22 he called Ambassador Castillo Nájera to the Department and handed him a new note to read. Written more in sorrow than anger, it nonetheless bristled with such phrases as "unfruitful negotiations," "astonishing theory," "bald" and "unadulterated confiscation." If the nations of the world were to follow Mexico's example, it declared, "human progress would be fatally set back." The note concluded by calling upon Mexico to settle the agrarian dispute through either regular arbitration or a mixed claims commission headed by an impartial arbitrator. Meanwhile, no more American lands should be taken without prompt payment.[68] After Castillo Nájera had digested these arguments, Hull offered to withhold the note if Mexico "could see its way clear to withdraw its last note." Without hesitation, the Ambassador flatly refused, pointing out that the Mexican note had been published in both countries. When Hull persisted, Castillo Nájera said that he would not even suggest such a course to his superiors. This left Hull with no option but to request that his note be transmitted to Mexico City. But before the Ambassador left, Hull tried to clarify the Department's position on the Yaqui Valley cases. Ambassador Daniels seemed to have the mistaken impression that Welles had rejected Mexico's offer to pay for these lands, he said. The United States view was that while Mexico was obligated to pay for all lands, it could, of course, make any arrangement it wished with the Yaqui Valley owners.[69]

"I am very glad you declined to comment on Cordell's latest note," Daniels wrote Roosevelt a few days later, after the State

Department had published the note. "Independent of his position, it was unduly severe. Spanking a nation that is desperately poor in public on account of debts, when there is not even a slap on the wrist for great countries that ignore their obligations, is a severe strain on the Good Neighbor Policy."[70] In these troubled days American policy ought to seek to preserve hemispheric unity at any cost, Daniels declared.

With a world on the verge of war, in fact portions of it at war, I feel that the success of your foreign policy and the good of our country depends upon the unity and friendship of the Pan American countries .... Today the Mexican masses as a whole are seeing daylight as never before. Given freedom from revolution and exploitation, another generation will be our best neighbors and best customers. With patience and devotion to the Good Neighbor policy, even when it hurts, we shall preserve on this hemisphere the hope of a drifting world.[71]

The forceful Hull note found considerable favor in the United States, however. The *New York Times* hailed its "devastating" logic and suggested that the time had come to demand the return of the oil properties.[72] But in Mexico the press reacted strongly against the note, and government officials were grimly silent. "The Mexicans talk very little about it," Daniels noted worriedly in his diary, "and I feel very much disturbed as to what answer they shall make."[73]

Daniels did not have long to wait. On September 1 President Cárdenas addressed the opening session of the Mexican Congress. While Daniels and the rest of the diplomatic corps listened attentively, Cárdenas bitterly attacked the recent American note as an attempt to impose the will of the strong on the weak. Mexico's land reform would proceed without special favors for foreigners, he declared. Nor could Mexico accept the principle of immediate compensation. But beneath the not unexpected bluster was a significant concession. The President offered to submit the American agrarian claims to a two-man commission subject to the ruling of a third impartial arbitrator.[74] Later that same evening Daniels was called to the Foreign Office where he was handed a note, equally unrepentant, which formally repeated this offer. Like the

Cárdenas speech, the note contained a sly dig at the New Deal's currency reform of 1933, noting that there were various forms of expropriation without compensation, such as compelling holders of gold or gold obligations to accept depreciated paper money.[75] Daniels was assured privately by Undersecretary Beteta, however, that the note did not really mean all it said about no special favors. Beteta was quite confident that very few American-owned lands would be expropriated in the future, and what little might be taken could be promptly assessed and paid for.[76]

Daniels begged Hull to overlook the provocative, defiant language of both President Cárdenas' speech and the Mexican reply, and recognize that Mexico had gone a considerable way toward meeting the United States demands. The Mexican government could hardly go on record as exempting Americans from the land reform program, but in practice the Beteta assurances, if lived up to, would amount to this, he argued. Americans, more fortunate in their political history and economic well-being, must not lose sight of the fact that for years Mexico had been the victim of exploitation by venal officials and foreigners, that its people were still desperately poor. "These conditions call on our part for Patience, and more Patience, and Persistence and more Persistence, toward just agreements," he declared, "even though such a course results in severe criticism from those who want the application of force." Dramatically, if somewhat extravagantly, Daniels posed the unwelcome alternatives to compromise:

To be sure, we could bring pressure to bear by refusal to buy silver, but that would hurt the American owners of the silver mines, thus reducing employment here with consequent suffering to the worker, and would be deeply resented as a Big Stick measure. We could encourage revolution by permitting the importation of arms by those who would wish to oust Cárdenas by force, with the consequent responsibility for the blood that would be shed; we could refuse to buy anything from Mexico, boycott its exports, and thereby reduce the necessities of life to the masses; we could denounce the country as dishonest and do much to strangle her; we could conquer it and put in a man as President who would be beholden to us; we could, after we had conquered it, make it a province or annex it and admit Mexican States to the Union. We could do any or all of these things, but what would be the result? The Good Neighbor policy, the brightest hope of the Roosevelt Administration, would receive a body blow, and the people who are on our nearest southern boundaries would regard us as imperialists and oppressors, and many Americans would be grieved that we had returned to what they would characterize the Big Stick and Dollar Diplomacy, which were execrated when practiced by former administrations.[77]

But to Cordell Hull, indignant over Mexico's continued refusal to acknowledge the sacredness of international law, these considerations were of little import. He put scant faith in the informal assurance that Mexico for all practical purposes would cease expropriating additional American lands, even when this promise was repeated by the Mexican Ambassador in Washington. Instead, twice within the next week he lectured Dr. Castillo Nájera on his government's dangerous disavowal of its plain responsibilities. Declaring that he had been "almost flabbergasted" at the last Mexican note, Hull said sternly that it would take Mexico "exactly one thousand years" to convince the United States that social reform, however worthwhile and necessary, should be based on the confiscation of private property. Mexico seemed to be "getting close onto Marxism or the Communistic basis," Hull remarked vehemently, adding that it was "a great pity" the Mexican government was persisting in its *ejido* or village communal land program, which "might have functioned to some extent two, three, or four centuries ago," but was hardly suited to modern times. Hull informed Castillo Nájera that the United States position was unchanged, but that he nevertheless intended to prepare a brief refutation of the latest Mexican arguments.[78] A visitor to the Department advised Daniels that sentiment there favored another detailed argumentative reply.[79]

Already fearful that the two countries might be heading for an open break, Ambassador Daniels appealed to President Roosevelt to call a halt to the "further exchange of notes for the public, which get us nowhere." Mexico was wrong to take American property without paying a fair price for it, and the United States should use every legitimate means to help its citizens secure com-

pensation. But, he warned, "to go to further lengths gets no payment unless we are ready to use force. And that would be a
blunder equal to a crime and I know you would never consider
such an Old Deal policy." Rather, the United States ought to
accept Mexico's offer to settle the dispute through a two-member
claims commission, bound by the rulings of an impartial arbitrator:

If, after agreeing to this, Mexico does not pay within a reasonable time,
we will be in a far better position than to turn down the only course
open that does not call for economic pressure (and suffering for Mexico's poor people) or force. I have made Mr. Hull acquainted with my
views and I hope they have had some weight with him. However, I fear
the State Department lawyers see nothing except from the standpoint
of creditor-and-debtor, and would like to see the Big Stick used to force
payment. They see none of the social implications growing out of the
Revolution and the absolute necessity for educating the people and
breaking up the big haciendas if Mexico is to be freed from feudalism.
And besides, to demand the whole amount in the thirty months of
Cárdenas' term is to try to extract blood from a turnip.[80]

The effect, if any, of Daniels' appeal to the President can only
be speculated. It is worth noting, however, that Roosevelt returned to Washington on September 14, after an absence of
nearly a week while his eldest son James was operated on in
Minnesota for a possible stomach cancer. Daniels' letter reached
him within the next two or three days. And on September 20 Secretary Hull called in Ambassador Castillo Nájera and suggested
that it might be well to end the public "hammer and tongs discussions" which "would soon estrange our two countries in every
important way." He offered instead to limit his reply to the latest
Mexican note to a simple acknowledgment. The two governments could then begin quiet oral conversations on the practical
details of a settlement based on a mixed claims commission.[81]

What had caused this apparent sudden shift in State Department thinking? Presidential intervention? Secretary Hull's concern over the disturbing situation in Europe, which was to come
to a head at the Munich Conference the following week? On the
basis of available information, the answer is unclear. It was evident, however, that the State Department still had strong reser-

vations about the value of a conciliatory approach. Pierre Boal warned Daniels from Washington that most officials doubted "whether it is really worth trying," and he stressed that "if no agreement can be reached now we are in for what may soon amount to an open break with Mexico."[82]

Over the next few weeks the two governments discussed the details of a settlement, and, as Duggan told Daniels, things seemed "to be 'inching' along."[83] Daniels was quite optimistic. The Mexicans seemed so genuinely eager to come to terms, he reported to Hull, that they were likely to make larger concessions than at any time in the past. "The compelling reason which has caused me to urge a course of conciliation, even of some sacrifice," he pointed out once more, "is that I believe the Good Neighbor policy must be undergirded if this hemisphere is to escape the contagion that threatens Europe."[84]

Nevertheless, a snag soon developed over the question of how much Mexico should budget for the agrarian claims payments each year. The State Department thought the first Mexican offer —$500,000—was inadequate.[85] Daniels conceded that this sum was not as much as the United States would like, but he suggested that it would be wiser to agree on some figure that Mexico could afford to pay regularly "than to insist upon larger promises which might not be met." He reminded his superiors that Mexico was already paying $500,000 a year under the 1934 special claims settlement, and noted that President Cárdenas was willing to give oral guarantees against the future taking of American lands without prompt compensation.[86]

These were valid considerations, but the State Department, more experienced than Ambassador Daniels in the rules of diplomatic poker, was determined to raise the ante as high as possible. On October 25 Undersecretary Welles proposed to Ambassador Castillo Nájera that Mexico pay $1,000,000 on agrarian claims in 1939, and the balance in four annual installments. Since the total debt would not be determined until after the claims commission had completed its work, this was asking the Mexicans to sign a blank check. As soon as he learned of Welles's plan, President Cárdenas called Daniels to the National Palace and protested that he could not get his Congress to approve an agreement committing the country to a series of undetermined payments. Cárdenas offered instead to pay $1,000,000 a year until the American agrarian claims were liquidated. Daniels promptly telephoned this welcome news to Washington, stressing that payments of this size would put a heavy strain on Mexico's limited resources.[87]

Not quite trusting the State Department, Daniels also sent a copy of the Cárdenas offer to the White House. Mexico would be "scraping the bottom" to pay a million dollars each year, he told President Roosevelt:

A million dollars for Mexico equals hundreds of millions for the United States. The bulk of the people are desperately poor, and you know what dire poverty means in revenues for public works as well as in undernourishment for the people. If Mexico should undertake to pay us more than a million dollars a year, it would require forced unemployment with consequent suffering, cessation of the irrigation works necessary for the needed crop production, the slowing up of the construction and carrying on of public schools and necessary public works and the much too small public health prevention work .... It is for these reasons that I sincerely hope, now that the principle Cordell enumerated with such vigor has been agreed to, that we will meet President Cárdenas more than half way.[88]

Again, one can only speculate whether Roosevelt acted upon this advice in any way. But significantly, a few days later the State Department advised Ambassador Castillo Nájera that the United States would accept the Cárdenas offer, provided that Mexico paid the first $1,000,000 within six months after the claims commission began its work. The two governments could agree upon subsequent payments after the commission had determined the value of the claims, but they must be at least $1,000,000 a year.[89] After making sure the Mexicans accepted these stipulations, the following week Secretary Hull formally outlined the settlement in a public note. Mexico promptly confirmed its approval, though with the reservation that the agreement must not be considered a precedent for any other dispute.[90]

A later generation, used to foreign aid programs costing billions, may find the 1938 Mexican agrarian settlement rather small change, if not completely incongruous. This should not obscure the fact that it constituted another important milestone in the history of the Good Neighbor Policy. With Europe on the brink of war, the Roosevelt administration had drawn back from a course that might have led to an open break with Mexico and imperiled U. S. relations with Latin America. Although the United States was to complain subsequently about the expropriation of several more American properties and to protest what it considered Mexican stalling on the claims commission, in the main the agreement justified Ambassador Daniels' high hopes. For the next three years Mexico annually presented a check for a million dollars, until the negotiation of a new and broader settlement in 1941.

Just how much credit Daniels should be given for the 1938 settlement is difficult to say. It is clear that he was prepared to accept considerably less than his State Department superiors eventually got from Mexico. Nor did the State Department trust Daniels to do much of the negotiating. One might say, therefore, that the settlement was largely the result of Hull's and Welles's unyielding defense of property rights and international law. On the other hand, the State Department accomplished little until it followed Daniels' advice and stopped calling the Mexicans names in public. For a time, indeed, the Department's firmness seemed more productive of gall than gold. Hull's tough approach on agrarian claims also had no apparent effect on the much more important oil dispute, other than to harden the opposition of the oil companies to any compromise settlement. This would subsequently be a matter of considerable embarrassment to the State Department. The agrarian claims agreement seemed to bear out Daniels' contention that American principles and rights could be upheld without resort to pressure tactics that might imperil the Good Neighbor Policy. The settlement was thus a happy blending of Daniels and the Department, with President Roosevelt perhaps acting as a quiet catalyst.

I am a confirmed optimist, and when the oil people
say "Never" and the Government says "Never" to
the various proposals, I say to myself, in the words
of the opera, "What, never? Well, hardly ever."
—Josephus Daniels[1]

CHAPTER X

A "Global" Settlement

During the negotiations for an agrarian settlement there had been little mention of the troublesome petroleum issue. The oil dispute had remained ominously in the background, however, ready to erupt at any moment like one of the gushers of the fabulous Mexican Golden Lane. Both countries knew that Secretary Hull's insistence upon compensation for American landowners was meant to apply with equal force to the much larger claims of the oil companies. But the oil problem was complicated by the seemingly irreconcilable stands taken by the two sides. The oil men refused even to discuss compensation, insisting upon the return of their properties, while the Mexicans declared they would neither return the properties nor pay for the oil in the ground, which under Mexican law belonged to the nation.

Toward the end of the agrarian discussions, President Cárdenas granted a personal interview to a visiting *New York Times* editor. He made a point of stressing his eagerness to settle the oil dispute through direct negotiations with the companies, promising that Mexico would pay back "every penny" the oil men had invested in their properties from the beginning of their operations.[2] The offer indicated that the Mexicans still had no intention of paying for the subsoil oil—by far the largest element of the companies' claims—and for this reason, a Jersey Standard official promptly advised Secretary Hull that the companies were not interested in such a settlement.[3] A few weeks later President Cár-

230

denas repeated to Daniels his hopes for early negotiations with the oil men, pledging a "reasonable and just" settlement. Cárdenas said that the government intended to retain control over the oil fields, but he suggested that the companies might be allowed to work the properties and handle oil exports.[4] Ambassador Daniels thought this offer should be pursued, and when he returned to the United States over the Christmas holidays, he urged Hull and Welles to try to get the companies to begin negotiating with the Mexicans.[5]

This was no easy assignment. The oil men were grimly convinced that if Mexico got away with the expropriation there would be no safety for their holdings in other ambitious, oil-rich countries. Company representatives in Mexico frankly admitted that they were in no hurry to discuss a settlement until after the 1940 elections on both sides of the Rio Grande. "They hope you will be succeeded by an apostle of the Big Stick," Daniels told Roosevelt, "and that the successor of Cárdenas will be a rightist."[6] The companies' strategy was simple yet dangerously unimaginative: quarantine the Mexican expropriation virus, sit tight, and hope for the day when a chastened or disillusioned Mexican government would invite them back. In ordinary times, and over the short run, these tactics might have succeeded, for they had usually worked in the past. But these were not ordinary times. Mexico's economic nationalism was symptomatic of a new and powerful force in the underdeveloped areas of the world, a force the oil men would have to learn to live with if they wanted to stay in business. Europe was on the verge of war, moreover, and already there was ample evidence that Mexican oil was entering into the strategic calculations of several of the future belligerents. Furthermore, the administration in power in Washington was committed—ideologically and strategically—to fostering inter-American solidarity through its Good Neighbor Policy. Consequently its freedom of action in dealing with Mexico was considerably limited. There is some question, therefore, whether the strategy of the companies was wholly suited to the times.

The oil men found plenty of support at home for their no-

compromise policy. Many Americans, including an important seg-
ment of the press, were exasperated by Mexico's perverse attitude,
which seemed to regard neighborliness as an invitation to steal
American property. Spare the rod, these critics argued, and the
results were as disastrous in dealing with small nations as small
children. What was needed, it was said, was the return to a more
forcible style of diplomacy, which, if it made Uncle Sam no
friends, at least compelled respect for his property. Even after the
agrarian settlement in November, 1938, criticism of Mexico continued. An army colonel sent President Roosevelt an unsolicited
set of plans for a naval blockade to frustrate Mexican oil exports.
The Texas Legislature passed a resolution protesting the oil seizure and complaining that cheap Mexican oil was hurting Texas
producers. An obscure group called the National Citizens Committee on Mexico began collecting a projected twenty million
signatures to a petition calling on Congress to use "our whole
armed might" to bring about a return of the oil properties.[7] Some
of this agitation was doubtless company-inspired, but clearly
much of it also reflected genuine public dismay.

In Congress, where the recent elections had increased the
strength of the Republicans and anti-administration Democrats,
the oil companies did not lack for vocal champions. Conservative
members of both parties expressed great dissatisfaction with
Washington's failure to deal sternly with Mexico. Senator Styles
Bridges of New Hampshire demanded an investigation to find out
if the oil expropriation had secret New Deal support, charging
that the Roosevelt administration had "encouraged and even con-
nived at the establishment of communism in Mexico."[8] Senator
Robert R. Reynolds of Daniels' home state also called for a probe
of the Mexican situation. With somewhat rubbery logic, Reynolds
asserted that Mexico's grant of asylum to Leon Trotsky was proof
that the country had gone communist, while its trade agreements
with Germany and Italy signified fascist control. In any case, the
Cárdenas government was "un-American," he reasoned, and the
United States had no business subsidizing it through silver purchases.[9] Representative Hamilton Fish of New York, a dedicated

critic of the administration, told the House that Washington had
been following a soft, supine policy, "where we have been the
good neighbor and they have taken our shirts and our pants, too."
"If we do not take a firm position and stop this communism and
this confiscation of property, including the oil properties," he
warned, "it means the end of our investments not only in Mexico
but throughout Latin America."[10]

The critics were inclined to blame Ambassador Daniels for at
least part of the trouble. Their suspicions were reinforced when
Hearst columnist H. R. Knickerbocker, a good friend of Assistant
Secretary of State George S. Messersmith, hinted that Daniels had
suppressed a strong American protest right after the oil expropriation. Knickerbocker described the secret note as "a bombshell
which contains explosives sufficiently powerful to blow up either
the Cárdenas government or the diplomatic relations between the
United States and Mexico."[11] Their curiosity aroused, several congressmen demanded an investigation of the Ambassador's role in
the oil dispute, and one, Representative Martin J. Kennedy of
New York, even introduced a resolution asking his recall.[12] "If we
had an Ambassador down there that meant business, and had
proper instructions from the State Department," the peppery
Ham Fish agreed, "we could settle this controversy in a short
time."[13]

The Roosevelt administration was not particularly disturbed by
these attacks, for it had the votes to block any embarrassing congressional action. But there were other reasons why Washington
hoped for an early end of the oil controversy. Ever since the expropriation, Mexico, blocked from its traditional export markets
by the companies' boycott, had been selling increasing quantities
of oil to the fascist bloc. Oil-poor Nazi Germany was an eager
bidder for Mexican oil after March, 1938. Acting through the
shadowy American speculator, William R. Davis, Germany soon
concluded a series of purchase agreements through which Mexico
exchanged crude oil for cash and German-made oil equipment
and other heavy machinery. Italy also made several barter deals
for Mexican oil, offering oil tankers and rayon yarn. And although

Mexico's oil industry was Atlantic Coast-oriented, Japan, too, promptly showed an interest in Mexican oil.[14] This attention from the fascist nations was rather embarrassing to the Mexican government, which was probably the outstanding champion of Loyalist Spain in all of Latin America. Officials from President Cárdenas down repeatedly emphasized that they would much prefer to sell their oil to the democracies. Indeed, during the Munich crisis in September, 1938, Cárdenas secretly proposed to President Roosevelt the establishment of an inter-American economic boycott against aggressor nations, even though such a move would cost Mexico the important German market for its oil.[15] At this time, it should be noted, Germany accounted for about a third of Mexico's not inconsiderable oil exports.[16]

Even before the oil expropriation, Ambassador Daniels had been concerned about the increasing threat of German economic and political penetration in Mexico. Fully a year before President Cárdenas seized the oil fields, Daniels had moved to block a plan to barter Mexican government-produced oil for German railroad equipment. This required a degree of political courage, for the proposal was tied to the sale of surplus American cotton, a fact of some interest to Daniels' own section. The scheme was being pushed, moreover, by a group of American speculators who had contributed generously to the Democratic Party in 1936 and who had good political contacts in Washington. These considerations failed to impress the Ambassador, however. He not only refused Embassy support for the deal, but gently rebuked the State Department official who had given a letter of introduction to the group, declaring: "I cannot see that the Embassy should promote it when it would exclude the use of American-made equipment."[17] When the Mexican press reported that Elliott Roosevelt was involved, Daniels straightway warned his father of some of the implications, pointing out that the proposal would hurt American manufacturers, and, more important, would "tend to encourage the Government in refusing to continue concessions to foreign oil companies in order to enlarge its own reserves." President Roosevelt was grateful for the information, and nothing came of the plan.[18] It might be news to American oil men that Daniels was looking out for their welfare, but his stand was consistent with his goal of closer ties with Mexico, including equitable commercial relations.

The post-expropriation barter deals caused the Ambassador even more concern. "If the Mexican Government should enter into arrangements to barter petroleum for goods made in Germany," he warned Secretary Hull shortly after the seizure, "it will seriously affect the commerce of United States manufacturers and turn the tide of Mexican purchases from American-made goods to German-made goods."[19] Daniels' fears were reinforced by figures showing that in the first year after the oil expropriation the United States suffered more than 90 per cent of the total decline in Mexican imports, which had been curtailed because of the post-expropriation financial crisis. In the same period, however, Mexico's trade with Germany, Italy, and Japan rose sharply.[20] Rather unhappily, Daniels defended Mexico's right to turn to the fascist bloc in the face of the oil companies' boycott. "We cannot properly object to such sale because the Standard Oil Company sold to Japan and Germany before the expropriation," he reminded Hull.[21]

One thing is assured: If, as is almost certain, Mexico must barter oil for German, Japanese and Italian goods or be drowned in oil, the United States business houses and manufacturers will lose the big market it has enjoyed in Mexico, and we know from experiences in some South American countries, that trade influences other associations. The loss of this market does not seem to concern the Standard Oil and other American oil companies. Just as long as they make money for themselves they seem indifferent as to what happens either to other business concerns or to the Good Neighbor policy upon which we properly set such store.[22]

Much as he deplored it, Daniels could do little to prevent the Mexican barter trade with the fascist countries. He did, however, advise a prominent American businessman in Mexico City to turn down an offer to serve as adviser to a Mexican mission trying to expand oil sales in Germany, pointing out that so long as the State Department regarded it as "stolen oil" no American should "have any part except acting for his country, no matter what his feelings were."[23] Another time, Daniels and the State Department managed to persuade the Mexican government not to go through with a plan to barter oil for German aircraft and military and technical advisers.[24] Needless to say, Daniels' efforts to sabotage German influence and trade in Mexico were a source of considerable annoyance to his colleague Baron von Rüdt, the German Minister.[25]

After Mexico agreed to settle American agrarian claims in November, 1938, the oil companies recognized that it would be difficult to justify a continued refusal to discuss an oil settlement with the Cárdenas regime. For the agrarian agreement showed, contrary to company claims, that it *was* possible to deal with the Mexicans. It was clear, too, that the Roosevelt administration was reluctant to intervene directly in the dispute until the companies had made some kind of effort at a negotiated settlement. Daniels had argued all along that it was incumbent upon the oil men to explore the various Mexican offers of compensation before turning to Washington for help. President Roosevelt agreed. In June, 1938, Roosevelt had told a Standard Oil attorney that the companies must accept the fact of the expropriation and discuss a financial settlement with Mexico.[26] He repeated this advice six months later, warning that he would not enter the controversy until the oil men had first tried to get an acceptable agreement. Significantly, the President indicated once more that a fair settlement should be based on the companies' actual investments in Mexico, not their estimates of potential profits.[27] Roosevelt was inclined to see Mexico in much the same perspective as Daniels. When, for example, a friend passed along some criticism of the Ambassador, Roosevelt responded:

Knowing all the angles of it and not just a few, I cannot help feeling that your friend has obviously been talking principally with the kind of people who would give anything to have old President Diaz reincarnated and restored to power in Mexico. His type of benevolent despotism is, they argue, the only permanent solution for the governing of a lot of ignorant natives. It is largely because of the ownership of Mexico by "successful business men" for so many years that the somewhat unhappy transition period of the last twenty-five years became inevitable.[28]

Within the State Department opinion was divided as to how much and what kind of support the oil interests ought to get. Daniels noted that Sumner Welles agreed "1,000 per cent" that the companies ought to do their own negotiating. Secretary Hull, on the other hand, was nearly as pessimistic as the oil men, believing that only stern words from Washington would bring results. Hull was convinced, too, that the Mexicans were trying to sell the rest of Latin America on the advisability of seizing U. S. investments. "He has no sympathy with them and wishes us to be as hard as nails to them, but says no forces can be employed," Daniels recorded after a conversation with the Secretary of State in January, 1939. "In heart he would like to use a Big Stick, but hopes strong language, very strong (almost threats) will enable him to dictate to them."[29]

There was another pressing reason for the major oil companies to make at least a half-hearted attempt at a negotiated settlement. Some of the smaller companies were becoming restive under the rigid no-compromise policy imposed by the dominant Standard Oil-Royal Dutch Shell interests. In fact, toward the end of 1938 the Sinclair group retained former Secretary of War Patrick J. Hurley to explore the possibility of a separate settlement with Mexico. Before expropriation, Sinclair had accounted for about 25 per cent of the production and 40 per cent of the refining and distribution capacity of the American companies in Mexico. Here, then, was a real threat to the companies' united front. Hurley went to Mexico, conferred with President Cárdenas and other top Mexican officials, and returned convinced that it might be possible to work out a satisfactory settlement with Cárdenas, whom he regarded as more conciliatory than some of his aides.[30]

A separate Sinclair settlement was a highly disturbing prospect to the rest of the companies. The other oil men recalled bitterly that Harry Sinclair had always been a lone wolf—witness his coming to terms with the Soviet Union while the other companies were boycotting Soviet oil, his sly attempt to outsmart his com-

petitors by getting access to the naval oil reserves at Teapot
Dome. Business considerations aside, if Sinclair should make
peace with Mexico, he would virtually demolish the contention
that it was impossible to get satisfaction without forceful support
from Washington.

Reluctantly, the major oil companies concluded that it was time
to send a negotiator to Mexico. They selected for this delicate
mission Donald R. Richberg, a former Bull Moose and La Follette
Progressive, railway labor expert, final head of the defunct National Recovery Administration, and currently a law partner of
Ambassador Joseph E. Davies. As an old line progressive and
former New Dealer, Richberg's political contacts in Washington
were excellent. Doubtless for this reason, shortly after the oil expropriation he had been retained by Walter C. Teagle, the board
chairman of Standard Oil of New Jersey, to represent the companies in their joint efforts to protect their Mexican interests. Like
his clients, Richberg thoroughly disapproved of the Mexican
seizure. As a realist, however, he believed that the companies must
consider the expropriation an accomplished fact, forget about a
return to the old order, and agree to a settlement based on recognition of Mexican ownership. His advice was opposed by some of
the more conservative company officials, especially the local
managers in Mexico, and it was not until the end of 1938, when
Pat Hurley began exploring the possibility of a Sinclair settlement, that Richberg was given authority to try to work out an
agreement that acknowledged Mexican ownership yet restored
the companies to management of their properties. Because Hurley
had already begun talks with the Mexicans along similar lines,
the two men originally planned to conduct joint negotiations. But
at the last minute Sinclair was asked to let Richberg handle the
initial discussions, and Hurley remained behind.

It is unnecessary to recount here more than the outlines of
Donald Richberg's unsuccessful year-long effort to arrange an oil
settlement, for much of the story is available elsewhere.[31] The
Richberg mission began auspiciously enough, with an assist from
President Roosevelt himself. Even before Richberg departed for

Mexico City the State Department persuaded the President to direct Ambassador Daniels to "make very clear" to President Cárdenas that the oil attorney was bringing with him an "eminently practical" plan. Roosevelt declared:

The proposal will make it possible for the companies to recoup the value of the properties over a period of years through a reasonable share of the profits obtained under a management contract, and will at the same time make it possible for the companies yearly to pay cash on the barrelhead to the Mexican Government in the form of a fanchise tax—or whatever it may be decided to call it—which tax will vary in amount depending upon the total profits made. As I understand it, when the contract is terminated, the companies have nothing further to do with the properties. Thus, there is as I see it, a tacit recognition of the right of the Mexican Government to expropriate without any further ado. The mere fact of the contract itself and of the payment of a franchise tax on a sliding scale, plus termination of any interest on the part of the companies at the end of the contract not only saves everybody's face but also brings cold cash to the Mexican Government. That is much to be desired. I wish you would do your utmost to impress upon President Cárdenas that I believe this proposal offers a fair basis for agreement and that I consider it of the utmost importance in the interest of the two countries that an agreement be found at a very early moment.[32]

Daniels promptly secured an appointment with President Cárdenas and read him Roosevelt's letter, but Cárdenas indicated that he had already been advised of the Richberg plan and was not overly impressed with the idea of a management contract with the companies. He nevertheless emphasized Mexico's willingness to compensate the oil interests, and declared that if necessary he could pay at once. This would involve getting the money from Germany and Italy, he hinted, with probably serious consequences for the present defensive alignment in the Western Hemisphere. Since Ambassador Castillo Nájera had already informed the State Department that Cárdenas was agreeable to some sort of long-term collaboration with the companies, this veiled threat was pretty clearly a combination of bluff and blackmail. But it was evidence of Mexico's determination to get the most out of the troubled international situation.[33]

Richberg got to Mexico early in March, 1939, just in time for

the heady celebrations of the first anniversary of the oil expropriation. Over the next three weeks he had a series of private conferences with President Cárdenas, both men relying on Ambassador Castillo Nájera as interpreter. From the first, Richberg
brushed aside Cárdenas' attempts to discuss the value of the oil
properties, for he was well aware that the two sides held irreconcilable views on the ownership of the subsoil, on which the companies based about 90 per cent of their claims. Candidly he explained to Daniels: "We could never agree, and if it were possible
to agree, Mexico cannot pay; therefore some other basis must be
found." Daniels quickly protested to Hull that this stand contra-
dicted a recent public statement by the Department on the scope
of the negotiations. He was reassured by Welles, who declared
that "sooner or later the question of valuation must be faced by
the companies in reaching a settlement."[34]

Richberg, however, was operating under fairly rigid instructions from his clients: "to seek the return of the properties in
Mexico to the management of the rightful owners under an arrangement that will secure to us our substantive rights, backed by
a treaty which will afford a guarantee of the permanency of such
a solution."[35] Accordingly, he offered the Mexicans a fifty-year
management contract under which the companies would operate
the oil industry, investing new capital as needed and sharing the
profits with the government; on its part, the government would
have to guarantee reasonable taxes and labor conditions. At the
end of the contract the properties would be turned over to
Mexico free of charge. Cárdenas, who suspected that at the end
of fifty years Mexico would be left with an impressive collection
of dry holes, had something quite different in mind. He proposed
the immediate valuation of the properties, arguing that this was
implicit in any profit-sharing arrangement. Otherwise, how could
one divide up the profits? Once the value was known, Mexico
would arrange compensation in oil. He offered to collaborate in
the future with a single company consortium that would be under
effective government control. Richberg had no authority to accept
such a settlement, and when he returned to the United States at

the end of March, the two sides were still far apart. He promised a meeting of the National Petroleum Association that the companies would not "consider legalizing the expropriation by waiving their fundamental rights and accepting the status of creditors relying on the unsecured promise of the Mexican government to pay a fractional compensation for their properties out of a future production of oil."[36]

Toward the end of April Richberg returned for further talks with President Cárdenas and Dr. Castillo Nájera in the picturesque north Mexico town of Saltillo. Here he was put in the awkward position of not daring to refuse Cárdenas' invitation to review a revolutionary May Day parade, surely an anomalous assignment for a Standard Oil man! This embarrassment over, Richberg presented Cárdenas with a modification of his original offer:

(1) The companies would consolidate their interests into four new companies having a Mexican majority on the boards of directors.

(2) The four companies would receive long-term contracts from Mexico to develop and operate the oil industry, investing new capital as required.

(3) Mexico would guarantee reasonable labor demands and fixed tax obligations. Besides taxes, Mexico would receive a share of the oil produced.

(4) Both sides could rest easy that the contracts would be enforced: through an Accounting Board, composed of government and company representatives, with access to pertinent records; and through a joint Board of Adjustment, which would settle any disputes, either on its own or with recourse to a neutral arbitrator.

Without exactly saying so, the Richberg plan took into account the companies' claims on the subsoil. Each of the new companies would expect, the proposal stipulated, "to produce in net income a fair return upon all its original and future contributions plus an amount sufficient to amortize or retire all such contributions, so that at the end of the contract all its claims and interests in pro-

ducing properties in Mexico will be released and transferred to
the Government without payment of any further consideration."[37]
As before, the new Richberg plan successfully skirted the delicate
matter of valuation, but it was hard to see how the scheme could
be put into operation without some value being assigned to the
companies' "contributions," "claims," and "interests."

Richberg left Saltillo convinced that Cárdenas was prepared to
accept a settlement on these terms. Later, after negotiations broke
down, he charged that Cárdenas had even helped to formulate
the plan, but that his more radical advisers subsequently talked
him into repudiating it. State Department records tend to sub-
stantiate the Mexican contention, however, that the proposal was
largely Richberg's, and that whatever Cárdenas' immediate reaction, he asked for further time to study the scheme before giving
a definite assent. In fact, when Richberg furnished the State
Department with a copy of the proposed settlement on his return,
he carefully noted that "all concerned have reserved judgment
and avoided any definite commitment."[38] Cárdenas and Richberg,
it should perhaps be recalled, had to rely for communication on
Ambassador Castillo Nájera, who because he regularly had to face
Hull and Welles was intensely eager to promote a settlement.
Thus the two principals may well have misunderstood what the
other meant by a Mexican majority on the boards of directors of
the new companies.

If, under Richberg's and Castillo Nájera's persuasion, Cárdenas
had actually given tentative approval to the Saltillo plan, he soon
had sober second thoughts. For more than two months he kept
Richberg waiting for a reply, though in the interval the State
Department and even President Roosevelt resorted to some judicious prodding, and Ambassador Castillo Nájera tried, evidently
on his own, to work out some changes in the Saltillo plan to make
it more acceptable to his superiors.[39] Finally in July Cárdenas
accepted the Saltillo plan as the basis for a settlement, but with a
fundamental modification. He stipulated that the Mexican government must appoint and control a majority of the boards of direc-

Josephus Daniels receiving a $1,000,000 check from Mexican Foreign Minister Eduardo Hay on June 1, 1939, the first payment of claims on expropriated American lands. Below, President Roosevelt and Daniels conferring in Washington on June 14, 1940.

United Press International photo

Mexican Ambassador Dr. Francisco Castillo Nájera presenting a check in payment of claims for expropriated American lands to Secretary of State Cordell Hull, June 29, 1940. Below, Daniels and Mexican President Manual Avila Camacho bidding farewell at the time of Daniels' retirement in November, 1941.

Library of Congress photo

tors and the presidents of the four new operating companies. This was hardly the sort of collaboration the oil men were interested in, and Richberg advised Castillo Nájera that on this basis "further negotiations would be useless."[40]

Rather than let the discussions collapse, on August 2 Sumner Welles, with President Roosevelt's approval, made a secret compromise proposal. To break the deadlock over management, Welles suggested that the companies and the Mexican government each name one-third of the directors of the new operating corporations. These would then select the remaining directors from a panel of neutral nominees—men of demonstrated business competence who were not citizens of any of the interested countries—originally agreed upon by Mexico and the United States. Welles stressed that this was only a temporary expedient, which could be modified after two or three years when both sides had a clearer idea of the sort of partnership arrangement they wanted. Like most compromise solutions, this one was received sourly by both sides. Cárdenas disliked putting control of the oil industry in the hands of the so-called neutral directors whose business background would presumably lead them to vote with the company-appointed directors. Richberg thought it "one of those amazing suggestions which under the appearance of 'compromise' gave everything to the other side."[41]

Enterprising Washington reporters soon published a garbled report of the Welles proposal, variously attributing it to Mexico and Richberg. The companies promptly issued an indignant disclaimer of responsibility for this "entirely unacceptable" plan, and called upon Washington to insist that Mexico return the properties. This gave the Mexicans a chance to blame the oil interests for the breakdown in negotiations, as well as to point out that there was evidently no further need to consider the neutral director scheme, for which they, too, denied responsibility.[42] Rather unhappily, Welles admitted that he was the unwitting cause of the rupture. He reminded both sides in a public statement, however, that while Mexico had an obligation to compensate the owners of expropriated property, the United States also expected its citizens to "give the most ample and attentive consideration to all constructive proposals."[43]

Both sides now withdrew like snapping turtles to their original uncompromising positions. President Farish of Jersey Standard told Secretary Hull that the Mexican partnership offer was "a mockery instead of a promise of justice," and he urged the State Department to demand the return of the properties.[44] President Cárdenas, in his state of the union message on September 1, 1939, declared that Mexico had completed an inventory of the companies' properties, and was now prepared to make an offer of compensation. The oil men could either accept it or challenge its fairness in Mexican courts, he said. Cárdenas appeared to be in dead earnest. "His whole attitude indicated that he considers this as his last word and that the matter is closed as far as he is concerned," commented one American newsman.[45]

Over the next few months the State Department tried hard to get the stalled negotiations under way again. At the Department's behest, President Roosevelt suggested to Cárdenas that, as part of a general settlement of Mexican-American problems, the oil dispute be submitted to impartial arbitration to determine the amount and form of payment to the companies. Daniels delivered Roosevelt's letter to Cárdenas on September 8, a week after the outbreak of war in Europe, and he found the Mexican President well aware of the increased need for continental solidarity. But Cárdenas was suspicious of arbitration, and explained that Mexican public opinion would not believe that a negotiated settlement was impossible.[46]

Neither side seemed very anxious to negotiate seriously, however, each believing that the war situation would hurt its opponent. The companies were sure that with Germany out of the market the Mexicans would quickly drown in oil. The Mexicans were equally confident that Italy could take over the German contracts, and that in any event the democracies would soon be needing all the oil Mexico could spare. By December, after the Mexican Supreme Court issued a final rejection of the companies' plea to set aside the expropriation decree, both Richberg and Castillo Nájera admitted to Welles that further negotiations seemed pointless.[47]

In order to convince the American public that Mexico was wholly responsible for the impasse, the oil companies brought the break into the open by publishing Donald Richberg's account of his unsuccessful mission. When his lengthy report appeared, under the title *The Mexican Oil Seizure*, Richberg was dismayed to see on the cover a drawing of a disreputable-looking Mexican, presumably a bandit or revolutionary. This, he later wrote, "could only have been motivated by a malicious effort to express a distaste and distrust for Mexicans that did not reflect my own feelings."[48] Richberg had suspected all along that his efforts toward a settlement were being sabotaged by conservative elements within the companies' leadership, especially the representatives in Mexico. Even before he went to Mexico, the local oil men had predicted to reporters that his mission was doomed to failure and was designed chiefly to satisfy the State Department that the companies could not obtain justice on their own. On his return to the United States after his first talks with Cárdenas, Richberg had twice felt obliged to speak out against those whom he described as "influential persons, in and outside the United States, who are exceedingly anxious to prevent an amicable settlement of controversies with Mexico." "Such persons," he declared, "desire to augment discord between the citizens and governments of the two countries."[49] Richberg's influence in company councils, never dominant, was by late 1939 definitely on the decline. When he later learned that the Jersey Standard men in Mexico were working against his further efforts at compromise, he withdrew in disgust.[50]

In any event, the publication of the Richberg report in January, 1940, virtually killed any hope of a negotiated settlement between Mexico and the companies. President Cárdenas and Ambassador Castillo Nájera were deeply offended by Richberg's breach of confidence, and the Mexican government promptly issued an indignant partisan reply. The companies, in turn,

retaliated with a long angry defense of their legal rights.[51] If anything, the two sides were further from agreement than ever.

With the collapse of the Richberg negotiations, pressures
mounted on Washington to take a more active hand in the dispute. The *New York Times* protested that a strong stand by the
United States was long overdue. "If we continue to temporize,"
it warned editorially, "the position of American investments not
merely in Mexico but in other countries may be placed in
jeopardy."[52] The outbreak of the war in September, 1939, led
both the British and the Dutch governments to urge the State
Department to stand firm in insisting upon the full rights of the
companies.[53] In Congress Hamilton Fish continued to attack the
administration for failing to look after American interests, accus-
ing President Roosevelt and Ambassador Daniels of "fawning on
the 'red' dictatorship in Mexico, practically ignoring the plunder-
ing of our citizens by our next-door neighbor."[54] Fish suggested
in a speech to a group of Tucson Republicans that the United
States settle its claims against Mexico by running the border due
west from Nogales to the Gulf of California, thus giving Arizona
a port![55]

Even some members of the President's family were critical.
Elliott Roosevelt (no doubt without his father's advance knowledge) told a Texas radio audience:

If conditions come to a head we may find ourselves right back where
we were in 1915 when we had to police Mexico to safeguard property
and the lives of Americans along the border .... A few blunt statements
from our State Department to Mr. Cardenas, who understands blunt
statements better than polite ones, probably would do that gentleman
some good and, at the same time, save us a lot of future trouble.[56]

The President was not overly receptive to this sort of advice from
his sons. When James Roosevelt passed along a letter from a
friend who was critical of Daniels and the Cárdenas regime in
Mexico, his father responded: "My reaction to it is that he is a
complete ass because he assumes that the only thing I know of
Mexico is what Ambassador Daniels tells me—and, incidentally, his

knowledge of what Mr. Daniels tells me is apparently extremely limited!"[57]

At the State Department the mood was one of growing frustration and exasperation. To overworked Department officials, dealing with a world coming apart at the seams, it seemed downright perverse of the Mexicans and the oil men not to settle their quarrel by amicable means. One reaction of the Department was to conclude an executive agreement with Venezuela in November, 1939, which gave that country the major share of the oil permitted to be shipped into the United States at preferential duty rates. Mexico was not listed among the exporting countries assigned quotas, and was thus forced to compete for the unassigned 3.8 per cent of the total. And the Department advised Ambassador Castillo Nájera that until the dispute was settled it would be unwise to try to ship even a drop of oil into the United States.[58] At the same time, there was increasing recognition that the oil companies were not blameless, either. "The State department's top men are thoroughly fed up with both sides of the controversy," reported Alan Barth in a news story that quickly drew an anguished protest from Jersey Standard's Washington lobbyist. "American oil companies, they charge, have made an admittedly bad situation worse by stubbornness," Barth wrote. "Hull doesn't want to ask .hem to accept anything less than a fair settlement. But informed sources expect him to insist that they get down to brass tacks, pare their claims down to what they genuinely believe they're worth."[59]

This was a thought that had already occurred to several of the smaller American oil companies. The smaller independents could ill afford to lose their Mexican investments, and they had less reason than Jersey Standard or Royal Dutch Shell to fear the international ramifications of a compromise settlement with Mexico. No doubt with these considerations in mind, the Seaboard Oil Company cautiously sounded out Washington in the fall of 1939 as to the advisability of conducting separate negotiations with the Mexican government. The State Department still had hope that Richberg would be able to arrange a general settlement, however, and it discouraged the Seaboard move.[60] Less easily dissuaded was Harry Sinclair, whose earlier restlessness had been one of the factors prompting the major companies to send Donald Richberg to Mexico. Throughout the Richberg negotiations Sinclair attorney Pat Hurley had been watching from the sidelines, alert to protect his client's interest. At one point he had even reminded the Mexicans that Sinclair was still interested in a separate settlement should Richberg fail.[61]

Once it was plain that Richberg was making no progress with his management contract idea, Hurley went to work in earnest. His ire was aroused by a report that Richberg had told the Mexicans not to worry about Sinclair, since the smaller companies would have no choice but to acquiesce in any settlement made by the majors.[62] Richberg subsequently denied ever making such a statement, hence the report may well have been a Mexican experiment in psychological warfare.[63] If so, it was a brilliant success. Sinclair now broke completely with the united front of the companies. Hurley offered to accept payment in oil for the Sinclair properties and hinted at the possibility of buying substantial amounts of Mexican oil. His first offer—thirty million barrels of oil as compensation and the purchase of another fifteen million—was rejected by the Mexicans as way out of line. Undismayed, he cheerfully conceded that he was only horse-trading, and continued to bargain. By February, 1940, negotiations had progressed to the point where the Mexicans were jubilantly predicting an early agreement. On March 1 Hurley confirmed to Secretary Hull that Sinclair was about to conclude a settlement, provided the oil received as compensation could be brought into the United States at the preferential tariff rate.[64]

Ambassador Daniels was impressed with Pat Hurley's shrewd yet realistic negotiating. Hurley was direct and candid, and unlike some of the resident oil men, left the impression that he both liked and trusted Mexicans. Nor did he waste time debating the legality of the expropriation or the merits of the Mexican Revolution. Instead, with the affability of a small-town Rotarian, he reminded Cárdenas that they were both military men and had

Indian blood, and with this in common no problem was insurmountable.[65] This was exactly the sort of let's-trust-each-other approach that Daniels had been urging upon the oil men since well before the expropriation. One cannot help but wonder whether there would have been any expropriation at all if the oil companies had called in men like Hurley and Richberg earlier.

The major oil companies and their sympathizers in the State Department did not share Daniels' enthusiasm for Hurley's progress. If Sinclair settled, the other companies would be on the spot. Newsmen were already cautiously pointing out what was painfully clear to the oil men—that a Sinclair settlement would raise the question of "whether the remaining companies were not perhaps unreasonable in their stand."[66] As in the past, the oil men looked anxiously to Washington.

Ever since the breakdown of the Richberg negotiations, the State Department had been considering the possibility of settling the oil dispute through arbitration, under terms that would permit the companies to manage the properties during the period Mexico paid whatever compensation was awarded. President Cárdenas had turned down the Department's earlier suggestion of arbitration, and had recently made a public statement against such a solution, but Welles and Hull continued to press the idea upon Ambassador Castillo Nájera.[67] During February, while Pat Hurley dickered with the Mexicans, the State Department consulted with Jersey Standard over the terms of an arbitrated settlement.[68] On March 2, the day after Hurley had informed him of the details of the proposed Sinclair settlement, Hull requested Dr. Castillo Nájera to find out if Cárdenas was still opposed to arbitration. Off-handedly, Hull pointed out the difficulty of increasing the import quotas for Mexican oil under a purchase agreement such as Sinclair contemplated.[69] If this was a subtle warning, it had no effect. Castillo Nájera declared, both before and after consulting his superiors, that Mexico had no intention of submitting the dispute to arbitration.

Acting, nevertheless, as if he knew nothing of the Mexican attitude, and was completely unaware of Sinclair's progress toward a negotiated settlement, Secretary Hull on April 3 formally demanded that the oil dispute be settled by arbitration, with the arbitral tribunal given authority to set both the amount of compensation and the means by which it should be paid. As he had during the angry 1938 dispute over agrarian claims, Hull released the text of his note without waiting for a reply, a move that was interpreted by some Washington observers as an effort to influence the coming Mexican presidential election.[70] The German Legation in Mexico City, on the other hand, always grateful for an opportunity to expand Nazi influence in Mexico, attributed the move to a desire to attract campaign funds for the coming presidential campaign in the United States![71] In either case, Hull's action was warmly applauded in Rockefeller Plaza. "The futility of private negotiations having been demonstrated," declared Eugene Holman, head of Jersey Standard's chief Mexican subsidiary, "it is now apparent that the only practical means of righting the wrong is for the United States Government, as it did in 1917 and 1925, to persuade Mexico to observe the rules of international law."[72]

The publication of Hull's arbitration proposal heightened anti-American sentiment in Mexico. *Ultimas Noticias,* a Mexico City paper that had often critized the Cárdenas regime in the past, summed up the general press reaction. "The international Pan-American New Deal of Roosevelt No. 2," it said, "is nothing but a branch grafted in the trunk of the big stick of Roosevelt No. 1."[73] Throughout Mexico there were demonstrations in support of the government, with some twenty-five thousand workers parading before President Cárdenas in Mexico City carrying anti-American banners. One showed a Mexican hitting Uncle Sam over the head with a club labeled "expropriation," while another portrayed a Mexican worker on a derrick squirting oil in Uncle Sam's eyes and saying: "Here's your oil. Take it!"[74] During April, while the government pondered its reply, the Mexican army significantly held parades commemorating the anniversary of Mexican resistance to the landing of American Marines at Veracruz in 1914.[75]

Ambassador Daniels had not been consulted about the State

Department's strategy, and, characteristically, he considered it rather uninspired. In fact, Daniels had been working along quite opposite lines. Two weeks before Hull's arbitration note he had sounded out the Mexicans on the possibility of improving relations by quietly exploring ways to settle certain longstanding problems on which no progress had been made since the oil expropriation. The reaction, he reported to Hull, was "most receptive." But the State Department view was that such discussions should wait until after Mexico agreed to an oil settlement, and Daniels' suggestion was rebuffed.[76] Without directly criticizing his superiors, Daniels indicated what he thought of the Department's tactics by sending President Roosevelt an editorial from the *Springfield Republican* which expressed doubt that Hull's tough policy would get results. "It is the best presentation of a delicate and difficult situation that I have read in any American newspaper," Daniels declared, "most of them seeing Mexican affairs through the eyes and influenced by the plentiful insidious propaganda of the oil companies."[77]

Mexico's reply to the arbitration proposal, handed to Daniels on May 1, contained no surprises. The note stressed that Mexico was a firm believer in the principle of arbitration, and cited the Mexican record in complying with arbitral decisions, at the same time politely reminding Washington that it still had not acquiesced in the adverse 1911 Chamizal decision. The note flatly declined to arbitrate the oil dispute, however, on the ground that it was a domestic matter.[78]

Timed to coincide with the publication of the Mexican reply was the government's proud announcement that it had concluded a financial settlement with the Sinclair interests. The State Department, kept informed by a nervous Jersey Standard lobbyist, had suspected such a development might be in the wind, and had recognized that an agreement with Sinclair would, as one official put it, "greatly strengthen the Mexican position." But both Duggan and Welles had concluded there was "nothing to be done," since they doubted that Mexico could be persuaded to withhold announcement of the settlement.[79] According to Finance Minister

Suárez' announcement in Mexico City, Sinclair would receive a total of $8,500,000 in cash over the next three years, with the first $1,000,000 to be paid at once.[80] At a meeting with top State Department officials, Pat Hurley admitted that there was more to the deal than that. Besides the $8,500,000 in cash, Sinclair had contracted to purchase twenty million barrels of oil over the next four years at a price averaging twenty-five to thirty cents below the market. The total compensation would thus come to between $13,000,000 and $14,000,000. Significantly, Hurley observed that his client's motto was "half a loaf is better than none."[81] In New York Harry Sinclair smiled expansively and declared himself well satisfied. "I am not worried about Mexican payments," he told a meeting of his stockholders. "They made the contract in good faith and I believe that it is going to be carried out literally."[82] Sinclair must indeed have been pleased with the settlement, for Hurley's authorized biographer asserts that for this assignment he received the largest fee of his career—reportedly a million dollars. The Mexican government was also deeply appreciative. For Hurley's yeoman service in shattering the companies' united front, Mexico subsequently bestowed upon him the coveted Aztec Eagle decoration.[83]

In spite of the Sinclair agreement, or perhaps partly because of it, Mexico was roundly berated in the United States for refusing Secretary Hull's bid to arbitrate the oil dispute. Some critics lashed out as well at the Roosevelt administration for what the New York *Daily News* called its "super-good neighborliness toward Mexico."[84] Even Hull's arbitration proposal was not immune from attack. "What is there to arbitrate, to compromise, about these Mexican confiscations anyway?" demanded Representative Dewey Short in Congress. "A horse-high, hog-tight, bull-strong case of robbery is standing against Mexico .... No one arbitrates with a thief."[85] Senator Robert Reynolds appealed for passage of his resolution to curb the entry of Mexicans into the United States, lugubriously reminding his colleagues of the "innumerable widows and orphans" who owned oil stock.[86] Warning that Mexico was consumed with "poisonous hatred" for the United States, Elliott

Roosevelt advocated stronger border defenses against Mexican-based fifth columnists and subversives.[87] Representative Thomas Hennings of Missouri called for a House investigation of Mexican expropriations, and tacitly acknowledged a report that he intended to ask for congressional letters of marque and reprisal against Mexican shipping.[88] The drive to end foreign silver purchases gained new vigor. Shortly after Mexico rejected arbitration, a bill repealing the Treasury's authority to buy foreign silver passed the Senate by a comfortable margin, but House leaders, jealously guarding their constitutional prerogatives, refused to act because the Senate bill also contained a tax revision.[89]

In oil circles mention of Harry Sinclair brought epithets and worse. Charging that Sinclair's imports of Mexican oil were damaging American producers, the other oil men managed to get the Texas Railroad Commission to hold a hearing on the matter in the summer of 1940. Hurley forestalled any action with a rousing defense of Sinclair's right to settle with Mexico, at the same time chiding his competitors for their obstinacy. Through shrewd cross-examination, he brought out that Jersey Standard was importing more than four times as much Venezuelan and Colombian oil as Sinclair planned to take from Mexico. "The Sinclair Companies," Hurley declared self-righteously, "respectfully decline to be the scapegoat."[90]

But the mutterings against the imports of Mexican oil by Sinclair and other American independents continued.[91] The two Texas senators, Morris Sheppard and Tom Connally, quietly induced their colleagues to approve without debate an obscure amendment to the National Stolen Property Act that would effectively block the oil purchase feature of the Sinclair agreement. Secretary Hull assured House leaders that he had "no objection" to the measure, but it failed to pass after a spirited debate in which even anti-Mexican members like Ham Fish came to recognize its far-reaching ramifications.[92] The State Department was more successful in persuading the Navy Department to reject a Sinclair bid on a sizable oil contract, pointing out that the Navy would first have to satisfy itself that Sinclair's oil did not come from "stolen" wells.[93] In the eyes of some Americans, it seemed, Sinclair *was* to be a scapegoat.

Having once again stated the United States position with dignity, force, and maximum publicity, the State Department was inclined to let the oil dispute rest for awhile. Consequently, Welles was noncommittal when Ambassador Castillo Nájera proposed early in June, 1940, that the two governments each appoint a commissioner to evaluate the remaining oil properties and determine the method of compensation. The Ambassador said President Cárdenas was willing to set a brief period—"even as short as two months"—for the deliberations, and was prepared to let any disagreements be settled by a neutral referee. This was a remarkable offer—the basis, in fact, for the settlement eventually concluded seventeen months later—but the State Department, suspicious of the *mañana* propensities of Mexican commissioners, let it pass.[94]

The Department's reluctance to explore a compromise settlement had strong Standard Oil support. President Farish of Jersey Standard reminded Secretary Hull that Mexico's flagrant attempt to confiscate the companies' subsoil rights "should again be openly and publicly contested." The companies had "never asked the Department of State to take any drastic action with respect to Mexico," he said. If, however, impartial arbitrators should decide that the Mexican expropriation was unlawful, the only remedy would be the restitution of the properties under a new management contract. On the other hand, if the seizure was upheld and compensation awarded, payment could be assured "only if administered by the expropriated companies…until the award had been fully liquidated."[95] Jersey Standard was clearly still out for the whole loaf.

Doubtless because of the oil dispute, Hull and Welles were hesitant about publicly praising the strongly anti-German stand taken by President Cárdenas and other Mexican leaders in the dark days immediately following the British rout at Dunkirk and the rapid collapse of the French armies. Ambassador Daniels was home on leave, but his second-in-command, Pierre Boal, appealed by cable and two telephone calls for some sign that Washington appreciated this evidence of Mexican-American solidarity.[96] The State Department was not yet ready to fawn over the Cárdenas government, but when Ambassador Daniels returned to Mexico City toward the end of June, he carried a personal message to Cárdenas from President Roosevelt expressing his friendship and esteem.[97]

One reason for the reluctance of both the State Department and Jersey Standard to pursue an oil settlement at this time was the fact that Mexico was scheduled to elect a new president on July 7, 1940. There was certain to be a change of administrations, because President Cárdenas was constitutionally ineligible for re-election. For the first time since the Revolution, moreover, there was a well organized and financed conservative party in the field, led by General Juan Andreu Almazán, whom some American Catholics enthusiastically described as another Franco. Almazán was making a spirited bid for the anti-government vote, promising stability, guarantees to capital, a curb on labor, and an end to socialistic education. He also declared he would never surrender to the oil interests, but the oil men and most foreign businessmen in Mexico were confident that this was only a matter of campaign tactics. They were certain he would prove much easier to deal with than the government party's candidate, General Manuel Avila Camacho. Shortly before the election Almazán threatened to lead a revolt if he were cheated of what he regarded as certain victory.

Despite President Cárdenas' apparently sincere hopes for peaceful balloting, the election was marked by widespread violence and intimidation by both sides. Each candidate claimed victory, and, charging an unfair count, the Almazán forces refused to submit their ballots for tabulation. When, as a result, General Avila Camacho was proclaimed the winner by a lopsided margin, Almazán angrily left the country, his followers predicting a revolution if he were not installed in the presidential palace. "At the proper time I will return to Mexico," he promised from a haven in the United States, "and claim the high office to which I am entitled by an overwhelming vote of the people."[98]

Ambassador Daniels, who had warned his staff to stay clear of local politics, was distressed by the violence of election day and the bitter contest over its results. But he was inclined to believe that General Avila Camacho was the legitimate winner, and he advised both the White House and the State Department that it was unlikely Almazán could find enough support for a successful revolution. The Mexican people, he noted, "prefer to bear the ills they have rather than to fly to those they suffered during the years after 1910."[99] Reluctantly, Daniels passed up an invitation to help President Roosevelt dedicate Great Smoky National Park in North Carolina, long a favorite *News and Observer* project, because it coincided with the opening of the Mexican Congress. The Ambassador feared his absence on this ceremonial occasion might be construed as tacit support for the rebellious General Almazán.[100]

The story of Almazán's efforts to find American backing for his revolutionary plans is by no means entirely clear. The General later charged that he had been betrayed by the United States, claiming that the oil companies had promised him $200,000 for arms, that his agents had sounded out President Roosevelt and apparently found him sympathetic, and that Elliott Roosevelt had agreed to use his Texas radio stations to support the revolution in Mexico. Until more of the pertinent corporate archives and personal papers are open, there is no way of knowing just how much and what kind of support Almazán found in the United States, or of determining whether, as seems likely, he mistook widespread sympathy for something more potent.

This much can be said with some assurance. Almazán partisans approached at least two prominent Democrats—Huston Thompson, a Washington attorney and former member of the Federal Trade Commission, and Homer S. Cummings, attorney general from 1933 to 1939—with offers of handsome retainers if they would influence the Roosevelt administration against recognizing the election of Avila Camacho. Thompson, who had recently visited Mexico and conferred with Daniels, was not interested, but Cummings apparently took the job, though without noticeable success.[101] Another well-known Democrat, publicist George Creel, was also induced to work for the Almazán cause. Creel begged Marvin McIntyre, a White House aide, for "some guarded word" as to the administration's attitude toward the general. "If we favor him, shutting our eyes to border activities, he can win easily and immediately," he pointed out enthusiastically. "If, on the other hand, we take a stand against him, he's whipped before he starts, and thousands of lives will be lost needlessly."[102] After consulting Roosevelt and Hull, McIntyre wired back simply: "My advice is Hands Off."[103] Creel took the hint, and when the Almazanistas came to him for help in tracking down a missing $15,000 arms shipment he refused to get involved.[104]

There is no evidence to support General Almazán's claim that the White House encouraged his revolutionary plans. Indeed, the McIntyre telegram to Creel supports the opposite conclusion. During the abortive Cedillo revolt in 1938, Roosevelt had advised Donald Richberg that there would be no overthrow of the Cárdenas regime. He did not change his mind when confronted with another disaffected general ready to march on Mexico City. After Avila Camacho had been officially certified as the victor, the State Department on several occasions went out of its way to demonstrate that Washington did not question his election.[105] The odds on Almazán plummeted to zero when the White House announced that Vice President-elect Henry A. Wallace would head the United States delegation at the inauguration of his rival. At this, General Almazán called off his revolution and quietly went home. The decision to send Wallace to Mexico—Daniels delightedly told Roosevelt it was an "inspiration"—was seen in both countries as proof that the United States accepted the election results and was eager for close relations with the new Avila Camacho government.[106]

Vice President Wallace's trip to Mexico marked the beginning of a concerted effort by Washington to strengthen its ties with

Mexico. It was virtually unprecedented for the United States to send such a high-ranking representative to a Latin American inauguration, let alone to a country which had not been regarded with much neighborly affection in recent years. But President Roosevelt's personal interest in the success of the Wallace mission doubtless quieted any lingering reservations within the State Department. With the instinct of a master politician, Roosevelt advised Wallace to be sure to lay a wreath on the monument honoring the young Mexican cadets killed defending Mexico City against American troops in 1847.[107] The new soft approach began to pay dividends almost at once. When Wallace and Daniels appeared with the United States delegation at the inaugural ceremonies, the assembled Mexican congressmen and government leaders rose to their feet for several minutes of warm applause. This remarkable ovation was exceeded only by the applause which followed President Avila Camacho's reference to inter-American solidarity in his inaugural address.[108]

Even before the change of administrations in Mexico, Sumner Welles had approached Ambassador Castillo Nájera with the suggestion that the two governments quietly explore the possibility of a global settlement—diplomatic parlance for a general settlement of all pending claims and disputes. In the circumstances, the term had an appropriate double meaning. With Germany triumphant in Europe, and Japan hungrily eyeing southeast Asia, Washington had reached the sound conclusion that the time had come to mend fences below the border, significantly, through a "global" settlement. Ambassador Daniels' proposal of such a settlement, which the State Department had rejected the previous March, made more sense now. As Duggan had reminded Welles during the fall of France, "an unfriendly Mexico, as it was from 1914 to 1918, could create manifold and difficult problems for us."[109] Since the outbreak of the war, moreover, American navy strategists had been advocating the creation of naval bases along Mexico's Pacific coast for use in the event of a war with Japan. While relations between the two countries remained cool, such bases were obviously out of the question.

In January, 1941, President Roosevelt asked Daniels to sound out President Avila Camacho on the possibility of building naval bases at such Pacific coast points as Acapulco and Magdalena Bay, a suggestion already tentatively advanced by Welles in his conversations with the Mexican Ambassador. Daniels reported that the new chief executive was anxious to strengthen Mexico's naval and air defenses. The chief obstacle was Mexico's poverty, however, and Daniels warned that "if any large construction is undertaken I am sure we will have to advance—or furnish—most of the money in a way that will not embarrass the President of Mexico."[110] Roosevelt replied that he was "greatly encouraged" by Avila Camacho's attitude, and promised, "If and when the necessity arises for financial assistance on our part, I shall have the situation explored promptly."[111]

Daniels advised Roosevelt that the oil dispute stood perversely in the way of a *rapprochement* with Mexico:

There is a general desire here that the negotiations reach a satisfactory settlement of old controversies. The lion in the path has been—it may be now—the greed of the oil companies. Mexico will never return the subsoil to private companies. They ought to be satisfied with fair payment of the real values. Doheny and Cowdray took many millions from the oil fields for which they made little return. The present owners ought to be paid, but up to now they have not been very cooperative. Quite the contrary. I know that you will not permit the more important matters to fail because the oil companies insist upon the old status quo. It is as dead as Julius Caesar.[112]

The oil men agreed with Daniels' premise—the importance of their dispute with Mexico—but they were not yet ready to accept his conclusions. Shortly after Welles opened negotiations with Ambassador Castillo Nájera, President Farish of Jersey Standard reminded Secretary Hull that both countries would benefit if Mexico could be persuaded to return the properties.[113] At the State Department's urging, Farish went to Washington for a secret conference with Dr. Castillo Nájera late in December, 1940, shortly after President Avila Camacho's inauguration. He reported that Mexico still refused to consider paying for subsoil rights and would not permit the companies to return except in an advisory capacity. "Under these circumstances," Farish told the Department, "we saw no possibility of reaching any common basis for discussion."[114] Jersey Standard's strategy, it was clear, was still based more on a concern for its assets outside of Mexico than on a desire to salvage something from its seized properties. But at the State Department there was increasingly less disposition to be guided by such considerations. Welles believed the time had come "when the two Governments themselves should try to work out a solution to the problem which they believe to be practicable and equitable."[115]

Throughout the first half of 1941 the two countries moved closer toward an understanding on important defense and economic matters. On April 1 Welles and Castillo Nájera signed an agreement pledging the right of transit and use of air fields for military aircraft of both nations.[116] The United States quietly contracted to buy Mexico's output of eleven strategic minerals.[117] Ambassador Daniels reported that Mexican officials were coöperating closely with the Embassy to frustrate German subversive activities.[118] The extent of the *rapprochement* was shown in late July, when President Avila Camacho intimated in a public address that Mexico would go to war if the United State were attacked.[119]

By the summer of 1941 the oil dispute was the chief remaining obstacle to a general settlement with Mexico, an accord which Washington hoped would open the way to closer collaboration on defense matters. At the State Department there was mounting exasperation over the oil companies' unwillingness to suggest some reasonable formula to end the controversy. And for the first time in the three-year-old dispute, the Department was armed with reliable figures showing that the companies' claimed valuations were absurdly high. At the State Department's request, petroleum experts in the Interior Department's Geological Survey had prepared an estimate of the value of the foreign-owned oil holdings in Mexico. They based their estimate on three factors: physical assets, estimated net profits receivable from 1941 to the exhaustion of the properties, and the estimated value of nonproducing but potentially productive lands. The latter two factors thus took account of subsoil claims. Even so, the Interior Department experts concluded that the remaining American properties were worth only $13,538,052. They valued the Sinclair properties at $10,320,322, whereas Sinclair, it will be recalled, had actually settled with Mexico for about $13,500,000.[120]

To say the least, the Interior Department study came as something of a shock to the State Department, which for more than three years had accepted without question the word of the oil men that their properties were worth hundreds of millions of dollars. Red-faced Department officials hastily decided to keep the report secret, since it was embarrassingly close to the Mexican government's valuation of the properties. Mexico would certainly have been willing to concede a much larger value earlier, the Department believed, and it might yet be persuaded to settle for more than the Interior Department figure. (Ambassador Castillo Nájera had intimated shortly after the expropriation, for example, that Mexico might consider paying $200,000,000 for the oil properties, instead of the $450,000,000 claimed by the companies.[121]) The Interior study was thus clearly useless for bargaining, except perhaps with the companies. Yet even discounting the Interior Department figure, which some State Department economic experts were inclined to do, other sources indicated that the companies' claims were way out of line. An oil geologist of many years' experience, currently working in the Petroleum Coördinator's office, advised a Department official that the holdings of Standard Oil of New Jersey—the largest of the American claims—were worth $15,000,000 to $20,000,000 at the most, using what he described as "very generous bases of calculation,...including physical assets, production and undeveloped lands."[122] A well-informed independent oil man went further, asserting privately that Jersey Standard was entitled to little if any compensation, except possibly as a face-saving device. The company had long since written off its Mexican properties, he said, and its investments had been returned many times over.

With these sobering estimates in mind, in July, 1941, the State Department began serious discussion of an oil settlement with

Ambassador Castillo Nájera. Already the two governments had tentatively agreed on other aspects of the global settlement: Mexico to pay $40,000,000 over a period of years on American agrarian and general claims; the United States to resume direct silver purchases and to make available long-term credits and a large loan for highway construction.[123] Early in July Ambassador Castillo Nájera repeated his suggestion, advanced unsuccessfully a year earlier, that each government appoint an expert to value the oil properties. He said Mexico would not object to a neutral third commissioner to settle any disputes, and he offered to pay $3,000,000 as a down payment while the experts completed their work.[124] The State Department was now prepared to accept responsibility for valuing the properties in this fashion, but with an eye on American public opinion, which for three years had been told that the companies' stake in Mexico was about $450,000,000, the Department insisted that the down payment must be $9,000,000. And the Department's legal adviser thought the agreement should specify that the $9,000,000 would not be returned if the two experts were unable to agree.[125] By early August the two governments had drawn up, and President Roosevelt had approved, a tentative oil agreement involving a $9,000,000 initial payment by Mexico and valuation of the properties by two government-appointed experts.

Ambassador Daniels had been cheering the progress of the Washington discussions from Mexico City, and he urged Roosevelt and Welles to speed up the negotiations so President Avila Camacho could make a favorable report, coupled with friendly references to the United States, in his first state of the union message on September 1.[126] Daniels also suggested to Hull that the United States could win a fund of goodwill in Mexico by including the longstanding Chamizal controversy in the settlement. The Mexicans were not pressing the matter, he noted, but they had already demonstrated that they were prepared to trot it out any time Washington proposed arbitrating some unpopular dispute. "We are big enough to go far to settle this matter, even though it involves a refusal to be bound by the legal objections filed by the State Department officials years ago," Daniels declared. "Until it is settled it will be a running sore."[127] Welles had already decided against reopening this ancient controversy, but he promised both Roosevelt and Daniels to try to expedite the settlement.[128]

By the end of August details of the proposed oil settlement began to leak out in Washington and Mexico City, to the great dismay of the holdout American oil companies. An enterprising *Newsweek* reporter even learned of the secret Interior Department appraisal of the oil properties.[129] Alarmed, President Farish of Standard Oil of New Jersey warned Hull against accepting a "confiscatory" settlement, especially one that did not include Royal Dutch Shell, since "the British may ultimately succeed in getting their properties back or making a better settlement, leaving the American companies in an unfortunate position." Farish still clung to the hope of an eventual return to Mexico:

It is our opinion, as previously observed, that the only possibility of a successful operation of the properties for the benefit not only of Mexico but of the United States and all parties concerned is to reinstate company management under a long-term contract which will give to Mexico and her people that economic advantage which Mexico has sought. A settlement not based on this principle would leave the matter in a worse position than it is now.[130]

Thomas R. Armstrong, a Jersey Standard vice president, explained to Department officials that his company was anxious "to preserve certain principles," and consequently wished to return to Mexico "under some sort of arrangement even if it were not a very satisfactory one."[131]

Farish's fear of Royal Dutch Shell evidently went only so far, because Jersey Standard officials lost no time in telephoning their rivals in London to urge them to get the British and Dutch governments to protest the proposed oil agreement. Jersey Standard's Washington office called in reporters and briefed them on the company's opposition, referring mysteriously to a complete dossier on certain American senators with the implication that the data could be used to obstruct a settlement. Not all of the reporters were impressed. The *St. Louis Post Dispatch* warned on September 11 that Jersey Standard's "stubbornness" might leave it "holding an empty bag."

Within the State Department there was still some support for the companies' position. Both Herbert Feis, the economic adviser, and Max W. Thornburg, the Department's recently acquired petroleum adviser, expressed fear that the proposed agreement might establish an "unfortunate precedent" with regard to other American oil holdings. Feis questioned whether "it might not be better for the Mexican oil question to remain unsolved until such time as Mexico's needs for foreign investments were such as to induce Mexico herself to solve the controversy." Thornburg—a former executive of Standard Oil of California who was subsequently dismissed in 1943 for what Secretary of the Interior Harold L. Ickes later said was a continuing oversolicitous concern for Standard Oil interests—was particularly vehement against the Interior Department study valuing the oil properties in Mexico. He described the appraisal as "a hoax," "absolutely worthless," and declared it "either incompetent or insincere."[132] Even Ickes, in his capacity as Petroleum Coördinator, reflected the companies' fear that a settlement with Mexico would prejudice other American oil holdings. He cautioned Hull against any agreement that might set off a chain of other Latin American expropriations, and several times over the next few months advised Roosevelt that the United States ought to buy the companies' rights in Mexico in order to insure adequate American defense reserves.[133]

But top State Department officials were under increasing Mexican pressure to proceed with the now virtually completed agreements, and with the international situation looking blacker daily, they hesitated to delay longer. On September 27 Secretary Hull met with a group of leading Standard Oil executives and pleaded for coöperation, stressing the danger of Axis subversion in Latin America and the consequent need of closer economic and defensive ties with Mexico. His arguments had little effect. W. S. Farish, Jersey Standard's uncompromising president, asserted that the fight against the Axis also involved the defense of international

agreements and property rights, and he chided the Secretary of
State for going back on his earlier strong stand. Farish wondered
if it was necessary to include the oil dispute in the general agreement with Mexico. Hull replied that oil was an integral part of
the picture, since the United States wanted many things from
Mexico, including naval bases, and he emphasized that it would
be highly undesirable to let the controversy drift along indefi-
nitely. He begged the companies not to try to undermine the
settlement, but to coöperate at least to the extent of suggesting
the American oil expert to value the properties. Farish declared,
however, that he was certain his board would prefer to see the
dispute remain unsettled, even if it meant losing the properties,
than to compromise on the vital issue of subsoil rights.[134] He repeated these objections in a letter to Hull on October 8.[135]

Secretary Hull still hoped to bring the oil men around, but
even he was beginning to resent their intransigence. At Hull's request, the Treasury Department had gone over Jersey Standard's
tax records, and Secretary Morgenthau reported that the company's own book value of its Mexican properties tallied closely
with the recent low geological appraisals received by the State
Department. Moreover, Mexican Finance Minister Eduardo
Suárez had come to Washington early in October on the understanding that the financial agreements were ready to be signed,
and officials found it rather embarrasing to put him off. It was
with some difficulty, indeed, that the State Department persuaded Secretary Morgenthau to hold back the financial agreements while Hull did further missionary work among the oil men.
Morgenthau, who frequently objected to State Department logic,
had no patience with Sumner Welles' admonition that "if the
Treasury does not cooperate, the other pieces...will not be put
together."[136]

Meanwhile, Ambassador Daniels had arrived back in the
United States, bringing with him President Avila Camacho's expressed hope that the agreements could be signed soon, since
after all the optimistic publicity in Mexico the continuing delay
was embarrassing the government. This was not, however, the

main reason for the Ambassador's return. For several years Addie Daniels had been suffering from increasingly painful attacks of arthritis. Medical specialists, including their physician son Worth, confirmed that she could no longer stand the social responsibilities or the high altitude of the Mexico City Embassy. Daniels discussed the matter with President Roosevelt at the end of October, and Roosevelt offered his old chief a quieter assignment if he wanted it, but Daniels had made up his mind to resign so that his ailing wife could return to their comfortable Raleigh home, close by her family and friends. Roosevelt, always sentimental about such partings, accepted the decision with genuine reluctance, for he and Daniels had worked together in government for nearly seventeen years. He urged his friend to return to Mexico for a proper leave-taking, and gave him a message of friendly greeting for President Avila Camacho.[137]

Leaving Mrs. Daniels at home, early in November the Ambassador flew back to Mexico City for a week of farewell banquets, receptions, and frantic packing. He found Mexican officials upset over Secretary Hull's continued reluctance to sign the long-completed general settlement without the consent of the oil companies. There was also resentment that in recent weeks the oil men had been working on the more conservative elements in the Mexican government, trying to promote another round of private negotiations between the companies and Mexico. Newsmen in Mexico City reported rumors, perhaps inspired by the oil men but in any event repeated by them to the State Department, that only the old Cárdenas faction liked the proposed oil agreement. President Avila Camacho, it was intimated, favored a management contract with the companies, but feared to break with the Cardenistas. The President's brother, General Maximino Avila Camacho, who had recently been entertained by Farish in the United States, was suggested as an ideal go-between to arrange an amicable working agreement with the companies.[138] The reports had some effect within the wavering State Department, for Welles asked Ambassador Castillo Nájera what his government's reaction would be if Jersey Standard should send a top-level negotiator to Mexico City.[139]

It may have been pure coincidence, but the day after Daniels arrived back in Mexico City, Foreign Minister Ezequiel Padilla answered Welles' query with a surprisingly blunt public statement. Referring to what he called the companies' recent press campaign, Padilla scotched rumors that the government was considering direct talks with the oil men. "It is to be hoped," he warned, "that in their own interest the expropriated companies will become persuaded that further delay in settling this question would not be without prejudice to the companies."[140] Mexican officials in Washington further advised the State Department privately that the oil controversy must be included in the general settlement or the whole deal was off.[141] Finance Minister Suárez, who had been waiting in Washington for over a month, threatened to go home if Secretary Hull did not make up his mind soon.

On November 13 Jersey Standard formally turned down another State Department plea to accept the oil agreement. As before, the company's chief objection was that the plan ignored subsoil rights—"the main element of value." Farish told Hull:

It may be needless to say that we are anxious to be helpful in promoting closer relations with Mexico. We believe that this can best be done by our government insisting that the Mexican Government enter into a long-term operating contract with the companies. We feel certain that, while this would be more beneficial from the Mexican as well as the American point of view than any other procedure, it would also result in making more secure the large investments of United States capital not only in Mexico, but also in other American countries to the South, to the mutual advantage of all concerned.[142]

Ambassador Daniels returned to Washington just as the State Department was pondering this rejection. Knowing the dangerous status of the current negotiations with Japan, Secretary Hull was anxious to settle the Mexican difficulties, but he still hesitated to proceed without the assent of the oil men. At a White House conference with President Roosevelt on November 18,

Daniels transmitted an urgent personal appeal from President Avila Camacho to break the deadlock. Roosevelt agreed that the time had come to act, but said it would first be necessary to convince Hull that it was futile to wait any longer for the companies' approval.[143] Daniels went immediately to see Hull and stressed that further delay would only alienate the friendly Avila Camacho government. "As the Ambassador says," Roosevelt also pointed out to Hull, "the Mexican Government is really concerned by the delay in the oil matter."[144] Daniels' arguments must have tipped the scales, for he had no more than started home to Raleigh than Laurence Duggan wired exultantly: "Agreements will be signed tomorrow afternoon. Many thanks for all you did."[145] Duggan elaborated on Hull's change of heart in a letter to Daniels several days later:

I suspect that the words which you brought back from the White House weighed heavily with the Secretary. When we saw him about 4:30 on Tuesday afternoon [November 18] the Secretary had apparently made up his mind. I know that your appointment with him was at 4:00 o'clock. Perhaps his decision was arrived at entirely independently of anything you may have told him, but in any case, it was a coincidence that the Secretary informed us of his decision so shortly after his conversation with you.[146]

The next afternoon, November 19, 1941, Secretary Hull and Ambassador Castillo Nájera met at the State Department and with a ceremonial flourish exchanged notes outlining the long-readied global settlement. Under the agreements Mexico promised to pay a total of $40,000,000 over the next fourteen years to settle all American general and agrarian claims. Each government agreed to appoint an expert to determine the amount Mexico owed the American oil companies, and Mexico promised an immediate down payment of $9,000,000. The United States agreed to spend up to $40,000,000 to stabilize the Mexican peso, to purchase 6,000,000 ounces of newly mined Mexican silver a month, or about $25,000,000 worth a year, and to negotiate a trade agreement. In addition, the American Export-Import Bank agreed to lend the Mexican government $30,000,000 for road construction, mainly to complete the Mexico City-Guatemala section of the Pan American Highway.[147] The agreements showed that Washington was now willing to pay a considerable price for a *rapprochement* with Mexico, for it was plain that the United States in effect would be underwriting the Mexican payments.

So, at least, thought the embittered oil men. After a strategy meeting in New York, the companies announced through President Farish of Standard Oil of New Jersey that the oil settlement was unacceptable, because "it purports to validate the original confiscation, which violated international law, and thereby jeopardizes all foreign investments."[148] Farish did not bother to explain just how an agreement to value and pay for expropriated property violated international law. After some hesitation, which worried the State Department, the companies agreed to coöperate in supplying data to help the experts value their properties. Farish urged Hull, however, to instruct the American expert, Morris L. Cooke, "to adhere to the established principles of international law so clearly set forth by your Department as applicable to this controversy."[149]

Cooke revealed later that he and his Mexican colleague, Manuel J. Zevada (whom he described as "straight as a string"), had no trouble reaching agreement on about three-fourths of the final award, using standard American valuation practices based on the prudent investment theory. Nevertheless, the American experts were shocked at the discrepancy between company claims and what they actually found in Mexico—obsolete equipment twenty-five years old and badly in need of repair, miles of pipeline corroded almost beyond use. "We were pretty embarrassed at times," recalls one of the American appraisers. "We insisted that Standard Oil had invested over $400,000,000 in their properties, only to have the Mexicans bring out the books of the oil company which plainly showed that they had put in much, much less."[150] Shortly before Cooke and Zevada made their report, the State Department had a visit from an apprehensive Jersey Standard board member, Wallace Pratt. Pratt, still hopeful that some form of management agreement could be worked out, declared that his company "would be willing to see that Mexico received 50% of the profits through royalties, taxes, et cetera, and that a working arrangement would be better than a fair or unfair evaluation."[151] In a day when the oil companies had not yet accepted the fifty-fifty sharing arrangements now standard in international oil concessions, this was a remarkable offer—undoubtedly far more than would have originally been required to avert the expropriation. The only trouble was that it came about four years too late! Two weeks later Cooke and Zevada reported that the American oil properties were worth $23,995,991, plus interest of slightly more than $5,000,000 from the date of expropriation. Of the total award, the Jersey Standard holdings accounted for $18,391,641, a figure that compared favorably with the company's own book values and the estimates made earlier for the State Department by reputable geologists.[152] The award was a far cry from the companies' earlier demands, but it was eloquent proof that the State Department had finally accepted what Ambassador Daniels and President Roosevelt had conceded from the start—that the oil men should expect to recover only their investments, not future profits on oil in the ground.

Daniels was unfortunately not on hand to witness the signing of the agreements on that chill November afternoon. He had returned to Raleigh and was enjoying his first real day of retirement after nearly nine years as an amateur diplomat. Nevertheless, as Larry Duggan and Ambassador Castillo Nájera and other insiders recognized, November 19, 1941, was in a real sense Josephus Daniels' day. Daniels had not, it is true, been permitted to do much of the negotiating that led to the global settlement. Hull and Welles had preferred to handle matters themselves in Washington, in consultation with the Treasury and other interested agencies. But more than any one, Daniels had kept the explosive oil dispute from wrecking Mexican-American relations. No one had argued more consistently or convincingly that nothing must be permitted to destroy the Good Neighbor Policy, the only effective long-run approach to Latin America. Some will protest that it was the threat of war, not Daniels' nagging, that forced the retreat of the State Department; it will be claimed that the 1941 settlement with Mexico was purchased only at the expense of American principles, oil company rights, and the U. S. taxpayer. No doubt this is partly true. Yet with the sobering perspective brought by postwar billion-dollar foreign aid programs, one may legitimately ask whether these "rights" and "principles" did not need re-examination. In this light, Daniels' neighborly approach seems realistic and, indeed, strikingly advanced. Had the oil men adopted it prior to 1938 they would probably still be in business in Mexico. It must be remembered, too, that the State Department got nowhere with Mexico until it stopped fingering its big stick and gave up the unrewarding practice of bluster and name-calling.

Ambassador Daniels' service in Mexico and the global settlement that climaxed it need to be assessed in light of their immediate substantial results. Within hours after the first Japanese bombs fell on Pearl Harbor on December 7, 1941, the Mexican government announced: "Associated with the United States in the common defense of democracy and of the destiny of America, we will omit no effort, by all possible means, to establish our spirit of solidarity and of close friendship."[153] With United States approval, Mexico did not declare war on the Axis powers immediately, lest American forces have to be diverted to help defend the Mexican coastline. But when Mexico did enter the war, it was one of the few Latin American nations to send a token fighting force overseas. Whatever his earlier reservations, even Secretary Hull had to admit after the war that Mexico had been an "outstanding example of helpful cooperation."[154] This alone would seem to be a satisfactory "global" return on the 1941 agreements.

Ambassador Daniels, rejected at first, viewed with
suspicion by the Mexicans, has demonstrated that he
was the man needed to bring about the closer relations necessary in these times of uncertainty regarding the future .... Led by the hand, our people can
be led anywhere; but by pushes, not even to glory.
—*La Opinión*[1]

CHAPTER XI

"By Pushes,
Not Even to Glory!"

Even today Josephus Daniels' nine
years of service in Mexico are the subject of controversy. Some
State Department officials, businessmen, and members of the
American colony in Mexico still think of Daniels with more than
a trace of bitterness. They see him as a personally charming,
but soft-headed and perhaps a little senile old man, a weak and
ineffectual idealist at a post that required tough-minded firmness. Whether because he was expiating his personal guilt feelings over the occupation of Veracruz in 1914, or because he
naively thought Lázaro Cárdenas was a Mexican New Dealer,
Daniels' "neighborliness," the critics charge, cost the United
States millions of dollars in expropriated investment. Others,
Mexicans and Americans alike, take an opposite view. Daniels
was truly an Ambassador Extraordinary, they argue, a wise and
far-seeing statesman who fought tenaciously to make the Good
Neighbor Policy a reality, and in the process charted an uncommonly sensible way to deal with Latin American nationalism.

Ambassador Daniels' own view of his mission was summed up
in a single sentence in his letter of resignation. "I went to
Mexico animated by a single purpose," he told President Roosevelt, "to incarnate your policy of the Good Neighbor." And as a
result, he added with justifiable pride, "the relations between

Mexico and the United States are on the most sincerely friendly basis in their history."[2] Asked by reporters what he considered the outstanding achievement of his turbulent stay in Mexico, Daniels replied simply: "It was in having a heart. I tried to be a good neighbor and to be in sympathy with the things the Mexicans were trying to do for the good of their country."[3]

President Roosevelt fully agreed with this assessment, and in his formal letter of acknowledgment, he told Daniels that he, perhaps more than anyone else, had "exemplified the true spirit of the good neighbor in the foreign field."[4] Newsmen noted that the President's voice was husky with emotion when he told them that he was "very, very regretfully" accepting his old chief's resignation. "I don't know that the country as a whole realizes," Roosevelt reminded his press conference, "that of all of the people in the last eight and a half years who have been in foreign posts in Central and South America...Mr. Daniels probably has done more to encourage and live up to the Good Neighbor Policy than anybody else I know. And today our relations with Mexico are on a basis of understanding and friendship; with a very great improvement, as we all know, over conditions that existed when he went down there in the spring of 1933."[5]

American business interests, while applauding Daniels' retirement, took a much less charitable view of his accomplishments. The New York *Journal of Commerce*, for one, immediately objected to the President's praise, asserting that Daniels could be said to have advanced the Good Neighbor Policy "only in a very special, Pickwickian sense." Roosevelt's remarks, the paper complained editorially, implied a wholly undeserved rebuke to other American diplomats in countries that had shown much more regard for American capital than Mexico:

Venezuela, for example, preferred to sell her petroleum production to Great Britain while Mexico was stocking the tanks of Germany, Italy, and Japan before the war halted such shipments. Venezuela has treated American capital fairly and equitably, thus encouraging new investments which expand the productivity of that country, raise the standard of living of its people and stabilize economic and political conditions for the future. Has Mr. Daniels done more to encourage the Good Neighbor policy than our envoys at Caracas?

Since Josephus Daniels took his post in Mexico City in 1933, American farmers in Mexico have been deprived of their holdings, American petroleum properties have been seized without compensation to their owners, and a policy of discouraging the collaboration of American capital and enterprise in Mexico's economic development has been pursued consistently. There is no evidence that Mr. Daniels has opposed these antagonistic policies. There have been many reports that his personal attitude has encouraged them.[6]

To this, a Mexican labor paper quickly retorted that "if Daniels had worked in Mexico as other U. S. diplomats did in Venezuela President Roosevelt's Good Neighbor policy would be anathema to Mexico."[7] Another Mexico City paper declared: "President Roosevelt is right; Daniels has surpassed all United States diplomats in Latin America with reference to a conscientious, frank, authentically Pan American interpretation of the Good Neighbor Policy."[8]

These varied comments, all made within a few days of Ambassador Daniels' retirement, illustrate the striking range of opinion regarding his service in Mexico. The debate has been muted by the passage of time, but its echoes can still be detected when Daniels' name is mentioned in certain circles. One reaction is the amused, condescending expression on the face of a young career official at the U. S. Embassy in Mexico City; another is the almost apoplectic response of an oil man in Rockefeller Center as he warms to a discussion of subsoil rights; still another comes from a retired American consul living in Mexico, who recalls his intense satisfaction when the do-gooder Daniels was replaced by the no-nonsense George S. Messersmith. A rather different reaction is the warm and obviously genuine admiration of Mexican officials who knew Daniels, and the continuing repect, loyalty, and affection of his close staff members. Inevitably, it seems, one's opinion of the Ambassador is determined by one's view of the Good Neighbor Policy.

In his dealings with the Mexicans, Josephus Daniels never forgot that he was in a proud, sensitive, but economically backward country which should be encouraged in its ambitious plans to better the condition of its people. "Mexico is emerging, after a long reign of feudalism and semi-feudalism, into a socialized democracy," he told a friend in 1938.[9] Veteran of many a battle for reform back home, Daniels possessed little of the concern for the status quo that seems so characteristic of diplomats. He took a long view of Mexico's problems and future, and found them exciting. "Mexico is the most interesting laboratory in the world," he once remarked enthusiastically to William Allen White. "Coming out of ages of feudalism, it is making experiments in government and social matters that we have been unwilling to essay. They are doing some of these things uncommonly well and many of them uncommonly crudely .... As a confirmed optimist, even when passing through a graveyard, I hold fast to the belief that the best is yet to come."[10] Daniels was convinced that a few years of sympathetic help by the United States would see Mexico fast developing into a stable and prosperous democracy, an expanding market for American trade, and a reliable ally in time of trouble. Washington should pay more attention to its relations with Latin America, he thought. When a North Carolina paper suggested in 1937 that he had earned a promotion to the vacant embassy in London, Daniels expressed appreciation but observed: "I firmly believe that the countries south of the Rio Grande are going to mean more and more to the interests of the United States as time goes on, and the proper representation will have a large part in bringing it to pass."[11]

Americans who took a similar view of Latin America naturally tended to become enthusiastic Daniels champions. Daniels had been at his post only a little over a year when an American returning from a visit to Mexico City reported to the State Department that he was "more genuinely popular among the Mexicans, official and unofficial, than any Ambassador this country had ever had at that capital."[12] A Boston businessman repeated a similar impression to Roosevelt in 1937.[13] After a trip to Mexico in 1940 John Steinbeck told Archibald MacLeish: "I went in to see Daniels the last time I was down and had one of those surges of pride in a democracy. That is a great and humble man. I don't much like the diplomatic class. But this man knows more about the Mexican people than his predecessors did, the common people. My admiration and affection for him are very great."[14] Edward Keating, the editor of *Labor*, expressed the same thought. "You are my favorite diplomat," he once told Daniels. "I don't like those career men in the State Department. They know little of America or Americans, and I am always nervous when they 'sit in' with the representatives of foreign governments. A democracy should be represented, in all of its activities, by men who are democrats, with a small 'd.' "[15] After the oil expropriation threatened to engulf the Good Neighbor Policy, a number of Americans voiced relief that Danels was on hand to tend to the crisis. "I don't envy you your job at this time," was a typical response, from William Allen White; "as a citizen of this country, however, I am resting easily because you are on the job."[16]

Perhaps because at heart he was one of them, Daniels generally made a good impression on American news correspondents working in Mexico. He was easily accessible to reporters, and did not hesitate to keep them informed through off-the-record briefings. This was taking a calculated risk, and the newsmen appreciated it. One of Daniels' assistants recalls that the only time he ever saw him really angry was after a Hearst reporter violated the confidence of one of these background briefings.[17] Even newsmen who did not share the Ambassador's optimistic view of the Mexican scene quickly came under the spell of his good-humored candor. Frank L. Kluckhohn, a *New York Times* correspondent whom the Mexican government subsequently expelled from the country for hostile reporting, wrote affectionately in 1937: "Mexican officials, who usually have no overweaning kindness for Americans north of the Rio Grande, love him .... He maintains unshaken his youthful belief in democracy and, particularly, in the common man. It is this that has made him loved in Leftist Mexico."[18]

Other American correspondents came to similar conclusions.

Howard Vincent O'Brien, a *Chicago Daily News* columnist, told his readers after a visit to Mexico that Ambassador Daniels was extremely popular with large segments of the Mexican population, but was hated by businessmen, socialites, the clergy, and those generally opposed to social change. The latter groups, he said, either blamed Danels for instigating all the wicked things Cárdenas had done, or considered him "a kindly simpleton, the dupe of men whose evil intent he has not the wit to understand." O'Brien firmly rejected both notions:

Make no mistake, either, about our Ambassador to Mexico being a benevolent old geezer who takes what is fed him and doesn't know what it is all about. It is my opinion, based on conversations with him, and, much more, on conversations I have had with others about him, that he has the low-down on Mexico as well as any American can hope to have it. He has looked on the Mexican kaleidoscope with a shrewdly quizzical eye, and he has kept his ears open. It may be that I think him a wise old owl because he has reached the some conclusions that I have. Whatever the reasons for my thought, I think we would be fortunate if we could always have ambassadors of his sort .... Mr. Daniels is not in the Metternich-Talleyrand tradition. He is the sort of person that I imagine Jefferson and Ben Franklin to have been.[19]

Raymond Clapper, one of the ablest of American news analysts, observed from Mexico in the spring of 1941 that there were two reasons for the improving relations between the United States and its southern neighbor. One was the war in Europe, which naturally drew both countries together. The other was "Uncle Joe Daniels, the American Ambassador."

By all of the rules he should be the most unpopular ambassador we have ever had. For as Secretary of the Navy under Wilson, he sent the fleet to Vera Cruz. He doesn't speak a word of Spanish—says he is too old to learn. Yet no ambassador has been more loved by the Mexican people. The reason is that they are convinced he is sympathetic and that he is not trying to gouge them. We have had ambassadors who have conceived it their duty to concentrate on nagging the Mexican Government, serving as a kind of police court lawyer for the oil companies. The oil companies don't like Daniels. They resent his not acting like the British did .... Ambassador Daniels could have been tough with the Mexican Government, but it wouldn't have got the oil properties back.

Nothing is going to get the oil properties back. Expropriation Day is the big national holiday here now. But the Mexicans do not take it out on the American Government and for a good deal of that we can thank Uncle Joe Daniels. He is an old-fashioned country editor, a William Jennings Bryan Democrat, and happens to be just the kind of person who inspires confidence among the Mexicans who are going through their Bryan period.[20]

Perhaps the best test of a man is how he measures up in the eyes of those who know him best—his subordinates. Here Ambassador Daniels comes off remarkably well. For the most part, he was well liked by his staff at the Embassy, and some of his close associates developed a real and continuing affection for their chief. The Ambassador's old-fashioned southern dress—his soft collar and black string tie, his broad brimmed flat black hat—along with certain of his personal mannerisms—his strict temperance views, his unconscious penny-pinching, and his eye for personal publicity—made him the butt of a certain amount of staff humor, most of which fortunately escaped his attention. The career men took with good-natured grace Daniels' joshing about the superiority of amateur "shirt-sleeve" diplomacy over the professional "silk-hat-and-spats" variety, for nobody in the Embassy ordinarily wore a silk hat or spats, any more than the Ambassador customarily worked in his shirt sleeves. They knew, too, that Daniels was well aware that the Embassy could not function without the trained knowledge and skills of the professionals.

Although Daniels frequently complained that most of the career men despised the Good Neighbor Policy, this was not true of his most trusted assistants, especially those who served with him the longest. Several of these men—all career foreign service officers who have since risen to high diplomatic posts—are today convinced that Ambassador Daniels was not only extremely effective in protecting the over-all long-range interests of the United States in Mexico, perhaps uniquely so, but that he also did all that might reasonably be expected of him to look after American private interests. Of the latter, Pierre Boal, Daniels' counselor from 1936 to 1941, declares: "Personally I doubt whether they could have come off much better than they did no matter what the action of the Embassy and the United States Government had been." Boal and other Embassy staff members make the point that Daniels always considered himself (and was considered by Roosevelt) the personal representative of the President, not the emissary of the State Department. They believe, too, that Daniels had standing instructions from the White House not to allow any relatively unessential matter to jeopardize good relations with Mexico. Hence he felt free on occasion to oppose, block, or water down what he regarded as ill-advised State Department policy. Boal says:

...the Ambassador, knowing the President's mind and sentiment allowed no action which might disturb our basic good relationship with the Mexican Government. He tread softly and got the blame for being "soft." The policy toward Mexico and its methods of execution were determined and currently followed up at the White House. What Mr. Daniels did, or did not do, represented the wishes of the President. Decisions were made at the White House (sometimes Mr. Hull may not have realized how far they went) but the action was taken in Mexico and Mr. Daniels shouldered the blame.

This may be somewhat overstressing Daniels' relationship with Roosevelt and the latter's personal interest in Mexico, but it nevertheless contains a shrewd insight into the Ambassador's *modus operandi.*[21]

All this is not to say that Josephus Daniels was without critics during his diplomatic service, for this book makes abundantly clear that such was not the case. It should be noted that some of the Ambassador's staff considered him too soft, too trusting in his dealings with the reform-minded Cárdenas government, and this was plainly the predominant view of his State Department superiors. Cordell Hull thought Daniels "a little too radical at times to suit me," a sentiment thoroughly shared by most of the American colony in Mexico.[22] The oil expropriation led one North Carolinian living in Mexico, for example, to express his "absolute contempt" for the Ambassador. "You would certainly be doing your country a service if you would resign the position," he advised Daniels. "As far as I personally know you are the laughing stock of the Americans as well as the more intelligent element of the Mexican population."[23] Anita Brenner reported that one American oil man had told her in all seriousness that the expropriation had been planned at a meeting attended by Cárdenas and other leading Mexican officials, Leon Trotsky, and, not least, Ambassador Daniels![24] Such criticism was not only unfair but absurd. It was proof, however, that Daniels was by no means universally beloved by his compatriots. Indeed, it is probably safe to say that none of Franklin D. Roosevelt's ambassadors received more condemnation and abuse from home in the course of his work. Yet Daniels took it all smiling, without bitterness, serene in the knowledge that he enjoyed the President's full confidence.

So much for the varied American reactions to Ambassador Daniels; what of the Mexican view? Some Mexicans, chiefly those who did not share Daniels' enthusiasm for their country's Revolution, never forgot nor forgave his role in the Veracruz occupation of 1914. *Omega,* the right-wing paper that had raised this objection to Daniels' appointment in 1933, was still complaining in 1941 that the banquets, receptions, and toasts honoring his retirement were "offensive to the martyrs of Veracruz."[25] Since *Omega* and its readers had little love for the Mexican Revolution, which the Veracruz intervention had been intended to aid, one may question the sincerity of this solicitude. The hostility to Daniels came mostly from conservatives. Upon receiving the news of Daniels' resignation, the head of the rightist Sinarquista movement issued a statement declaring that Washington now had "a magnificent opportunity to demonstrate that the Good Neighbor Policy would begin to be a reality." How?—"by naming a Catholic as the new ambassador."[26]

But such lingering hostility was the exception rather than the rule. Most Mexicans were prepared to forget Veracruz, once Daniels had revealed his genuine interest in their problems and aspirations, his sure grasp of the nuances of Mexican life. Some even took to defending his role at Veracruz on the ground that he was merely carrying out orders, and besides, had only wanted to save the Revolution from the conservative Huerta coup. After a small bomb had been exploded outside the Embassy in the summer of 1935, presumably by anti-American radicals, one Mexico City newspaper reminded the unknown perpetrators that Daniels, unlike some of his predecessors, was a fair-minded friend, not simply the guardian of American investments in Mexico. "What do you want, then," it asked angrily, "intelligent and humane ambassadors, or international police?"[27] The Mexican government, which had accepted Daniels' appointment only very reluctantly, had by 1936 so changed its mind about the despoiler of Veracruz that it wanted to give him the highest decoration it could bestow upon a foreigner.[28] The popular magazine *Hoy* accounted for the transformation thus:

Mr. Daniels arrived in Mexico and immediately disillusioned those melodramatic souls who had imagined him to be a terrible conquistador. Instead of the grip of a Caesar, there was a gentle hand, full of cordiality; in place of an overbearing frown and the fulgent eyes of Zeus, a limpid and tranquil gaze, eager to establish a friendly relationship. The memory of Veracruz would make one fear that he was a vulture; but talking to him for five minutes was sufficient to convince one that he was as gentle and peaceful as a dove .... No diplomat in Mexico was as important as Mr. Daniels, for behind him was the richest and most powerful country of the world. Nevertheless, far from demonstrating his power, the Ambassador kept it courteously from view, and anyone unfamiliar with him might have assumed that he was from a small nation. Never did he offend us with the threat of the crushing might of his country, as previous ambassadors and ministers used to do.[29]

Daniels' long political experience helped greatly to make him *simpático* with the mass of Mexicans. As is true of successful politicians everywhere, some of his actions were apt to strike sophisticates as undignified or even a trifle corny, but they were nonetheless effective in winning the hearts of ordinary folk. Wherever he went, and Daniels probably saw more of the Mexican countryside than any previous American envoy, he gave the impression that he was among friends, that he considered Mexico his second home. He sometimes jokingly used the expression "we

Mexicans" in his public speeches, to the evident delight of his
audience.[30] John Steinbeck reported that his Mexican camera-
man, Felipe, after photographing Daniels in action at a social
gathering, had remarked wonderingly: "He ate one tamal and
he ate two tamales and he ate three—*and he liked them.*" "You
cannot imagine how that won him," Steinbeck told the Ambassador.[31] Instinctively, Daniels seemed to know the right gesture,
the right phrase, to conquer Mexican suspicions. Mexicans sometimes commented that he was the first real representative of the
American people, as distinguished from their government, ever
to be sent to Mexico. The intelligentsia no doubt smiled when
Daniels donned his *charro* suit and sombrero, and Mrs. Daniels
her *China Poblana* dress (especially since the *China Poblana* cos-
tume had at one time been the uniform of courtesans), but ordinary Mexicans found the gesture appealing. Newspapers noted
approvingly that Daniels not only was an avid sports fan (aside
from bull fights), but that he abandoned diplomatic aloofness to
mingle with the the crowd and the players. "The Ambassador has
a face so kind, a smile so frank, and a handshake so sincere that
he attracts all to him," declared a Mexican sports writer after
observing Daniels at a football game. "He gives you the impression of being your grandfather or some dear old relative."[32] Dr.
Francisco Castillo Nájera, Daniels' opposite number in Washington, recalls that he once stopped an old woman on Calle Morrow
in Cuernavaca, where Ambassador Morrow had lived, and asked
her if she knew how the street had got its name. She nodded, and
replied, "Mr. Morrow was a good ambassador to the Mexicans
like Mr. Daniels."[33]

Mexican officials, dedicated to their Revolution, found Daniels
a kindred liberal spirit, youthful in his ideas, unafraid of reform
and social change. He spoke their language, even though he knew
scarcely a word of Spanish. But even more that this, his candor
and utter sincerity impressed them. "God made us neighbors; we
should try to become friends," he liked to say.[34] Ambassador Castillo Nájera remembers Daniels as "an astute and subtle psychol-

ogist, at the same time candid, ingenuous, incapable of believing in trickery; to him deception was monstrous."[35] "He was Washington's representative, yet he understood Mexico's problems."[36] Once when a Mexican had questioned something Daniels had said in a speech, Foreign Minister Ezequiel Padilla reminded him, "All the same, there is one thing that must not be forgotten— the good faith of Mr. Daniels is not open to question." Finance Minister Suárez, who was listening, said emphatically, "*absolutamente*."[37] Ambassador Daniels "always kept in constant touch with Mexican realities, without ever encroaching on our sovereignty," declared Padilla after Daniels resigned; the Ambassador had rightly earned the reputation of a Good Neighbor, but even more, "that of a great and sincere friend of Mexico."[38] When he learned of Daniels' decision to retire, former President Lázaro Cárdenas, living in provincial retirement, hastened to write him —"from this, your home"—of his concern for Mrs. Daniels' health. "Your great civic virtues leave here a deep imprint," Cárdenas asserted, "which will cause you to be remembered always as an exemplary man, noble and gentlemanly, who by his understanding attitude knew how to draw more closely together two peoples who aspire to the same destiny of peace and freedom."[39]

Daniels' last gesture as Ambassador was typical, and it won sentimental Mexican hearts, Misty-eyed, his cheeks smeared with the lipstick of girl employees of the Embassy, he turned in the doorway of the plane that was to take him home, and said softly to the assembled crowd of Mexican and American well-wishers, "¡Que Dios os bendiga!"—May God bless you! Commented one popular Mexico City newspaper: "It was seldom that we had the opportunity to hear him say a word in our language, but on saying farewell he wanted to do it that way, even at the risk of doing it badly, as a demonstration of affection for the people with whom he had lived for more than eight years."[40] Returning the compliment, two other papers headlined their farewell editorials in English, saying: "Good Bye, Mr. Daniels!" "Come Again, Mr. Daniels!"[41] But the comment Daniels would have appreciated most

came in Spanish, in the pro-government newspaper, *El Nacional.*
"To Daniels," it declared, "goes the glory of having been our best
interpreter."[42]

Farewells, like obituaries, are suspect, because at such times
one speeds even an enemy on his way with appropriate expressions of sadness and praise. But in Ambassador Daniels' case, the
Mexican esteem was genuine and lasting. Some time after Daniels
had retired, President Avila Camacho sent him a large silk Mexican flag with the admonition that he must "never live a day" without being under its folds.[43] In 1946 President-elect Miguel Alemán, who had first known Daniels while governor of the state of
Veracruz, instructed the Mexican Embassy in Washington to urge
the eighty-four-year-old former Ambassador to be Mexico's guest
at Alemán's inauguration. Daniels accepted with delight, but
asked that Alemán understand that his first social obligation when
he arrived would be to pay his respects to another old friend, Lázaro Cárdenas. Cárdenas, who does not give his friendship lightly,
least of all to American diplomats, arranged instead to call first on
Daniels, and later entertained him at a private dinner party, as
did former presidents Rodríguez and Avila Camacho.[44] Daniels'
return to Mexico in 1946 was thus in the nature of a real homecoming. The State Department thoughtfully delegated Stephen E.
Aguirre, an Embassy staff member throughout most of Daniels'
mission, to escort him to and from Mexico. Everywhere there
were affectionate Mexican *abrazos* to show that he had not been
forgotten. Indeed, American newsmen reported that he was
"practically lionized."[45]

The following year when Daniels published his warm autobiographical *Shirt-Sleeve Diplomat,* he told Salvador Duhart, a
prominent Mexican newspaperman, that his one hope was that the
book might some day be translated into Spanish so the Mexican
people could know how he felt about them. Duhart agreed to do
the translation, and former Ambassador Castillo Nájera offered
to write an introduction, but Daniels died in January, 1948, before
the Spanish edition was ready. *Novedades,* an influential Mexico
City paper with rather conservative leanings, declared editori-

ally: "Mexico has lost a great friend."[46] This was perhaps the finest tribute of all, for one of *Novedades'* popular columnists had taken some unflattering digs at Daniels at the time of his retirement.[47] Daniels would also have been gratified to know that *Novedades* arranged to serialize the Spanish version of his book—*Diplomático en mangas de camisa*—in advance of its publication in 1949.[48]

Daniels is still remembered with affection in Mexico. In 1957, when a new United States ambassador, Robert C. Hill, arrived in Mexico City, one paper greeted him with a graphic cartoon. It showed Daniels as the smiling representative of the Good Neighbor Policy, and Henry Lane Wilson, Díaz' and Huerta's partisan, clutching money bags, as the symbol of Dollar Diplomacy. Ambassador Hill was shown walking between them, and the caption read: "Choose Your Path, Mr. Hill."[49]

It is, of course, possible to view Josephus Daniels' mission to Mexico as an abysmal failure. From the standpoint of American private interests, it might be argued that his determination to be a good neighbor sometimes blinded him to the injustices of the Mexican Revolution. His interest in the growth of public education in Mexico affronted some Roman Catholics in both countries. He stood by while Mexico expropriated American-owned lands and oil resources without acting vigorously to save American property rights. He studiously refrained from applying the sort of diplomatic pressure that might have prevented further expropriations, and perhaps might have secured larger compensation for past seizures. American property-holders, used to an Embassy that went to great lengths to protect their interests, were understandably bitter about the new and unwelcome diplomacy of Ambassador Daniels.

Those who reject Daniels' policy of the good neighbor in favor of something more stern and forceful ignore the restless stirring, the yearning, the extraordinary appeal and vigor of nationalist movements in the underdeveloped parts of the world today. Some readjustment of the old order in Mexico was inevitable in the twentieth century. Those foreigners who were unwilling to compromise with the Mexican Revolution, who insisted on continuing to work *over* instead of *with* the Mexican nationalists, tended to lose more than those who made a more realistic adjustment. As one of Ambassador Daniels' staff members has wisely observed: "At times it seemed that some of the oil company administrators, standing in their foreign shoes, had never really had contact with the soil of Mexico."[50] If the oil men had been willing at the beginning of the dispute to make even a few of the concessions—now commonplace—which they offered when it was too late, there probably would have been no expropriation. And today the storage tanks at Tampico and Tehuantepec would still bear the brand names Huasteca and El Aguila, instead of Petróleos Mexicanos' proud slogan, *"al servicio de la patria."* Even after expropriation, the oil men would very likely have salvaged more from the debacle had they not adopted a stubborn, essentially all-or-nothing attiude. Mexico, with a timely assist from World War II, taught the oil companies an expensive lesson: never assume that your opponent has only deuces; his determination, his technical skill, and his staying power may surprise you.

Ambassador Daniels recognized that the days of forceful diplomacy, economic pressure, and old-style dollar imperialism were numbered. The United States could get much further with its smaller neighbors, he believed, by means of tact, discretion, patience, and understanding. He rejected the Big Brother approach for the friendship-between-equals approach of the Good Neighbor Policy. Daniels thought that the United States, with its wealth and highly developed industrial economy, could well afford to go more than halfway in helping countries like Mexico to lift themselves out of ignorance and feudalism. Consequently, he sought to encourage the sort of reforms that would build a Mexico the United States would find advantageous as a neighbor in the future. Some American interests with vested rights in the old Mexico would inevitably suffer, but in the long run a higher standard of living would bring a greatly expanded demand for American goods and capital in Mexico. Besides, Daniels was convinced that change was bound to come, and must be accepted gracefully in order to salvage whatever possible for the affected American interests.

Daniels' work in Mexico has generally been overlooked in favor of the more spectacular, if ephemeral, achievements of Dwight W. Morrow. Morrow is usually credited with the reorientation of American policy toward Mexico in the late 1920's that led to the Good Neighbor Policy and the restrained diplomacy of Josephus Daniels. Unquestionably, Morrow's work was important in improving Mexican-American relations, and he stands in dramatic contrast with his immediate predecessors. But while his genuine contributions must not be overlooked, it is misleading to assume that he and Daniels had the same outlook on their work. Both were astute students of Mexican psychology; both became close friends of influential Mexicans and developed a real regard and affection for the Mexican people. But there the similarity ends. Morrow used his influence to gain concessions for American business interests, and his friendship with Mexican leaders to resolve disputes in favor of American property rights. Daniels did so to a much lesser extent. His was a wider vision that looked beyond the interests of American investors to include the common interests of the people of both countries. As more than one Mexican has since observed, Dwight Morrow was the able and effective representative of American capital in Mexico; Daniels represented the American people.

Basic to Daniels' work in Mexico was his belief in the need for more people-to-people contacts between the two countries. For if the *rapprochement* between the two governments was to have any enduring significance, there must be more interest and understanding between the ordinary citizens of both nations. This conviction no doubt stemmed from the Ambassador's long political and newspaper experience. Under his direction, the Embassy made studies leading to exchange student programs between American and Mexican universities. He threw his support behind such cultural projects as the Townsend linguistic groups among Mexican Indians, the American summer work camps in Mexico, the Pan American Indian Congress at Pátzcuaro. He helped to secure the establishment of the Benjamin Franklin Library in Mexico City, which ultimately became one of the very first State Department-operated libraries and information services. He became one of the most eloquent spokesmen for Mexican tourism, in order to persuade more Americans to get to know their southern neighbors firsthand. He himself took advantage of every opportunity to reach the Mexican people at every level, in the provinces as well as the capital. Without doubt, his efforts would have been even more effective had he known Spanish, but in spite of this handicap, Daniels was an important pioneer in the field of international cultural exchange, now considered so significant a part of American foreign policy.

It is interesting to speculate on the alternatives to Daniels' diplomacy of patience and understanding. Under Cordell Hull the State Department flirted with a number of harsh policies designed to aid those American private interests adversely affected by Mexican reforms. To rescue the oil companies from a dilemma at least partly of their own making, the State Department wrote strong notes, applied economic pressure, and even toyed with the idea of a diplomatic break. None of these tactics was particularly effective, except at conjuring up the old Latin American image of the threatening Colossus of the North. Even more forceful measures, by an outright imperialistic administration, would probably not have succeeded in winning back the lost American properties in Mexico. Such efforts had failed to accomplish much under Woodrow Wilson and the Republican administrations of the 1920's. Only when, under the threat of World War II, it adopted Ambassador Daniels' neighborly approach, was the State Department able to get a settlement, realistic if not wholly satisfactory. The shocking thing about that settlement was that it, or perhaps even a better one, could probably have been achieved earlier, without risking the Good Neighbor Policy. Indeed, the State Department chose to embark on three years of fruitless get-tough diplomacy before undertaking an independent assessment of the major problem—the oil companies' monetary claims. In the end, the United States probably suffered an important strategic loss, for the 1941 settlement did not guarantee any sharing of Mexican oil output, something President Cárdenas had freely offered earlier.

To aid the oil men in their desire to return to Mexico, the State Department risked, it seems clear, the creation of a hostile southern neighbor, one that might have been neutral in World War II, a rallying point for anti-U. S. sentiment in Latin America, and a haven for German submarines, spies, and saboteurs. It jeopardized, too, the safety of other American private interests in Mexico, such as the multimillion-dollar investment in the mining industry, for a hostile Mexico might well have been emboldened by the initial Axis military triumphs to undertake further expropriations. Fortunately, thanks partly to Josephus Daniels, this disagreeable prospect never materialized. Mexico, instead, was a reliable ally in war, and it has since continued to justify Daniels' faith as an increasingly stable democracy and an expanding market for American trade and investment. In this case, neighborliness clearly paid off.

The Good Neighbor Policy, as this book makes plain, was never a single, neatly defined, universally applied doctrine. Ambassador Daniels worked with a humanitarian version, one that seemed closer to Franklin D. Roosevelt's definition, incidentally, than to the legalistic absorption in property rights of Cordell Hull and Sumner Welles. In short, the Good Neighbor Policy, like Topsy, just grew. And in the growing, much depended on the diplomats in the field, on their ideas and actions, and, in some instances, on their influence at the White House. In the case of Mexico—the crisis country that largely established the tone of good-neighbor diplomacy in these years—this last point was of special importance. For Welles has admitted that "at the personal insistence of President Roosevelt," the issues between Mexico and the United States were "not permitted to occasion any such high-handed and domineering attitude on the part of the United States as would undoubtedly have been adopted in earlier years."[51] Welles might have added that one important reason for this was that Roosevelt possessed both a dedicated disciple and an eloquent mentor in his Good Neighbor Ambassador in Mexico.

Mexico D.F., Apr. 6, 1938.

Dear Franklin :— I read last night (I
don't get much time for reading these hectic
days) a letter which Theodore Roosevelt
wrote to Taft on Dec. 22, 1910 :

"As I utterly disbelieve in the policy
of bluff, in national and international of
fairs or any violation of the frontier
maxim "Never draw unless you mean
to shoot" I do not believe in keeping any position
anywhere unless we can make good."
That sound maxim has present day
applications.

Faithfully
Josephus Daniels

REFERENCE MATTER

ESSAY ON SOURCES

This study is based primarily on manuscript sources which are described in a general way below. Specific references for all quotations and other important documents will be found in the footnotes. This essay does not attempt to describe every source consulted or mentioned in the footnotes. It merely seeks to survey in an orderly fashion the materials most significant and useful for an understanding of Mexican-American relations in the 1930's.

Manuscripts

The most important single source for any study of the career of Josephus Daniels is, of course, the massive collection of Daniels' private papers in the Library of Congress. Contained in approximately 1100 file boxes and open to scholarly use without restriction, the Daniels Papers are particularly rich in materials relating to the administrations of Woodrow Wilson and Franklin D. Roosevelt. For the purposes of this book the most useful parts of the collection are the separate files of Ambassador Daniels' correspondence with key Mexican and American officials between 1933 and 1942, though there are also many documents of importance in the bulkier general correspondence. The collection also contains a file of detailed and sometimes revealing diary letters that the Ambassador wrote once or twice a week for the benefit of his sons back home, as well as scrapbooks of newspaper clippings and other personal items. The many hundreds of photographs which accompanied the collection are now housed in the Library's Print and Photograph Division.

While Ambassador Daniels retained some of his official despatches in his private papers, during his incumbency the Mexico City Embassy sent more than 14,000 despatches to the State Department and received in return an equally impressive number of instructions. Most of these communications are to be found only in the official records of the Department. They are invaluable in showing not only how Ambassador Daniels reacted to specific diplomatic problems but also how his superiors reacted to Daniels and his ideas. Here are outlined in detail many of the policy disputes between Daniels and his State Department chiefs, Cordell Hull and Sumner Welles. The records for the period through 1939 are now housed in the National Archives; those for more recent years are still in the possession of the Department of State. In both instances the Department grants prior permission and reviews notes on materials dealing with the period after 1930.

The Papers of Franklin D. Roosevelt in the Roosevelt Library at Hyde Park constitute another major manuscript source. The Roosevelt Papers are a useful supplement to the Daniels Papers because they include a number of holograph letters from Daniels that are not in the Daniels collection. The Roosevelt Papers, now partially indexed, also include material indicating the President's attitude toward Daniels, various problems in Mexican-American relations, and Good Neighbor diplomacy in general.

Other manuscript collections of lesser value for this study include: the William E. Borah Papers in the Library of Congress, useful in connection with the motivation behind the Borah Resolution of January 31, 1935, to investigate religious persecution in Mexico; the Arthur Bliss Lane Papers in the Sterling Memorial Library, Yale University, for the views of a career diplomat who served under Ambassadors Morrow and Clark in Mexico and for six months as Daniels' first Counselor; the James R. Sheffield Papers in the Sterling Memorial Library, Yale University, for the views of one of Ambassador Daniels' recent predecessors; and the presently scanty and disappointing Donald R. Richberg Papers in the Library of Congress, for some light on the views and activities of a prominent representative of Standard Oil of New Jersey after the expropriation crisis of 1938.

Newspapers and Periodicals

The *New York Times* is by far the best American newspaper source on Ambassador Daniels' work in Mexico, not only because of its helpful index but also because of its unusually thorough coverage. Most other American newspapers ordinarily showed little interest in Latin America and relied on the wire services to supply the stories they did print. The *New York Times*, however, maintained a resident correspondent in Mexico City during Ambassador Daniels' entire tenure and in addition published the reports of two of the wire services. Throughout late 1937 and 1938 the dispatches of *Times* correspondent Frank L. Kluckhohn often displayed a marked anti-Mexican bias that led to protests by the Cárdenas Government and eventually to his expulsion from the country. Greater objectivity was achieved by Kluckhohn's successors, Raymond Daniell and Arnaldo Cortesi.

Ambassador Daniels' newspaper, the Raleigh *News and Observer,* is useful chiefly in showing some of his extracurricular interests while a diplomat. After he became Ambassador the paper had a policy of printing nothing on Mexico except what originated with the wire services or other newspapers. Daniels wrote some book reviews and offered a few editorial suggestions in these years, but by and large he left the paper's management in the hands of his son Jonathan, who stayed clear of the editorial controversies involving his father and Mexico. Other North Carolina newspapers, such as the Charlotte *Observer*, the *Greensboro Daily News*, and the *Winston-Salem Journal*, sometimes took editorial notice of Daniels' work or defended him from attack.

Useful contemporary comment may also be found in the *Wall Street Journal* and the New York *Journal of Commerce*, both of which reflected business sentiment, and the *Nation* and the *New Republic*, which viewed Mexican matters from the sympathetic left. The *Oil and Gas Journal* published useful data on the Mexican oil industry after its nationalization in 1938. The American Catholic press was intensely interested in Ambassador Daniels and Mexico during the years 1934–1936. The Catholic periodicals most intemperate in their criticism of Daniels and of Mexican religious and educational policies include: the *Brooklyn Tablet*, the *Baltimore Catholic Review*, *Our Sunday Visitor*, a widely circulated midwestern weekly, and *Light*, the monthly publication of the International Catholic Truth Society. *America*, the Jesuit weekly, sparked the American Catholic drive against Daniels and waged intermittent editorial warfare against Mexican religious policies. *Columbia*, the monthly organ of the Knights of Columbus, regularly criticized Daniels and the Roosevelt administration for their failure to speak out against alleged Mexican outrages. Liberal Catholic sentiment on the Mexican issue is reflected in *Commonweal*. Other useful Catholic periodicals are *Catholic Action*, the *Catholic Mind*, *Ave Maria*, *Pax*, and *Truth*.

Mexican newspapers throughout the country showed considerable interest in Ambassador Daniels and his Good Neighbor diplomacy, but the most sustained coverage is naturally to be found in the Mexico City press. The large Mexico City dailies must, however, be used with the knowledge that they were at least partly responsive to government pressure in editorial matters. *Excélsior* and *El Universal*, the two largest papers in Daniels' day and still highly successful commercial enterprises, generally provided thorough news coverage along with an English language page and a cautiously conservative point of view pleasing to Mexican businessmen and the sizable American and British colonies in the capital. *El Nacional*, the daily organ of the ruling National Revolutionary Party, consistently reflected the attitude of the government.

Of the two dailies established while Ambassador Daniels was in
Mexico City, *El Popular* displayed a left-wing socialist orientation,
while *Novedades* generally took a more conservative point of view.
La Prensa, a somewhat sensational tabloid, occasionally took editorial
notice of diplomatic matters. Three irregular biweekly papers are
worth mention because of their right-wing orientation and their strong
criticism of both Ambassador Daniels and the Mexican government.
Both *Omega* and *La Palabra* liked to remind their rather limited
audiences of Daniels' connection with the American occupation of
Veracruz, while the small Catholic paper, *El Hombre Libre,* generally
critical of the government, led the attack on Daniels after his famous
Seminar speech endorsing public education in 1934. The sophisticated
weekly magazine *Hoy* sometimes commented editorially on Daniels
and Mexican-American relations.

Published Documents and Official Records

Documents pertaining to the diplomatic relations of the United
States and Mexico are to be found in the Department of State's ambitious and valuable series, *Foreign Relations of the United States* (Washington: Government Printing Office), of which the volumes dealing
with Mexico are presently complete through 1939. The Department
edits the text of documents published in *Foreign Relations* with
scrupulous regard for accuracy, but it occasionally omits significant
items (see, for example, note 46 of Chapter VI). Other useful State
Department publications are its *Executive Agreement Series,* containing
the text of executive agreements between the United States and other
nations, and its *Press Releases,* superseded by the *Bulletin* in 1939,
containing the text of press conference and other remarks by Department officials. The State Department has also published some interesting German archival material on Mexico in its continuing series,
Documents on German Foreign Policy, 1918–1945 (Washington:
Government Printing Office). The *Congressional Record* for the years
covered by this study contains a wealth of comment on Mexican-
American relations, some of it specifically directed at Ambassador
Daniels.

The Mexican government unfortunately has no publications program
comparable to the State Department's *Foreign Relations* series. The
texts of laws and official decrees are regularly published in the *Diario
Oficial* and from time to time the government has issued other important materials. Thus the Spanish royal ordinances and later laws
regulating land ownership and mining may be found in Secretaría de
Industria, Comercio y Trabajo, *Documentos relacionados con la legis-*

lación petrolera mexicana (México: Talleres Gráficos, 1919), and many of the relevant documents pertaining to the dispute that led to the oil expropriation of 1938 are reproduced in *Mexico's Oil: a Compilation of Official Documents in the Conflict of Economic Order in the Petroleum Industry, with an Introduction Summarizing Its Causes and Consequences* (Mexico City: Government of Mexico, 1940). Other official material on the oil dispute is in *The True Facts about the Expropriation of the Oil Companies' Properties in Mexico* (Mexico City: Government of Mexico, 1940), including records of the Richberg negotiations; and Secretaría de Relaciones Exteriores, *Tribunales extranjeros reconocen el indiscutible derecho con que México expropio los intereses petroleros* (México: Talleres Gráficos de la Nación, 1940), concerning legal cases involving the shipment of Mexican oil abroad. The controversial six-year plan of 1934 is reproduced in Partido Nacional Revolucionario, *Plan sexenal del P.N.R.* (México: 1934). The text of the notes leading to the diplomatic break between Mexico and Great Britain in 1938 is given in *Correspondence with the Mexican Government Regarding the Expropriation of Oil Properties in Mexico*, Cmd. 5758 (London: His Majesty's Stationery Office, 1938).

The various pronouncements of President Roosevelt on the Good Neighbor Policy are included in *The Public Papers and Addresses of Franklin D. Roosevelt*, Samuel I. Rosenman, comp. (New York: Random House, 1938–50), 13 vols. A not always judicious or complete selection of the correspondence between Daniels and his onetime assistant over the years is given in *Roosevelt and Daniels: a Friendship in Politics*, Carroll Kilpatrick, ed. (Chapel Hill: University of North Carolina Press, 1952).

Memoirs and Biographies

While he was in Mexico Ambassador Daniels began work on what turned out to be five somewhat disjointed and rambling volumes of autobiography: two on his early life in North Carolina and his introduction to Democratic politics, two on his service as Secretary of the Navy in the Wilson administration, and one on his work in Mexico. The last was of course the most useful for this study, though the other volumes helped greatly to fill in the picture of the man and his ideas. Daniels' autobiographical reminiscences suffer from the ordinary human failings of faulty memory, omission, and occasional distortion, but they nevertheless constitute an important source of information on many subjects. See Josephus Daniels, *Tar Heel Editor; Editor in Politics; The Wilson Era: Years of Peace; The Wilson Era: Years of War and After;* and *Shirt-Sleeve Diplomat* (Chapel Hill: University of North Carolina Press, 1939–47), 5 vols. The volume on Mexico also appeared in an abridged Spanish edition with a revealing foreword by former Ambassador Francisco Castillo Nájera under the title *Diplomático en mangas de camisa,* Salvador Duhart, translator (México: Talleres Gráficos de la Nación, 1949).

Several other participants have also prepared accounts outlining their roles in the events of this period. Both Cordell Hull, *Memoirs* (New York: Macmillan, 1948), 2 vols., and Sumner Welles, *The Time for Decision* (New York: Harper, 1944) touch briefly and incompletely on certain aspects of Mexican-American relations during the Roosevelt administration. Donald R. Richberg's autobiographical *My Hero: the Indiscreet Memoirs of an Eventful but Unheroic Life* (New York: Putnam, 1954) supplements his earlier account of his unsuccessful negotiations with the Mexican government on behalf of the oil companies in Richberg, *The Mexican Oil Seizure* (New York: Standard Oil Company of New Jersey, 1940).

The number of useful biographies of prominent Mexican and American leaders of the twentieth century is rapidly increasing. The work of Ambassador Dwight W. Morrow in Mexico between 1927 and 1929 is covered in sketchy and uncritical fashion in Harold Nicolson's official life, *Dwight Morrow* (New York: Harcourt, Brace, 1935). Alan S. Everest's specialized study, *Morgenthau, the New Deal, and Silver: a Story of Pressure Politics* (New York: King's Crown Press, 1950), contains an interesting chapter on the Roosevelt administration's silver policy and Mexico, spiced with revealing comments from the famous and currently restricted Morgenthau diaries. Don Lohbeck's authorized biography, *Patrick J. Hurley* (Chicago: Regnery, 1956), is a completely uncritical journalistic portrayal of its subject, but contains some interesting information, presumably from Hurley's files, regarding his negotiations with Mexico on behalf of the Sinclair oil interests. Kenneth E. Trombley, *The Life and Times of a Happy Liberal: a Biography of Morris Llewellyn Cooke* (New York: Harper, 1954), recounts the experiences of the United States expert named to appraise the value of the expropriated American oil properties in Mexico in 1941.

Carleton Beals, *Porfirio Díaz: Dictator of Mexico* (Philadelphia: Lippincott, 1932), gives background for the Mexican Revolution in a portrait now generally regarded as inaccurate and biased. The best full-length English biography of the initial leader of the Mexican Revolution is Stanley R. Ross, *Francisco I. Madero: Apostle of Mexican Democracy* (New York: Columbia University Press, 1955), which is complemented by Charles C. Cumberland, *The Mexican Revolution: Genesis under Madero* (Austin: University of Texas Press, 1952). Emile J. Dillon, *President Obregón: a World Reformer* (Boston: Small, Maynard, 1923), and Francisco Javier Gaxiola, *El presidente Rodríguez, 1932–1934* (México: Editorial "Cultura," 1938), are flattering portraits of two of Mexico's post-revolutionary presidents. William C. Townsend's completely uncritical and indifferently written *Lazaro Cardenas: Mexican Democrat* (Ann Arbor: Wahr, 1952), is of less value than the earlier incomplete review by Nathaniel and Sylvia Weyl, *The Reconquest of Mexico: the Years of Lázaro Cárdenas* (New York: Oxford University Press, 1939).

General Works

There are a number of useful general works in English on the subject of Mexico and Mexican-American relations. Herbert Corwin, *These Are the Mexicans* (New York: Harcourt, Brace, 1947), and Lesley Byrd Simpson, *Many Mexicos* (New York: Putnam, 1941, revised, 1952) are good introductions to Mexico. Perhaps the best one-volume history of Mexico in English is Henry B. Parkes, *A History of Mexico* (Boston: Houghton Mifflin, 1950). Now outdated in parts and written for the non-specialist, it covers Mexican development through the administration of Lázaro Cárdenas to 1940. Ernest H. Gruening, *Mexico and Its Heritage* (New York: Appleton-Century-Crofts, 1928), is a dated sympathetic account of Mexican history through the first fifteen years of the Revolution. Frank Tannenbaum, *Mexico: the Struggle for Peace and Bread* (New York: Knopf, 1950), attempts with considerable success to explain the development of the Mexican Revolution in terms of long-standing problems stemming from the Conquest. A heated view of Mexico by an American Catholic is to be found in Joseph H. Schlarman, *Mexico: Land of Volcanoes* (Milwaukee: Bruce, 1950).

For the diplomatic relations between the United States and Mexico, Samuel F. Bemis, *The Latin American Policy of the United States: An Historical Interpretation* (New York: Harcourt, Brace, 1943), is the standard general survey. Specifically concerned with Mexican-American relations are J. Fred Rippy, *The United States and Mexico* (New York: Crofts, 1931), and James M. Callahan, *American Foreign Policy in Mexican Relations* (New York: Macmillan, 1932), both pioneer works now partly superseded by Howard F. Cline, *The United States and Mexico* (Cambridge: Harvard University Press, 1953). The latter work treats economic and cultural relations between the two countries as well as diplomatic relations. Charles W. Hackett, *The Mexican Revolution and the United States, 1910–1926* (Boston: World Peace Foundation, 1926), is a still useful specialized survey.

Specialized Studies

In addition to the works already mentioned, many of which treat special aspects of Mexican history or Mexican-American relations, there are a number of other useful specialized studies. There is unfortunately no authoritative history of the Mexican Revolution. A good Mexican work on the subject is Miguel Alessio Robles, *Historia política de la Revolución* (Mexico City, 1946). Frank Tannenbaum, *The Mexican Agrarian Revolution* (New York: Macmillan, 1929) and *Peace By Revolution* (New York: Columbia University Press, 1933) are somewhat dated sympathetic accounts by an American scholar who influenced Ambassador Daniels' views. Tannenbaum's more recent views are given in his article, "Reflections on the Mexican Revolution," *Journal of International Affairs*, IX (1955), 37–46. Anita Brenner and George Leighton, *The Wind That Swept Mexico: The History of the Mexican Revolution, 1910–1942* (New York: Harper, 1943) is a short popular account with some excellent photographs. René Marchand, *L'Effort democratique du Mexique* (Paris: Editions Fistier, 1938) is a French socialist view. For a defense of the Revolution by a prominent Mexican official, see Ramón Beteta, *Economic and Social Program of Mexico (a Controversy)* (Mexico City, 1935), and *The Mexican Revolution: a Defense* (Mexico City: DAPP, 1937). Emilio Portes Gil, *The Mexican Schools and the Peasantry* (Mexico City: Ministry of Foreign Relations, 1936), gives the official government justification of its educational policies at the height of the American Catholic protests against Mexico's "socialistic" education. For other titles on the subject of Mexican education and Church-State relations, see footnote 1 of Chapter IV.

On Mexican agrarian policy, Eyler N. Simpson, *The Ejido: Mexico's Way Out* (Chapel Hill: University of North Carolina Press, 1937) is a sympathetic and comprehensive scholarly treatment of the early efforts toward agrarian collectivism. Nathan L. Whetten, *Rural Mexico* (Chicago: University of Chicago Press, 1948), gives more recent data on land reform. Marjorie R. Clark, *Organized Labor in Mexico* (Chapel Hill: University of North Carolina Press, 1935) is a good treatment of the early development of the Mexican trade union movement after the Revolution but is now dated. The problem of Mexican indebtedness after the Revolution is considered by Edgar Turlington, *Mexico and Her Foreign Creditors* (New York: Columbia University

Press, 1930), while Abraham H. Feller, *The Mexican Claims Commissions, 1923–1934* (New York: Macmillan, 1935), discusses the handling of claims by the various international claims commissions to 1934. Both works are dated but contain useful data. The record of the Bucareli Conference of 1923 is to be found in Department of State, *Proceedings of the United States–Mexican Commission Convened in Mexico City, May 14, 1923* (Washington: Government Printing Office, 1925).

For background on the struggle for control over Mexican oil, see Ludwell Denny, *We Fight for Oil* (New York: Knopf, 1928). The Morrow-Calles oil agreement of the late 1920's is discussed by an informed participant in J. Reuben Clark, Jr., "The Oil Settlement with Mexico," *Foreign Affairs*, VI (July, 1928), 600–614. Several of the official publications by the Mexican government on the oil controversy have already been mentioned in the section on "Published Documents and Official Records." Jesús Silva Herzog, *Petróleo mexicano: historia de un problema* (México: Fondo de Cultura Económica, 1941) is a useful Mexican account of the oil controversy by the chief author of the experts' report on the 1936–38 labor dispute and later the director of the government agency operating the expropriated industry. The oil companies' side of the dispute is thoroughly covered in a number of books and pamphlets issued by the chief American concern, Standard Oil of New Jersey, of which the following are a fair sample: *Mexico: Labor Controversy, 1936–1938* (1938); *They Took What They Wanted* (1939); *Diplomatic Protection* (1939); *Whose Oil It It? The Question of Subsoil Rights in Mexico* (1939); *The Reply to Mexico* (1940); *Investments and Trade* [1940]; *The Fine Art of Squeezing* (1940); *Denials of Justice* [1940]; *Present Status of the Mexican Oil "Expropriations," 1940* (1940); *Confiscation or Expropriation? Mexico's Seizure of the Foreign-Owned Oil Industry* (1940). The Jersey Standard trade organ, *The Lamp*, is also a valuable source for company opinion. Other contemporary works reflecting the companies' viewpoint are William E. McMahon, *Two Strikes and Out* (Garden City: Country Life Press, 1939); Roscoe B. Gaither, *Expropriation in Mexico: The Facts and the Law* (New York: Morrow, 1940); and John Serocold, *Oil in Mexico* (London: Chapman & Hall, 1938), the latter a critical British view of the Mexican expropriation.

The best study in English of Mexico's operation of the expropriated oil industry is J. Richard Powell, *The Mexican Petroleum Industry, 1938–1950* (Berkeley and Los Angeles: University of California Press, 1956). The same author's article, "Some Financial Aspects of the Mexican Petroleum Industry, 1938–1950," *Inter-American Economic Af-*

fairs, VI (Winter, 1952), 14–31, is a helpful summary. Harvey O'Connor, "Mexican Oil: a Study in Nationalization," *Monthly Review,* IV (December, 1952), 263–74, enthusiastically describes the progress of Mexico's nationalized oil industry after World War II while minimizing its problems. José Domingo Lavin, *Petróleo* (México: E.D.I.A.P.S.A., 1950), is a Mexican account of some of the industry's problems after expropriation. Some useful material, presented in a pedestrian fashion, is to be found in William S. McCrea, "A Comparative Study of the Mexican Oil Expropriation (1938) and the Iranian Oil Nationalization (1951)" (unpublished Ph.D. dissertation, Georgetown University, 1955). Mexico's early difficulties and success in operating the oil industry in the face of the companies' boycott are discussed at length in three articles by Ruth Sheldon, "Mexico Faced Many Problems in Operating Refineries," "Poza Rica Field Backbone of Oil Industry in Mexico," and "Marketing Harasses Mexican Oil Industry Officials," *Oil and Gas Journal,* XXXVIII (May 18, 25, and June 1, 1939), 39–41, 50; 26–29, 104; and 18–20. The diplomatic settlement of the oil dispute in 1941–42 is treated in Harlow S. Person, *Mexican Oil: Symbol of Recent Trends in International Relations* (New York: Harper, 1942). An excellent analysis of the legal, economic, and international aspects of the various Mexican expropriations, including the oil industry, may be found in Wendell C. Gordon, *The Expropriation of Foreign-Owned Property in Mexico* (Washington: American Council on Public Affairs, 1941).

There is as yet no authoritative history of the Good Neighbor Policy. Laurence Duggan, *The Americas: the Search for Hemisphere Security* (New York: Holt, 1949), gives the views of an influential State Department official under the Roosevelt administration. Edward A. Guerrant, *Roosevelt's Good Neighbor Policy* (Albuquerque: University of New Mexico Press, 1950), is based chiefly on published materials and throws no new light on Mexican-American relations under the Good Neighbor Policy. Some interesting Mexican reactions to the Good Neighbor Policy are given in Oscar Morineau, *The Good Neighbor* (Mexico City, 1938); Tarsicio Marquez Padilla, *Consideraciones sobre la interpretación mexicana de la política del buen vecino* (México: Universidad Nacional Autónoma de México [1944?]); and Francisco Cuevas Cancino, *Roosevelt y la Buena Vecindad* (México: Fondo de Cultura Económica, 1954).

The following articles by the present author, all based chiefly on manuscript sources, discuss at greater length several of the aspects of Ambassador Daniels' career covered in this book: "Josephus Daniels as a Reluctant Candidate," *North Carolina Historical Review,* XXXIII

(October, 1956), 457–82; "American Catholics and Mexican Anticlericalism, 1933–1936," *Mississippi Valley Historical Review,* XLV (September, 1958), 201–30; "A Southern Progressive Looks at the New
Deal," *Journal of Southern History,* XXIV (May, 1958), 151–76; and
"Interpreting the New Good Neighbor Policy: the Cuban Crisis of
1933," *Hispanic American Historical Review,* XXXIX (November,
1959), 538–67.

The following manuscript collections are referred to in abbreviated form in the notes:

The Papers of Josephus Daniels (Library of Congress).

The Papers of William E. Borah (Library of Congress).

The Papers of Donald R. Richberg (Library of Congress).

The Papers of Franklin D. Roosevelt (Roosevelt Library, Hyde Park, N.Y.).

The Papers of Arthur Bliss Lane (Sterling Memorial Library, Yale University).

The Papers of James R. Sheffield (Sterling Memorial Library, Yale University).

The Papers of the Department of State (in the National Archives for the years through 1939, and thereafter still in the possession of the Department). These papers are ordinarily cited in the notes as DS, followed by the file number of the particular document. Where the Department of State has published the text of a document in its *Foreign Relations* series, the published source is cited for the convenience of the reader.

Chapter I

1 *The Public Papers and Addresses of Franklin D. Roosevelt,* comp. Samuel I. Rosenman (New York: Random House, 1938), II, 14.

2 Franklin D. Roosevelt, Washington, to Eleanor Roosevelt (August 5, 1914), in *F.D.R.: His Personal Letters, 1905–1928,* ed. Elliott Roosevelt (New York: Duell, Sloan and Pierce, 1948), p. 243.

3 Roosevelt, Albany, to Josephus Daniels, June 16, 1932, Daniels Papers.

4 Daniels, Raleigh, to Roosevelt, September 26, 1932, Daniels Papers. See also *New York Times,* September 27, 1932.

5 Roosevelt, Albany, to Daniels, November 17, 1932, Daniels Papers.

6 Daniels, Raleigh, to O. Max Gardner, January 14, 1933, O. Max

Gardner Papers (in possession of the Gardner family). I am indebted to Mr. William M. Geer of Chapel Hill for calling this letter to my attention.

7 Daniels to Roosevelt, undated [January, 1933], Daniels Papers.

8 H. E. C. Bryant, Washington, to the *News and Observer,* January 29, 1933, Daniels Papers.

9 Raleigh *News and Observer,* February 8, 1933.

10 Josephus Daniels, *Shirt-Sleeve Diplomat* (Chapel Hill: University of North Carolina Press, 1947), p. 16.

11 *Ibid.*

12 Daniels to Roosevelt, March 3, 1933, Daniels Papers (from Daniels' rough draft).

13 Daniels, *Shirt-Sleeve Diplomat,* p. 17.

14 Charlotte *Observer,* March 7 and 11, 1933; *New York Times,* March 11, 1933; Daniels, Raleigh, to John B. Glenn, February 21, 1933; Hiram R. Williamson, Dallas, to Daniels, March 4, 1933, Daniels Papers.

15 Isaac C. Wright, Wilmington, to Daniels, March 11, 1933, Daniels Papers.

16 Cordell Hull, *Memoirs* (New York: Macmillan, 1948), I, 182.

17 Daniels, Mexico City, to Lister Hill, October 10, 1938, Daniels Papers; Daniels, *Shirt-Sleeve Diplomat,* p. 22.

18 James A. Farley, New York, to the author, April 29, 1953. See also Farley, *Jim Farley's Story: the Roosevelt Years* (New York: Whittlesey House, 1948), pp. 97–98.

19 See Daniels, Mexico City, to Cordell Hull, September 25 and October 4, 1933; Daniels, Mexico City, to William E. Dodd, January 12, 1934, Daniels Papers; Daniels, *The Wilson Era: Years of Peace* (Chapel Hill: University of North Carolina Press, 1944), pp. 180–207.

20 See Daniels, Washington, to Moorfield Storey, June 11 and October 24, 1913; Daniels, Washington, to Erving Winslow, October 23, 1913; Daniels, Washington, to Newton D. Baker, November 15 and 26, 1918, Daniels Papers.

21 Luis Matus, Luis Espinoza, Ignacio Mori, and the Governors of the Eight Towns, translation of undated manifesto, Daniels Papers.

22 *Chicago Tribune,* May 8, 1914.

23 Daniels, Washington, to Woodrow Wilson, June 10, 1918, Daniels Papers.

24 Daniels, Washington, to Wilson, December 4, 1919, Daniels Papers; Daniels, *The Wilson Era: Years of War and After*

(Chapel Hill: University of North Carolina Press, 1946), pp. 521–23.

25 Raleigh *News and Observer*, April 23, September 1, November 2, and December 31, 1923, October 1, 1927, and October 6, 1931; Daniels, Raleigh, to *Literary Digest*, January 19, 1927, Daniels Papers.

26 Bernard M. Baruch, New York, to Daniels, March 16, 1936; M. A. Boyle, New York, to Daniels, April 29, 1936, Daniels Papers.

27 William B. Oliver, Washington, to Daniels, March 13, 1933, Daniels Papers.

28 Arthur Bliss Lane, Mexico City, to Daniels, March 28, 1933, Daniels Papers; Daniels, Washington, to Lane, undated [April, 1933], Lane papers.

29 *Greensboro Daily News,* March 15, 1933.

30 Lane, Mexico City, to Arthur H. Springer, March 9, 1933, Lane Papers.

31 Raleigh *News and Observer,* March 20, 1933.

32 Quoted in Daniels, *Shirt-Sleeve Diplomat,* p. 6.

33 *Ibid.,* pp. 4, 7–8; *New York Times,* March 29 and 30, 1933.

34 Daniels, Mexico City, to Roosevelt, November 17, 1936, Daniels Papers; Daniels, *Shirt-Sleeve Diplomat,* p. 6.

35 Quoted in Daniels, Mexico City, to Roosevelt, November 17, 1936, Daniels Papers; Daniels, *Shirt-Sleeve Diplomat,* pp. 8–9.

36 Arthur Bliss Lane, Mexico City, to Herschel V. Johnson, March 29, 1933, Lane Papers.

37 See, for example, *Philadelphia Inquirer,* March 19, 1933; *New York Sun,* March 14, 1933; New York *Herald Tribune,* March 14, 1933.

38 Hartford *Courant,* March 15, 1933; *Winston-Salem Journal,* March 14, 1933; Gerald W. Johnson, "Josephus in Mexico," Baltimore *Evening Sun,* March 16, 1933.

39 Daniels, Mexico City, to Roosevelt, November 17, 1936, Daniels Papers; Herschel V. Johnson, Washington, to Lane, March 24, 1933, Lane Papers; Daniels, *Shirt-Sleeve Diplomat,* p. 7.

40 Raleigh *News and Observer,* March 31, 1933; *New York Times,* March 31, 1933.

41 Raleigh *News and Observer,* April 7, 1933.

42 Quoted in Lane, Mexico City, to H. V. Johnson, March 29, 1933, Lane Papers.

43 Dr. M. J. Ferguson, Mexico City, to Roosevelt, March 13, 1933, Daniels Papers.

44 *El Universal* (Mexico City), March 29 and 30, 1933; *New York*

Times, March 29, 1933; *Omega* (Mexico City), March 31, April 2 and 7, 1933.

45   *El Universal,* March 26, 1933.
46   Quoted in Daniels, *Shirt-Sleeve Diplomat,* p. 6.
47   *La Palabra* (Mexico City), March 11, 1933.
48   *New York Times,* March 14, 1933; *El Nacional* (Mexico City), March 14, 1933.
49   Quoted in Arthur Constantine, Mexico City, to Tom Wallace, undated [April, 1933], Daniels Papers.
50   Lane, Mexico City, to James T. Williams, March 29, 1933, Lane Papers.
51   *La Palabra,* March 13, 1933; *Omega,* March 17, 1933; *Excélsior* (Mexico City), March 20, 1933.
52   Quoted in Daniels, *Shirt-Sleeve Diplomat,* pp. 9–10.
53   *New York Times,* March 29, 1933; *La Palabra,* March 29, 1933.
54   Quoted in *New York Times,* March 29, 1933.
55   *La Palabra,* April 1, 1933.
56   *Omega,* March 31, April 2, 7, and 10, 1933.
57   Lane, Mexico City, to Daniels, March 28, 1933, Daniels Papers; *New York Times,* March 30, 1933.
58   Daniels, Mexico City, to Roosevelt, April 19 and May 15, 1933, Daniels Papers.
59   *New York Times,* April 5, 1933; *El Universal,* April 5, 1933; *La Palabra,* April 5, 1933.
60   *Omega,* April 7, 1933. See also *La Palabra,* April 6, 1933; *Excélsior,* April 6, 1933; *El Nacional,* April 6, 1933; *La Prensa* (Mexico City), April 6, 1933.
61   *New York Times,* March 30, 1933; New York *Daily Mirror,* quoted in Raleigh *News and Observer,* March 30, 1933; Alvaro Espinoza, New York, to the editor, *New York Times,* April 4, 1933.
62   Charlotte *Observer,* March 30, 1933.
63   Durham *Sun,* March 30, 1933.
64   *Textile Bulletin,* XLIV (April 6, 1933), 15.
65   *Greensboro Daily News,* March 31, 1933.
66   Raleigh *News and Observer,* April 12, 1933. See also *El Universal,* April 12, 1933; *Excélsior,* April 12, 1933.
67   Quoted in Daniels, *Shirt-Sleeve Diplomat,* p. 11. See also Daniels, Mexico City, to Roosevelt, April 18, 1933; Daniels, Mexico City, to Cordell Hull, April 19, 1933, Daniels Papers; *New York Times,* April 13, 1933.
68   Daniels, Diary, April 15, 1933; Daniels, Mexico City, to Roose-

velt, April 18, 1933, Daniels Papers; Daniels, *Shirt-Sleeve Diplomat,* pp. 12–14.

69 *New York Times,* April 15, 1933; *Excélsior,* April 15, 1933. See also *New York Times,* April 16, 1933; *El Universal,* April 16, 1933; *Excélsior,* April 16, 1933.

70 Robert Hammond Murray, Mexico City, to Daniels, April 4, 1933, Daniels Papers; *New York Times,* April 15 and 16, 1933; *El Universal,* April 16, 1933; *Excélsior,* April 16, 1933; *La Prensa,* April 16, 1933; *La Palabra,* April 16, 1933; Daniels, *Shirt-Sleeve Diplomat,* p. 13.

71 Daniels, Mexico City, to Roosevelt, April 18, 1933, Daniels Papers.

72 Arthur Constantine, Mexico City, to Tom Wallace, undated [April, 1933], Daniels Papers. This was also the reaction of the Mexico City correspondent of the *Chicago Daily News,* who cabled his paper that neither the Ambassador's American friends nor the Mexican police "needed to have worried about him .... Two hours after his arrival Daniels had won the esteem of Mexican reporters," *Chicago Daily News,* April 17, 1933.

73 *Excélsior,* April 17, 1933; *La Palabra,* April 17, 1933; *New York Times,* April 18, 1933. See also *La Prensa,* April 17, 1933; *El Universal Gráfico* (Mexico City), April 17, 1933; *El Nacional,* April 16, 1933.

74 Lane, Mexico City, to J. Reuben Clark, May 9, 1933, Lane Papers.

75 Daniels, Mexico City, to Roosevelt, April 18, 1933, Daniels Papers; *New York Times,* April 18, 1933; Daniels, *Shirt-Sleeve Diplomat,* p. 14.

76 Agnes D. Rogers, Raleigh, to Addie Daniels, July 12, 1933, Daniels Papers.

77 *Omega,* April 17 and 19, 1933.

78 Daniels, Mexico City, to Roosevelt, April 19, 1933, Daniels Papers.

79 Daniels, *Shirt-Sleeve Diplomat,* pp. 25–26; *New York Times,* April 25, 1933.

80 Daniels, *Shirt-Sleeve Diplomat,* pp. 519–20.

81 Daniels, Mexico City, to Roosevelt, April 26, 1933, Daniels Papers.

82 *Omega,* April 28, 1933; Jesús Guisa y Azevedo, "Solicitamos Empleo de Mr. Daniels," *La Palabra,* April 27, 1933; *Excélsior,* April 26, 1933; *El Universal,* April 26, 1933. See also *El Nacional,* April 26, 1933. Daniels thought well enough of the *El*

Universal editorial to have it reprinted in the *News and Observer* of May 5, 1933.

83 H. E. C. Bryant, Washington, to Daniels, May 5, 1933, Daniels Papers.

CHAPTER II

1 Daniels, Mexico City, to Claude G. Bowers, August 31, 1934, Daniels Papers.

2 Frank Tannenbaum, *Mexico: the Struggle for Peace and Bread* (New York: Knopf, 1950), pp. 137, 140; Cora B. Older, *William Randolph Hearst: American* (New York: D. Appleton-Century, 1936), pp. 64–65, 434.

3 *Mexico's Oil* (Mexico City: Government of Mexico, 1940), pp. xxxii–xxxiii; Robert G. Cleland, *The Mexican Yearbook, 1920–1921* (Los Angeles: Mexican Yearbook Publishing Co., 1922), pp. 290–97; *New York Times,* April 4, 1957.

4 *Mexico's Oil,* pp. xxvi–xxviii. For the text of the Spanish royal ordinances and the Díaz mining laws see Secretaría de Industria, Comercio y Trabajo, *Documentos relacionados con la legislación petrolera mexicana* (México: Talleres Gráficos, 1919), pp. 21–29, 40–43.

5 For the full text of Article 27 see Eyler N. Simpson, *The Ejido: Mexico's Way Out* (Chapel Hill: University of North Carolina Press, 1937), pp. 749–55; for the text of the entire Constitution, see Department of State, *Foreign Relations of the United States, 1917* (Washington: Government Printing Office, 1926), pp. 951–81.

6 For further discussion of the revolutionary theory of property rights see especially Tannenbaum, *Mexico: the Struggle,* pp. 102–12, 136–53, 182–92; Simpson, *Ejido,* pp. 3–97; Charles W. Hackett, *The Mexican Revolution and the United States, 1910–1926* (Boston: World Peace Foundation, 1926), pp. 339–446; James M. Callahan, *American Foreign Policy in Mexican Relations* (New York: Macmillan, 1932), pp. 572–624; J. Fred Rippy, *The United States and Mexico* (New York: Crofts, 1931), pp. 365–85; J. Fred Rippy, José Vasconcelos, and Guy Stevens, *American Policies Abroad: Mexico* (Chicago: University of Chicago Press, 1928), *passim;* Ernest Gruening, *Mexico and Its Heritage* (New York: Appleton-Century-Crofts, 1928), pp. 99–105, 111–66; Wendell C. Gordon, *The Expropriation of Foreign-Owned Property in Mexico* (Washington: American Council on

Public Affairs, 1941), pp. 1–9; Howard F. Cline, *The United States and Mexico* (Cambridge: Harvard University Press, 1953), pp. 204–7; Green H. Hackworth, *Digest of International Law* (Washington: Government Printing Office, 1942), III, 655–65; *Mexico's Oil*, pp. xxvi–xxxiii; *The True Facts about the Expropriation of the Oil Companies' Properties in Mexico* (Mexico City: Government of Mexico, 1940), pp. 21–38.

7 Simpson, *Ejido*, pp. 74, 79, 87, 96–97, 612; Embassy Memorandum, "Brief Survey of the Mexican Agrarian Situation," Daniels Papers.

8 Tannenbaum, *Mexico: the Struggle*, pp. 140–41; "Brief Survey," Daniels Papers.

9 *Mexico's Oil*, p. 18.

10 Lansing to Parker, January 22, 1917, 5 P.M., in *Foreign Relations, 1917*, pp. 947–49.

11 *Affairs in Mexico*, 66 Cong., 2 sess., *Senate Report* 645, pp. 62–67. See also *Investigation of Mexican Affairs*, 66 Cong., 2 sess., *Senate Doc.* 285.

12 Simpson, *Ejido*, pp. 221–22; Embassy Memorandum, "Mexican Agrarian Bonds," Daniels Papers.

13 "Draft Treaty of Amity and Commerce between the United States of America and Mexico," *Foreign Relations, 1921* (1936), II, 397–404; Mexican Foreign Office to the American Embassy, Mexico City, June 4, 1921, *ibid.*, p. 412.

14 The official American record of the Bucareli Conference may be found in Department of State, *Proceedings of the United States-Mexican Commission Convened in Mexico City, May 14, 1923* (Washington: Government Printing Office, 1925).

15 *Foreign Relations, 1925* (1940), II, 517–18.

16 *Ibid.*, pp. 518–20.

17 For a sampling of the Mexican and American arguments, see *Foreign Relations, 1925*, II, 529–31, 537–40, and *Foreign Relations, 1926* (1941), II, 643–72.

18 Sheffield, New York, to William Williams, December 4, 1928, Sheffield Papers.

19 Sheffield, Mexico City, to Secretary of State, April 11, 1927, *Foreign Relations, 1927* (1942), III, 181–83.

20 Sheffield, New York, to George W. Hinman, July 23, 1929, Sheffield Papers.

21 Sheffield, New York, to Maj. Gen. James G. Harbord, November 5, 1928, Sheffield Papers.

22 Sheffield, New York, to William H. Taft, June 12, 1928, Sheffield Papers.

23 For a discussion of the Morrow-Calles agreement by a participant, see J. Reuben Clark, Jr., "The Oil Settlement with Mexico," *Foreign Affairs*, VI (July, 1928), 600–614.

24 Simpson, *Ejido*, p. 582.

Chapter III

1 First Inaugural Address, March 4, 1933, in *The Public Papers and Addresses of Franklin D. Roosevelt*, comp. Samuel I. Rosenman (New York: Random House, 1938), II, 14.

2 Josephus Daniels, Mexico City, to Franklin D. Roosevelt, September 9, 1933, Daniels Papers.

3 *New York Times*, March 17, 1923, and April 16, 1933. The quotations are from Daniels, *Shirt-Sleeve Diplomat* (Chapel Hill: University of North Carolina Press, 1947), pp. 29–30, 33.

4 Daniels, Mexico City, to Roosevelt, April 26, 1933, Daniels Papers; Daniels, *Shirt-Sleeve Diplomat*, pp. 438–41, 450, and illustrations facing p. 28 and p. 440; interview with Arturo Arnáiz y Freg, June 28, 1955.

5 Daniels, Mexico City, to R. Walton Moore, March 27, 1936, Daniels Papers.

6 Interview with Ezequiel Padilla, June 28, 1955.

7 Interviews with Robert Newbegin, January 15, 1953; R. Henry Norweb, May 2, 1953; Salvador Duhart, June 16, 1955; Arturo Arnáiz y Freg, June 28, 1955; also Francisco Castillo Nájera, Mexico City, to the author, June 12, 1953; Narciso Bassols, Tacubaya, to the author, June 4, 1953; Emilio Portes Gil, Mexico City, to the author, June 6, 1953; Ramón Beteta, Rome, to the author, June 23, 1953; Stephen E. Aguirre, El Paso, to the author, June 24, 1957; Pierre de L. Boal, Boalsburg, to the author, July 21, 1957.

8 Frank Daniels, Raleigh, to Mr. and Mrs. Josephus Daniels, September 4, 1933, Daniels Papers; Daniels, *Shirt-Sleeve Diplomat*, pp. 32–33.

9 Daniels, Mexico City, to Antenor Sala, September 17, 1936, Daniels Papers.

10 Daniels, Mexico City, to Roosevelt, July 7, 1939, Daniels and Roosevelt Papers.

11 Arthur Bliss Lane, Mexico City, to J. Reuben Clark, May 9, 1933, Lane Papers.

12 *Excélsior*, May 13, 1933. See also *El Universal*, May 13, 1933.

13 Quoted in Daniels, Diary, September 11, 1933, Daniels Papers.

14   Compare, for example, *La Palabra,* July 7, 11, and November 30, 1933.

15   *El Universal,* June 21, 1933. See also *Excélsior,* June 10, 1933; *El Nacional,* June 8, 1933; Daniels, *Shirt-Sleeve Diplomat,* pp. 93–95.

16   *Excélsior,* May 10 and 11, 1933; *El Nacional,* May 11, 1933; *El Universal,* May 10, 1933; *La Palabra,* May 10, 1933; *La Prensa,* May 11, 1933; *New York Times,* May 10, 1933.

17   Daniels, Fourth of July Address, 1933, Daniels Papers.

18   Daniels, Mexico City, to Robert W. Bingham, July 13, 1933, Daniels Papers.

19   *Cronos* (Puebla), July 8, 1933. See also *Excélsior,* July 5 and 6, 1933; *El Universal,* July 5 and 6, 1933; *El Nacional,* July 5 and 7, 1933; *Omega,* July 7 and 10, 1933; *La Prensa,* July 6 and 15, 1933; *La Palabra,* July 7, 1933; *Actualidad* (Mexico City), July 19, 1933; *Servicios Publicos,* July 15, 1933; *El Jalisciense* (Guadalajara), July 13, 1933.

20   Orelia R. de Lozano, Monterrey, to Daniels, July 7, 1933, Daniels Papers.

21   Clark, Salt Lake City, to Lane, August 7, 1933, Lane Papers.

22   Interview with Robert Newbegin, January 15, 1953.

23   Daniels, Mexico City, to Cordell Hull, October 8, 1936 [possibly not sent], Daniels Papers.

24   See Herschel V. Johnson, "Mexico in 1932," lecture given at the Army War College, December 2, 1932, Daniels Papers.

25   Daniels, Mexico City, to Roosevelt, May 15, 1933, Daniels Papers.

26   P. Elías Calles, El Sauzal, to Daniels, May 6, 1933, Daniels Papers.

27   Daniels, Mexico City, to Calles, May 15, 1933; Calles to Daniels, May 29, 1933, Daniels Papers.

28   *El Universal,* July 31, 1933. See also Daniels, Mexico City, to Calles, August 2, 1933, Daniels Papers; Daniels, Mexico City, to Roosevelt, August 7, 1933, Roosevelt Papers.

29   Daniels, Mexico City, to Hull, August 14, 1933, Daniels Papers.

30   Daniels, Mexico City, to Claude G. Bowers, August 22, 1933, Daniels Papers. See also Daniels, Diary, August 15, 1933; Daniels, Mexico City, to Hull, August 15, 1933; Daniels, Mexico City, to Roosevelt, August 15, 1933; Daniels, Mexico City, to Jonathan Daniels, August 15, 1933; Daniels, Mexico City, to Louis M. Howe, August 16, 1933, Daniels Papers.

31 Daniels, Mexico City, to Roosevelt, March 12, 1934, Roosevelt Papers. See also Daniels to Roosevelt, undated [March, 1934], Daniels Papers.

32 Roosevelt, Washington, to Daniels, March 22, 1934, Daniels Papers. See also Roosevelt, Washington, to Calles, March 22, 1934; Daniels, Mexico City, to Roosevelt, March 25, 1934, Daniels Papers.

33 Francisco Javier Gaxiola, *El Presidente Rodríguez, 1932–1934* (Mexico City: Editorial "Cultura," 1938), pp. 120–24; Daniels, *Shirt-Sleeve Diplomat*, p. 54.

34 Daniels, Mexico City, to Roosevelt, April 6, 1934, Roosevelt Papers.

35 Daniels, Mexico City, to Calles, April 4, 1934, Daniels Papers.

36 Daniels, *Shirt-Sleeve Diplomat*, p. 55.

37 *El Nacional,* November 3, 1934; *New York Times,* November 4, 1934; Daniels, Mexico City, to Secretary of State, November 5, 1934; William W. Schott, Mexico City, to William J. Kenealy, February 18, 1936 [not sent], Daniels Papers; Gaxiola, *Rodríguez,* pp. 124–28; Daniels, *Shirt-Sleeve Diplomat*, pp. 50–51.

38 Daniels, Mexico City, to Claude G. Bowers, August 22, 1933, Daniels Papers.

39 Daniels, Mexico City, to R. Walton Moore, March 27, 1936, Daniels Papers.

40 See, for example, Daniels, Mexico City, to Hull, May 9, 20, and 25, and September 1, 1933, Daniels Papers.

41 Daniels, Mexico City, to Daniel C. Roper, April 27, 1933; Roper to Daniels, June 14, 1933; Daniels, Mexico City, to William Phillips, July 5, 1933, Daniels Papers.

42 Daniels, Mexico City, to Hull, May 20, 1933, Daniels Papers.

43 See, for example, Laurence Duggan, Washington, to Daniels, February 15, 1938, Daniels Papers.

44 Daniels, Mexico City, to Hull, September 1, 1933, Daniels Papers.

45 Daniels, Mexico City, to George H. Dern, May 4, 1933, Daniels Papers.

46 Daniels, Mexico City, to Hull, May 26, 1933, Daniels Papers. See also Daniels to Hull, May 9, 1933, Daniels Papers.

47 Dern, Washington, to Daniels, May 15, 1933, Daniels Papers.

48 Daniels, Mexico City, to Dern, May 26, 1933, Daniels Papers.

49 See, for example, Sumner Welles, Havana, to Secretary of State, May 13, 6 P.M., August 7, noon, August 8, 9 P.M., and August

9, 10 A.M., 1933, in Department of State, *Foreign Relations of the United States, 1933* (Washington: Government Printing Office, 1952), V, 287–90, 336–37, 340–45.

50 Daniels, Mexico City, to Roosevelt, July 15, 1933, Daniels Papers.

51 Daniels, Mexico City, to Hull, August 9, 1933, Daniels Papers.

52 Welles, Havana, to Secretary of State, August 19, 1933, noon, in *Foreign Relations, 1933*, V, 367–69.

53 Welles, Havana, to Secretary of State, September 7, 1933, noon, 3 P.M. and 6 P.M., *ibid.*, pp. 396–98, 400–401. See also various despatches and memoranda of telephone conversations between Welles and the State Department, September 5 and 6, 1933, *ibid.*, pp. 379–90.

54 Hull, Washington, to Welles, September 7, 1933, 8 P.M., *ibid.*, p. 402.

55 Daniels, Mexico City, to Roosevelt, September 5, 1933, Daniels Papers. See also Daniels, Mexico City, to Secretary of State, September 6, 1933, 9 P.M., in *Foreign Relations, 1933*, V, 394.

56 Daniels, Mexico City, to Roosevelt, September 9, 1933, Daniels Papers; Roosevelt to Hull, September 13, 1933, Roosevelt Papers.

57 Memorandum of telephone conversation, September 9, 1933, 1 P.M., in *Foreign Relations, 1933*, V, 412–13. Several hours later, after conferring with Foreign Minister Puig about Latin American sentiment, Daniels cabled that "the feeling against intervention by the United States is deep-seated and unanimous." *Ibid.*, p. 413.

58 Daniels, Mexico City, to Hull, September 9, 1933, *ibid.*, pp. 414–15. See also Hull, *Memoirs* (New York: Macmillan, 1948), I, 316.

59 Daniels, Mexico City, to Hull, October 3, 1933, Daniels Papers.

60 Welles, Havana, to Secretary of State, September 5, 1933, 4 P.M. and 9 P.M. in *Foreign Relations, 1933*, V, 384, 388.

61 Welles, Havana, to Secretary of State, September 11, 1933, 6 P.M., *ibid.*, pp. 422–24.

62 Welles, Havana, to Secretary of State, September 25, 1933, 1 A.M., *ibid.*, pp. 457–58.

63 Hull, Washington, to Welles, September 26, 1933, 5 P.M., *ibid.*, p. 459.

64 Daniels, Mexico City, to Roosevelt, October 6, 1933, Daniels Papers.

65 Daniels, Mexico City, to Hull, October 4, 1933, Daniels Papers.

66 Hull, Washington, to Daniels, September 28, 1933, 8 p.m., in
    Foreign Relations, 1933, IV (1950), 17. See also Daniels, Mexico
    City, to Hull, September 29 and October 6, 1933, *ibid.,* pp.
    18–27; Daniels to Hull, October 5, 1933, Daniels Papers.
67 Lane, New York, to Daniels, October 15, 1933, Daniels Papers.
68 Daniels, Mexico City, to Hull, October 17, 1933, Daniels Papers.
69 Hull, Washington, to Daniels, October 24, 1933, Daniels Papers;
    Hull, instructions to Montevideo delegation, November 10, 1933,
    in *Foreign Relations, 1933,* IV, 137–41.
70 Daniels, Mexico City, to Hull, December 4, 1933, Daniels
    Papers.
71 Hull, Montevideo, to Acting Secretary of State, December 19,
    1933, midnight, in *Foreign Relations, 1933,* IV, 201–2.
72 Hull, *Memoirs,* I, 333–35.
73 *Foreign Relations, 1933,* V, 525–26.
74 William Phillips, Washington, to Hull, November 25, 1933, 7
    p.m., *ibid.,* IV, 41–42. See also Phillips to Hull, November 28,
    1933, 6 p.m., *ibid.,* V, 527–28.
75 Hull, Montevideo, to Acting Secretary of State, December 19,
    1933, midnight, *ibid.,* IV, 201–2; Hull, *Memoirs,* I, 333–35.
76 Roosevelt, *Public Papers and Addresses,* II, 545–46. In his an-
    nual message to Congress on January 3, 1934, Roosevelt ob-
    served: "We have, I hope, made it clear to our neighbors that
    we seek with them future avoidance of territorial expansion and
    of interference by one Nation in the internal affairs of another."
    Ibid., III, 11.
77 Daniels, Mexico City, to Roosevelt, December 29, 1933, tele-
    gram, Daniels Papers. See also Daniels' letter to Roosevelt of
    the same date, Daniels Papers.
78 C. P. Nutter, Washington, Associated Press dispatch, December
    29, 1933, Daniels Papers.
79 Hull, Washington, to Jefferson Caffery, January 23, 1934, in
    Foreign Relations, 1934, V (1952), 107.
80 Daniels, Mexico City, to Hull, July 24, 1934, Daniels Papers.
81 Daniels, Mexico City, to Hull, July 10, 1934, Daniels Papers.
    The Cuban crisis of 1933 and the intra-administration debate
    over the application of the Good Neighbor Policy, are discussed
    at greater length in E. David Cronon, "Interpreting the New
    Good Neighbor Policy: the Cuban Crisis of 1933," *Hispanic
    American Historical Review,* XXXIX (November, 1959), 538–67.
82 Daniels, Diary, April 29, 1933, and January 22, 1934, Daniels
    Papers; Daniels, *Shirt-Sleeve Diplomat,* p. 123. For background

on the Mexican claims situation, see Abraham H. Feller, *The
Mexican Claims Commissions, 1923–1934: a Study in the Law
and Procedure of International Tribunals* (New York: Macmillan,
1935), pp. 1–7, 15–23; Edgar Turlington, *Mexico and Her
Foreign Creditors* (New York: Columbia University Press, 1930),
especially pp. 263–341.

83 Department of State, *Proceedings of the United States-Mexican
Commission Convened in Mexico City, May 14, 1923* (Washing-
ton: Government Printing Office, 1925), pp. 53–62; Feller,
Mexican Claims Commissions, pp. 49–55.

84 Daniels, Mexico City, to Secretary of State, October 2 and November 1, 1933, in *Foreign Relations, 1933,* V, 802–8; A. Moreno, memorandum on claims, Daniels Papers; Daniels, *Shirt-
Sleeve Diplomat,* p. 118.

85 Daniels, Mexico City, to Roosevelt, April 18, 1933, Daniels
Papers. See also Daniels to Roosevelt, April 26 and May 2, 1933,
Daniels Papers.

86 Daniels, Mexico City, to Secretary of State, May 12, 1933, in
Foreign Relations, 1933, V, 800–801.

87 Daniels, Mexico City, to Lane, December 28, 1933, Lane Papers.

88 Daniels, Mexico City, to Secretary of State, November 1, 1933,
in *Foreign Relations, 1933,* V, 805–8. See also Daniels, Mexico
City, to Lane, November 2, 1933, Daniels Papers.

89 Daniels, Mexico City, to Secretary of State, December 6, 1933,
in *Foreign Relations, 1933,* V, 809–13. See also Daniels, Mexico
City, to Moreno, December 5, 1933, Daniels Papers.

90 Phillips, Washington, to Daniels, December 9, 2 P.M., December
16, and December 26, 1 P.M., 1933, in *Foreign Relations, 1933,*
V, 813–23.

91 Daniels, Mexico City, to Secretary of State, January 26, 1934,
ibid., 1934, V, 398–403. See also Daniels, Mexico City, to Phillips, January 8 and 9, 1934; Daniels, Mexico City, to Roosevelt,
undated [January, 1934 (?)]; Daniels, Mexico City, to Hull,
January 26, 1934, Daniels Papers.

92 Daniels, Mexico City, to Hull, January 26, 1934, Daniels Papers.

93 Daniels, Mexico City, to Hull, February 14, 1934, Daniels
Papers. See also Daniels to Secretary of State, February 10, 1934,
in *Foreign Relations, 1934,* V, 408–13; Daniels to Hull, February 20, 1934, Daniels Papers.

94 Johnson, Washington, to Daniels, February 16, 1934, Daniels
Papers.

95 Hull, Washington, to Daniels, April 7, 1 P.M., and April 11, 11

A.M., 1934; Daniels, Mexico City, to Secretary of State, April 9, 4 P.M., April 13, 4 P.M., April 14, 3 P.M., and April 15, 4 P.M., 1934, in *Foreign Relations, 1934*, V, 450–61.

96 Hull, Washington, to Daniels, April 17, 1934, 3 P.M., *ibid.*, pp. 461–62.

97 Daniels, Mexico City, to Secretary of State, April 19, 1934, noon, *ibid.*, p. 463.

98 Daniels, Mexico City, to Hull, April 19, 1934, Daniels Papers.

99 Phillips, Washington, to Daniels, April 21, 1934, 4 P.M., in *Foreign Relations, 1934*, V, 464–65.

100 Moreno, Mexico City, to B. L. Hunt, April 25, 1934, Daniels Papers.

101 *New York Times*, April 25, 1934; *Foreign Relations, 1934*, V, 467–76.

102 Daniels, Diary, April 24, 1934, Daniels Papers.

103 Daniels, Washington, to Key Pittman, May 26, 1934; Daniels, Raleigh, to R. Henry Norweb, May 17, 1934, Daniels Papers; Hull, Washington, to Roosevelt, November 26, 1934, Roosevelt Papers; *New York Times*, May 26, 31, and June 16, 1934, January 4, 1935; Daniels, *Shirt-Sleeve Diplomat*, p. 121.

Chapter IV

1 Portions of this chapter, and additional related material, have appeared in E. David Cronon, "American Catholics and Mexican Anticlericalism, 1933–1936," *Mississippi Valley Historical Review*, XLV (September, 1958), 201–30. For further background on the conflict between Church and State in Mexico, see Frank Tannenbaum, *Mexico: the Struggle for Peace and Bread* (New York: Knopf, 1950), pp. 122–35, 154–72; Ernest Gruening, *Mexico and Its Heritage* (New York: Appleton-Century-Crofts, 1928), pp. 171–286, 515–30; Charles W. Hackett, *The Mexican Revolution and the United States, 1910–1926* (Boston: World Peace Foundation, 1926), pp. 398–400; Howard F. Cline, *The United States and Mexico* (Cambridge: Harvard University Press, 1953), pp. 201–3; Josephus Daniels, *Shirt-Sleeve Diplomat* (Chapel Hill: University of North Carolina Press, 1947), pp. 127–95; George F. Kneller, *The Education of the Mexican Nation* (New York: Columbia University Press, 1951); George I. Sánchez, *Mexico: a Revolution by Education* (New York: Viking, 1936); George C. Booth, *Mexico's School-Made Society* (Stanford: Stanford University Press, 1941); Ramón Beteta, *The*

Mexican Revolution: a Defense (Mexico City: DAPP, 1937), pp.
5, 11–18, 59–63; Emilio Portes Gil, *The Catholic Clergy against
the Mexican Government* (Mexico City: Trens News Agency,
1934), and *The Conflict between the Civil Power and the Clergy*
(Mexico City: Ministry of Foreign Affairs, 1935); Michael J.
Curley, *Mexican Tyranny and the Catholic Church* (Brooklyn:
International Catholic Truth Society, 1926); Francis C. Kelley,
Blood Drenched Altars (Milwaukee: Bruce 1935); Michael
Kenny, *No God Next Door* (New York: Hirten, 1935); Wilfred
Parsons, *Mexican Martyrdom* (New York: Macmillan, 1936);
William F. Montavon, *The Church in Mexico Protests* (Wash-
ington: National Catholic Welfare Conference, 1935); Charles
S. Macfarland, *Chaos in Mexico* (New York: Harper, 1935).
2   Herschel V. Johnson, "Mexico in 1932," Daniels Papers.
3   *Catholic Action*, XV (February, 1933), 5.
4   Wilfred Parsons, "An Open Letter to Ambassador Daniels,"
America, XLVIII (April 1, 1933), 619.
5   John J. Burke, Washington, to Daniels, June 20, 1933, Daniels
Papers. See also Burke to Daniels, July 21, 1933, Daniels Papers.
6   Patrick R. Duffey, Brookland, to Daniels, April 18, 1933, Daniels
Papers.
7   Daniels, *Shirt-Sleeve Diplomat*, p. 519.
8   *Baltimore Catholic Review*, April 28, 1933.
9   P. H. Callahan, Louisville, to Daniels, July 28, 1933, Daniels
Papers.
10 Daniels, Mexico City, to J. P. B. Connell, July 15, 1933, Daniels
Papers.
11 *New York Times*, June 30, 1933.
12 Daniels, Mexico City, to William F. Montavon, August 16,
1933, Daniels Papers.
13 Daniels, Diary, September 11, 1933, Daniels Papers.
14 Daniels, Mexico City, to P. H. Callahan, September 6, 1933,
Daniels Papers.
15 Daniels, Mexico City, to Secretary of State, February 16, 1934.
See also Daniels, Mexico City, to Antonio de P. Araujo, February 16, 1934, Daniels Papers; Daniels, *Shirt-Sleeve Diplomat*,
pp. 132–34.
16 Partido Nacional Revolucionario, *Plan sexenal del P.N.R.* (Mexico:
1934), pp. 83–90.
17 Daniels, Mexico City, to Secretary of State, April 25, 1934. See
also Raleigh *News and Observer*, May 4, 1934; *Washington
Post*, May 6 and 8, 1934; *Winston-Salem Journal*, June 15 and

October 6, 1934; *El Sol* (Monterrey) May 9, 1934; *San Luis Potosí Vanguardia,* July 7 and 8, 1934; *Excélsior* (Mexico City), July 9, 1934; *El Nacional* (Mexico City), July 10, 1934; *New York Times,* July 9, 1934.

18 *El Nacional,* June 22, 1934.
19 Quoted in "Ambassador Daniels 'Explains,'" *America,* LI (September 22, 1934), 554–55.
20 *New York Times,* July 26, 1934.
21 Daniels, Seminar Address, July 26, 1934, Daniels Papers.
22 José María Rodríguez to Daniels in *El Hombre Libre* (Mexico City), August 3, 1934.
23 Daniels, Mexico City, to José María Rodríguez, August 11, 1934, Daniels Papers.
24 See *El Hombre Libre,* August 3, 6, 13, 15, 17, and 20, 1934.
25 "Dark Days in Mexico," *America,* LI (August 25, 1934), 459.
26 "Daniels Should Resign!" *ibid.,* 483–84.
27 *Denver Catholic Register,* September 16, 1934.
28 *Baltimore Catholic Review,* September 21, 1934.
29 Joseph H. Wels to the editor, *America,* LI (September 22, 1934), 573.
30 *Baltimore Catholic Review,* October 5, 1934; Agnes G. Regan, Washington, to Franklin D. Roosevelt, October 23, 1934, Roosevelt Papers.
31 Raleigh *News and Observer,* October 8, 1934.
32 See Callahan, Louisville, to Daniel C. Roper, September 4, 1934; Callahan to Wilfred Parsons, September 17, 1934; Callahan to Daniels, September 18, 1934, Daniels Papers.
33 Callahan, Louisville, to Daniels, September 17, 1934, Daniels Papers.
34 Callahan, Louisville, to Barry Bingham, January 14, 1935, Roosevelt Papers.
35 William F. Montavon, Washington, to Daniels, September 17, 1934, Daniels Papers. See also Montavon to Daniels, August 31, 1934; Daniels to Montavon, September 4, 1934, Daniels Papers.
36 *Greensboro Daily News,* October 18, 1934. See also *Winston-Salem Journal,* October 6, 1934.
37 Presidential press conference 151, October 17, 1934, Roosevelt Papers, IV, 133.
38 Transcript of conversation, October 17, 1934, Daniels Papers.
39 Memorandum of press conference, October 17, 1934, Department of State Papers (hereafter cited as DS).
40 *Dallas News,* October 19, 1934.

41 "The New Deal and Mexico," *Commonweal*, XX (October 26, 1934), 599–600.
42 "Contrasts and Inconsistencies," *Ave Maria*, XL (November 10, 1934), 600–601.
43 *New York Times*, November 17, 1934.
44 "A Citizen of the U.S." to Daniels, undated, Daniels Papers. See also "A Lay Soldier of Gesus [*sic*]," Los Angeles, to Daniels, October 30, 1934, Daniels Papers.
45 Peter M. Dengus, Goldsboro, to Daniels, June 5, 1935, Daniels Papers.
46 Daniels, Mexico City, to Laurence Nason, November 7, 1934, Daniels Papers.
47 Edward L. Reed to Salmon, December 4, 1934; Reed to Sumner Welles, March 27, and May 3, 1935, DS, file nos. 812.404/1366 and /1650 1/2.
48 *New York Times*, December 3, 1934.
49 *Ibid.* See also *ibid.*, February 6, 15, and 19, 1935; Charles H. Dillon to the editor, *Commonweal*, XXII (May 3, 1935), 21–22; Edward L. Reed, memorandum of conversation with Michael Kenny, January 5, 1935, DS, 812.404/1416; Daniels, Mexico City, to Roosevelt, June 28, 1935, Daniels Papers.
50 *New York Times*, December 24, 1934.
51 *Ibid.*, November 24, 28, December 1, 10, 1934, and May 26, 1935; *Truth*, XXXIX (July, 1935), 3–4; Robert W. Hull, Huntington, to Dr. Don Enrique Bordonave, April 3, 1935, DS, 812.404/1666; R. W. Hull to the editor, *Commonweal*, XXI (December 28, 1934), 258–59.
52 Hubert C. Herring, New York, to Daniels, February 12, 1935, Daniels Papers. See also Daniels, Mexico City, to Roosevelt, November 6, 1934; Daniels to William Phillips, November 7, 1934, Daniels Papers.
53 Francis W. Durbin, Lima, to P. H. Callahan, December 20, 1934, Daniels Papers.
54 G. G. Herr, Southern Pines, to Daniels, February 23, 1935, Daniels Papers.
55 Callahan, Louisville, to J. A. O'Brien, September 22, 1936, Daniels Papers.
56 Callahan, Louisville, to Anthony J. Beck, January 29, 1935, Daniels Papers.
57 Callahan, Louisville, to Vincent dePaul Fitzpatrick, December 15, 1934, Daniels Papers.

58 Callahan, Louisville, to Daniels, January 16, 1935, Daniels Papers.
59 John P. Higgins, Washington, to Roosevelt, January 15, 1935, Roosevelt Papers. See also Higgins to Roosevelt, December 19, 1934, DS, 812.404/1408; *New York Times,* January 9, 1935.
60 "A Dubious Victory," *Chicago New World,* January 18, 1935.
61 Louisville *Courier-Journal,* January 9, 1935.
62 Cordell Hull, Washington, to Higgins, December 23, 1934, DS 812.404/1408; Roosevelt, Washington, to Higgins, January 23, 1935, Daniels and Roosevelt Papers.
63 R. Walton Moore, Washington, to Daniels, January 7, 1935, Daniels Papers.
64 *Congressional Record,* 74 Cong., 1 sess., LXXIX (January 10, 21, and 31, 1935), 246–47, 680, and 1296–97; Martin H. Carmody to Hull, January 21, 1935, DS 812.404/1475; *New York Times,* January 22, 1935.
65 Senate Res. 70, *Congressional Record,* 74 Cong., 1 sess., LXXIX (January 31, 1935), 1298; *New York Times,* February 1, 1935.
66 *New York Times,* February 2, 1935.
67 Jonathan Daniels, Raleigh, to Josephus Daniels, February 8, 1935, Daniels Papers. The William E. Borah Papers in the Library of Congress do not resolve this question of a possible political trade in connection with the World Court proposal. They do show, however, that Borah's interest in Mexican religious conditions began only at this time, and that Senator David I. Walsh, a Catholic Democrat from Massachusetts, had a hand in persuading him to introduce his Mexican resolution. See Carmody, Buffalo, to Borah, January 31, 1935, telegram, Borah Papers.
68 *Milwaukee Journal,* February 2, 1935.
69 *New York Times,* February 14, 22, and March 2, 1935; press releases, Daniels Papers.
70 Edwin M. Borchard, New Haven, to Borah, February 5, 1935, Borah Papers.
71 *El Hombre Libre,* February 8, 1935. For other adverse comment in the Mexico City press, see *Excélsior,* February 2 and 3, 1935; *El Universal,* February 3, 1935; *El Nacional,* February 2, 3, and 4, 1935; *La Prensa,* February 2, 3, and 5, 1935; *La Palabra,* February 3 and 6, 1935.
72 Stephen E. Aguirre, memorandum of conversation, April 13, 1935, Daniels Papers.

73 Hull, Washington, to Daniels, February 19, 1935, Daniels Papers.

74 Hull, Washington, to Key Pittman, February 12, 1935, Roosevelt and Borah Papers.

75 *Congressional Record,* 74 Cong., 1 sess., LXXIX (February 5, 1935), 1485–89; *New York Times,* February 6, 1935.

76 *Congressional Record,* 74 Cong., 1 sess., LXXIX (February 8, 1935), 1745–59; *New York Times,* February 9, 1935.

77 "Maligning a Good Man," *New York Times,* February 9, 1935.

78 *Congressional Record,* 74 Cong., 1 sess., LXXIX (April 25, 1935), 6420–33; *New York Times,* April 26, 1935.

79 74 Cong., 1 sess., House of Representatives: Joint Res. 311; Concurrent Res. 3, 7, 8, 12, 17, and 28; Res. 70, 179, 194, 277, 282, 283, and 286.

80 *New York Times,* February 28, March 6, 7, and 17, 1935.

81 John P. Higgins and Clare G. Fenerty to Roosevelt, July 16, 1935, Roosevelt Papers. See also *New York Times,* July 17, 1935.

82 Sam D. McReynolds, Washington, to Daniels, April 6, 1935, Daniels Papers. See also *New York Times,* January 23, 1935.

83 Roosevelt, Washington, to Daniels, July 12, 1935, Daniels Papers.

84 Daniels, Mexico City, to Secretary of State, November 5, 1934, Daniels Papers. See also Daniels, Diary, October 31, 1934; Daniels, Mexico City, to Roosevelt, October 26, 1934; Daniels, Mexico City, to William Phillips, November 7, 1934; Daniels, Mexico City, to Hull, November 7, 1934, Daniels Papers.

85 *Our Sunday Visitor,* January 20, 1935. See also William J. Kenealy, "The Mexican Religious Persecution," *Catholic Mind,* XXXIII (December 8, 1935), 453–55; *Michigan Catholic,* December 27, 1934; *El Hombre Libre,* November 9, 1934.

86 *Our Sunday Visitor,* January 20, 1935. See also "Meet Mr. Canabal," *Ave Maria,* XLI (February 16, 1935), 216–17.

87 Daniels, Diary, December 11, 1934, Daniels Papers.

88 Edward L. Reed to Secretary of State, February 18, 1935, DS, 811.91212/79. See also Daniels, Mexico City, to Secretary of State, April 12, 1935, in Department of State, *Foreign Relations of the United States, 1935* (Washington: Government Printing Office, 1953), IV, 766–70.

89 Daniels, Mexico City, to Secretary of State, July 11, 1935, DS 812.404/1756; Daniels to Secretary of State, July 11, 1935, 2 P.M., in *Foreign Relations, 1935,* IV, 804.

90 Daniels, Mexico City, to Roosevelt, July 23, 1935, Daniels Papers.

91 Daniels, Mexico City, to Secretary of State, May 26, 1936, DS, 812.404/1892; Daniels, Mexico City, to Eduardo Hay, May 20, 1936; Pierre de L. Boal, Mexico City, to Daniels, May 23 and 30, 1936, Daniels Papers; Daniels, *Shirt-Sleeve Diplomat,* pp. 148–50.

92 *El Hombre Libre,* May 24, 1936.

93 John L. Bazinet, Washington, to Daniels, March 9, 1937, Daniels Papers.

94 Daniels, Mexico City, to P. H. Callahan, November 12, 1936, Daniels Papers.

95 Daniels, *Shirt-Sleeve Diplomat,* pp. 191–93; Daniels, Mexico City, to Roosevelt, June 28 and November 18, 1935; William Franklin Sands, Washington, to P. H. Callahan, July 20, 1935; Sands to Daniels, March 20, 1936, Daniels Papers; Edward L. Reed, memorandum of conversation with Sands, July 24, 1935, DS, 812.404/1770.

96 Sands, Washington, to Marvin H. McIntyre, July 25, 1935, Roosevelt Papers.

97 John Mitchell, Brooklyn, to Daniels, November 27, 1934, Daniels Papers.

98 *New York Times,* March 26, 1935.

99 *Congressional Record,* 74 Cong., 1 sess., LXXIX (April 25, 1935), 6429.

100 Carmody to Roosevelt, October 25, 1935 (press release), Borah and Daniels Papers; *New York Times,* October 28, 1935. See also *New York Times,* August 21, 22, and November 18, 1935, and August 21, 1936; Cincinnati *Catholic Telegraph,* April 2, 1936; *Columbia,* XIV (February, 1935), 12; (March, 1935), 12; (April, 1935), 12; (June, 1935), 12; (July, 1935), 12–13; XV (November, 1935), 13; (December, 1935), 11–13; (January, 1936), 6–7, 18–19; (February, 1936), 3; (June, 1936), 3; XVI (October, 1936), 8–9.

101 For details of the Ambassador's protracted indecision, see E. David Cronon, "Josephus Daniels as a Reluctant Candidate," *North Carolina Historical Review,* XXXIII (October, 1956), 465–82. Daniels' keen interest in New Deal reform is shown in Cronon, "A Southern Progressive Looks at the New Deal," *Journal of Southern History,* XXIV (May, 1958), 151–76.

102 Daniels, Mexico City, to Daniel C. Roper, February 18, 1936, Daniels Papers.

103 Roper, Washington, to Daniels, March 2 and 13, 1936, Daniels Papers.

104 See Daniels, Mexico City, to Roper, February 18, 1936, Daniels Papers.
105 *Ibid.*
106 Daniels, Mexico City, to Roosevelt, undated draft [February, 1936], Daniels Papers.
107 See Daniels, Mexico City, to Roosevelt, July 7, 1939, Daniels and Roosevelt Papers.
108 Roosevelt, Washington, to Daniels, February 27, 1936, Daniels Papers.
109 See Daniels, Mexico City, to James A. Farley, January 22 and August 3, 1936; Daniels, Mexico City, to Roosevelt, February 28, March 30, and undated draft, 1936, Daniels Papers; Daniels, Philadelphia, to Roosevelt June 22, 1936, Roosevelt Papers.
110 Farley, New York, to Daniels, July 27, 1936, Daniels Papers.
111 Daniels, Mexico City, to Sam Rayburn, August 24, 1936, Daniels Papers.
112 Roper, Washington, to Daniels, September 5, 1936, Daniels Papers.
113 Hull, Washington, to Daniels, September 12, 1936, 2 P.M., Daniels Papers.
114 Hull, Washington, to Daniels, September 18, 1936, Daniels Papers.
115 Roosevelt, Washington, to Daniels, November 9, 1936, Daniels Papers.

CHAPTER V

1 Peabody, Warm Springs, to Daniels, January 17, 1938, Daniels Papers.
2 Daniels, Mexico City, to Peabody, January 21, 1938, Daniels Papers.
3 Daniels, Mexico City, to Roosevelt, September 20, 1940, Daniels Papers.
4 Daniels, Mexico City, to Creel, March 23, 1936, Daniels Papers.
5 Daniels, Mexico City, to Frank W. Buxton, June 28, 1939, Daniels Papers.
6 Kirk H. Porter and Donald B. Johnson (eds.), *National Party Platforms, 1840–1956* (Urbana: University of Illinois Press, 1956), p. 333.
7 Daniels, Mexico City, to Hull, August 17, 1934, Daniels Papers.
8 Daniels, Mexico City, to Hull, October 4, 1933, Daniels Papers. See also Daniels to Hull, April 20, 1934, Daniels Papers.

9 Thomas W. Lamont, New York, to Daniels, April 14, 1933, Daniels Papers.

10 Daniels, Mexico City, to Robert L. Durham, September 4, 1934, Daniels Papers.

11 Daniels, Mexico City, to Secretary of State, April 1, 1936, Daniels Papers. See also Daniels to Sumner Welles, April 6, 1936, Daniels Papers.

12 Welles, Washington, to Daniels, April 24, 1936; Daniels, Mexico City, to Welles, May 14, 1936, Daniels Papers.

13 Daniels, Mexico City, to Welles, May 8, 1936, Daniels Papers.

14 Welles, "The Roosevelt Administration and Its Dealings with the Republics of the Western Hemisphere," January 17, 1935, Department of State press release, Daniels Papers.

15 Daniels, Mexico City, to Secretary of State, February 4, 1936, in *Foreign Relations of the United States, 1936* (Washington, Government Printing Office, 1954), V, 770–72.

16 Welles, Washington, to R. Henry Norweb, February 19, 1936, *ibid.*, p. 772.

17 Daniels, Mexico City, to Welles, November 7, 1938, Daniels Papers. See also Daniels to Welles, December 3 and 6, 1938; Daniels, Diary, November 9, 1938, Daniels Papers.

18 Memorandum of conversation between Daniels and Cárdenas, October 7, 1936, Daniels Papers. See also Daniels, Mexico City, to Secretary of State, October 9, 1936, Daniels Papers, and *Foreign Relations, 1936*, V, 715–19.

19 Moore, Washington, to Daniels, November 23, 1936, *ibid.*, pp. 723–25.

20 Moore, Washington, to Daniels, November 23, 1936, Daniels Papers. See also Moore to Daniels, November 27, 1936, Daniels Papers.

21 Daniels, Mexico City, to Moore, November 30, 1936, Daniels Papers.

22 Daniels, Mexico City, to Secretary of State, November 28, 1936, in *Foreign Relations, 1936*, V, 725–28.

23 Daniels, Mexico City, to Moore, November 30, 1936, Daniels Papers.

24 Moore, Washington, to Hull, December 3, 1936, in *Foreign Relations, 1936*, V, 728–30.

25 Quoted in Moore, Washington, to Daniels, December 10, 1936, 1 P.M., *ibid.*, p. 730.

26 Daniels, Mexico City, to Moore, December 7, 1936; Daniels to Hull, December 7, 1936, Daniels Papers.

27   Daniels, Mexico City, to Secretary of State, December 16, 1936, in *Foreign Relations, 1936*, V, 709–15.

28   Pierre de L. Boal, Mexico City, to Daniels, December 17, 1936, Daniels Papers.

29   Daniels, Mexico City, to Claude G. Bowers, April 20, 1940, Daniels Papers.

30   For a general account of the expropriation of the Mexican National Railways, see Wendell C. Gordon, *The Expropriation of Foreign-Owned Property in Mexico* (Washington: American Council on Public Affairs, 1941), pp. 136–42.

31   See Boal, Mexico City, to Secretary of State, June 23, 1937, midnight, and June 24, 1937, 5 P.M.; Welles, memorandum of conversation with Francisco Castillo Nájera, June 24, 1937, in *Foreign Relations, 1937* (1954), V, 678–81, 683–84.

32   Boal, Mexico City, to Welles, June 24, 1937, Daniels Papers.

33   Hull, Washington, to Daniels, August 31, 1937, Daniels Papers.

CHAPTER VI

1   Daniels, Mexico City, to Ben Dixon MacNeil, December 2, 1936, Daniels Papers.

2   Cordell Hull, Washington, to Daniels, September 29, 1936, 5 P.M., in Department of State, *Foreign Relations of the United States, 1936* (Washington: Government Printing Office, 1954), V, 701.

3   Daniels, Mexico City, to Franklin D. Roosevelt, May 2, 1933, Daniels Papers.

4   Estados Unidos Mexicanos, Departmento Agrario, *Memoria, 1935–1936* (México, D.F., 1936), p. 67; *ibid., 1940–1941* (1941), p. 177; Eyler N. Simpson, *The Ejido: Mexico's Way Out* (Chapel Hill: University of North Carolina Press, 1937), p. 612; Frank Tannenbaum, *Mexico: the Struggle for Peace and Bread* (New York: Knopf, 1950), p. 149; Daniels, *Shirt-Sleeve Diplomat* (Chapel Hill: University of North Carolina Press, 1947), p. 200.

5   Simpson, *Ejido*, pp. 221–23; Embassy staff memorandum, "Mexican Agrarian Bonds," Daniels Papers.

6   "Agrarian Code of the United Mexican States," quoted in Simpson, *Ejido*, pp. 806–7.

7   Stanley Hawks, "The Agrarian Problem in Mexico," Daniels Papers.

8   "Brief Survey of the Mexican Agrarian Situation," Daniels Papers. See also R. Henry Norweb, Mexico City, to Secretary

of State, June 13, 1935, in *Foreign Relations, 1935* (1953), IV, 770–76.

9 Daniels, Diary, February 7, 1934, Daniels Papers.

10 Daniels, Mexico City, to Roosevelt, September 28, 1936, Daniels Papers.

11 Daniels, Mexico City, to Roosevelt, August 17, 1934, Daniels Papers.

12 William P. Blocker, Monterrey, to Daniels, November 19, 1936; Daniels to Blocker, November 30, 1936, Daniels Papers.

13 Daniels, Mexico City, to Roosevelt, September 28, 1936, Daniels Papers.

14 Daniels, Mexico City, to William E. Dodd, December 10, 1936, Daniels Papers.

15 Hull, Washington, to Joseph R. Baker and Peter H. A. Flood, April 4, 1935, in *Foreign Relations, 1935*, IV, 753–54.

16 Norweb, Mexico City, to Secretary of State, June 13, 1935, *ibid.*, pp. 770–76.

17 Quoted in Daniels, Mexico City, to Hull, July 9, 1935, Daniels Papers. For a frank estimate of Baker and Flood as negotiators, see Norweb, Mexico City, to Edward L. Reed, June 4, 1935, Daniels Papers.

18 Daniels, Mexico City, to Hull, July 9, 1935, Daniels Papers.

19 Hull, Washington, to Daniels, July 18, 1935, Daniels Papers.

20 Daniels, Mexico City, to Secretary of State, September 19, 1935, in *Foreign Relations, 1935*, IV, 776–78.

21 Hull, Washington, to Daniels, September 28, 1935, *ibid.*, p. 778.

22 Daniels, Mexico City, to Secretary of State, October 10, 1935, *ibid.*, pp. 778–79.

23 Hull, Washington, to Daniels, October 23, 1935, *ibid.*, p. 780.

24 See, for example, R. Walton Moore, Washington, to Daniels, November 2 and 14, 1935, *ibid.*, pp. 754–57, 759–60.

25 Daniels, Mexico City, to Moore, November 9, 1935, *ibid.*, pp. 757–59.

26 Moore, Washington, to Daniels, November 14, 1935, *ibid.*, pp. 759–60.

27 Daniels, Mexico City, to Secretary of State, November 27, 1935, *ibid.*, pp. 760–64.

28 Daniels, Mexico City, to Secretary of State, January 21, 1936, in *Foreign Relations, 1936*, V, 750–54.

29 Daniels, Mexico City, to Secretary of State, January 23, 31, February 1 and 6, 1936, *ibid.*, pp. 754–58.

30 Hull, Washington, to Daniels, February 4, 1936, 8 P.M., *ibid.*, pp. 756–57.

31   Daniels, Mexico City, to Secretary of State, April 16 and September 17, 1936, *ibid.*, pp. 692–98.

32   Norweb, Mexico City, to Secretary of State, June 13, 1935, in *Foreign Relations, 1935*, IV, 770–76.

33   Laurence Duggan, memorandum of conversation, December 14, 1937, in *Foreign Relations, 1937* (1954), V, 640. See also Hull, memorandum of conversation, April 20, 1937, *ibid.*, pp. 605–6.

34   A. F. Yepis, Guaymas, to Secretary of State, September 21, 1936, in *Foreign Relations, 1936*, V, 698–700.

35   Hull, Washington, to Daniels, September 29, 1936, 5 P.M., *ibid.*, p. 701.

36   Daniels, Mexico City, to Secretary of State, October 9, 1936, *ibid.*, pp. 715–19; memorandum of conversation between Daniels and Lázaro Cárdenas, October 7, 1936, Daniels Papers.

37   See above, pp. 122–26.

38   Daniels, Mexico City, to Sumner Welles, October 14, 1936, Daniels Papers.

39   Daniels, Mexico City, to Secretary of State, October 17, 1936, in *Foreign Relations, 1936*, V, 704–7.

40   Daniels, Mexico City, to Secretary of State, October 20, 1936, *ibid.*, pp. 707–8.

41   Moore, Washington, to Daniels, November 20, 1936, 6 P.M., *ibid.*, p. 709.

42   Daniels, Mexico City, to Secretary of State, December 16, 1936, *ibid.*, 709–15.

43   Pierre de L. Boal, Mexico City, to Daniels, December 18, 1936, Daniels Papers.

44   Daniels, Mexico City, to Secretary of State, December 16, 1936, in *Foreign Relations, 1936*, V, 709–15.

45   Richard C. Tanis to Moore, December 30, 1936, in *Foreign Relations, 1937*, V, 602–3.

46   Roosevelt, Washington, to Moore, January 16, 1937, Roosevelt Papers. This directive is worth quoting at length, especially since after some hesitation the State Department chose to delete it from the documents compiled for the *Foreign Relations* series. The Department did, however, publish the memorandum (see above, note 45) to which Roosevelt objected, thereby leaving the impression that it represented the clear policy of the Roosevelt administration. The belated decision not to print Roosevelt's order explains why the earlier Tanis memorandum, dated December 30, 1936, appears by itself, clearly out of place, in the 1937 volume.

47   Hull, Washington, to Roosevelt, March 26, 1937, Roosevelt Papers.

48   Boal, Mexico City, to Daniels, January 12, 1937, Daniels Papers.

49   Daniels, Mexico City, to Secretary of State, October 22, 1937, 8 P.M., in *Foreign Relations, 1937,* V, 614–15.

50   Daniels, Mexico City, to Secretary of State, October 28, 1937, midnight; Presidential *acuerdo,* October 27, 1937, *ibid.,* pp. 616, 622–24.

51   Daniels, Mexico City, to Secretary of State, October 28, 1937, *ibid.,* pp. 616–19.

52   Daniels, Mexico City, to Secretary of State, October 29, 1937, *ibid.,* p. 619.

53   Ramón Beteta, Mexico City, to Daniels, October 29, 1937, *ibid.,* pp. 625–26.

54   Daniels, Mexico City, to Secretary of State, December 23, 1937, *ibid.,* pp. 642–44. See also Daniels to Secretary of State, January 24, 1938, in *Foreign Relations, 1938* (1955), V, 660–61.

55   Daniels, Mexico City, to Welles, November 6, 1937, Daniels Papers.

56   *New York Times,* December 7, 1937.

57   *Ibid.,* December 9, 1937.

58   Daniels, Mexico City, to Welles, December 9, 1937, Daniels Papers.

59   Daniels, Mexico City, to Welles, December 14, 1937, Daniels Papers. See also Daniels to Welles, December 10, 1937, Daniels Papers.

60   Daniels, Mexico City, to Duggan, January 29, 1938, Daniels Papers.

Chapter VII

1   Daniels, Mexico City, to Franklin D. Roosevelt, September 14, 1937, Daniels Papers.

2   Josephus Daniels, *Shirt-Sleeve Diplomat* (Chapel Hill: University of North Carolina Press, 1947), pp. 217–20.

3   Richard C. Tanis, memorandum of conversation, September 21, 1934, DS, 812.6363/2791.

4   Daniels, *Shirt-Sleeve Diplomat,* pp. 221–22.

5   Daniels, Mexico City, to Hull, undated draft [November, 1934; apparently not sent], Daniels Papers.

6   Daniels, Mexico City, to Hull, November 14, 1934, Daniels Papers.

7 R. Henry Norweb, Laredo, to Daniels, November 24 [1934], Daniels Papers. This presumably meant that Norweb thought the plan would be vetoed either by the companies' home offices in New York, or by the State Department in Washington.

8 Norweb, Cleveland, to Daniels, December 4, 1934, Daniels Papers.

9 Edward L. Reed, memorandum of conversation, December 10, 1934, Daniels Papers. See also Sumner Welles to Reed, December 11, 1934, DS, 812.6363/2814.

10 Reed, Washington, to Daniels, December 12, 1934, Daniels Papers. See also Daniels, Mexico City, to Norweb, December 15, 1934; Daniels to Reed, December 22, 1934, Daniels Papers.

11 Norweb, Cleveland, to Daniels, December 19, 1934, Daniels Papers.

12 Hull, Washington, to Daniels, March 23, 1935, in Department of State, *Foreign Relations of the United States, 1935* (Washington: Government Printing Office, 1953), IV, 764–65.

13 Daniels to [Hull?] undated draft [March, 1935?], Daniels Papers.

14 Daniels, Mexico City, to Secretary of State, April 12, 1935, in *Foreign Relations, 1935*, IV, 766–70; Huasteca Petroleum Company to the Department of State, April 29, 1935, DS, 812.5045/213.

15 "Confidential Memo for the Embassy," May 20, 1935, DS, 812.6363/2849. See also Norweb, Mexico City, to Secretary of State, May 23, 1935, DS, 812.5045/226; *Mexico: Labor Controversy, 1936–1938* (New York: Huasteca Petroleum Company, 1938), pp. 1–46.

16 See, for example, *Mexico: Labor Controversy*, p. 56; *Mexico's Oil* (Mexico City: Government of Mexico, 1940), pp. xli–xliii, 518; Wendell C. Gordon, *The Expropriation of Foreign-Owned Property in Mexico* (Washington: American Council on Public Affairs, 1941), p. 106; Nathaniel and Sylvia Weyl, *The Reconquest of Mexico: the Years of Lázaro Cárdenas* (New York: Oxford University Press, 1939), pp. 293–94; *El conflicto del petróleo en México, 1937–1938* (México, D. F.: Universidad Obrera, n.d.), pp. 11–13.

17 Pierre de L. Boal, Mexico City, to Daniels, June 7, 1937, Daniels Papers.

18 Boal, Mexico City, to Daniels, June 11, 1937, Daniels Papers. See also Thomas H. Lockett, Mexico City, to Daniels, June 9, 1937, Daniels Papers.

19 Boal, Mexico City to Daniels, June 16, 1937, Daniels Papers;

Boal to Secretary of State, July 2, 6 P.M., July 6, 5 P.M., and July 7, 3 P.M., 1937, in *Foreign Relations, 1937* (1954), V, 644–46; Lockett, Mexico City, to Daniels, July 3, 1937, Daniels Papers.

20 Hull, Washington, to Boal, July 9, 1937, 5 P.M., in *Foreign Relations, 1937*, V, 646–47.
21 Certain American oil companies to the Secretary of State, July 14, 1937, *ibid.*, pp. 649–52.
22 Boal, Mexico City, to Secretary of State, July 15, 1937, *ibid.*, pp. 652–54.
23 Boal, Mexico City, to Secretary of State, July 10, 5 P.M., and July 14, 4 P.M., 1937; Boal, memorandum of conversation with Ramón Beteta, July 10, 1937, *ibid.*, pp. 647–49, 654–56.
24 Boal, Mexico City, to Secretary of State, undated [July 8, 1937], *ibid.*, pp. 686–87.
25 Hull, Washington, to Boal, August 2, 1937, 7 P.M., *ibid.*, pp. 657–59.
26 Boal, Mexico City, to Secretary of State, August 4, 1937, 8 P.M., *ibid.*, pp. 659–61.
27 *Mexico's Oil*, pp. 591–603.
28 *Ibid.*, pp. 591–92; Jesús Silva Herzog, "Mexico's Case in the Oil Controversy," *International Conciliation*, No. 345 (December, 1938), p. 517.
29 Boal, Mexico City, to Secretary of State, August 4, 1937, 8 P.M., in *Foreign Relations, 1937*, V, 659–61.
30 F. C. Pannill, New York, to Laurence Duggan, August 11, 1937, in *Foreign Relations, 1937*, V, 662–64.
31 William P. Blocker, Mexico City, to Secretary of State, August 16, 1937, *ibid.*, p. 665. See also Boal, Mexico City, to Daniels, August 14, 1937, Daniels Papers.
32 Duggan, memorandum of conversation, August 18, 1937; Certain American oil companies to the Secretary of State, August 18, 1937, in *Foreign Relations, 1937*, V, 666–69; *Mexico: Labor Controversy*, pp. 47–49.
33 Walter C. Teagle, New York, to Hull, September 1, 1937, DS, 812.6363/3002.
34 Hull, Washington, to Daniels, August 31, 1937, Daniels Papers.
35 *New York Times*, September 6 and 7, 1937; Daniels, Mexico City, to Secretary of State, September 6 and 11, 1937, DS, 812.6363/2994 and /3006.
36 Daniels, Mexico City, to Hull, September 7, 1937, Daniels Papers.

37 Daniels, Mexico City, to Hull, September 9, 1937, Daniels Papers.

38 Daniels, Mexico City, to Hull, September 24, 1937, Daniels Papers.

39 Daniels, Mexico City, to Franklin D. Roosevelt, September 14, 1937, Daniels Papers.

40 Duggan to Legal Adviser [Green H. Hackworth], September 24, 1937, DS, 812.5045/567. See also Duggan to Secretary of State, September 4, 1937, DS, 812.5045/541.

41 Daniels, Mexico City, to Secretary of State, October 20, 1937, 2 P.M., in *Foreign Relations, 1937*, V, 672–73.

42 Daniels, Diary, November 6, 1937, Daniels Papers. See also Daniels, *Shirt-Sleeve Diplomat*, pp. 223–24.

43 Daniels, Mexico City, to Secretary of State, November 10, 1937, 10 P.M., DS, 812.5045/580.

44 Daniels, Mexico City, to Hull, October 29, 1937, Daniels Papers.

45 Hull, Washington, to Daniels, November 17, 1937, Daniels Papers. See also Welles to Hackworth, November 6, 1937, DS, 812.5045/587.

46 *New York Times*, November 17, 18, and 21, 1937.

47 Daniels, Mexico City, to Secretary of State, November 17, 1937, 5 P.M., in *Foreign Relations, 1937*, V, 674–75. See also Duggan to Welles, November 24, 1937, DS, 812.6363/3048.

48 Daniels, Mexico City, to Hull, November 26, 1937, Daniels Papers.

49 Duggan, memorandum of conversation, January 5, 1938, DS, 812.52/2542.

50 Daniels, Mexico City, to Hull, November 19, 1937, Daniels Papers.

51 Allan S. Everest, *Morgenthau, the New Deal, and Silver: a Story of Pressure Politics* (New York: King's Crown Press, 1950), p. 83.

52 *New York Times*, November 21, 1937.

53 Daniels, Mexico City, to Welles, December 9, 1937, Daniels Papers.

54 Henry Morgenthau, Jr., Diary, CI (December 13, 1937), 298, quoted in Everest, *Morgenthau*, p. 86.

55 Duggan, memorandum of conversation, December 15, 1937, DS, 812.5045/623. See also Duggan, memorandum of conversation, December 14, 1937, in *Foreign Relations, 1937*, V, 639–42.

56 Morgenthau, Diary, CII (December 16, 1937), 178 f., quoted in Everest, *Morgenthau*, p. 86.

57 *Ibid.*, p. 87.

58 *New York Times,* December 19, 1937; *Mexico's Oil,* pp. 697–803.
59 Daniels, Diary, December 20, 1937, Daniels Papers.
60 *Ibid.,* December 23, 1937, Daniels Papers.
61 *Wall Street Journal,* December 30, 1937; New York *Journal of Commerce,* December 30, 1937; H[erbert] F[eis], memorandum of conversation, December 30, 1937, DS, 812.5045/622.
62 Everest, *Morgenthau,* p. 87.
63 Morgenthau, Diary, CIV (December 31, 1937), 285 f., quoted in *ibid.,* pp. 87–88.
64 Welles, memorandum of conversation, December 29, 1937, Daniels Papers. For the Treasury's disclaimer of politics, see *New York Times,* December 31, 1937.
65 Welles to Feis, December 30, 1937, DS, 812.5045/622.
66 H[erbert] F[eis] to Welles, December 31, 1937, DS, 812.5045/637.
67 Daniels, Mexico City, to Secretary of State, December 30, 1937, 7 P.M., in *Foreign Relations, 1937,* V, 675–76.
68 Welles, Washington, to Daniels, December 31, 1937, 2 P.M., *ibid.,* pp. 676–77.
69 Hull, Washington, to Daniels, December 31, 1937, 7 P.M., *ibid.,* pp. 677–78.
70 Daniels, Diary, January 8, 1938, Daniels Papers.
71 Daniels, Mexico City, to Welles, January 10, 1938, Daniels Papers.
72 Daniels, Mexico City, to Lockett, January 14, 1938, Daniels Papers.
73 Daniels, Mexico City, to Secretary of State, January 21, 1938, DS, 812.5045/636. For a Mexican official's candid opinion of Armstrong, see Lockett, Mexico City, to Daniels, July 6, 1938, Daniels Papers.
74 Memorandum of conversation between Thomas R. Armstrong and Antonio Villalobos, January 29, 1938, DS, 812.5045/645.
75 Daniels, Mexico City, to Lockett, January 28, 1938, Daniels Papers.
76 Lockett, Mexico City, to Daniels, July 6, 1938, Daniels Papers.
77 Daniels, Mexico City, to Secretary of State, February 24, 1938, 7 P.M., in *Foreign Relations, 1938* (1956), V, 721–22.
78 *Ibid.* See also Daniels, draft account of incidents pertaining to the oil controversy, February 18 and 24, 1938, Daniels Papers.
79 Daniels, draft account of incidents, February 21 and 22, 1938, Daniels Papers.
80 "To Duggan," February 21, 1938, *ibid.*

81 *Ibid.*
82 Adolf A. Berle, Jr., memorandum of conversation, October 4, 1938, DS, 812.5045/821.
83 Daniels, Mexico City, to Secretary of State, February 25, 1938, noon, in *Foreign Relations, 1938,* V, 722–23.
84 *New York Times,* March 2, 1938; *Mexico's Oil,* pp. 847–73.
85 *New York Times,* March 2, 1938.
86 Daniels, Mexico City, to Welles, March 4, 1938, Daniels Papers.
87 Daniels, Mexico City, to Secretary of State, March 11, 1938, in *Foreign Relations, 1938,* V, 723–24.
88 Daniels, Diary, March 5, 1938, Daniels Papers.
89 Daniels, Diary, March 12, 1938, Daniels Papers.
90 *New York Times,* March 16, 1938.
91 Daniels, Mexico City, to Secretary of State, March 16, 1938, 7 P.M., in *Foreign Relations, 1938,* V, 724–25. See also Daniels to Secretary of State, March 19, 1938, DS, 812.5045/705.
92 Lockett, Mexico City, to Daniels, July 6, 1938; Daniels, Mexico City, to Hull, July 26, 1938; Daniels, Mexico City, to Roosevelt, July 30, 1938, Daniels Papers.
93 Boal, Boalsburg, to the author, July 21, 1957.
94 Duggan, memorandum of conversation, March 16, 1938, DS, 812.5045/725.

Chapter VIII

1 Daniels, Mexico City, to Hull, March 22, 1938, Daniels Papers.
2 Hull, memorandum of conversation, April 2, 1938, in Department of State, *Foreign Relations of the United States, 1938* (Washington: Government Printing Office, 1956), V, 743.
3 *Mexico's Oil* (Mexico City: Government of Mexico, 1940), pp. 877–79.
4 *New York Times,* March 20 and 21, 1938; Daniels, Mexico City, to Secretary of State, March 19, 1938, 3 P.M., DS, 812.6363/3093.
5 Daniels, Diary, March 19, 1938, Daniels Papers.
6 *New York Times,* March 20, 1938.
7 *Ibid.,* March 19 and 20, 1938.
8 Hull, Washington, to Daniels, March 19, 1938, 7 P.M., in *Foreign Relations, 1938,* V, 727.
9 Daniels, Mexico City, to Secretary of State, March 20, 1938, 1 P.M., DS, 812.6363/3097. See also Daniels to Hull, March 25, 1938, Daniels Papers.

10 Daniels, Mexico City, to Secretary of State, March 21, 1938, 10 P.M., *Foreign Relations, 1938,* V, 728–29.

11 Daniels, Mexico City, to Secretary of State, March 22, 1938, 9 P.M., *ibid.,* pp. 733–34; Daniels to Hull, March 22, 1938, Daniels Papers.

12 Daniels, Mexico City, to Hull, March 22, 1938, Daniels Papers.

13 Daniels, Mexico City, to Franklin D. Roosevelt, March 22, 1938, Daniels Papers.

14 H[erbert] F[eis], "The Consequences of Ending the Treasury Arrangement for the Purchase of Mexican Silver," March 24, 1938, DS, 812.515 Silver Purchase/736.

15 Allan S. Everest, *Morgenthau, the New Deal, and Silver: a Story of Pressure Politics* (New York: King's Crown Press, 1950), p. 88.

16 Henry Morgenthau, Jr., Diary, CXVI (March 24, 1938), 406, *ibid.*

17 Morgenthau, Washington, to Roosevelt, March 25, 1938, 2:26 P.M., Roosevelt Papers.

18 *New York Times,* March 28, 1938; Department of State, *Press Releases,* XVIII (April 2, 1938), 435.

19 *New York Times,* March 29 and 31, 1938.

20 Morgenthau, Diary, CXVII (March 28, 1938), 267, in Everest, *Morgenthau,* p. 89.

21 Hull, Washington, to Daniels, March 26, 1938, 2 P.M., quoted in Daniels, *Shirt-Sleeve Diplomat* (Chapel Hill: University of North Carolina Press, 1947), pp. 232–35.

22 Hull, Washington, to Daniels, March 26, 1938, 3 P.M., in *Foreign Relations, 1938,* V, 734–35.

23 See, for example, *New York Times,* March 24, 1938; Daniels, Mexico City, to Welles, March 25, 1938, Daniels Papers; Daniels, *Shirt-Sleeve Diplomat,* pp. 246–47.

24 Daniels, Mexico City, to Secretary of State, March 27, 1938, 1 A.M., DS, 812.6363/3167.

25 Daniels, Mexico City, to Secretary of State, March 27, 1938, 9 A.M., in *Foreign Relations, 1938,* V, 735.

26 Hull, Washington, to Daniels, March 27, 1938, 2 P.M., DS, 812.6363/3190B.

27 Hull, Washington, to Daniels, March 27, 1938, 3 P.M., in *Foreign Relations, 1938,* V, 735–36.

28 Daniels, Mexico City, to Secretary of State, March 27, 1938, 9 P.M., *ibid.,* p. 736.

29 Daniels, Mexico City, to Secretary of State, March 29, 1938, 1 P.M., DS, 812.6363/3203.

30 *New York Times,* July 20 and 21, 1938.
31 Hull, Washington, to Daniels, July 20, 2 P.M., and July 21, 1938, 6 P.M., in *Foreign Relations, 1938,* V, 755–57; Laurence Duggan, press release, July 21, 1938, DS, 812.52/2942.
32 Daniels, Mexico City, to Hull, July 24, 1938, Daniels Papers. See also transcript of telephone conversation between Hull and Daniels, July 21, 1938, DS, 812.52/2968; Daniels, Diary, July 23, 1938, Daniels Papers; Daniels, Mexico City, to Secretary of State, July 21, 1938, noon; Welles, memorandum of conversation, March 31, 1938, in *Foreign Relations, 1938,* V, 756, 737–38.
33 Hull, Washington, to Daniels, July 21, 1938, 6 P.M., *Foreign Relations, 1938,* V, 757.
34 Daniels, Mexico City, to Secretary of State, March 30, 1938, 3 P.M., DS, 812.6363/3215; Daniels, *Shirt-Sleeve Diplomat,* p. 236.
35 Lázaro Cárdenas to Daniels, March 31, 1938, in Department of State, *Press Releases,* XVIII (April 2, 1938), 435–36; Daniels, *Shirt-Sleeve Diplomat,* pp. 236–37.
36 Daniels, Mexico City, to Secretary of State, March 31, 1938, 9 P.M., in *Foreign Relations, 1938,* V, 739–41.
37 *Ultimas Noticias,* February 6, 1939; *New York Times,* February 7, 1939.
38 Ramón Beteta, Rome, to the author, June 23, 1953.
39 Daniels, Mexico City, to Roosevelt, March 29 and 30, 1938, Daniels Papers.
40 Morgenthau, Diary, CXVIII (April 1, 1938), 27 ff., quoted in Everest, *Morgenthau,* p. 90.
41 Laurence Duggan, memorandum of conversation, April 6, 1938, DS, 812.6363/3450.
42 *New York Times,* April 15, 1938.
43 H[erbert] F[eis], memorandum, April 18, 1938, DS, 811.515 Silver Purchase/726.
44 Daniels, *Shirt-Sleeve Diplomat,* pp. 249–50. A table listing the Treasury's total annual purchases of Mexican silver between 1934 and 1941 may be found in Everest, *Morgenthau,* p. 177.
45 Everest, *Morgenthau,* pp. 90–91.
46 Presidential press conference 447, Warm Springs, April 1, 1938, 1 P.M., Roosevelt Papers, XI, 266–68. See also *New York Times,* April 2, 1938; Associated Press dispatch, April 1, 1938, Daniels Papers.
47 Welles, memorandum of conversation, March 31, 1938, in *Foreign Relations, 1938,* V, 737.

48 Welles, memorandum of conversation, March 21, 1938, *ibid.*, p. 730.
49 Hull, memorandum of conversation, April 2, 1938, *ibid.*, p. 742.
50 Daniels, Mexico City, to Roosevelt, April 6, 1938, Daniels Papers.

CHAPTER IX

1 Cordell Hull, Washington, to Francisco Castillo Nájera, July 21, 1938, in Department of State, *Foreign Relations of the United States, 1938* (Washington: Government Printing Office, 1956), V, 676.
2 Josephus Daniels, Mexico City, to Claude G. Bowers, September 6, 1938, Daniels Papers.
3 Daniels, Mexico City, to Hull, April 2, 1938, Daniels Papers.
4 Daniels, Mexico City, to Secretary of State, April 4, 1938, 11 P.M., in *Foreign Relations, 1938*, V, 746.
5 Daniels, Mexico City, to Hull, April 14, 1938, Daniels Papers.
6 Daniels, Mexico City, to Hull, April 9, 1938; Daniels, Diary, April 9, 1938, Daniels Papers.
7 Sumner Welles, Washington, to Daniels, April 11, 1938, Daniels Papers.
8 *Correspondence with the Mexican Government Regarding the Expropriation of Oil Properties in Mexico*, Cmd. 5758 (London: His Majesty's Stationery Office, 1938), pp. 2–3.
9 *Ibid.*, pp. 13–14.
10 Mexico to Great Britain, May 13, 1938, *ibid.*, pp. 14–15.
11 Henry Morgenthau, Jr., Diary, CXXIV (May 12, 1938), 346 f., in Allan S. Everest, *Morgenthau, the New Deal, and Silver: a Story of Pressure Politics* (New York: King's Crown Press, 1950), p. 91.
12 Daniels, Mexico City, to Hull, August 19, 1938, Daniels Papers.
13 *New York Times*, April 22, 1938.
14 Welles, memorandum of conversation, and Welles to Castillo Nájera, May 9, 1938, in *Foreign Relations, 1938*, V, 664–65, 749–52; *New York Times*, May 12, 1938.
15 *New York Times*, May 13, 1938.
16 Castillo Nájera, Washington, to Welles, May 26, 1938, DS, 812.52/2981; *New York Times*, May 27, 1938.
17 Daniels, Raleigh, to Franklin D. Roosevelt, May 29, 1938, Roosevelt Papers.
18 Laurence Duggan, memorandum of conversation, May 31, 1938, in *Foreign Relations, 1938*, V, 752–55.
19 T. R. Armstrong, *Various Aspects of the Mexican Oil Confisca-*

tion (New York: Committee on Mexican Relations, 1938), p. 15.

20   Daniels, Raleigh, to Roosevelt, June 4, 1938, Daniels Papers.

21   See, for example, *New York Times,* March 27, April 1, and August 24, 1938, February 1, July 15 and 23, 1939; México, Secretaría de Relaciones Exteriores, *Tribunales extranjeros reconocen el indiscutible derecho con que México expropio los intereses petroleros* (México: Talleres Gráficos de la Nación, 1940); *The True Facts about the Expropriation of the Oil Companies' Properties in Mexico* (Mexico City: Government of Mexico, 1940), p. 14; Ruth Sheldon, "Mexico Faced Many Problems in Operating Refineries," and "Poza Rica Field Backbone of Oil Industry in Mexico," *Oil and Gas Journal,* XXXVIII (May 18, 1939), 40, and (May 25, 1939), 29, 104.

22   Daniels, Mexico City, to Hull, February 24, 1939, Daniels Papers.

23   Hull, Washington, to Claude A. Swanson, May 2, 1939, DS, 812.6363/5736. See also Herbert S. Bursley, memorandum, April 25, 1939, DS, 812.6363/5735.

24   Welles, memorandum of conversation, July 26, 1939, DS, 800.014 Antarctic/230.

25   Green H. Hackworth, memorandum of conversation, September 26, 1940, DS, 812.6363/7113 1/2.

26   Mexican Embassy, Washington, to Department of State, October 2, 1940; Duggan, memorandum, October 2, 1940; J. F. Stone, memorandum, October 10, 1940; and Adolf A. Berle, Jr., memorandum, October 11, 1940, DS, 812.6363/7119 1/2; /7120 1/2; /7159; and /7160. The State Department, without passing judgment on the Sinclair settlement, finally decided that Sinclair's oil imports from Mexico would not be considered "confiscated" (and banned for government purchase), provided the oil came from Sinclair's old properties in Mexico. Hull told Secretary of the Navy Frank Knox: "Where any such oil is offered to the Navy, it would seem to be a question of fact for its determination whether or not the oil falls within this category." Hull to Knox, October 14, 1940, DS, 812.6363/7123A.

27   Bursley, memorandum of conversation, May 3, 1940, DS, 812.6363/6846.

28   Department of State, *Executive Agreement Series,* Nos. 191 and 192 (Washington: Government Printing Office, 1941).

29   Daniels, Mexico City, to Secretary of State, August 30, 1938, in *Foreign Relations, 1938,* V, 759; Daniels, *Shirt-Sleeve Diplomat* (Chapel Hill: University of North Carolina Press, 1947),

pp. 255–56; Standard Oil Company (N.J.), *Looking at Mexico* [excerpted from *The Lamp*], I (April 28, 1939).

30 William Miller, Cleveland, to Paul Y. Anderson, November 28, 1938; Miller to Daniels, January 5, 1939, Daniels Papers.

31 *Ibid.*; Upton Close, New York, to Daniels, September 15, 1938, Daniels Papers; Close to Hull, August 20, 1938, DS, 812.52/ 3238; Henry J. Allen, *The Mexican Confiscations: Together with a Careful Survey of the Present Revolutionary Trends in Mexico* (August, 1938); Allen, "Mexico's Kilowatt Crooks," *Reader's Digest*, XXXIII (November, 1938), 58.

32 See, for example, *Salt Lake Tribune*, October 18, 1938; *New York Times*, November 23, 1938.

33 Daniels, Mexico City, to Bowers, September 6, 1938, Daniels Papers.

34 "The Atlantic Presents," *Nation*, CXLVII (September 3, 1938), 217.

35 Marshall, "Mexico Cuts Off Her Nose," *Collier's*, CIV (November 25, 1939), 16; Daniels, Mexico City, to Secretary of State, February 27, 1940, DS, 812.6363/6552; Quintana, *Facts on Mexican Oil.*

36 Daniels, Mexico City, to Duggan, September 29, 1938, Daniels Papers.

37 Burt M. McConnell, *Mexico at the Bar of Public Opinion* (New York: Mail and Express Publishing Company, 1939).

38 Carroll Kilpatrick, Montgomery, to Daniels, September 5, 1938, Daniels Papers.

39 *New York Times*, May 19, 20, 22, and 23, 1938; Daniels, *Shirt-Sleeve Diplomat*, p. 259.

40 Duggan, memorandum of conversation, May 31, 1938, in *Foreign Relations, 1938*, V, 754.

41 *New York Times*, June 8 and November 22, 1938.

42 Daniels, Mexico City, to Roosevelt, July 12, 1938; Daniels to Welles, undated draft [July, 1938], Daniels Papers.

43 Daniels, Mexico City, to Roosevelt, April 8, 1938, Daniels Papers.

44 Daniels, Mexico City, to Secretary of State, April 20, 1938, DS, 812.6363/3573.

45 Welles, memorandum of conversation, May 9, 1938, in *Foreign Relations, 1938*, V, 750–51; Castillo Nájera, Washington, to Welles, May 26, 1938, DS, 812.52/2981. For a discussion of the Yaqui Valley claims, see pp. 141–53.

46 Welles, Washington, to Castillo Nájera, June 29, 1938, in *Foreign Relations, 1938,* V, 667–72.

47 Daniels, Mexico City, to Welles, July 7, 1938, Daniels Papers.

48 Frank Tannenbaum, Mexico City, to Daniels, July 6, 1938, Daniels Papers.

49 Morgenthau, Diary, CXXXIV (July 13, 1938), 164 f., in Everest, *Morgenthau,* p. 91. Interestingly, only a few days before, Hull had flatly denied that the United States was putting financial pressure on Mexico. *New York Times,* July 1, 1938.

50 Daniels, Mexico City, to Roosevelt, July 2, 1938, Roosevelt Papers. See also Daniels to Hull, July 8, 1938; Daniels to Roosevelt, July 12, 1938, Daniels Papers.

51 Daniels, Mexico City, to Roosevelt, July 14, 1938, Roosevelt Papers.

52 Presidential press conference 447, Warm Springs, April 1, 1938, 1 P.M., Roosevelt Papers, XI, 266–68. See also *New York Times,* April 2, 1938; Associated Press dispatch, April 1, 1938, Daniels Papers.

53 Hull, Washington, to Castillo Nájera, July 21, 1938, in *Foreign Relations, 1938,* V, 674–78.

54 *New York Times,* July 22 and 23, 1938.

55 Armstrong, New York, to Hull, July 28 and 29, 1938, DS, 812.52/2985 and /3001.

56 *New York Times,* July 23, 1938.

57 New York *Journal of Commerce,* August 18, 1938.

58 *New York Times,* July 24, 1938.

59 *Ibid.,* July 28, 1938.

60 Daniels, Mexico City, to Hull, August 2, 1938, Daniels Papers.

61 Daniels, Mexico City, to Welles, July 29, 1938, Daniels Papers.

62 Daniels, Mexico City, to Roosevelt, July 30, 1938, Daniels Papers.

63 *New York Times,* August 4 and 5, 1938; Duggan, Washington, to Daniels, August 6, 1938, Daniels Papers.

64 Eduardo Hay, Mexico City, to Daniels, August 3, 1938, in *Foreign Relations, 1938,* V, 679–84.

65 Daniels, Mexico City, to Hull, August 7, 1938, Daniels Papers.

66 Pierre de L. Boal, Boalsburg, to Daniels, August 21, 1938, Daniels Papers.

67 "Anti-Daniels Grumbling," *Newsweek,* XII (August 22, 1938), 7; Close, New York, to Hull, August 20, 1938, DS, 812.52/3238. Rather embarrassed, Hull agreed that the *Newsweek* story was

"shameful." Hull to Close, September 6, 1938, DS, 812.52/3238.

68 Hull, Washington, to Castillo Nájera, August 22, 1938, in *Foreign Relations, 1938*, V, 685–96.

69 Hull, memorandum of conversation, August 22, 1938, DS, 812.52/3178.

70 Daniels, Mexico City, to Roosevelt, August 27, 1938, Daniels Papers [not sent?].

71 Daniels, Mexico City, to Roosevelt, August 31, 1938, Daniels Papers.

72 *New York Times*, August 27, 1938.

73 Daniels, Diary, August 29, 1938, Daniels Papers; *New York Times*, August 27 and 28, 1938.

74 *New York Times*, September 2, 1938.

75 Hay, Mexico City, to Daniels, September 1, 1938, in *Foreign Relations, 1938*, V, 696–702.

76 Daniels, Mexico City, to Hull, September 2, 1938, Daniels Papers.

77 Daniels, Mexico City, to Hull, September 3, 1938, Daniels Papers.

78 Hull, memoranda of conversations, September 6 and 10, 1938, in *Foreign Relations, 1938*, V, 702–7.

79 J. R. O'Connor, New York, to Daniels, September 17, 1938, Daniels Papers.

80 Daniels, Mexico City, to Roosevelt, September 15, 1938, Daniels Papers.

81 Hull, memorandum of conversation, September 20, 1938, in *Foreign Relations, 1938*, V, 707–9.

82 Boal, Washington, to Daniels, September 21, 1938, Daniels Papers.

83 Duggan, Washington, to Daniels, September 28, 1938, Daniels Papers.

84 Daniels, Mexico City, to Hull, September 27, 1938, Daniels Papers. See also Daniels to Secretary of State, September 16, 1938, noon, DS, 812.52/3296.

85 Hull, memorandum of conversation, September 26, 1938, in *Foreign Relations, 1938*, V, 709–10.

86 Daniels, Mexico City, to Welles, October 12 and 14, 1938; Daniels to Hull, October 18, 1938, Daniels Papers. The quotation is from the letter to Hull.

87 Bursley, memorandum of telephone conversation, October 26, 1938, DS, 812.52/3534; Daniels, Mexico City, to Secretary of

State, October 26, 1938, in *Foreign Relations, 1938,* V, 710–13.

88 Daniels, Mexico City, to Roosevelt, October 29, 1938, Daniels Papers.

89 Hull, Washington, to Daniels, November 2, 1938, 5 P.M., in *Foreign Relations, 1938,* V, 713–14.

90 Hull, Washington, to Castillo Nájera, November 9, 1938; Hay, Mexico City, to Daniels, November 12, 1938, *ibid.,* pp. 714–19.

CHAPTER X

1 Daniels, Mexico City, to Reuben B. Robertson, February 9, 1939, Daniels Papers.

2 *New York Times,* October 23, 1938.

3 T. R. Armstrong, New York, to Cordell Hull, October 26, 1938, DS, 812.52/3444.

4 Daniels, memorandum of conversation, December 10, 1938, Daniels Papers.

5 Daniels, memorandum of conversation, January 14, 1939, Daniels Papers.

6 Daniels, Mexico City, to Franklin D. Roosevelt, January 31, 1939, Daniels Papers.

7 Sumner Welles, Washington, to Stephen Early, January 18, 1939, Roosevelt Papers; *New York Times,* January 10, 22, and February 14, 1939.

8 *New York Times,* March 3, 1939; Senate Res. 177, 76 Cong., 1 sess., *Congressional Record,* LXXXIV (July 29 and 31, 1939), 10411, 10464.

9 Senate Res. 72, 76 Cong., 1 sess.; *New York Times,* January 28, 1939.

10 *Congressional Record,* LXXXIV (April 4, 1939), 3806.

11 I.N.S. dispatch, February 1, 1939, quoted in *ibid.* (July 29, 1939), p. 10413. After a conversation with Knickerbocker, Daniels reported to Hull that the newsman "seemed to know more about the note of March 27th than anybody else." Daniels, Mexico City, to Hull, February 7, 1939, Daniels Papers.

12 House Res. 102, 76 Cong., 1 sess., *Congressional Record* LXXXIV (February 22, 1939), 1795. See also House Res. 78, 107, and Senate Res. 177, *ibid.* (February 7, March 8, July 29 and 31, 1939), pp. 1181, 2463, 10411–18, and 10464.

13 *Ibid.* (April 4, 1939), p. 3807.

14 *New York Times,* March 23, 24, 26, 27, 31, April 3, 7, 10, 28,

May 15, 16, July 24, October 24, December 10, 24, 1938, January 21, 23, February 11, 15, 24, April 6, 7, 21, June 25, and July 15, 1939; Department of State, *Documents on German Foreign Policy, 1918–1945* (Washington: Government Printing Office, 1953), Series D, vol. V, 829, note 5; Ruth Sheldon, "Marketing Harasses Mexican Oil Industry Officials," *Oil and Gas Journal*, XXXVIII (June 1, 1939), 18–19.

15 Lázaro Cárdenas, Mexico City, to Roosevelt, September 28, 1938; Daniels, Mexico City, to Roosevelt, September 29, 1938, Daniels Papers.

16 Sheldon, *op. cit.*, p. 18. According to Sheldon, Mexico managed to export 12,616,951 barrels and 56,955 metric tons of crude oil and refined products, worth $12,313,411, in the first year after expropriation. This was about half what the companies had annually exported in 1934–36. See tables in *Mexico's Oil* (Mexico City: Government of Mexico, 1940), pp. 567–69.

17 Daniels, Mexico City, to R. Walton Moore, January 23, 1937, Daniels Papers.

18 Daniels, Mexico City, to Roosevelt, April 16, 1937; Roosevelt, Washington, to Daniels, April 23, 1937, Daniels Papers.

19 Daniels, Mexico City, to Hull, June 30, 1938, Daniels Papers. See also Daniels to Hull, July 8, 1938, Daniels Papers.

20 Daniels, Mexico City, to Hull, February 9, 1939, Daniels Papers.

21 Daniels, Mexico City, to Hull, August 20, 1938, Daniels Papers.

22 Daniels, Mexico City, to Hull, August 22, 1938, Daniels Papers.

23 Daniels, memorandum of conversation with John R. O'Connor, September 7, 1938, Daniels Papers.

24 Welles, memorandum of conversation, February 18, 1939, in Department of State, *Foreign Relations of the United States, 1939* (Washington: Government Printing Office, 1957), V, 667–68; *New York Times*, February 24, 1939.

25 See Freiherr von Rüdt, Mexico City, to German Foreign Ministry, April 8, 1938, in *Documents on German Foreign Policy*, Series D, vol. V, 827–29.

26 See Daniels, Mexico City, to Roosevelt, July 12, 1938; Daniels, Mexico City, to Welles, undated draft [July, 1938], Daniels Papers.

27 Daniels, memorandum of conversation, January 14, 1939; Daniels, Mexico City, to Roosevelt, January 22, 1939, draft, Daniels Papers.

28 Roosevelt, Washington, to George T. Bye, March 7, 1939, Roosevelt Papers.

29 Daniels, memorandum of conversation, January 14, 1939, Daniels Papers.

30 *Ibid.*

31 See Donald R. Richberg, *The Mexican Oil Seizure* [New York: Standard Oil Company of New Jersey, 1940]; Richberg, *My Hero: the Indiscreet Memoirs of an Eventful But Unheroic Life* (New York: Putnam, 1954), pp. 248–68; *The True Facts about the Expropriation of the Oil Companies' Properties in Mexico* (Mexico City: Government of Mexico, 1940), pp. 103–28; *Oil: Mexico's Position* (Mexican Bureau of Information, 1940); *Foreign Relations, 1939,* V, 667–719; Don Lohbeck, *Patrick J. Hurley* (Chicago: Regnery, 1956), pp. 147–50.

32 Roosevelt, Washington, to Daniels, February 15, 1939, Daniels and Roosevelt Papers. This letter was originally drafted by Sumner Welles and subsequently revised by the President. The most significant change by Roosevelt was his deletion of the word "simultaneous," which Welles had twice used in referring to compensation for expropriated property.

33 Daniels, memorandum of conversation, February 25, 1939; Daniels, Mexico City, to Roosevelt, February 28, 1939, Daniels Papers; Welles, memorandum of conversation, February 18, 1939, in *Foreign Relations, 1939,* V, 668.

34 Daniels, Mexico City, to Hull, March 17, 1939; Welles, Washington, to Daniels, March 23, 1939. Daniels Papers.

35 Richberg, *My Hero,* p. 252.

36 Richberg, "The Mexican Oil Problem," address given before the National Petroleum Association, Cleveland, April 14, 1939, Richberg Papers; *New York Times,* April 15, 1939.

37 See Richberg, Washington, to Green H. Hackworth, September 25, 1940, DS, 812.6363/7103.

38 Richberg, Washington, to Laurence Duggan, May 18, 1939, in *Foreign Relations, 1939,* V, 674–75; Richberg to Hackworth, September 25, 1940, DS, 812.6363/7103.

39 Welles, memorandum of conversation, May 29 and June 20, 1939, in *Foreign Relations, 1939,* V, 679–80, 683–84; *New York Times,* June 16, 17, and 18, 1939.

40 Richberg, Washington, to Francisco Castillo Nájera, July 17, 1939, in *Foreign Relations, 1939,* V, 693–96.

41 Welles, memorandum of conversations, August 2 and 10, 1939, *ibid.,* pp. 688–90, 696–97. The quotation is from Richberg, *My Hero,* p. 262.

42 *New York Times,* August 10, 11, 12, 16, 17, and 18, 1939; W. S. Farish, New York, to Hull, August 10, 1939, in *Foreign Relations, 1939,* V, 609–93.

43 Welles, press statement, in *Foreign Relations, 1939,* V, 697–700; *New York Times,* August 15, 1939.

44 Farish, New York, to Hull, August 10, 1939, in *Foreign Relations, 1939,* V, 690–93.

45 *New York Times,* September 2, 1939.

46 Roosevelt, Washington, to Cárdenas, August 31, 1939, in *Foreign Relations, 1939,* V, 703–6; Daniels, Mexico City, to Roosevelt, September 12, 1939, Daniels Papers; Duggan, Washington, to Welles, September 29, 1939, 6 P.M., DS, 812.6363/6177A.

47 *New York Times,* December 3, 1939; Standard Oil Company (N.J.), *Denials of Justice* (New York: 1940), pp. 49–167; *Mexico's Oil,* pp. 807–73; Daniels, Mexico City, to Secretary of State, December 5, 1939, in *Foreign Relations, 1939,* V, 712–13.

48 Richberg, *My Hero,* p. 265.

49 *New York Times,* February 24 and 26, 1939; *Washington Post,* April 7 and 8, 1939; Daniels, Mexico City, to Herbert S. Bursley, April 8, 1939, Daniels Papers. The quotation is from Richberg, "Mexican Oil Problem," April 14, 1939, Richberg Papers.

50 Richberg, *My Hero,* p. 267. See also *ibid.,* pp. 250, 252–53.

51 *New York Times,* January 14 and 31, 1940; Mexico, *Oil: Mexico's Position* and *True Facts;* Standard Oil Company (N.J.), *Denials of Justice,* and *The Reply to Mexico,* and *Present Status of the Mexican Oil "Expropriations"* (New York: 1940).

52 *New York Times,* August 16, 1939.

53 Hull, memoranda of conversations, September 19 and October 6, 1939; British aide mémoire, December 12, 1939, in *Foreign Relations, 1939,* V, 707, 709, 716–19.

54 *Congressional Record,* LXXXVI (March 28, 1940), 3638.

55 Bursley to Briggs and Welles, January 10, 1940, DS, 812.6363/6445.

56 *New York Times,* August 6, 1939.

57 Franklin D. Roosevelt to James Roosevelt, September 26, 1939, Roosevelt Papers.

58 Department of State, *Executive Agreement Series,* No. 191 (Washington: Government Printing Office, 1941); Welles, memorandum of conversation, December 11, 1939, in *Foreign Relations, 1939,* V, 715. Shortly after this agreement went into

effect, the quota for "other foreign countries," including Mexico, was raised to 5.1 per cent of the total. *Executive Agreement Series,* No. 192 (1941).

59 Santa Barbara *News Press,* December 11, 1939; Bursley to Briggs, January 4, 1940, DS, 812.6363/6423.

60 Duggan, memorandum of conversation, October 6, 1939, in *Foreign Relations, 1939,* V, 708–9.

61 Welles, memorandum of conversation, May 29, 1939, *ibid.,* p. 680.

62 Lohbeck, *Hurley,* pp. 147–48.

63 Richberg, *My Hero,* p. 266.

64 Welles, memorandum of conversation, November 24, 1939, in *Foreign Relations, 1939,* V, 710–11; Welles, memorandum of conversation with Eduardo Suárez and Castillo Nájera, January 11, 1940; Duggan, memorandum of conversation between Hull and Hurley, March 1, 1940, DS, 812.6363/6451 and /6594; *New York Times,* February 21, 25, 29, March 2, 6, and 10, 1940.

65 Daniels, *Shirt-Sleeve Diplomat* (Chapel Hill: University of North Carolina Press, 1947), p. 265.

66 *New York Times,* March 10, 1940.

67 *Ibid.,* January 31 and February 1, 1940; Welles, memorandum of conversation, December 11, 1939, in *Foreign Relations, 1939,* V, 715; Welles, memorandum of conversation with Castillo Nájera, February 5, 1940; Duggan, memorandum of conversation between Hull and Castillo Nájera, February 19, 1940, DS, 812.6363/6486 and /6529. See also Department of State to the British Embassy, January 11, 1940, DS, 812.6363/6436.

68 Green H. Hackworth to Welles, February 9, 1940, DS, 812.6363/6527.

69 Duggan, memorandum of conversation between Hull and Castillo Nájera, March 2, 1940, DS, 812.6363/6595.

70 Hull to Castillo Nájera, April 3, 1940, in Department of State, *Bulletin,* II (April 9, 1940), 380–83; *New York Times,* April 6, 1940.

71 Hans Thomsen, Washington, to German Foreign Ministry, May 4, 1940, 6:06 P.M., in *Documents on German Foreign Policy, 1918–1945* (1956), Series D, vol. IX, 282–83.

72 *New York Times,* April 8, 1940.

73 *Ibid.,* April 7 and 8, 1940.

74 *Ibid.,* April 12, 1940.

75 *Ibid.,* April 22, 1940.

76 Daniels, Mexico City, to Hull, March 13, 1940; Hull to Daniels, March 23, 1940, DS, 812.6363/6626.

77 Daniels, Mexico City, to Roosevelt, April 27, 1940, Daniels Papers.

78 Eduardo Hay to Daniels, May 1, 1940, in Department of State, *Bulletin*, II (May 4, 1940), 465–70.

79 Bursley to Duggan and Welles, May 2, 1940, DS, 812.6363/6845.

80 *New York Times*, May 8 and 9, 1940.

81 Hackworth, memorandum of conversation between Welles and Hurley, May 6, 1940, DS, 812.6363/6899. See also Daniels, Mexico City, to Secretary of State, May 7, 1940, DS, 812.6363/6864.

82 *New York Times*, May 16, 1940. See also *ibid.*, April 12 and August 7, 1941.

83 Lohbeck, *Hurley*, p. 150.

84 New York *Daily News*, May 25, 1940.

85 *Congressional Record*, LXXXVI (May 6, 1940), 5625–26.

86 *Ibid.* (April 8, 1940), p. 4142. See also *ibid.* (May 6, 1940), p. 5568.

87 *New York Times*, June 1, 1940.

88 *Washington Times Herald*, April 4, 1940; *Congressional Record*, LXXXVI (April 16, 1940), Appendix, 2171–72.

89 Allan S. Everest, *Morgenthau, the New Deal, and Silver: a Story of Pressure Politics* (New York: King's Crown Press, 1950), pp. 75–78.

90 Hurley, address before the Texas Railroad Commission, August 1, 1940, DS, 812.6363/7031; *New York Times*, August 3, 1940; Lohbeck, *Hurley*, pp. 148–49.

91 *New York Times*, September 5, 1940.

92 *Congressional Record*, LXXXVI (October 1, 1940), 12971–94.

93 Duggan to Adolf A. Berle, Welles, and Hull, October 2, 1940; J. F. Stone, memorandum, October 10, 1940; Berle, memorandum, October 11, 1940; Hull to Frank Knox, October 14, 1940, DS, 812.6363/7120 1/2; /7159; /7160; and /7123A.

94 Welles, memorandum of conversation, June 4, 1940; Duggan to Welles, June 7, 1940, DS, 812.6363/6952, and /6965.

95 W. S. Farish, New York, to Hull, June 20, 1940, DS, 812.6363/6981.

96 Pierre de L. Boal, Mexico City, to Secretary of State, June 11, 1940; Duggan, memorandum of telephone conversation with Boal, June 12, 1940, DS, 711.12/1473, and /1482.

97   Daniels, Mexico City, to Secretary of State, June 25, 1940, DS, 711.12/1488; Daniels to Roosevelt, June 28, 1940, Daniels Papers.

98   *New York Times,* September 3, 1940. See also *ibid.,* July 3, 7, 8, 9, 11, 12, 13, 28, August 2, 15, and 16, 1940.

99   Daniels, Mexico City, to Secretary of State, July 5, 1940, DS, 812.00/31150 and Roosevelt Papers. See also Daniels to Roosevelt, September 20 and October 8, 1940; Daniels to Secretary of State, October 28, 1940, Daniels Papers.

100 Daniels, Mexico City, to Roosevelt, August 27, 1940, Daniels Papers.

101 Huston Thompson, Washington, to Daniels, September 4 and November 5, 1940, Daniels Papers.

102 George Creel, San Francisco, to Marvin H. McIntyre [September 11, 1940?], Roosevelt Papers.

103 Roosevelt to Hull, September 18, 1940; McIntyre, Washington, to Creel, September 21, 1940, Roosevelt Papers.

104 Creel, San Francisco, to John R. O'Connor, January 31, 1941; Creel to Daniels, January 31, 1941, Daniels Papers.

105 *New York Times,* September 14, 15, and October 6, 1940.

106 *Ibid.,* November 13, 14, and 19, 1940; Daniels, Mexico City, to Roosevelt, December 2, 1940, telegram, Daniels Papers.

107 See Welles to Roosevelt, December 16, 1940, Roosevelt Papers.

108 *New York Times,* December 2 and 4, 1940.

109 Duggan to Welles, June 12, 1940, DS, 711.12/1482.

110 Daniels, Mexico City, to Roosevelt, March 11, 1941, Daniels Papers. See also Daniels to Roosevelt, February 4, 1941, Daniels Papers; *New York Times,* October 30 and December 17, 1940; William S. McCrea, "A Comparative Study of the Mexican Oil Expropriation (1938) and the Iranian Oil Nationalization (1951)" (unpublished Ph.D. dissertation, Georgetown University, 1955), pp. 238–40.

111 Roosevelt, aboard U.S.S. "Potomac," to Daniels, March 28, 1941, Daniels Papers.

112 Daniels, Mexico City, to Roosevelt, March 11, 1941, Daniels Papers.

113 Farish, New York, to Hull, September 16, 1940, DS, 812.6363/7387.

114 Farish, New York, to Welles, January 24, 1941, DS, 812.6363/7329.

115 Welles to Roosevelt, January 10, 1941, DS, 711.12/1549 1/2.

116 *Congressional Record,* LXXXVII (April 3, 1941), 2987–89;

Daniels, Mexico City, to Roosevelt, April 5, 1941, Daniels Papers.

117 *New York Times,* July 29 and September 4, 1941; *The Secret Diary of Harold L. Ickes,* Vol. III, *The Lowering Clouds, 1939–1941* (New York: Simon and Schuster, 1955), pp. 575–76.

118 Daniels, Mexico City, to Roosevelt, May 2 and June 3, 1941, Daniels Papers.

119 *New York Times,* July 29, 1941.

120 Allan Dawson to Duggan, June 6, 1941, DS, 812.6363/7306 1/2.

121 Welles, memorandum of conversation, May 9, 1938, in *Foreign Relations, 1938* (1956), V, 751.

122 Bursley to Duggan, August 12, 1941, DS, 812.6363/7354 5/11.

123 See, for example, Lawrence M. Lawson, El Paso, to Bursley, July 17, 1941; Duggan to Welles, August 1, 1941, DS, 812.52 Agrarian Commission /236 2/6, and 812.6363/7354 1/11.

124 Bursley, memorandum of conversation between Castillo Nájera and Duggan, July 5, 1941, DS, 812.6363/7317 1/11. See also Bursley to Duggan, June 30, 1941; Bursley, memorandum of conversation between Castillo Nájera and Duggan, July 14, 1941, DS, 812.6363/7317 4/11, and /7317 8/11.

125 Duggan to Welles, August 1, 1941, DS, 812.6363/7354 1/11.

126 Daniels, Mexico City, to Roosevelt, July 25, 1941; Daniels to Welles, July 25, 1941, Daniels Papers.

127 Daniels, Mexico City, to Hull, July 29, 1941, Daniels Papers.

128 Welles to Roosevelt, March 19 and August 8, 1941, Roosevelt Papers; Welles, Washington, to Daniels, August 8, 1941; Roosevelt, Washington, to Daniels, August 18, 1941, Daniels Papers.

129 "Mexican Oil Embarrassment," *Newsweek,* XVIII (August 25, 1941), 8. See also *New York Times,* August 21, September 3, 4, and 5, 1941; *Excélsior* (Mexico City), August 27, 1941.

130 Farish, New York, to Hull, August 27, 1941, DS, 812.6363/7329.

131 Bursley, memorandum of conversation between Duggan and T. R. Armstrong, August 21, 1941, DS, 812.6363/7346 9/9.

132 Bursley to Duggan, September 3, 1941; Petroleum Adviser, memorandum, October 4, 1941, DS, 812.6363/7354 10/11, and 7359 2/3. For Ickes' explanation of Thornburg's dismissal, see *New York Times,* February 2, 1946.

133 See, for example, Ickes, *Secret Diary,* III, 629, 649; Ickes, Washington, to Roosevelt, October 18, 1941, Roosevelt Papers.

134 Hull, *Memoirs* (New York: Macmillan, 1948), II, 1141.

135 See also *New York Times,* October 10, 1941.

136 Henry Morgenthau, Jr., Diary, CDXLVIII (October 6, 1941), 99, quoted in Everest, *Morgenthau,* p. 86. See also *New York Times,* October 7, 1941.

137 Daniels, *Shirt-Sleeve Diplomat,* p. 511.

138 See, for example, *New York Times,* October 23, 24, 26, November 2 and 4, 1941.

139 See Welles to Duggan, November 5, 1941, DS, 812.6363/7353.

140 *New York Times,* November 5, 1941.

141 See, for example, *ibid.,* November 7, 1941.

142 Farish, New York, to Hull, November 13, 1941, DS, 812.6363/7430.

143 Daniels, Raleigh, to Roosevelt, November 13, 1941, Roosevelt Papers; *New York Times,* November 19, 1941; Castillo Nájera, "Prólogo," in Daniels, *Diplomático en mangas de camisa,* trans. Salvador Duhart (México: Talleres Gráficos de la Nación, 1949), pp. xv–xvi.

144 Roosevelt to Hull, November 21, 1941, Roosevelt Papers.

145 Duggan, Washington, to Daniels, November 18, 1941, Daniels Papers.

146 Duggan, Washington, to Daniels, November 25, 1941, Daniels Papers. Daniels himself evidently believed that his intervention had been decisive in persuading the reluctant Hull to act. See F. J. McGurk, Mexico City, to Daniels, November 25, 1941, Daniels Papers.

147 Department of State, *Bulletin,* V (November 22, 1941), 399–403; *New York Times,* November 20, 1941.

148 *New York Times,* November 22, 1941.

149 Farish, New York, to Hull, December 29, 1941, DS, 412.11 Oil/27.

150 Kenneth E. Trombley, *The Life and Times of a Happy Liberal: a Biography of Morris Llewellyn Cooke* (New York: Harper, 1954), pp. 212–13.

151 Bursley, memorandum of conversation, April 1, 1942, DS, 412.11 Oil/91.

152 Department of State, *Executive Agreement Series,* No. 419 (Washington: Government Printing Office, 1945); *New York Times,* April 19, 1942; Hull, *Memoirs,* II, 1141–42.

153 [F. J. McGurk, Mexico City] to Secretary of State, December 7, 1941, Daniels Papers.

154 Hull, *Memoirs,* II, 1423.

CHAPTER XI

1 *La Opinión* (Los Angeles), July 20, 1934.
2 Josephus Daniels, Washington, to Franklin D. Roosevelt, October 30, 1941, Daniels and Roosevelt Papers; also quoted in Daniels, *Shirt-Sleeve Diplomat* (Chapel Hill: University of North Carolina Press, 1947), pp. 513–14.
3 *El Universal* (Mexico City), November 4, 1941. See also *New York Times*, November 4, 1941.
4 Roosevelt, Washington, to Daniels, October 31, 1941, Daniels and Roosevelt Papers; quoted in Daniels, *Shirt-Sleeve Diplomat*, p. 515.
5 Presidential press conference 780, Washington, October 31, 1941, 11 A.M., Roosevelt Papers, XVIII, 267; *New York Times*, November 1, 1941.
6 New York *Journal of Commerce*, November 1, 1941.
7 *Mexican Labor News* (Mexico City), November 4, 1941.
8 *El Popular* (Mexico City), November 4, 1941.
9 Daniels, Mexico City, to George Foster Peabody, January 21, 1938, Daniels Papers.
10 Daniels, Mexico City, to William Allen White, January 10, 1938, Daniels Papers.
11 Daniels, Mexico City, to Lamont Smith, December 30, 1937, Daniels Papers.
12 W. R. M., memorandum of conversation, August 1, 1934, DS, 810.154/616.
13 George Harding, Boston, to Roosevelt, April 2, 1937, Roosevelt Papers.
14 Quoted in Archibald MacLeish, Washington, to Daniels, January 24, 1941, Daniels Papers.
15 Edward Keating, Washington, to Daniels, November 13, 1937, Daniels Papers.
16 White, Emporia, to Daniels, April 5, 1938, Daniels Papers.
17 Stephen E. Aguirre, El Paso, to the author, June 24, 1957.
18 *New York Times*, May 16, 1937.
19 Howard Vincent O'Brien, "All Things Considered," *Chicago Daily News*, March 25, 1937.
20 Raymond Clapper, "Capital Comment," *San Francisco News*, April 22, 1941.
21 Pierre de L. Boal, Boalsburg, to the author, July 21, 1957. Also Aguirre to the author, June 24, 1957; Thomas H. Lockett, Algiers, to the author, May 28, 1953; interviews with Robert

Newbegin, January 15, 1953, and R. Henry Norweb, May 2, 1953.

22   Cordell Hull, *Memoirs* (New York: Macmillan, 1948), I, 182.

23   H. G. Brackus, Chihuahua, to Daniels, March 22, 1938, Daniels Papers.

24   Daniels, Diary, July 2, 1938, Daniels Papers.

25   *Omega* (Mexico City), November 13, 1941.

26   *Novedades* (Mexico City), November 1, 1941.

27   *Todo* (Mexico City), June 25, 1935.

28   Boal, Mexico City, to Daniels, December 17, 1936, Daniels Papers.

29   "Good Bye, Mr. Daniels!" *Hoy* (Mexico City), November 8, 1941.

30   See, for example, *La Opinión*, April 21 and July 20, 1934; *La Prensa* (San Antonio), May 4, 1934.

31   John Steinbeck, Pacific Grove, to Daniels, February 20, 1941, Daniels Papers.

32   *El Mundo* (Mexico City), October 2, 1933.

33   Francisco Castillo Nájera, "Prólogo," in Daniels, *Diplomático en mangas de camisa*, trans. Salvador Duhart (México: Talleres Gráficos de la Nación, 1949), p. xiv.

34   "Come Again, Mr. Daniels!" *La Prensa* (Mexico City), November 10, 1941.

35   Castillo Nájera, "Prólogo," p. xiii.

36   Castillo Nájera, Mexico City, to the author, June 12, 1953.

37   W. B. Richardson, Mexico City, to Daniels, December 9, 1940, Daniels Papers.

38   Ezequiel Padilla, Address, November 7, 1941, quoted in Daniels, *Shirt-Sleeve Diplomat*, pp. 522–24. Padilla stressed in this farewell address that he spoke with "deep and genuine feeling." Talking with him nearly fourteen years later, it was evident that he had not changed his mind. Interview June 28, 1955.

39   Lázaro Cárdenas, Jiquilpan, to Daniels, November 5, 1941, Daniels Papers.

40   *El Universal Gráfico* (Mexico City), November 11, 1941. See also *New York Times*, November 10, 1941.

41   *Hoy*, November 8, 1941; *La Prensa*, November 10, 1941.

42   *El Nacional* (Mexico City), November 10, 1941.

43   Daniels, *Shirt-Sleeve Diplomat*, p. 92.

44   Interview with Salvador Duhart, June 16, 1955; Daniels, "Visit to Mexico, November 29–December 5, 1946," Daniels Papers.

45   W. J. Hooten, "Everyday Events," *El Paso Times*, undated

clipping [December 10, 1946?], Daniels Papers. See also *New York Times*, December 6, 1946.

46 "Se va un amigo," *Novedades*, January 17, 1948.
47 Lord Lyon, "Entre los cuernos," *ibid.*, November 3, 4, 8, and 10, 1941.
48 Interview with Duhart, June 16, 1955.
49 Betty Kirk, "U. S. in Latin America: Policy of the Suction Pump," *Nation*, CLXXXV (October 5, 1957), 221.
50 Boal to the author, July 21, 1957.
51 Sumner Welles, *The Time for Decision* (New York: Harper, 1944), p. 203.

agrarian negotiations, 137, 138, 139; opposes Roosevelt view on expropriations, 146–47; notes interest in oil dispute, 158, 169, 173–74; objects to oil royalty plan, 163–64; denies U.S. pressure on Mexico, 178; uses pressure tactics in oil dispute, 185, 188, 191–98, 201, 208, 215–16, 237, 248–54; fears Axis role in Mexico, 187; and 1938 agrarian settlement, 212–29 *passim;* seeks oil companies' approval of settlement, 247, 264–65, 267; hesitates to praise Cárdenas, 254–55; J.D. helps persuade to sign agreement, 267–68; praises Mexican role in World War II, 271; opinion of J.D., 279; contrasted with J.D., 288–89

Hurley, Patrick J.: negotiates Sinclair settlement, 237–38, 248–53

Ickes, Harold L., 264
Illinois (state): opposes Mexican anticlericalism, 102
Illiteracy: in Mexico, 84
Immigration: J.D. aids from Mexico, 87; Senator Reynolds opposes from Mexico, 252
Imperialism: J.D.'s opposition to, 10, 68, 71–72; Communists accuse J.D. of, 20
Insull scandals: cited by J.D., 122
Interior Department (U.S.): J.D.'s early service in, 4; values of properties in Mexico, 260–61
International Committee of Bankers on Mexico: J.D.'s suspicions of, 118–20
Intervention: by Wilson administration in Mexico, 10–11, 31; as barrier to J.D.'s appointment, 15–16; Pan American Conferences disapprove, 32, 73–75; Calles warns U.S. against, 48; J.D.'s opposition to, 67–69, 70–72, 73, 75–76, 87;

U.S. suggestions for in Mexican religious dispute, 99–103; Senator Pittman's views on, 218. *See also* Veracruz
Investment, foreign: J.D.'s views on, 11–13, 57–58, 76, 115–27, and *passim;* in Mexico, 32–36, 41; State Department concern for, 76, 117–18, 121, and *passim. See also* Claims; Land reform; Foreign oil companies in Mexico; Petroleum industry in Mexico
Italy: trade with Mexico, 233, 244; Cárdenas hints closer ties to, 239

Japan: interest in Mexican oil, 234, 235
Jefferson, Thomas: J.D.'s admiration for, 90
Johnson, Gerald W., 16–17
Johnson, Herschel V.: advises J.D. on Mexico, 17, 85; backs J.D. on claims agreement, 79
Jones, T. A. D., Company: and Mexican oil, 209
Journal of Commerce (New York): supports oil companies, 218; criticizes J.D., 273–74
Juárez, Benito: anticlerical policies of, 82; J.D. praises, 90, 113

Keating, Edward: praises J.D., 276
Kellogg, Frank B.: hostility to Mexico of, 47–48, 49
Kennedy, Martin, J., 233
Kluckhohn, Frank L., 276
Knickerbocker, H. R., 233
Knights of Columbus: demand reprisals against Mexico, 96, 98–99; criticize J.D. and Roosevelt, 106, 109
Ku Klux Klan, 86

Labor: Cárdenas' interest in, 114; unionism in Mexico, 159–60
La Follette, Philip F., 117
Lamb, Hugh L., 95–96
Lamont, Thomas W.: heads bond-